ORALKHAN BOKEEV
The Man-Deer and Other Stories

Published by The Kazakh Pen Club, © 2018

Translation copyright © Simon Hollingsworth, 2018

ISBN-13: 978-1984180711

ORALKHAN BOKEEV
The Man-Deer and Other Stories

Translated into English by Simon Hollingsworth

Edited by Simon Geoghegan

Published under the supervision of
President of the Kazakh PEN Club
Bigeldy Gabdullin

ACKNOWLEDGEMENTS

The publishers would like to thank the Kazakh PEN Club for their continual support on this project. The project was initiated by Kazakh PEN Club President Bigeldy Gabdullin, designed to expose the best works of classic Kazakh writers to the global literary stage through their translation into the English language. Through the tireless efforts of Mr Gabdullin, the project gained the financial and logistical support needed from influential Kazakh state organisations and private companies. The translation of these stories by Oralkhan Bokeev was possible thanks to the generous support of Kazakhtelecoom JSC.

Kazakhtelecom JSC, established in 1994, is Kazakhstan's largest infocommunication operator. Kazakhtelecom offers fixed telephony services, broadband internet access, paid digital television and various innovation services. It enjoys a presence across the country with a network of 264 service points, 16 datacentres and contact centres. Kazakhtelecom is actively involved in the development of promising cyber security, IoT technology, smartcity, smarthome and other solutions.

The international ratings agency Standard&Poor's has raised Kazakhtelecom's credit rating from "BB-Positive" to "BB+-Stable". On the national scale, Kazakhtelecom JSC's rating has increased from "kzA+" to "kzAA-".

The company is listed on the Kazakhstan Stock Exchange (KASE), ensuring a high level of transparency for investors, partners and other interested persons.

Major shareholders of Kazakhtelecom JSC: FNP Samruk-Kazyna JSC (51% ordinary shares) and SobrioLimited (24.47% ordinary shares).

TABLE OF CONTENTS

SHORT STORIES

THE LIGHTNING TRAIL

The people had decided that Kiyalkhan, the poor soul, had lost his mind.

As the evenings drew in, he hoped the sun would not leave the sky. But it invariably disappeared beyond the horizon. Each morning he did not want the day to begin, but this wish was also never granted: the restless course of life continued uninterrupted. However hard he tried to avoid it, uneasy reality would force its way into his consciousness. Not a single ray of joy shone within him and it seemed that he no longer expected anything new from the world; the blazing battle between light and day, the struggle between good and evil, white and black, was everywhere: in unknown, distant corners of the world and right there, beside him. But perhaps this sense of unease that Kiyalkhan felt could be explained by the simple feeling of regret for the speed with which his life was passing him by, lost in this cruel world amidst a host of other lives, with no hope of ever being heard or understood.

Inevitably the morning would arrive, rising above the mountains as it broke free from its captivity in the dark ravines. The sun that appeared with a smile and which departed in the evening with a red face, shed its bright light equally generously on good and evil, without distinguishing between the two. The hustle and bustle of the little *aul* continued from the moment it rose to the moment it set. Only the sinister long-eared bats hung the entire day in their caves, waiting for dusk to fall, so they could venture out on the hunt.

As Kiyalkhan walked to the river to wash, the third-grade teacher Toiganbai, twitching like a buffoon in the yard in front of his log cabin, caught sight of him. This young teacher was performing his morning exercises to raise his spirits. Straightening up, he cried out,

"Ki-ake-e, Ki-ake!"

"Eh?"

"The collective farm is calling for extra hands; shall we stay or shall we go?"

"We could go," Kiyalkhan replied.

"Ah, sod 'em! If you give them an inch, they'll soon get used to it and start dragging us into the fields every day," Toiganbai objected. "Hey, let's head over to the herdsmen, instead and get ourselves a belly full of *kumiss*."

"They give us *kumiss* at work too..."

"That stuff is nothing but swill! They water it down... Well, you do what you want. I can't be doing with that haymaking. Old Mother Idleness won't let me go. He-he!" roared Toiganbai.

In the small, crowded mountain *aul* of Stozhary, there was a primary school and Kiyalkhan worked there as a teacher, having graduated from the university's philosophy faculty. He had been to visit the year before to see his uncle, who had found him through the newspaper, and he had never returned to the town since. It couldn't be said that he had any particular fondness for his new-found family, without whom he had managed quite happily for thirty years and whom he couldn't be sure were actually family at all, but he was quite overwhelmed and enchanted by the powerful beauty of the mountains and he had simply wanted to stay. There was another thing, too: here was where he could immerse himself in all the thinking he wanted; no-one got in his way and the people here had their own things on their minds as it was. Back in the hustle, bustle and disordered life of the town, this was a state of affairs that this philosophy graduate could only dream of and it was at this time when he had been living alone in a tiny place he rented from someone or other, that he had read an announcement in the newspaper that mentioned his name. Kiyalkhan had gone to the *aul* unburdened by doubt. His uncle had been searching for his nephew, of whom all trace had been lost during the war.

Kiyalkhan, having seen his uncle and the numerous members of his family, never did understand why this man had needed to spend time looking for a nephew to supplement his household. There were seven children swarming around the uncle's house, which was kept by his sluggish, lethargic wife. At first, the young philosopher thought the master of the house might be a little weak in the head, a holy fool, who took everything lying down; you could lead a whole flock of sheep over him and he would just lay there chuckling, foolishly and embarrassed. He was the shepherd of the *aul's* small herd. A dishevelled woman, Kiyalkhan's aunt, would spend days on end sitting by the river, lazily washing the children's clothes.

And here she was now, at this ungodly hour, sitting at the water's edge, scrubbing the clothes against a stone. Noticing the approaching Kiyalkhan, she hurriedly buttoned up her dress that was open at the chest.

"You're up early, nephew, dear," she said affably. "Or did the cock crow earlier than usual?"

"I'm off to help with the haymaking," replied Kiyalkhan, stopping. "And where's uncle?"

"Your uncle has gone off to tend to the herd, where else would he be?" Saying this, the woman slapped the wet linen in the water and went on angrily, "What do you want to go helping those cursed idlers for? All they know is how to spend the entire summer drinking *kumiss* and eyeing up the girls from the bushes. And then in the winter all they do is drag their half-famished calves round to other people's homesteads hoping someone will give them something to eat."

Walking further along the bank, Kiyalkhan turned his head several times to look with pity at his aunt's shaggy-looking back. He found it hard to believe that this woman, drearily doubled-up by the

10

water, could have once had a slender figure and swan-like neck. Perhaps she had had a decent voice, to sing like the flowing river, in which she now rinsed her dirty linen.

Oh well, the only thing you can say is truly beautiful is that which doesn't grow old. Or that which drifts further back in the memory and, the further back it goes, the more beautiful it becomes. Kiyalkhan's gaze lingered on a lone pine, standing on the other side of the stream. The strange, incredible similarity struck him: he had seen a pine tree just like it only recently in a dream. Kiyalkhan closed his eyes, trying to bring this vision up once more, only in waking life. But to no avail. All he could imagine was the sparkling stream, the sprawling pine with its red-brown, scale-like bark and, instead of a girl in red, who was supposed to be riding a swing, he saw his aunt, washing the linen and looking as unkempt as an old witch.

But at dawn, this is what he had dreamed. At first, the rain was falling in red and green streaks, which flickered and crisscrossed like falling arrows. Having flown past like a screen of colour, these streaks revealed multicoloured, dappled mountains behind them. However, this was not a peculiar landscape, while the people walking meekly in a procession, holding candles, struck the dreamer profoundly, along with the fact there was a complete lack of black anywhere to be seen. But most important of all was the tall pine on the river bank, with sprawling, multicoloured, red and blue branches, endowed with the remarkable ability to pronounce human words when stroked. A swing made of snow-white yarn was tied to a large bough of this tree; on the swing sat a girl in a red dress, swinging quietly, and the colourful mountains sang. This country where the girl lived could have been called Mamyrstan: the country of tenderness. The idea pierced the dreaming philosopher's mind that there was no death in this country. These meek people from the procession, walking with their candles, were the most odious criminals and villains the world had ever seen, but now they were repenting and, pacing softly one after the other, they were singing songs of kindness. The sky here was clear and bright, like an emerald; the crows and magpies sang enchanting melodies; a large, grey donkey was getting excited and running in circles like some fairytale, winged horse, while, among the doves over the multicoloured pine, cherubic-bottomed infants soared, mewling songs in their slight voices... (*Get up, son, get up!*)

"Get up! The sun is already high in the sky!" the old woman Ak-apa said, shaking him by the shoulder. He shot up, sat on the edge of the bed and blurted out without a moment's hesitation,

"Two tonnes of coal cost 22 roubles and, if you carry the coal in buckets, you get 150 buckets. Ah-h..." he said hoarsely and then rubbed his eyes with his fists. "It's you, *apa*. It's a good thing you woke me, as I was having a bad dream. Perhaps I would have died if you hadn't..."

"Don't talk about dreams like that! Is there such a thing as a bad dream? I'll talk to you about that tonight. For now, though, son, get yourself down to the river and have a decent wash, then you'll have some breakfast... The supervisor came over to summon the teachers over to do some voluntary Saturday work and you'd better go, son..."

So here Kiyalkhan was now, sitting on the riverbank, with a vacant look on his face, dipping his hands in the water and thinking to himself, *if every morning a person doesn't do something new, will their life ever actually get going? So that's it: a decent day's work is what's needed. And what about that shepherd of the third-graders Toiganbai? He can read a lecture on public conscience and workers' morals for two hours but would never go out haymaking himself. How quiet it is here. Such a sleepy, quiet and peaceful life. It looks like nothing could happen here. Most people are content with a full belly and they couldn't care less about anything else. It seems that the people here are quite content and happy with their lives. But I think it's Dostoyevsky who says that you cannot be happy if there are those around you suffering...*

"Hey, nephew, what are you muttering about there?" a shrill voice reached Kiyalkhan. "Hasn't Ak-apa taught you how to pray yet?"

"No, auntie, I was just thinking..." replied Kiyalkhan involuntarily and he got up and shuffled home. When he was walking past his aunt, she grabbed her tub of linen from the ground and walked along beside him.

"People are chattering about how miraculous it was finding our nephew, just as if he had risen from the dead, but that his aunt has set him up in the old woman's apartment. Of course, you can't stop others talking, so let them gossip, but it hurts all the same. It would be better if you lived with us, but would you really be able to manage with all our noise and clutter? After all, a house with children is no home for those who write or draw. But at least you could dine with us, Kiyalkhan, so you don't have to spend extra money on food. It's just a bit awkward, that's all."

"Don't worry, auntie, things are fine for me at the old woman's place. And my giving you money is just my way of helping uncle. Don't you worry about a thing. Anyway, it's no fun for Ak-apa, living all on her own. And it's easier for her with me around."

"Well, you know what's best. And Ak-apa is almost part of the family. We have the same roots, you see, distant relatives. But still, come round to see us more often, so the neighbours don't gossip so much. Your uncle, you see, only came to his senses and rushed off to find you when he was forty... and he found you, see! So you do your best not to hurt his feelings. He is a quiet man and it is that kind that grief that hits the hardest. There are times I get to thinking where he might be, wandering about with his herd all alone. Who knows, perhaps he has suddenly dropped dead or something." And, turning around, his aunt sniffed.

"Don't say that, auntie. Uncle is not the sort to die just like that. Those who herd livestock live longer than everyone else."

When making the hay, Kiyalkhan fell into deep thought, recalling his vivid, multicoloured dream, and he even failed to notice that he had dropped his fork. The elderly stacker, who had long been looking askance at him, could not hold himself back and screamed out, red in the face from so much anger that his ears shone:

"Hey, you there, teacher! Quit playing the fool and get some proper work done. This is no place to be daydreaming about your books, you know! All you seem to know about is giving the kids a hard time."

"Alright, alright. Keep your hair on!" cried another from below, pausing from wrapping the hay onto what was now a tall stack. "You're just giving the teacher a hard time because your idiot son can't hack his studies. Off you go and have a break, teacher," he said, turning to Kiyalkhan. "It is no easy matter doing this dirty work if you are not used to it."

"If he can't do the work, what was the point of him coming here in the first place?" the man up above continued to scream. "A waste of space, people like him shouldn't be allowed within two kilometres of the *aul*! What do we need them for? We don't go creeping into their town, now do we? And we have to pay taxes for them, give them chickens and wool and butter, and it's never enough, is it?! Those that plough, sow, clean and so on – they mean nothing to them. And they only *think* they can, but they can't even hold a hay fork properly."

"Shut it, will you!" cried the stacker from below, an old man with a pockmarked face and bulging eyes. "You're just one big gob from ear to ear. He's really off on one this time! I once read this book called *Alitet Goes to the Hills*; it's all about an idiot just like you. Get down from there, before I get you with my fork! Born with such a black heart, forever blowing your top, like some black cauldron... Get down, I tell you!"

Kiyalkhan walked quietly away, while they continued to curse and bicker over him.

Returning home, he walked with his head down in a gloomy fashion. It would have been better if he had remained at home, like Toiganbai, as then he would never have heard those hurtful words. How can people be so intolerant of others! And yet the only sense in it all is quite the opposite. The future of humanity and all of its hope is linked with people's ability to live in brotherly harmony and not to pounce on one another.

Ak-apa was looking out for him to put the dinner on the table. She brought out a pitcher and poured water onto his hands.

"What are you so gloomy about, young man? Are you tired?"

"Oh, I am tired, but not from the work, grandmother," sighed Kiyalkhan. "I have been tormented by various thoughts. They get into my head like flies in sugar, swarming and buzzing..."

"Oh, you poor thing! That's why your face looks so wan. Don't you worry about a thing, my son!"

"Oh, grandmother, and I am tormented by the strangest of dreams."

"You have something to eat and then I'll tell you the kind of dreams people have."

If only the sun wouldn't set, thought Kiyalkhan gloomily. *At least just this once.*

But set it did. The dinner made by the old woman's caring hands was tasty but it brought Kiyalkhan no joy. He thought dark thoughts that, after Hiroshima, it was hardly likely that any person in their senses could exult in what little joys the world had to offer. Sighing, the philosopher turned to the small, wrinkled, old woman:

"Well then... you wanted to tell me about a dream, Ak-apa?"

"Ah, yes, yes! Listen up," the old woman said, coming to life, "There once was a man, they say, who lived in some distant wintering camp. He went off hunting and got held up, while his pregnant wife remained at home. And she had a dream that two wolves sank their teeth into her breasts and ate them away. She awoke, gasped and ran to the *aul*, so the fortune-teller could tell her what her dream had meant. It was winter and a blizzard was blowing and the wife found it hard going. She finally made it to the *aul*, but the fortune-teller was not at home, just his wife. Well, so the woman tells the fortune-teller's wife about her dream and the latter, young and foolish, blurted out without much thought: 'Well, that means that wolves will eat away your body for real.' The woman was stupefied, jumped up and ran back to the camp even faster than she had come. Well, the fortune-teller comes home and his wife tells him who had visited and what had happened. He says to her: 'You should not have said that. You understand nothing about all this! You must only interpret each dream in a positive light. She shall have twin boys, that's what you should have said. Now, though, I fear that a misfortune will indeed befall her.' He took to his horse and galloped off, following the tracks that the woman had left. But what must be must be. He never managed to reach her and the wolves had indeed mauled the woman. But two new-born infants lay there on the bloodied snow... So there you have it, son: there has never been an instance when a dream did not come true. And, as the fortune-teller said, they should only be interpreted in a positive light. And that is how they will come to pass."

Finishing her tale, the old woman turned, looked at Kiyalkhan and noticed with a fright that he was staring into the fire with strange, motionless eyes and that he was unlikely to have heard anything, like a

14

deaf and mute person, who hears only his own, silent thoughts. His appearance, too, was pitiful, suffering and anxious.

"Son," the old woman called to him, touching his cheek lightly with her hand, "you are all alone in the world. Who do you have to be sad about?"

"If I were all alone, *apa*, I still wouldn't be sad." The warm touch of another person seemed to give Kiyalkhan new strength and he smiled. "I am not speaking of myself. And how can I be alone, *apa*, when I am here with you?"

"I knew your mother. She had a disposition like silk, she did! You were five months old when they held your father's funeral. She could not bear the grief and passed away and you were handed over to an orphanage. Oh, Allah, it's as if it was only yesterday! So much grief and certainly no less than in the olden days, during the Steppe Plague. We never even set eyes on our enemy yet so many died at its hands."

"What am I to do, Ak-apa? I feel so sad that it is hard to live on even for another day. Why is that, *apa*?" Kiyalkhan complained quietly to the little, old woman. "I don't know what it means to rejoice in life because I have never been caressed by a mother's hand. And I am tired of it, *apa*. I am tired of forever having to wait for some new misfortune to be visited on me by the world. It is only with you, *apa*, that I am at ease! You are like the mother I once dreamed about and you give off that warm, motherly smell. Oh, Ak-apa!" Kiyalkhan, his faced pressed against the old woman's shoulder, wept like a fragile adolescent, broken by grief. Ak-apa, touched by this, stroked his hair and wiped the tears that had welled up.

"You have a good old cry, my little colt," she muttered. "All your sadness will well up from your soul like bile and your grief will be washed away by your tears. Cry, light of my life, cry like a new-born child first cries as he comes into this world. And let it be the last time you weep for your mother and father, whom you never knew. I will weep with you too, my little orphan: I will light up my own memory once more and remember my own son, who perished thirty years ago in some foreign land from an enemy bullet."

But each day passed, each the same and as meaningless as the other, while during the nights he would be plagued more and more by sleeplessness and, unable to withstand it all, he would leave his bed and leave the house to wander in the quiet of the night, in which the mountains, forests, birds and people all slept as if in a single moment that stretched to infinity. Stepping quietly, he silently reached the stream that babbled in the thick half-light; the crests of the little waves flickered faintly, reflecting the light of the distant stars. They were like jewellery, jingling in the dark plaits of the night and, one day, Kiyalkhan involuntarily cried out:

"Oh, but that is poetry!" and he took fright at the sound of his own voice and continued, this time in his mind's eye: *Yes, this is nothing but the sorcery of poetry. With the rising sun, the spells disperse and real-life proceeds. Why does the world appear like this, as if it has been handed over forever to the power of magical poetry? What a load of rubbish! What deceit! Not peace and serenity but the ghost of peace, quiet and serenity... All of this round, little world blazes from within, tormented by its own heat, a deep, intolerable heat. In the spaces of the night, it is fanned by the tender coolness from the mountains; the beautiful full moon floats up above, as if rejoicing in blessed motherly affection, quietly immersing its quivering fingers into the waves of the mountain stream and, from this touch, the black waters flare up and lovers' games are afoot, and shepherds' wolfhounds bark loudly in the distance; all this seems to remind us accidentally that the eternal bird of life still flies and performs good deeds above the mists of the night.*

However, a lone pine appeared on Kiyalkhan's way, standing apart from the other trees on the bank of the stream, returning his memory to that vivid dream. He was also completely alone, like this pine, although all around was the thick, never-ending forest of his compatriots. One day, approaching the tree, he touched one of its long branches, arched low, recalling that here and now he had to hear a human voice. And there in front of him flashed the dress as red as fire of that girl in his dream...

"What is it you need in the world of dreams?" she asked.

"You," replied Kiyalkhan.

"But I am not accessible to mortal man."

"Then I need the key to all the secrets of the universe."

"What for?"

"I would like to find happiness, if not for myself, then at least for my people."

"And where is this happiness to be found?"

"In immortality, I suppose."

"No. Without dying, people will infest the world. They will be at each other's throats."

"Let them squabble, just as long as they don't perish."

"And you think this will be a good thing for them? No, you cannot be trusted with the key to the universe."

"Then ensure that not a single enemy weapon fires on this earth and that people die a natural death and not at the hands of evil-doers."

"You know yourself how to achieve this."

"I have to seek the zhasyn, *the arrow of lightning that has fallen to earth?"*

"Yes. And climb and stand atop the peak of the highest mountain with this arrow and remain there, vigilantly protecting the

world. While the arrow of lightning is in your hand, not a single villainous shot will ever ring out."

"*Bismillah, Bismillah*, wake up, my son! What's the matter with you? Why are you moaning and groaning like that?" said Ak-apa early the next morning, shaking him and anxiously looking at his face.

Kiyalkhan sat up in bed, shook his head and mumbled, "Two tonnes of coal makes 150 buckets full."

"Oh, Lord, I do hope he has not taken sick here," sighed Ak-apa. "Of course, fretting in one's dreams is not a bad omen. It means that in reality, something good is sure to happen. I hope to Allah this is right. And now get up, my dear, and wash yourself in cold water."

Let the sky cloud over, let the rain fall, implored Kiyalkhan, but the sky remained completely placid. There was not a single cloud, not the slightest breeze; the sun's rays were blinding, a rare thing that year. All around was good but soon, very soon, Kiyalkhan was bound to lose his mind. For now, though, he was strolling under this blue, overturned sky, which he could reach up and touch, admiring the snowy peaks of the surrounding mountains and the dark trees of the taiga, scattered over their slopes, like the innumerable khanate forces of the *Sarbazi*. Walking through the forest, he could see small glades with quivering, crimson and yellow flowers on long, thin stalks; the grass in these glades was thick and wild and it was immediately apparent that no human had ever set foot here. The narrow, woodland path led further and further up into the heavens, enticing the traveller into the unknown limits of the silent mountains. From the abundant rains that had fallen, the earth had absorbed the surplus moisture to bursting point, making the ground soft underfoot, while the tracks in the supple soil, unable to endure their emptiness, filled instantly with water.

And if one were to climb up the jubilant, green hill and tumble down, a broad, flattened trail would be left from top to bottom. And in the place where the bright-green peaks of the hills meet the blue of the heavens, it seems that a placating breath of life passes by, solemnly and peacefully watching over its innumerable herd of clouds, sheep, people and wild animals.

The weather had been like this for some ten days in a row. Then, one day, something changed, as if an error had made its way into the regular course of these halcyon days: a wind rushed in from the north onto the mountain meadows and a long storm cloud, like some small, grey, felt saddle-cloth, appeared over the distant ridge. It covered the sky more and more and, suddenly, it was followed from beyond the ridge by the entire entourage of its restless kinsfolk. The cloud brought all of its fluffy, stormy family into a single whole and a foreboding, heavenly army formed overhead. Somewhere in the distance, out of sight, the first thunderclaps roared like cannons.

17

A sense of curative coolness entered Kiyalkhan's mind, long since pitted with fruitless thoughts like the stings of countless ants. His eyes stopped stinging, there was no longer any pressure or knocking in his temples and the invisible bellows that had blown heat into the red-hot furnace of his heart had temporarily stopped blowing. Kiyalkhan himself, as if relieved of a heavy burden, became as lively and frisky as a young camel. He immediately rushed in leaps and bounds from the mountain, setting his open chest to the incoming north wind. He ran as if joyfully welcoming a clarity and epiphany in his soul, but from this moment on everything he did appeared like the actions of a madman. The thunder roared overhead and fiery lightning flashed simultaneously, long and intertwined, like the veins on a hand. And the young man, with his long hair flying in the wind, raised his arms to the sky and jumped high. The lightning cracked once more and he bent down to the ground, bursting into fits of loud, derisive laughter, slapping himself across the thighs. The black sky and the descending north wind, which instantly turned every leaf inside out, completely changed the image of the earth. The tops of the enormous pines were filled with a sonorous din and they swayed from side to side. Kiyalkhan whirled in this wind like a spinning top, released by a powerful hand. Suddenly something unimaginable occurred. For a moment the wind died down, breathing in all the air around, and then it all blew out in a single, squall-like gust and felled all the trees that lay in its path, forming an enormous opening. Kiyalkhan froze to the spot, at once overcome with terror and admiration.

Up above, it lashed all the more often across the sky, from both the right and the left like a rapid, fiery crop. Unable to withstand these impacts, the sky broke out into violent tears. How these tears clear the heart! And once the heart is cleared, the soul becomes merrier and the world stops scowling darkly, from its virulent, reckless abandon, in all its brightly luminiferous, distant spaces. Having calmed, Mother Nature will again lay its bountiful table and will drink tea until its brow breaks out in droplets of perspiration. The green, bathed forests, the rivers overflowing and the thundering, muddy waters of the ravine will all be present at the feast...

But there is still a long time to wait until this blessed armistice, while, for now, it was not shrapnel from an exploded bomb that showered the head of the bent-double Kiyalkhan, but large, finger-sized, icy hailstones. The philosopher's life, no longer subject to his will, had been removed to some no-man's land between reality and non-entity. The hail fell a long time and stopped wholly unexpectedly, as if it had been switched off by a switch, and, in that instant, grey-sheep storm clouds unravelled and the still nóonday sun, impetuous and bright, broke through to the earth, coated in a sweaty sheen of rain. The mighty, wounded forest with its dependent shrubbery was still unable to come to its senses and it smoked quietly, deafened and hammered down by the hail...

However, a squirrel poked its head out of the hollow of an old tree and a steppe eagle, perched on a black, wet, mossy boulder, yawned broadly and gave out a cry. A dog in the *aul* barked merrily. Life went on.

Kiyalkhan, wet and dishevelled, got up from the ground and headed off to the *aul*, where the residents were once again bustling about its streets, busy with their affairs like mice, saved from a flood. Kiyalkhan's aunt was already seated next to the stream, washing the linen.

But the prostrate pine lay on the ground, fumes smoking from it! The same, lone pine on the bank that had preoccupied Kiyalkhan so much, both in real life and in his dreams. It had been split in two by the lightning, its trunk torn asunder in such a way that white splinters stuck out like bones between the charred branches. Kiyalkhan froze as if rooted to the spot and looked at the tree, killed by the lightning. His aunt cried out in a merry voice,

"Hey there, nephew! Where have you been wandering? Ak-apa has already come running, looking for you!"

At any other time, Kiyalkhan would not have failed to notice the irony, be it out loud or to himself, that his closest relatives should be the ones to search for him and not some old woman, but that was the last thing on his mind right now. His attention was tensely focused on the pine, struck down by the lightning. Noticing this, his aunt gladly changed the subject:

"Oh, look how much free firewood there is lying about! Any other time you would be fined for breaking off the odd branch but, here, Allah himself has broken the wood for us, so let them fine him!"

But her nephew failed to respond to this as well and remained motionless, strangely and with a tormented, tense look on his face, gazing at the smoking remains of the enormous tree. It was as if lightning flared once more in the mind of Kiyalkhan, who had only just been at the mercy of the squally wind and hail of an unprecedented thunderstorm. And it was at that moment that a strange thought entered his pained mind: that he should dig up the *zhasyn*, the cooled arrow of lightning that must have gone underground and must be lying in the roots of the dead pine.

And so Kiyalkhan remained for three days, digging a hole beneath the burnt pine. He would not emerge from there to go for his dinner and the old Ak-apa had to bring him food from home. Back in the *aul* the people were at a loss. They decided not to approach the hole and stood a short distance away, shaking their heads and, clucking their tongues in bewilderment, they went their separate ways, away from that sinful place. On that third day, though, Toiganbai sat down at the edge of the hole and remained there for some time, looking with bulging eyes at

Kiyalkhan, covered in earth. He opened his mouth, evidently wanting to say something, but he did not venture to utter a word. Only when he got up to go did he mutter,

"They say you want to get the, you know... so there won't be any war and all that. Hm! That's a load of nonsense you've got into your head, Kiyalkhan if you ask me."

"Damn it, I am declaring war on wars!" screamed Kiyalkhan from the hole. "But you are my first enemy! I declare war on you, too! Get out of my sight, while you're still in one piece!"

Then Kiyalkhan's uncle the shepherd came. He stood there and then, unable to find words to say what he wanted, he departed. Finally, the supervisor arrived, poked his whip into the void and cried,

"Hey! You, there, you half-wit! What are you looking for, eh? You could have spent your time digging me a silo pit instead of rooting out this burnt-out old stump!"

Kiyalkhan did not respond and the supervisor likewise went on his way.

It was at the end of this day that the poor philosopher came to realise for himself that he was digging in vain. His temperance and composure gradually returned to him thanks to this long and hard stint of work. Kiyalkhan threw down his shovel, sat down, his back against the wall of the pit he had dug and, throwing back his head and looking up at the sky, he fell into a deep, childlike sleep, with a smile on his face as if he sensed that happiness would soon come. And once more he dreamed of the girl in the red dress. Laughing happily, she poured water onto his hands from a copper jug and then cut his nails and gave him a camel skin gown that was whiter than white...

He awoke and saw a wonderful, blue sky high up above and next to him a girl in a blue dress. She was sitting on her haunches and, smiling quizzically, she picked off the lumps of dry clay that had stuck to his cheeks.

"Who are you, dream girl?" asked Kiyalkhan, smiling with a mock solemnity.

"I am Gulgul," the girl replied simply.

"Where did you appear from into this dull, sad world?"

"I'm from the *aul* here but I am studying in town. I came home for the holidays and I've been here ten days already. I heard that you were digging the earth to dig up the...to get hold of the fabled *zhasyn*, the lightning trail... Is that true?"

"And what if it is?"

"Can I help you?"

"What? Do you believe in miracles, too?"

"Just the same as you do."

They looked attentively at one another and then burst out laughing.

20

"And now," she said, taking him by the hand and pulling him after her. "Up you get and go and wash yourself in the river."

"Gulgul," he said later, "how come you weren't frightened of me?"

"But I was afraid... You see, everyone was saying that you had gone mad. But today I made up my mind, crept up to the pit and looked in. And there you were sitting, fast asleep, and your face appeared so tormented. And you were talking aloud in your sleep, saying, 'Oh, creator, take away my reason.' And then I realised that a man who asks for his reason to be taken from him cannot be a madman."

"Gulgul, well done, you! And now I'll go over to that hill and sit in the sun and rest. In the meantime, you head over to the *aul* and tell everyone this: tell them that Kiyalkhan is not looking for lightning after all, but for treasure. Say it's an ingot of gold, that in olden times was buried under this pine, and that it is the size of a horse's head."

"But why?"

"You'll see for yourself what will happen..."

And, climbing to the top of the hill, from where he had a broad view all around, he looked over to the *aul* with a smile on his face... Kiyalkhan could see his aunt sitting calmly by the river with her washing. He could see his uncle, too, on his short-tailed, ginger colt, cantering near the herd and turning it about. But from the *aul*, the supervisor and the teacher Toiganbai were running, tripping over one another's heels with shovels in their hands. And they were running to the pit that Kiyalkhan had dug, where previously they had had no intention of going to help him retrieve the *zhasyn*. But now they were the ones who were going to do the digging. And Kiyalkhan said,

"The poor people! They must be out of their minds."

But perhaps it was also true that Kiyalkhan himself had lost his mind. That said, very soon afterwards, he made a full recovery. And on the day he recovered and returned home under Ak-apa's wing, he wrote in his diary: *20 million Soviet people alone died during the Second World War. They included my father, a soldier. But is the number of people who perished from grief, like my mother, ever taken into account? And is there a list for the likes of me?*

THE THAW

If I had realised that the most terrible thing had happened and you were no longer here, then I think the grief would not have killed me. The painting remained, which had always linked you and me and I can view it without end. Do you remember how I told you about this painting in great detail, trying to convey what I understood in it; the joy of springtime warmth that the painter had expressed so sincerely and simply? I don't know what the true joy of life involved, but I think the artist succeeds in conveying this in bright splashes of nature, just like you find in spring.

You were sitting there, staring at a single point, motionless and tensing your whole being in an attempt to imagine this. And I could only understand from the fitful breathing that interrupted your concentrated silence how much you wanted just once to see the white light with your own eyes and then die.

You poor thing, you slender sapling, fully grown in this endless steppe! When I hear your sad and painfully lonely melody so clearly, I am prepared to run out into this steppe, find you, wrap my arms around you and weep, weep in long desperation over my loss. And the last of this March snow, which seems warm in the painting, but which had remained where it was in my soul since that time, would melt away in my impossibly hot tears.

I fell in love with the painting and its dusky thaw through the yellowed varnish; a thaw in which your wisdom and my secret interpretation of its meaning were as if hidden. After all, you probably know that a person cannot do without this, cannot do without another person understanding them and, in moments of genuine suffering, they seek something complete and perfect, which is able to assuage the pain of a wounded soul. Before, I never stopped to think how many wonderful moments could flash by in just one day, if the vivacity of perception is not suppressed by the mundane. I followed your tracks, holding your delicate fingers in my hand, those tracks of endless sorrow, and it seemed to me that I was coming to understand the secrets of an uncovered sense of the beauty of moments. When you were by my side, everything was different, more meaningful.

I had never spent time at a health resort but, that spring, I agreed on a last-minute ticket to Tasbugen; that winter I had suffered a bout of pneumonia. Just before leaving, I bought a painting, to ensure things would not be that dull when I set out on my journey.

The coach's wheels found every pothole and splashes of liquid snow would splash in all directions from the deep puddles. The seated passengers were jolted about and they merrily knocked into one another. I saw a girl, looking motionlessly out of the window and who was taking no part in this general merriment. I was struck by the beauty of her face, slender and so transparent, that I even wanted to look through her at the world flashing by outside, as if through a pretty little window.

I asked her to hold my painting, which was getting under my feet; after all, I found myself spending most of the journey standing on one foot. She placed the painting carefully on her lap without looking at me and continued to look at the cliffs and hills that flashed by; I could not bring myself to talk with her. She was very young, but her inner austerity gave her appearance a particular charm.

The path to the health resort from the bus stop was made of steep stone steps, rising upwards, and it became lost behind the trees, which were already reflecting the full vigour of spring and which were discarding the last clumps of loose snow from their branches. The painting, which I had taken back, having thanked you, was again under my arm but I was nonetheless curious as to why you had not given it the slightest attention; after all, it conveyed a truly remarkable sense of springtime. So I decided that this was simply out of a lack of any kind of coquetry, which I had always disliked in girls. I foolishly found cheer in this thought and took to following you up the steps, thinking of the first words I would say.

You were walking very slowly as if you wanted your feet to feel every last step. You stopped, in an attempt to let me pass.

"Sorry, but I wanted to ask if you liked my painting or not. I think there is the same spirit of spring here and the snow has softened in the same way, only it doesn't squelch underfoot, does it?"

At that moment a large clump of snow broke away from a branch and burst onto the path behind you and you shuddered. I looked at your face, smiling and delighted at your splendid courage, at the sun and at my conversation with you, but you remained serious and, slowing a little, you said,

"I couldn't see..."

"I understand... I must appear rather persistent to you and you probably don't want to talk to me, do you?"

And here you moved your eyes away and your cheeks went a little pale. I felt a little dismayed by your lifeless, yet beautiful eyes.

"I am blind."

For a second I lost the ability to feel anything. The painting fell from under my arm and hit me on the foot; I quickly bent down to pick it up.

"You didn't get it dirty did you? It is very wet."

"No, it's alright. Let's go."

We continued to walk slowly up the steps and at times I couldn't believe what you had said and looked at you shyly, but you were calm and continued looking ahead.

"What is your name?"

24

...Your name is Zhanar. When you said your name, I felt something shiver inside. Your voice... Then I became lost in its sounds, which reminded me of a flute's melodies, dazzling me with their tender charm. I thought then that this enchantment would never end for me, just as my wonder for the richness of your soul and your world of purity and serenity will never end, Zhanar.

* * *

Life at the health resort began with the exercises that they sent us on (except for you, that is), like a herd of silly, sleepy rabbits, and then they fed us with medication, which, by the end of our treatment, we simply hid anywhere we could or quietly dropped from our hands on the way to breakfast.

We went almost everywhere together and I was delighted that you didn't have to see the men's eyes, which contained so much greedy curiosity and so little kindness. We never missed a single film, because you perceived the words and music so well, that all I could do was marvel at your ability to listen. Then we went for walks, crunching the icy cover of the earth with our feet; on those moonless, dark nights, I held your hand tightly, finding it hard to work out where to go, yet we never stumbled or fell into the mud even once. These were the nights when you led me.

During the day we liked to sit on a wooden bench in the sun, which still offered only a little warmth. You sometimes enjoyed dozing, with your head on my shoulder and it was at these times that I would gaze unsuppressed into your face. It seemed completely transparent beneath your thick, black hair and I imagined that I could see your pure soul with pale blue veins. Anger boiled up inside me at fate and at nature for mutilating such young beauty. Suddenly, you opened your eyes and asked me,

"You were looking at me so intently...Why?"

I didn't know what to respond...

"How could you see that, Zhanar? That's incredible..."

"Well, I can see with my senses, that's all. Otherwise, I would probably be unable to live. I close my eyes when I want to sleep, but I often find I am unable to drop off. There is a thick darkness before my eyes, but this is not like a never-ending dream, do you understand? This darkness is sometimes torn apart by a gentle light that tickles my eyes. Do you understand what this light is? I think you understand everything that I find difficult to express in words."

"But what if you are mistaken, Zhanar?"

"You know, I also have what I call a premonition, only it is more than just a premonition. It is a kind of conviction in something that only I understand and I have never been proved wrong once."

I listen to your gentle breathing and I look at your closed lashes and suddenly a warm ray enters me. This is a particle of your warmth being conveyed to me and I ask myself with a sense of pain, what will happen to you tomorrow and thereafter... I want to press you close and pity fills my soul... But:

"Don't you pity me, okay? I know and I can imagine that there may be pity in people's eyes and I am afraid of these eyes! I don't like compassion; it is a bad thing. You see, if there is a person in this world, capable of giving me my sight, he would do this not from a sense of pity but, for the most part, because he could do it, isn't that right?"

From that moment, it was as if something turned head over heels inside me. I began learning the clarity of your thoughts from you and now I am seldom wrong and I never lie to myself. Words settled in my consciousness, whose sacred meaning I perceived then like a prayer: may fate rid me of the blindness of my reason and my heart and I am not ashamed that I sometimes pray for you and for me, Zhanar.

You and I wandered in the uncertainty of timid feeling which was like a child at the moment of a mesmeric vision, who freezes and opens their eyes wide. People took us for lovers, but they were unable to discern the full meaning of our feelings. For me, this was a state of peaceful, strange dreaming, lived out in reality, which was unlike anything else in the world. I was ten years older than you, but I was like a small boy compared to you.

* * *

The evening dances at this health resort reminded me of the vanity of human desires, hopes and secret affliction, which was explained by the fact that the arena for self-expression appeared simply as a wooden dance floor. However, the people rushed here in a delight that rounded off each regular day at the resort.

Once I took my girl there and we danced. It was then that I thought that the ability to give oneself up to the rhythm is what creates the harmony between the dancers. Suddenly, someone uttered loudly, "Hey, that blind girl isn't a bad dancer." The state we had enjoyed for many days was destroyed in an instant. My arms now held the tense and leaden body of my girl. After that evening she did not come down for breakfast and I went to see her over the waterlogged soil. I felt sad that I could not release her from her solitude, that she would soon lose sight of me and that she would not find her happiness in me. Although I realised that the charm of youth that had returned to me would disappear at any moment, while I was together with this girl, I now enjoyed being her silent captive. Then a joy awoke inside me and I had a hazy understanding that I was finally finding tranquillity and the correct tone for our relationship.

26

We loved walking to the old hovel, which still sported a hat of snow but which grew smaller and smaller with each passing day.

We would sit in silence for hours on a log in front of the hovel, our arms wrapped around our knees, understanding what it meant to have the serenity of mind that joined and cradled us. The dilapidated old hovel, the blindingly white snow all around, the mountains, the absolute peace and quiet – these were the riches that can put a soul at ease. I recalled Lake Karakol with its lustrous surface, located in the spurs of the Altai among the cool cliffs. It is surrounded by pines and cedars, like the lashes around your eyes. And however clear its waters may be, both day and night, it always seems impenetrably black. I thought that it motionlessly clenched suffering in its embrace. The herdsmen in the region never stopped by Karakol, herding their flocks from the valleys into the mountains. There were rumours that the lake harboured evil, that a water cow lived there, emerging at night to graze on the shore. And everyone had long known that a mermaid swam in its depths.

I went there when my father and I travelled out to the pasture of Shamanbai. My father had advised me not to go to the lake, but I spent the night there. At sunset, the crimson rays of the sun fell onto the fine ripples of the water and the lake, which had just been cheerless and foreboding, was suddenly bathed in gold. I could not imagine anywhere else quite so beautiful. The fresh mountain breeze, the cool night at the pasture and me, drunk on the enchanted air – all this was created for dreams and I only dropped off to sleep near morning. At this point I imagined that a pale girl emerged from the water with black hair and that she stood there, staring at me. Her eyes shone, just like yours, Zhanar. She smiled and disappeared under the water. I woke up. The sun had only just appeared from beyond the mountains.

I have never told this to anyone before now and I often thought to myself that perhaps this beautiful girl had been aggrieved with life and had drowned, cursing the human race as she went. You look very much like that girl and I was even rather afraid of you in the first days.

You also once admitted to me that you were afraid of all that is evil and terrible in the world. The beauty of the outside world barely exists for a blind person, which is why they value spirituality all the more. Therefore, you had become attached to me and sometimes you had been unable to take your eyes off me, thinking about me. You had searched long and hard for the warmth and understanding of an elder brother and you thought you had now found it.

You said all this quietly and freely and I felt touched when I looked into your face, which was concentrated yet bright at the same time, and again I valued your lack of coquetry and affectation.

"I have never spoken to you quite so openly before and now I would like to clear the air. We conceal everything from ourselves but

27

there will come a day when the questions will ask themselves and demand explanations."

I was astonished at your delicate femininity and I listened to you with humility and with pride for you. You suddenly broke into a cheerful, serene smile and told me you had seen me in a dream. Such nights give you more than days because you can see when you are dreaming. The dream struck me as odd.

"You are slightly taller than average, you have black hair, a bent nose and brown eyes. You were leading me across a bridge, the breadth of a horse's hair, which crossed a violent mountain river. 'Don't look around,' you said to me, 'for if you do, we'll both fall into the river and perish.' I walked behind you, my eyes tightly screwed up and I opened them only once we had emerged on the other bank... And this is what I saw: a deep-black night, a sky much the same, and people. Suddenly, everything became coloured in red and white. The river filled with blood. I burst into tears of happiness as I could see, but it was not tears flowing from my eyes but my own two pupils. You caught them deftly in your hand and threw them into the bloody river. Then you looked displeased and said, 'You should not have cried, as you are only allowed to laugh here, loudly and merrily! Here you must scream and laugh with joy, nothing else, do you understand?' And with these words, you led me back across the bridge. I said goodbye to you forever and returned back again to my home on the island of the blind where I had always lived in black darkness."

When you were relating your dream, water dripped from the beam inside the hovel. I thought then that these were the tears of the black hovel but I didn't tell you that. Then I was overcome by a strange sense of fatigue. This was the fatigue of a traveller, returning from an incredibly long journey. I rested my weary soul and tired body by your side, listening to the sounds of a familiar voice and envying you a little for your youth. I was even happy to have fallen ill and now be resting here in Tasbugen; it was here that I met a girl who filled my soul with a clear, cool liquid of purity. Zhanar, you are the thaw in my soul!

The day before you left, we walked along now-familiar paths, from which the snow had already receded. The earth was already swollen and juicy and the birds had returned to their nests and were singing.

We didn't go to dinner and strolled until dusk, said our farewells to the old hovel, walking for the last time along the only pathway that led to it. Then we went up to Tasbugen. Alma-Ata shone with a sea of lights down below and you wanted to view the city through my eyes. You breathed in the aroma of the unfamiliar city with the wind. Looking up at the black sky, I said, "A star has fallen."

"Perhaps it is my eyes flying; the ones that fell in my dream?"

"Zhanar, I don't recognise you. What is this darkness all of a sudden?"

28

"I don't understand myself today. I have a feeling as if I have been trying really hard to swim to the shore, but all my efforts were in vain. I am really tired. Decent people probably meet so that they can part like this."

You pressed your head against my shoulder and I realised you were crying. I ran my palm over your cheeks, and they were flowing with tears. I said, "Let's go back," but you replied that you wouldn't let me go today. That you understood how important it is for a person to have not only eyes but an honest, loyal friend as well. You ran your quivering fingers over my face so carefully, as if you were worried they would leave a mark.

The night was growing cool. It seemed that a hitherto unknown, hazy sadness was now hanging between heaven and earth. I strained to keep myself together, suppressing the sudden urge inside. It was after midnight when we returned and the thought suddenly occurred to me that we should hide at the dacha, which was all alone, its lifeless windows dark. A lingering sense of something unsaid slipped from the heart. We happily entered the house, having broken a window. A fresh wind repelled the smell of a home that had not been lived in. A bed stood in the corner, onto which I threw an old goatskin that the owners had left there.

I remember the silhouette of Alatau, like a camel, and our last conversation in the darkness of that unfamiliar home. You asked me to tell you a story but I could not remember one and nor did I want to recall any tales with happy endings. You quickly sensed this, interrupting me in mid-sentence. Then you asked softly if you could kiss me on the cheek, to which I replied with a question: could I kiss you on the eyes. Nearer to morning, you fell asleep and I thought that you would never see this dawn when the night loosens its hold on heaven and earth under the first rays of the sun: the earth and the heavens say their farewells to one another, full of regret. I knew you and I would part in a few hours, but I wondered if you had become even just a little bit happier.

After seeing you to your train, I returned to the hovel, where I read your letter.

* * *

Soon I will be alone and I am writing you my explanation of what happened. I now feel a terrible void as, in the thirty days of our acquaintance, I experienced what would probably fit into thirty years.

I want to tell you that my heart bears a heavy burden and I would like to be rid of it. Oh, how important it is to me that you understood my real pain.

I cannot deny that you behaved wonderfully, that you took upon yourself to behave discreetly, something that in other circumstances would have appeared ridiculous. But I now feel even more alone and, therefore, what you did, you did in vain.

29

You met a person who lived in hope of finding a friend who was able to understand that a physical ailment, be it blindness, lameness or anything else, is no impediment to loving life for all the joys that it holds. These joys are simple and they are plentiful, and who doesn't want the happiness of living with these joys to the full? And if you saw and appreciated my soul, as you once admitted to me you did, then how could you and why did you sink to pitying me when I am stronger than you. Why did you not kiss me that night, like everyone else; why did you never grasp me and spin me about, forgetting that I could not see? Why did I constantly feel this maddening, cautionary attitude? And you know why. It hurts me bitterly to realise this now. You should not have deceived me; after all, I have been hurt enough as it is. Is that not true? And heaven forbid the thought that we could be happy together...

I am sorry, but what happened was that you spent thirty days admiring yourself. Self-admiration can go unnoticed if one assumes the role of such a respectable man as you showed yourself to be. But I think this is awful. I do not want to teach you, but this really hurts me right now, because you are, all the same, a kind and decent person and I somehow trusted you from the very beginning. But all the same, you need to be more attentive to people, after all, you have eyes and that really counts for a lot.

Farewell.

* * *

Now I live boldly and at ease, as if I have rid myself of some long-running ailment. That is because you cured me, Zhanar. Do you understand? Do you hear me?

BURA

To the lonely, little camel,
left tethered
The author

With a roar, Bura shot through the *aul* of Kazakbai. And there was a curse in his cry.

1

When a person waits for the morning as a release, their eyes become round in the night. Sadness leans over them, chasing away scary dreams. Any living creature pines in much the same way if they are deprived of the friends with whom they have spent days on end in merry play and good-natured squabbles. Bura did not regret the past, which had slipped by like a ray of sunshine. However, he often plodded about the soft dunes of a time gone by, aching from his sweet memories, and the Sahara was his reality. The wind caressed the tender fur on his slender neck as he continued walking after his mirage, after the hope that is always the last thing to die in one's soul. Even the most attentive onlooker would have seen nothing but a serene, gallant giant, rhythmically chewing the cud and viewing the land around with indifference. Bura was too proud to allow his feelings to break through to the surface. He paced along in silence, leading a caravan of shadow-days and the pain he suffered was unknown and unspoken. Although people could say *as weepy as a double-humped camel,* his large eyes were dry and only the flecks of the sunset floated in them. Bura had lost everything, but no-one heard a moan from him. Since the reeds had issued tassels and the grass had burst through towards the sun, he had been passing the *aul* by. Had he really forgotten his home, where he had been surrounded by warm, caring caresses? No, there was no place more homely and wonderful, warm and close to Bura's heart. But he had left it. He would have remained if he could forget the moist eyes of his mother, the she-camel, who had been butchered for meat before his very eyes. He would have remained, but the tight-knit host of his brothers had suddenly disintegrated into shards, each of which sent a searing pain into his heart. His small, warm tribe had been expelled to an *aul*, far beyond the Bukhtarma River.

They had been dispersed without compassion to all corners, ripping apart the tender bonds that had held them together, repelling them like lepers, innocent before God and people. A spear had been plunged into his heart by a cruel hand, as terrible as a snake's forked tongue. Of what were they guilty?

A beast, too, is capable of feeling anguish. For six months, Bura had not recalled his *aul*. No sooner had the green shoots broken through, however, he felt an irrepressible calling to the mountains. The Altai is

31

rich and beautiful. Forty tribes and peoples call it home and there is space aplenty here for them all. The snowy peaks offer shelter to the clouds floating by. The valleys are green and peaceful.

A shrill wind whistles constantly from the mountains, swaying the thick, silvery feather grass, and it then becomes like a furious ocean under the angry gusts of a storm. This plain stretches to the very mountains, mirthless and void of people. Only in the spring does it come to life, when the people wander into the mountains and all around fills with laughter, whooping and singing. Occasionally, the hills and mounds raise their heavy heads but, otherwise, a monotonous steppe stretches as far as the mountains. Here and there the ruins of deserted homes or old mausoleums can be seen. Patches of land, burned white by the sun, are like salt marshes. It is a grey place. But what of it? Be it picturesque or sombre, there was no place more like home for Bura. He paced on ahead and the hill flowed by beneath his hooves.

This was not the first time he had had to take this difficult, winding road to the pasture land, but this was the first time he had felt so alone. In previous years, this journey had been easy-going and merry. No sooner had the steppe turned green than the people gathered together their possessions and set out on their way. And they all walked off together. The strong and experienced camels and horses carried the heaviest burdens. The colts and young camels skipped along with their light loads, keeping pace with the camp, and no-one whipped them along. When the autumn spread its golden robe and the grass obediently yellowed, the people descended into the valleys and the caravan stretched in a line along the old path, like the large shadow of a flock of cranes, hurrying on their way to warmer climes. Everyone was in good health and in good spirits. Even the working camels, who knew no peace, had fat, healthy humps. These were happy times indeed.

Bura came to a stop right by the pass. It was here, before the difficult ascent, that his mother had normally fed him her warm milk. Perhaps he recalled that precious time from the distant past. Perhaps he was simply tired from his long, monotonous journey. His nostrils had been torn by a rope loop. Bura reluctantly sniffed the grass; he didn't really want to eat. He extended his long neck and looked at length at the pass. Then he slowly turned his head and looked back. On the right, the old wintering ground stood in the foothills of Tasshoky Mountain. This was where the flock would find refuge from the frost and, as soon as the snow cleared, they would be herded beyond the pass. And it was to the enclosure that Bura now headed. This was a truly miserable place. Broken sledge runners, smashed bottles, old bootlegs, heaps of sheep dung and dirty poultry feathers. The air reeked of the stench of marsh rot. Treading slowly, Bura approached a wooden trough, cracked from the sun, wind and the passing time. Rusty water had accumulated at one end after the recent heavy rains, while the other end was caked in coarse, dirty salt. Bura lowered his head and licked greedily at the salt. However, someone had poured old fuel oil here and the camel lifted his head and snorted with displeasure. Then he moved on to the empty enclosure. Large, yellow flies swarmed in droves around the moist manure and flew away loudly under Bura's squelching steps. The farmyard was already overgrown with thistles. Here and there, stiff stalks of dry grass lay scattered, the remains of the sheep fodder. Bura stretched out his neck and munched on the stalks, even though there was enough fresh grass all around. Then he scratched himself against a wooden corner post, shredding his mangy sides with pleasure, and headed on toward the pass.

From a distance, he looked like a giant beetle. No longer a huge camel, more a grain of sand in this deserted kingdom, and he was the only living soul in the entire land. The load he was carrying was unusually heavy: the full burden of ages of silence and solitude. Time had outrun his measured pace. Having fallen behind the age, he slowly plodded on alone and there was no sign of life in his eyes. Bura did not know that he was still very much needed by the people and that his current solitude was the result of a misunderstanding. Grievance and pain had taken him far away. And pain is blind. On walked Bura, a giant among people, but an insect in the mountains. But why talk of a camel, when people, too, desert their native homes when aggrieved, dooming themselves to anguish and yearning, profound and eternal?

The sun was beginning to set when Bura emerged at the pass. From here, the edge of the summer pasture, so familiar to Bura, could be seen. Hills stretched onward, overgrown with thick coppice woods.

The nearer Bura got to the places he knew, the more sprightly his step became. Along the way he drank his fill from the mountain stream, the Kairakty, bubbling in a cold rage, and he chewed on a little grass on the bank; it smelled of mint and had a bitter taste, like a distant recollection. He did not remain here for long. Bura caught sight of a round, scorched clearing; it was here that the yurt had stood. He stood there a good while, breathing in the familiar smells, and he was unable to leave without recalling something very important. Neither the sun, red from fatigue and returning to its golden palace, nor the amicable concert put on by the frogs in their emerald, velvet doublets, nor even the cries of the mountain goats could distract him. He searched, obstinately and in considerable torment. Wise but ill-natured crows sat on a post, dried out by the sun and the wind. *Those rotten birds!* thought Bura, his lip protruding in contempt, and he began scratching himself against this post. The crows departed ponderously. And then the black Bura appeared to recall something. Turning his head, he looked at the place where the yurt had stood. Smoke once more plumed above this hearth. A large, six-panel yurt had risen on this scorched circle. Fifteen magnificent racers pawed the soil nearby. A little to one side, fluffy lambs were bleating and a small shepherd boy was gnawing on a piece of sour *kurt*. The camel

33

herder Abish emerged from the yurt, his staff in his hand. Everyone was here, only Bura could not see his fellow camels. They weren't there in this farm *aul*. He imagined he could hear the pitiful crying of a new-born, white-faced camel calf in the woodland. Bura's nostrils flared in compassion and he sobbed loudly. The white yurt disappeared, the hot-blooded steeds were gone and the crying of the camel calf fell quiet. Coolness drew in from the mountains. The north wind rushed in and the tulips belatedly bowed their heads to it as it passed.

The old stopping place could not hold Bura for long, either, and he moved on, into the mountains. Here he knew every last tree and every last stone. A warm shiver spread beneath his coat and a new desire took hold of Bura. It used to be jolly and noisy in the old nomad camps but not once had he found himself at the peak of a mountain. And what was there for him to do back then, on that bare peak, when he was surrounded by friends and there was plenty of sugar-sweet grass all over the slopes? But who knows where desperation, the desperation of solitude, might take one and not just Bura, but people as well! His legs were already stumbling from fatigue and his heavy head was bowed to the ground, but he nevertheless made it up the mountain. The human settlement now lay at his feet and the Bukhtarma twisted and turned like a silver ribbon. His native *aul* was down there in the hazy mist. Bura had not seen it for a long while. It seemed so small and sad to the camel and he had not noticed it when he had lived there. Perhaps now he only noticed the grey and unsightly in things. His grievance was like leucoma in his eye. Bura looked attentively all around: at the ravines, the peaks and the forests. Stretching out his neck, he looked to all four corners. Oh, Lord! How had he not seen it before? A road wound its way up Mount Ulystau, beaten there by nomadic camps. Where did it begin and where did it lead? Whose road was this? Who had travelled it? A desolate trail stretched over the bald mountain, winding its way like a ribbon and sliding like a snake. The years had gone by and the path was still not overgrown. And it was unlike the other routes that Bura had walked in the past. No, he had never walked this path and nor had his brothers, from whom he had now been separated. His ancestors had beaten this path. Heavy, shaggy and even wilder than he was, they had marked this path, pacing steadily and patiently. It had then been drenched and, since that time, no grass had grown there. Back then they would walk to different ends of the earth, obedient to the will of the people, their masters. They carried the people's loads, bales of goods, tears, hopes and joys on their deformed humps. There were times when they saw blood. They had cause to carry wounded masters from death, too, ensuring unfortunate souls were not left in enemy hands. Strange creatures, these slaves of Allah, who spend their time killing one another! Many times the she-camels' milk had saved their masters and their still-bald infants from starvation. Life flowed with the camel's milk.

34

Oh, long, distant road! We passed by and you remained in our memory. You were trodden out by camels. Let that not be a reproach to you.

A sense of unease overcame Bura. His eyes burned with rage. He wanted to strike the earth out of desperation. *Let me carry the full load of the* aul *and I would feel its weight; I would walk whatever distance along this path and I would never know fatigue. Why am I alone?!* Bura wanted to cry, but he could not.

His tender childhood had begun with affection and joy. When he lay, still wet and helpless, he had been taken from his mother and carried into the yurt, beyond the red, cambric canopy. They had kept him there for ten days, concealing him from view. The pockmarked wife of Abish the camel herder had never left the little camel's side. When he had started getting to his disobedient, shaking legs and his large, black eyes misted over with fear, Abish's wife had fed him melted broadtail fat from the big sheep and her pockmarked face had been full of kindness. When he had been let outside for the first time, onto the clearing in front of the yurt, he had swayed on his still-weak legs, his head spinning from delight, and he had tried to run to the sugar-sweet mountains but could only sway all the more. He would never forget that happy, infant happiness when he was caressed by the work-worn hands of Abish and the warm fingers of his pockmarked old woman. Oh, what a life!

Barely had the little Bura been able to stand on his own feet when he lost his mother. She had been loaded up with salt and led away somewhere. How bitter was that salt, both for the she-camel and for the little Bura. In his search for his white mother, he had wandered off into a birch forest. Everything around him had been lit by the moon and its light had been somehow similar to the she-camel's milk. Black shadows had slid heavily and silently above the trees. Disturbed birds had flapped their wings. The little camel could no longer weep, so overwhelmed had he been by terror. He had simply wanted to hide and see nothing. But suddenly his fear had dissipated and he had felt a part of this mysterious nature and neither the restless birds nor the frisky hares had frightened him any longer. Everything had become like an old dream he had once dreamed, centuries ago and he was a part of this dream. Suddenly something had whistled in the night and cracked down like a snake onto his long neck. A rope lasso! A terrible force had pulled him back and he had felt a sharp pain in his throat. The little camel did not understand what had happened thereafter. He had submitted to this brute force. How could he have done anything else? All he had understood was that strange people had captured him and that they had not smelled of Abish. When he had regained his senses, he had sensed familiar hands caressing his neck where the iron hands of the strangers had inflicted such pain. He had opened his eyes and seen Abish and calm had returned. Once more he had heard the familiar voice of his master: "Oh, my silly little camel...

35

How could anyone want to butcher you? Did those wolves think your meat would last them the winter? Eating the meat of such a stripling is nothing more than murder. Such wicked people!"

Bura shed pea-sized tears into the age-old dust of the nomads' path.

Sounds came from afar, filling the silent mountains and the lifeless rocks with life. Barely audible, they came here like the breathing of a sleeping child. These were no cries of a herdsman, no voice of a ranger and no screeching of nocturnal birds. It seemed that a quiet song was playing wistfully somewhere in the distance. These melancholy sounds floated over the mountains, calling up remarkable dreams. The Tasshoky Pass was dreaming. There was not the slightest breeze; all was calm. The loud wings of the ducks had fallen silent, the merry crickets were quiet and only sorrowful sounds continued to grow, touching the heart with their sad melody.

This beautiful song was full of regret, supplication and expectation. It seemed that the mountains had turned black from pity. The mysterious forest was also silent, also listening. The heart ached from this song. But was it really a song? The sounds were not like the usual weeping of a camel; this was something different, something unknown, never heard before and not like any song. Was this a cry from an aggrieved heart, an entreaty, or desperation? Oh no! Perhaps it was a grievance, flying over the mountains, a grievance such that, even here, it was cramped and hemmed in? No. Or was this a weeping song of remembrance? No! This was incurable grief and anguish, hidden deep within. This was horror before the misty, grey dawn, which promised nothing good. Indeed, these laments could not be repeated. The weeping melody that broke into the night was unlike any *Yelimai, Korlan* or *Zhanbotu*, or even the light *Mendy kyz* or *Aimazhan*. The mountains were flooded with black. The night was setting in. Weeping, Bura remained on the path, while the darkness became thicker and thicker.

2

The disappearance of the black Bura had had no particular impact on life in Kazakpai *aul*. Bura had already been more than a year old. In the past, when they had wandered along the Kyzylkain, this could never have happened. Back then, everyone would have taken to their horses, they would have searched and they would have found even a button, not to mention a camel. From that time the *aul* had grown, with many new houses and the farmstead had become large. The people visited one another less often now and only grief or special occasions brought them together. The loss of the black Bura had only left Abish worrying. He had spent his entire life with camels and perhaps this was why this last one, Bura, was so dear to him. When the camel had gone missing, old Abish sorely cursed the management of the collective farm.

He even refused to go to work. He thought the supervisor would call him out but he never came even remotely close to his front door. Abish waited and hoped in vain, and he suffered bitterly. This proud and stubborn old man dreamed up an acute back pain, and he spent many days without rising from his bed. He was not accustomed to displays of reverence. The man's grandson would pop in occasionally.

"Ata," he would say, "Our Bura is wandering at the foot of Tasshoky. He's been seen at Terkuys."

Abish's grandson conveyed rumours about Bura, endeavouring to set the old man at ease. Abish thought about heading out himself on a search but he had no steed to saddle and he could not bring himself to go and ask a favour of the manager.

"Bura has been torn to pieces by wolves!" his grandson burst in on one occasion.

The old man sprung up from his bed, his face distorted in anger.

"Don't talk nonsense!" he roared. "Remember this, lad: Bura and I will never be fodder for wolves or enemies!"

3

At the same time, Bura had crossed over to the sands of Naryn. The days were now cold. A light drifting of snow had become a full blizzard and it would rage for several days. The cheegrass thicket quivered obediently under the gusts of wind and crunched under Bura's cold, heavy steps. For a good while, he hadn't wanted to succumb to the cold, but the blizzard lashed wickedly against his now sunken flanks, crushing his bones. Bura wandered along a railway line; the cheegrass was thicker here, offering him more to eat.

Several years before, when ore material was found in these places, Bura had still been very much wet behind the ears. Construction work had begun on a rail line. Regardless of his advancing years, an order had been issued to train Abish in surfacing work. Bura had not been as headstrong as his brother Akpas and quickly grasped this simple art. He had dragged sleepers, sand, rock and heavy rails. This was a time when not even a little camel calf was left in the *aul* of Kazakpai; all the animals had been herded off to work in the construction. The entire camel tribe had experienced the full burden of labour on this line, which now stretches far to the east. After this, the camels were no longer fit for such heavy work and this work was their last.

Black Bura had been placid and obedient since childhood, unlike his brother Akpas. The worst thing he did was to spit abundantly during the mating season. That said, seeing red, he would sometimes also chase after those around him. One February, though, Akpas had gone particularly wild. He charged about, roaring loudly and dropping large amounts of foam from his grinning mouth. The stock breeder from the collective farm was passing by at that time, not suspecting a thing, but

37

suddenly he found the crazy Akpas was chasing after him. It was a good thing the man had a fast horse beneath him. At first, the distance between them did not decrease, but Akpas, blind with fury, actually began to catch the horse. In several jumps, the frightened horse made it across the ice of the River Karasu which they met on their way. Akpas, while still running, fell to his forelegs, spread his rear legs wide and, sliding, literally flew across the river. He appeared to realise that his legs would not hold him. The stock breeder, clearly not expecting such a thing from a camel, became quite terrified. Urging his horse on with all his might, he made for the forest. He would not have managed to get away and the stock breeder understood this. He struck the horse with his crop and, passing under a tall tree, he caught himself on a branch and flew up, almost to the top, like a cat. Akpas rubbed up against the trunk of the tree, trying with all his might to topple it together with this man. Then, pulling back his head, he looked up. Foaming at the mouth and pawing at the ground in bursts, he then lay under the tree, prepared to wait an eternity for his enemy to appear. His jaw moved evenly, gathering up plenty of evil-smelling spit as he chewed his cud.

At that time, Abish was sick and was lying in the district hospital. He was the only one who could have got the camel to move from there. The stock breeder needed to be saved and so they shot Akpas dead.

Bura was not like his brother but now something happened to him. He ate nothing for two weeks, resigned to the call of nature. His eyes filled with blood, blinding and terrible, as it was during the mating season. Perhaps his lengthy solitude had taken its toll. Yet he wandered on, restless and troubled, spitting foam and grinding his teeth as he went. All tied up in knots, Bura rushed about, roaring with a sound like a short hum. The deserted steppe heard his desperation: *Boo! Boo!* Had he encountered anyone in his path, Bura would have trampled them, squashed and destroyed them, but there was no-one out here in this naked steppe other than Bura himself. Not even a mouse ran out in front of him and not a single bird cast its shadow over the plain.

Bura was now in a similar state to his wicked brother Akpas. Akpas, though, had gone mad from nothing to do, while this creature had been affected by solitude. His eyes were sunken from hunger, his unshorn coat hung down in clumps from his sides, moulting old fur mixed with new growth. Bald patches had appeared on his body; his humps had become emaciated and hung to the sides, not firm and upright as before.

Bura was not himself. His *Boo! Boo!* could be heard more and more often. It appeared that the short, winter's day had only just dawned and it was already approaching the evening in this still, lifeless steppe plain. The snowstorm that had raged all night like a she-wolf finally let up. Bura, though, was still looking for any other living creature. He looked at length out into the deceptive and hopeless distance. He looked until his eyes hurt. He wanted to roar from desperation but his mouth was full of bitter spit. He wanted to weep, but he had no tears. He wanted to die but death was somehow in no hurry. What could he do? Where could he go? To the *aul*? Heaven forbid! They would shoot him on the spot, just like Akpas, and he did not deserve such a death. *Boo-boo-boo-boo!*

Oo-oo-oo-oo! a railway engine responded shrilly. Bura started. He didn't know it was a train coming. A voice! He had heard a voice! His ageing memory told him he had already heard this sound in the past. Perhaps this was how males called to one another to fight over a white she-camel with large, wet eyes that dreamed of the impossible. His anguish faded once more and Bura went forth toward the powerful voice that was calling him.

A black plume of smoke hung over the turn; the wheels clattered over the rails. Wagons stretched out in a caravan, laden with timber, coal and iron. The train drew up to Bura. The camel roared out and foolish rage overcame him. He gave no thought to the fact he was weak and small compared with this giant and he threw his haggard body right into the train. Foam flew from his mouth in snow-like flakes. Jets of steam poured from his nostrils. Bura was urged on by a single desire to topple and trample the train. And he flew chest first into one of the wagons. A terrible force crushed him and threw him a considerable distance to the side. The engine gave out a shriek and the indifferent wagons rushed past the prostrate Bura.

Bura lay to the side of the railway line, his chest crushed. Blood spilt from his mouth, mixed with foam. Agony crashed through his body. He walked over a golden, sultry ocean, breathing in the aromas of strong spices and a bronze bell around his neck foretold a long-long journey.

Convulsions overcame his legs. A gruff breath darted out, his last in this world, and a late, clear tear ran from his dead eyes. The steppe turned to stone in grief. It was arrested in a lengthy silence. It was abandoned without Bura. And that was how the last camel from the *aul* of Kazakpai finally perished.

* * *

Hearing of Bura's death, the old camel herder Abish, who had not risen from his bed, went the same day to the manager to ask for a horse.

"After all, he had been plenty useful in his time. It would be cruel to leave his bones out there in the steppe. He should be brought back and buried properly. Perhaps his coat could be used for something."

"Come off it! Humans are mortal too. Why send a horse out because of some dumb camel?!" the manager said by way of a refusal. The aggrieved Abish returned home, his bridle concealed behind his back. But the old man did not forget the black Bura.

Barely had the snow begin to thaw and it had begun to grow warmer, than he took his grandson and went out on foot to the sands of the Naryn. There he brushed away the odious flies from the already rotting corpse and he buried Bura. He had carried a wooden stake with him the entire journey and now he positioned it on Bura's grave. It was actually more a column than a stake. He instructed his grandson to inscribe the words: *Here rests Bura, who died in a battle with a train.* However, the rains came and washed away these clumsily written words.

Trains pass by this place twice a day. The people in the warm compartments, seated on comfortable seats, pay no attention to the column that stands on a hill, turned white by the sun and heavy rains. Even if they do notice it, they believe it is a surveyor's boundary marker. They have no idea whose sweat has watered this comfortable railway line. And they also have no idea that not a single camel remains in the *aul* of Kazakpai. But perhaps the people will not forget the black camel known as Bura. After all, the railway engine whistles its welcome each time it passes here. The mournful whistle drowns out the wheels, hurriedly telling the tales of the lone Bura. No, this is by no means a keening song for Bura, buried in eternal sleep in the golden sands...

The train rushes, hurries, flies on its way...

What force could hold it back? There is no such force!

ARDAK

Many years ago, a modest yurt stood on the banks of Lake Markokol, at the point where the Sharykty stream flows in. Like a grey goose, who had lost its mate, this yurt stood forlornly in one and the same place, while livestock grazed over a wide pastureland around it. Goats, sheep and calves were joined in a single, cohesive herd, never dispersing and, rising up above them, like an attentive shepherd, stood a white camel with broad, keen nostrils. At times, standing amidst his flock, the master's chestnut gelding would appear, bowing his head as if in prayer and sinking his teeth into the grass. Put out to pasture with his legs fettered, the chestnut horse hobbled clumsily after the other animals, keen to fill his immense belly as fast as he could.

Kozha, the old master of the yurt and the herd, was not a man without kith and kin. There had been a time when he had lived in a village. And just as a mane and tail are the tell-tale signs that you're looking at a horse, the mere existence of relatives is a sure sign that a person has them. When Kozha was just twenty-five and his father, the youngest son of Kozha's grandfather Yesirkegen, passed away, his uncles Shalabai and Dalabai descended down on him, split the property of the deceased into three parts and, each with their own considerable share, hurriedly made their departure. As a farewell, Uncle Shalabai told the young man, "The deceased was your father, but to us, he was our brother, our own flesh and blood!" And so Kozha was left all on his own with his mother at his now destitute wintering ground.

How about that for relatives! Kozha was never one to be lazy and, in a few years, he had multiplied his share of his father's property. He found himself a decent bride and arranged an opulent wedding feast, even though he had only recently been walking around in tatters and rags. The uncles Shalabai and Dalabai, although invited, refused to come, saying, "That snotnosed brat got married and didn't even seek our advice. We won't go!" But if only this had been the last of it... The jealous relatives spread a rumour that, when Yesirkegen's property had been divided, the old woman Kadisha, Kozha's mother, had hidden a couple of sheep for her son and they claimed that these had produced another five head. So in broad daylight, Shalabai and Dalabai stole five sheep from their nephew's flock. Old Kadisha then flew into a rage at her brothers-in-law: "What an outrage! Have you no shame, plundering your own kin before the eyes of the entire village? It would be better never to set eyes on such relatives than live by their side and put up with their humiliation! No! Your father never brought you into the world to behave like that. We will take down our yurt and at dawn, we will leave for Lake Markokol; the pasture by the Sharykty spring has no owner and we will make our home there."

The following day, smoke was already billowing from Kozha's yurt on the wasteland next to Lake Markokol. Some twenty-five years had galloped by since that day and the years had not brought Kozha any particular prosperity to speak of but he could not say that his new home was an unhappy one either. A quarter of a century had passed by in hard work, Kozha already looked like an old man and his entire fortune barely covered the cost of providing guests with tea as is right and proper. The old woman Kadisha had long since departed this world, but into it came the comely, strong Ardak. She was Kozha's only child and, despite his grumbling and her efforts, his wife was unable to provide him with any more.

Before she died, the old woman made her final wishes known to her son:

"While it is still not too late, be sure to return back to our people in the village. We are like the fools in the story who, exasperated by the bed bugs, end up burning their entire house down! Aggrieved at our relatives, we left our village and, since then, neither you nor I have spent a day without yearning for the company of other people. What is there to hide, now I am facing death? So, people lied to us, but we didn't always tell the truth ourselves, let Allah be the judge. They also say that a problem shared is a problem halved. Go back to our native village, my son, even if they set the dogs on you. Let them kick you in the head but when your leg or your head feel pain, at the end of the day it is only people that will come to your aid. I am like a lost sheep in this lonely and unfortunate house and we don't even have a shroud to wrap me up in. And we have no neighbours we could ask. This is how things have turned out and evidently, it is God's will. Allah has clearly chosen to punish us for some sin or other."

The moment his strict yet wise mother was no more, Kozha came to sense the truth in these words. It had been easier for her to meet her death than it had been for her son to witness it, as she had long since—her whole life, in fact—prepared herself for this meeting with her maker, knowing that there would come a time when she would leave forever with her eyes closed. Her son, however, was unprepared for this loss and in that difficult hour, there were no kind people to sit by his side and lessen his sorrow. He even had to dig the grave himself; at least the soil was soft and there were no rocks. And the three of them stood over the freshly heaped burial mound: Kozha, his wife and their five-year-old daughter Ardak. She was astonished that they had buried her sleeping grandmother in the ground but she was soon distracted and seeing the wet clay she set about moulding a *kibitka* cart out of it. In the meantime, Kozha moved his lips in prayer, masking his brow and face with his hands.

Time, however, moves on, like water through a man's fingers, and Ardak, who had only recently been moulding playthings from the

42

clay next to her grandmother's grave, had grown into a young woman. Like the blossoming of the spring flowers, she had bloomed into a sixteen-year-old maiden.

Good-looking and a fine shepherdess, Ardak was both a daughter and a son to her mother and father and a great helper to boot. The virtues of this delightful girl were countless but she had one shortcoming. She was unable to roll her "r's", perhaps because, spoiled by her loving parents, she still felt and behaved like a small child, for whom burring and lisping were only natural. And so she never learned how to pronounce a hard "r-r-r" and this drove her kind parents to despair. They knew and lamented the fact that this little defect would render her virtues worthless.

"You see, wife, it is just as people say: *some are destined to have fine leather fall into their laps, but a poor man never has enough to even patch a hole in his coat*," Kozha would complain angrily. "Yes, we'll be forever clutching our heads and berating ourselves for having an only daughter who is as good as mute... It's not as if she's a lad who, slouching on his horse, could bark at his future in-laws: *You think you can laugh at me? Well, listen up! I've blought you a fine herd of horses! So shut your tlaps and hand over your plitty little daughter!* And anyone would hand over their daughter, no matter how dock-tongued the lad was. But who on earth would ever court a tongue-tied lass? You'll see, mother, it's not her face they'll be looking at but her tongue..."

"Ardak, thanks be to Allah, is both a son and a daughter to you. So if no-one takes her in marriage; what of it? Are we going to put her in the pot and eat her? It just means that she'll remain at home and we'll watch over her. She'll be a great help to you and me as well."

"Oh, we are to blame for this! If she had lived among the people in the village, she would no longer be babbling like a little child."

Kozha spent many a sleepless night, worrying terribly that his daughter's tiny defect would end up bringing her much unhappiness. And then his head would swell and ring like a copper cauldron... One night, tormented by his lack of sleep and his endless ponderings, Kozha suddenly lost his temper and thumped his peacefully sleeping wife in the side.

"You old crone! All you do is doze all the hours of the day and the night. Do you have nothing else on your mind other than getting a good night's sleep? Why don't you think about your daughter's future, you old crone? God, I hope you never get another wink of sleep again!"

His wife knew that at times like this her best course of action was to keep her peace and not rise to the old man's bait. She only asked him shortly to be a little quieter so as not to wake Ardak. And, with a lingering yawn, she fell silent.

However, her indifference only made him madder. Kozha prodded her in the ribs with his elbow, jumped up from the bed and with shaking hands groped around in the dark for his trousers.

"You old fool!" screamed Kozha in his rage. "No-one will take your daughter in marriage! Do you understand, you idiot?!"

Only then did his dishevelled wife rise from the bed and try to calm her husband's nerves with tender words. Having somehow calmed the old man down, she put him back to bed and, with a yawn, lay down beside him.

"Oh, I was having such a lovely dream until you woke me up."

"Well, you know what you can do with your damned dream," Kozha cursed.

For a while, they lay there in silence. Then he spoke once more:

"Wife, we at least have to be ready, just in case. We need to start putting something away for a dowry. Let Shalabai and Dalabai gossip all they like that my daughter is dock-tongued. We'll find a decent man for our Ardak all the same... And rather than wine and dine Shalabai that time, I should have treated him to my horse whip and sent him packing, may he rot in hell... And you...you are to blame for all this. That is what I wanted to do but you had to cut in, snivelling with your *But he is your flesh and blood* nonsense. And now this flesh and blood is spreading rumours about our daughter here, there and everywhere... Hey, are you listening to me?"

In response, his wife merely whiffled quietly through her nose.

"Ugh, I hope you never wake up. All you ever do is lie there, you old hag! If it weren't for this gossip, I would have long since moved to the village."

Kozha was referring to the last and only visit that his Uncle Shalabai had made, after which word had spread around the entire region that Kozha's daughter was short of tongue and that all she could do was lisp and mumble as if her mouth was full of gruel. This had been a few years earlier. Shalabai and his son Almas had been travelling to visit his wife's relatives and had dropped into his nephew's yurt, which was on the way. Kozha still remembered the old grievances and he particularly resented the fact that his uncle had not even come to his mother's funeral.

"*Assalamualaikum!*" Shalabai said as he poked his head into the yurt, his eyes swivelling this way and that, not sure if he should enter or if it would be better if he were on his way.

Kozha had only managed to purse his lips and fix him with an angry stare when the old woman flew out to meet them, gabbling away:

"Oh, look! My brother-in-law has come to see us! And he's brought his son with him! Come in, come in!" And she set about kissing the boy, who was the same age as Ardak.

After that she winked to her husband unnoticed, calling him outside, and there she said to him,

44

"Well, you know what they say Kozha, the only way to beat someone who throws stones is to kill them with hospitality! Why are you being so stubborn? After all, he is your flesh and blood, your only family. What is the good in cutting off your own hand? We'd be much better off offering due hospitality as is right and fitting and let your mother's spirit on the other side rest in peace."

After that Kozha gave in. He brought in the flock, selected a sheep and, leading it to Shalabai, who had wandered outside, said to him,

"Well, uncle, give it your blessing if it is to your liking!"

He wanted to shame his uncle with his generosity and hospitality. But he had ended up with nothing to show for it...

Shalabai's son quickly made friends with Ardak. At first, they spent many an hour running about, playing hide-and-seek near the yurt. Then, short of breath, Ardak made a suggestion,

"It's loasting hot?! Almas, let's go and bathe in the lake!"

They both stripped naked and ran full pelt into the water. It was at that moment that Ardak, who had never seen another child in her life, let alone a boy, understood that they were different...

Shalabai, meanwhile, had taken a keen interest in the twelve-tailed crop that was hanging from Kozha's yurt pole. He admired the whip for some time and when his hosts had left the yurt, he quickly took it down and stuffed it into his boot. Shalabai was most pleased with his visit to his nephew. Having already made his farewells, the uncle was sitting on his horse when Ardak came up, crying happily,

"Almas, make sure you come liding to us again!"

Shalabai gaped with his mouth open, staring at the girl in amusement.

"Hey, what was that? Do mean to tell me that your Ardak has a docked tongue?"

"Of course not!" replied Kozha, scowling in annoyance. "The girl is just a little spoiled, and speaks as if she is still a child..."

However, on their way, Almas told his father that Ardak hadn't behaved like a child when she was with him and that indeed she had a terrible lisp and, what's more, she didn't even know the difference between a boy and a girl. Listening to his son, Shalabai grinned merrily. He was already beginning to imagine how he would recount this tale to Dalabai and everyone else and, in so doing, cause his Clever-Dick nephew considerable annoyance and perhaps even some grief. Now in high spirits, Shalabai struck his lazy, quailing horse with his whip and galloped off at a sprightly pace.

Soon the whole district knew that *One-Yurt* Kozha's daughter was so dock-tongued that she was practically mute. Kozha heard rumours of this and harboured a dark animosity, planning to get his own back on his uncle when the occasion arose. And the occasion presented itself pretty soon thereafter.

Kozha was on his way to Zhakibai the blacksmith to get his one and only chestnut horse shod. It was a wet day and the road was muddy and soft, just the thing for a horse with worn-out shoes. Once the frost set in, there would be no way of riding an unshod animal on it. The sun was straying somewhere up in the grey clouds and a damp wind blew in from the north. Crows sat atop a bare poplar and loudly discussed their plans for the coming winter. Kozha was out of sorts at the sight of the inclement, autumnal weather. He knitted his brow and wrapped his long quilted *chapan* tightly round his chest.

He got to thinking that in the half-century he had lived on this earth, he had been blessed with only one great joy and that was his charming daughter. She was all he needed to be happy. But wicked people had chosen to envy him and their enmity had caused his tranquillity to dissolve like the remains of the teal's droppings in the waters of the lake. He had no recollections of any great joys but he also had no recollections that made him involuntarily clutch his head or want to slap himself. He had never let any worries about the future ever get the better of him, just so long as there was food on the table today. He also kept his dreams to himself, just as a prudent man keeps his horse tethered. There were times when he would climb to the top of Mount Akshoky and stand there for a long time looking out mournfully towards the village he had left behind. The mountains and mirages loomed up before him and an old pain smouldered in his chest. Then he would return home, without consolation, weary and with a haggard face. There was only one thing he wanted and that was never again to be affected by other people's animosity and deceit. But now, these very same things were going to affect his daughter.

This was what dominated Kozha's thoughts on the road that muddy season and his head swelled and rang like a copper cauldron from these morose and mirthless thoughts. Kozha now imagined that his entire life had been as joyless as this weather, as comfortless as the autumn cold and as unsteady as the stumbling steps of his unshod horse. At the Akshoky pass, Kozha caught sight of another rider coming towards him. There was only one path here and it would soon bring the two of them face to face. From the rider's stooping position and the fact that he held his whip in his left hand, Kozha recognised his Uncle Shalabai from quite a distance. "Oh, Allah," thought Kozha, closing his eyes, "thank you and give me strength! I'll meet my enemy with the crushing breast of my horse! Well, my chestnut steed, let's show him, what's what!" Jumping down from his horse, he tightened his saddle strap and tied his hat fast in preparation for battle. Leaping nimbly back into the saddle, he grasped his whip and his expression changed in an instant, his teeth clenched in rage. Then he launched into the charge against his uncle, calling loudly on the spirit of his ancestor to help him:

"Yesirkegen! Yesirkegen!"

As Shalabai, who had never in his life wavered when faced with his opponent, also called upon the spirit of his ancestor for help, they both ended up uttering one and the same battle cry:

"Yesirkegen!" And with that same cry, the uncle galloped out to meet Kozha, waving his whip as he went.

As they drew nearer to each other on the narrow pass, they exclaimed simultaneously "I see my enemy!", angrily thrashed at one another with their whips and parted at full gallop, neither of them stopping their horses, turning back or even looking around. They both felt ashamed, for each of them had called upon their common forefather in bad faith and, in so doing, had disturbed Yesirkegen from his slumbers in the grave. They receded away from each other along the pass, both knitting their brows darkly, both feeling their mutual hatred, born in their oppressive strife, in the fumes of their cooking pots and in their crowded yurts. This was a hatred that had grown and strengthened over the years and one day it might have devoured the pair of them, ensuring that neither would ever enjoy happiness again. If only Kozha had known then, overwhelmed as he was by the hatred that boiled up inside him, that in a mere five years from that day, Shalabai, who had just aimed his whip at his own nephew, would meet an untimely death and that he himself would be wailing, "My dear uncle! My flesh and blood!" striking the ground next to the grave of his reconciled kinsman? Or that the poor chestnut horse on which he now sat would be butchered in his uncle's honour and eaten at his funeral feast.

* * *

Yet this reconciliation was still a long way off. For now, Kozha would continue to live on the banks of the Markokol and tend to his herd with the help of his beautiful daughter.

Despite the peaceful tranquillity of her shepherd's life, Ardak's soul became troubled. Previously, the only people she had known were her mother and father, the white camel and the chestnut gelding. To her everyone else seemed to appear from far away or ride past like the characters from distant fairytale lands. Now, though, after the visit of her relatives, everything had changed. Although Ardak could not understand the meaning of this mysterious anxiety, it became all the clearer to her that she was no longer able and no longer wished to live like this, far away and isolated from other people.

Her boyish manners gradually disappeared and she came to look more and more like a girl. Her roguish and mischievous behaviour was replaced with a caring, sensitive attention to her parents and the latter, although touched to tears concealed their hidden anxiety. They understood that it would be difficult for this newly awoken girl to withstand the natural and sacred forces welling up inside her, but who

47

would reveal this secret to her and who would be the one to crown her with the first feelings of deserved happiness?

It was as if Ardak was floating in a no-man's land between dreams and reality and no force in the world could have ever torn her away from her strange, sweetly tantalising visions. She spent almost no time in the yurt now, wandering at length over the lakeside grass, walking far into the mountains and standing hidden in some gorge, as if waiting for an arranged rendezvous of two dear friends. Or she would sit motionless for hours on the banks of the Markokol, her arms clutched around her knees, looking out at the shimmering waves as one raced in after another. They appeared to promise some kind of solace and appeasement and Ardak, at last heeding their long, monotonous summons, would throw off her stuffy clothes and rush into the bitterly cold embrace of the lake. Cooling her hot body with the fresh water, Ardak would swim to the shore and walk along the dry earth, rubbing her hands against the cool skin of her body, which sprang back in response. Leaning over the smooth, shallow water, she would look with pained bewilderment at the reflection of her youthful, white, flowing and shivering flesh. This newfound knowledge was a source of persistent confusion to Ardak.

It had first assailed her that day when she went swimming with Almas in the lake. A long time had passed since then and the winter was behind her when her rebellious dreams had been sultry and fanciful amidst the surrounding snows, but now spring was walking the land, plentiful, verdant and warm, while Ardak stood at the blue edge of the lake, as naked as a white cloud.

Increasingly, the old couple would spend their sleepless nights, discussing the sad situation in which their grown-up daughter now found herself. And on each occasion, these watchful nocturnal hours would end with the couple squabbling and still no nearer a solution.

One night, after the latest altercation, when they had settled down and fallen unobtrusively into sleep's embrace and an abrupt, simultaneous, rhythmical snoring, Ardak quietly got out of bed and left the yurt, dressed only in her nightshirt.

The spring night drifted invisibly into the verges of the pending summer, the freshness was already pleasant and at times wafted warmly like bated breath along the night-time shores of the Markokol. Ardak sat by the water's edge, as white and motionless as a mermaid and the moonlit, sleepy waves lapped at her feet. Embracing the upturned basin of her knees, she rocked her head and sang her mother's favourite song in a barely audible voice:

> *Grey horseman with your gun,*
> *the village you call home*
> *is just beyond the mountain, yon,*

that mountain blue, alone...

She broke off from her song suddenly, as if discarding it angrily to one side and lay with her face in the sand, sobbing passionately. Then she jumped up, waded decisively into the lake right up to her neck and, with the water's moonlit sheen almost touching her lips, she whispered, "Almas, why don't you come? I am bathing here all alone." Having not seen any other boy bar her young relative, Ardak simple-mindedly believed that they had only to splash about together in the lake and all her dark yearnings would simply dissipate and disappear. The lake passionately cradled her face in its dense and glistening glare.

* * *

That year, the shores of Markokol dried up and blossomed riotously. The young grass greedily shot up from under the previous year's dried growth. Drowning in the heat haze, the spring's open expanses melded softly into the foothills of the blue sky. The smooth lake reflected this bright, spotless firmament and a long cloud, like a white yarn, stretching horizontally from Mount Tarbagatai, divided the snowy peaks of the mountains from the earth, making them seem as if they were floating up in the heavens. It was as if the air that day was filled with the aroma of fresh *kumiss*. Teals on the wing descended impetuously, cutting the water with their breasts as they landed onto the lake and rocked among the waves.

Kozha had long since grown accustomed to these scenes; with each passing year they repeated themselves and at times nature seemed monotonous, dull and artless to him, as did so much of his day-to-day life. It was at moments like this that he wanted to abandon everything and leave for some new, unknown land. But where could he go?! A wild horse gallops across the steppe, faster than the wind, but can you really gallop away from yourself? No! It was clear that he could not leave the shores of Lake Markokol; he and his family were bound here by some strong, rope-like force.

At the foot of Akshoky, the herd grazed their way up a hill, receding ever higher like Kozha's hairline. This was the entire sum of his life's fortune and hopes. Screwing up his eyes he looked at length at his livestock. If Azrael, the angel of death had come for him then, he would undoubtedly have had to take the shepherd's flock along with him. Year in year out, Kozha's flock remained the same. It neither grew nor shrank; his husbandry followed the same cycle each year, never bringing in an abundant income but never a cause for worrying about the future. Kozha had long since stopped hoping that his size of his herd would ever significantly increase; he had come to terms with his lot and was at ease. There was now only one thing that filled him with anxiety and that was his daughter's future.

"So I have lived to see another summer," Kozha muttered, gazing at the mountains. "My whole life has passed by like a horse that has been tethered to a stake for the night... and a tethered horse who hasn't even had his saddle removed."

He went back to the yurt, his hands clasped firmly behind his back. The old woman, who had already risen, was preparing breakfast. Kozha returned her surly look.

"Is Ardak up yet?"

"Probably. I just can't seem to wake her up..."

"So she's still slumbering, is she? Well, what's to be done, if she takes after her mother?"

And so there they sat, the three of them, drinking tea, like the three legs on a cooking pot. The canopy of the yurt was open and Akshoky, the White Mountain, could be seen in the distance. A cool breeze fanned the yurt and the hot sun lit up the front corner. Kozha was sitting over his tea with a morose, unhappy frown on his face as if he was counting his losses. Suddenly, his eyes came to life and sparkled: he had seen a horseman in the distance, descending from the direction of Akshoky.

"Look woman!" Kozha exclaimed, knocking over his bowl of tea in his agitation. "There's someone coming in this direction! Quick, tidy the yurt up. And make yourself more amiable!" and, with that, he hurriedly jumped up.

While the women were putting the yurt in order, Kozha brought over a bundle of dried dung cakes and threw them down in front of them.

"Stick this under our pile of belongings over there and cover it up with a carpet."

"But what on earth for?"

"So he'll think we're richer than we are, of course, you foolish woman! Or do you think your daughter's dowry is so abundant that it's about to burst through the roof? Now stick it under there, I tell you! And get on with it."

Ardak could not fathom the reason for this sudden flurry of activity until her father barked at her,

"Put on your newest clothes! And don't you dare open your mouth while our guest is here, do you understand? Don't you say a word!"

At last, the guest arrived at the yurt. A tall, pockmarked horseman he was, a little on the old side; either a little over or under thirty years of age. Kozha invited him into the yurt, sat him in the seat of honour and, seating himself opposite, he looked into the guest's eyes, hoping to discern some traces of kindness.

"Tell me, son, who are you and from which village do you hail?"

50

"I am from Mametek and our family hails from Kozhambet," the young man began confidently and without embarrassment. "I decided to shoot myself an animal on this side of Akshoky, saw your yurt standing here and thought I would drop in. I have heard much about you..."

"Well, good on you for coming! You are most welcome, my dear fellow. And how is the *biy* of Mametek doing? Is his livestock in good shape? And is he still going strong?"

"Thanks be to Allah, all is well, yes."

"And what is your name, son?"

"Salyk."

They butchered a sheep and, while the old man and his wife were preparing it, the stranger remained alone with Ardak in the yurt. The young man looked at the comely girl avidly. He could not take his eyes off her tender face and white neck, shining like a precious necklace between the collar of her quilted gown and her shining black crown of hair. He was ready to throw himself upon her there and then and yet Ardak understood nothing. It was the first time in her life she had ever seen a fine young *dzhigit*, yet his passionate stare roused nothing in particular within her. So what if he was looking at her with those bulging, glittering eyes; she guessed that was just how things were meant to be. There was only one thing she couldn't dispel from her head that made her uncomfortable: why had her father forbid her from speaking with their guest? She would have liked to ask him if, by chance, he knew Almas, and what it was like living in a village, and why his eyes were bulging in that funny way. Unable to hold back, a smile broke out across Ardak's face.

"What is so amusing, my sister?" the guest enquired politely.

Silence.

"You don't want to speak..? Oh, well, clearly only feasts and festivals could bring joy to such an angel as you. And is your name not Ardak?"

Ardak nodded slowly. She so wanted to talk and laugh and chatter and chatter she could have burst. But her father was nearby and he had been forbidden her to do so. Oh, what wouldn't she have given to go swimming right now! And the strange way that this young man was looking at her was clearly making him come over all hot. If only she could lure him away to the lake and push his enormous head that was as black as cooking-pot under the water...

"Ardak!" came her father's voice. "Come and help your mother with the innards and the tripe."

The meat had been eaten. Everyone was full. It was time to sleep and the lady of the house set about preparing a bed for the guest. The young man had just gone outside to get some air. The old woman turned to her husband:

"Where should I lay a bed for our guest?"

51

"Stop fussing," Kozha replied lazily, half asleep. "Make him a bed wherever you see fit..."

And so everyone turned in for the night. Ardak couldn't sleep. The old couple, began snoring the moment their heads hit their pillows, perhaps on purpose or perhaps not? Their guest lay quietly by the far wall. The coals were still glowing in the hearth and, looking at the flickering, red spots, barely audibly Ardak whispered her thoughts out loud: *The fire doesn't want to sleep and neither do I. Mama likes her sleep... and this young man likes his slumbers too... that makes him just as silly as her.* Without making a sound, Ardak quietly rose from her bed. The guest coughed in the dark and turned over. The girl stood there, waiting for the quiet to descend once more and then she threw on her gown and carefully made her way out of the yurt.

It was the season known as *Oliara*, the dark period between the moons, and over the land lay a soft, cool darkness, which was full of large stars that hung low in the sky. The lake gently lapped in the dark, filling the air with a keen freshness, and the breeze carried the flowery aroma of the grass. Somewhere a horse whinnied anxiously and loudly: the chestnut was missing the herd. Not even a horse wants to live in solitude, thought Ardak.

She approached the lake and it seemed that the Markokol was somehow angry with her. The darkness of *Oliara* concealed the lake's sparkling, night-time visage. Ardak cast off her clothes and was walking down to the water when then she heard a noise behind her.

Accustomed to the dark, she could instantly make out the figure of the guest, approaching. He came up to her, testing the ground gingerly beneath his feet. However, approaching the naked girl he took her boldly in his arms and, with a stifled laugh, said,

"My dear girl, what sort of place is this that people do their bathing in the middle of the night?! I have never heard of such a thing!"

"But I...I always go bathing," replied Ardak innocently.

"Aren't you afraid?"

"No."

"Won't you freeze in there?"

"I don't fleeze in the water," said Ardak, standing tall and white like a mermaid. "Do you want to swim together? Out to the velly middle of the lake?"

"Well, you see, I don't know how to swim," the young man replied, although he hurriedly removed his clothes all the same. "Oh well, I suppose if we have to swim, swim we shall!"

Drawing near to the girl, he nonchalantly, as if by accident, placed his hand on her broad, white, smooth hip. Ardak, like a frightened animal, jumped away and the man lost his nerve, thinking the wild thing would turn and savagely maul him. However, stopping a few steps away, he froze to the spot.

52

"What's the matter, Ardak?" asked the young man, growing bolder.

"Don't glasp or touch me," replied the girl plaintively. "I don't like being tickled, Salyk."

And with that, she rushed into the lake. He ran in after her and began embracing her young, supple, ample body under the water, while she escaped his clutches, splashing his face with water. But again and again, he thrust himself upon her. Like a pair of enormous, white river perch, gambolling in the dark pool, they twisted around each other, splashing and jumping out of the dark water. Ardak seemed to have lost her senses and she no longer feared Salyk's tickling and crude fumbling: she grabbed the young man by the throat and the hair and dunked his head under the water several times. He felt that if this went on just a little more, he would have no strength left to fight with her; he was all in, had taken his fill of the water and was growing weak in the girl's frenetic embrace. But somehow he contrived to entwine himself tightly around her shivering figure and he began kissing her lips and neck, embracing her until she calmed down in his arms and relented. And then he pulled her out of the water and, lifting her high in his arms, he carried her to the shore. He placed her down on their dry clothes. She was as submissive and beautiful as the daughter of King Solomon the sovereign of the waters, and her enchanted body passively obeyed what passion dictated. But then it suddenly started, cowered, rebelled and revolted. Salyk was cast aside and the frightened Ardak rushed off like a bird into the darkness with a pitiful wail, her indistinct, white and desecrated body concealed by the dark corners of the night.

The following morning, when he awoke, Kozha could find no sign of his guest. His boots remained but the man was gone.

* * *

A fair while passed and Kozha no longer harboured any hopes that anyone would ever come courting his daughter again. Salyk had disappeared completely and not so much as the crown of his head ventured from the other side of the mountains. Now, though, it was not the fact that his daughter might remain unmarried that tormented the poor father but the increasing heaviness of her gait and girth. Only recently, the old woman had begun to suspect something and came whispering about it to her husband. So fierce was his rage that he dragged her out of the yurt by the hair and gave her an almighty thrashing. And the shame that had caused him to raise his hand to his wife for the first time in twenty-five years of married life became more evident with each passing day. Kozha felt like dropping dead on the spot or jumping on his horse and riding off to wherever his good steed's legs would carry him. He was overcome with despair. After all, he thought, they say that even if a war

53

drags for forty years, only those who are fated to be killed will perish. Such is the nature of fate...

Then one day, Kozha's anger deflated and petered out altogether; he no longer kicked up a fuss or raged, lashing out at the old woman at the slightest provocation. It was as if he had become dull, calm and indifferent to everything. He now regretted more than ever that he had not moved back to the village when he had had the chance.

Ardak, too, was unrecognisable. She was incapable of understanding the condition she was in and only when surprised by its first signs, did she tell her mother everything that had happened. The old woman pressed Ardak's head to her breast and wept bitterly. Then, drying her tears, she told her daughter about Adam and Eve. "At first," her mother explained, "humans were two creatures moulded into one. They say it had four legs and four arms. God then realised that in this form, people would never reproduce and so he took the human and split it in half. And that, they say, is how we got the boy and the girl, the Adam and the Eve, and they fell in love."

"And what does that mean?" asked Ardak curiously.

Her mother sobbed and fell silent. Hesitatingly and at some length, she tried to find the right answer to her daughter's question. Wracking her brains and still failing to think of anything, as a precaution, she decided to tell her all the ancient folk tales she could recall about famous lovers. Then, having greedily listened to all her old mother had to say, Ardak asked excitedly:

"But did you and father also have love, mama?"

The old woman again fell silent and sighed. Finally, she said:

"I don't know, my little calf, I don't know... He would often come visiting our village. And, one day, he just came and stole me away..."

For Ardak, these conversations might have been useful had she heard them earlier. Now, though, they could not help the girl unravel the secrets of this complex world. From where had this Salyk appeared, where had he gone and would he ever return? Not one of the three of them knew the answers to these questions.

Time passed and the birth was drawing nearer and Ardak became more troubled with each day that passed. In one fell swoop, her carefree childhood had been swallowed up by the brittle eggshell of motherhood and now there was no recognising the young shepherdess. Her legs and hips swelled and spread, her beautiful, clear face was now covered with spots and the end of her nose was marked with dark blemishes. She was continually sick but she still greedily devoured her food and could never seem to eat her fill. For the first time in her life, she came to know emotional unrest, groundless anxiety and dark fears. Her living offspring only had to stir in her womb and Ardak would run screaming to find her mother.

54

And so the night came when Ardak could not close her eyes until almost morning. Her parents, lying by the door as they always did, were fast asleep. They had long kept watch that night, but as morning approached, sleep got the better of them. The flame in the twisted oil wick smoked and faltered. It was gloomy and stuffy in the smoky yurt. Ardak lay sweating, her lips dry and bitten. Frightened, she decided that whatever happened she would endure. However, the more the new child wanted to emerge into the bright, new world, the more turbulent it became and it tormented its mother, kicking her and draining her of her strength. Ardak got out of her bed, barely managing to regain her breath from the pain. The old couple, deep asleep, did not hear a thing. Ardak realised that she would be unable to stop herself from screaming out loud. Clutching her stomach with both hands, she got up with great difficulty, stepped over her father and walked out of the yurt.

Dawn was already on its way. Sheaves of hot rays were breaking through from behind the Black Mountain. The sleepy, lakeside world was still silvery but it was gradually beginning to separate into different colours. A predawn mist was floating over the lake like a blue canvas... Sad, restless dreams still reigned over the quiet and impassive foothills. Yet this sadness held no anxiety, rather it displayed a hope and a trusting anticipation of the future...

Ardak fell down, not even making it to the water. Oh, how much she wanted to dive into the lake now! To be done with the awful pain of her life, with all its troubles; after all, Ardak had been wholly innocent... And yet it was as if the lake, which had always consoled and lulled her with its waves, had moved away from her, becoming unattainable like her departed childhood. "Water!" Ardak uttered noiselessly through her dry, thirsty lips and she crawled towards the lake. The lake seemed to be her only saviour from the torments of her life.

Meanwhile, the dispassionate world completely ignored Ardak's screams and moans, absorbed as it was in the anticipation of hearing another's cry. A lark flapped its wings and flew up, singing, bringing word of the coming of the new day: "The sun will soon rise and the world will be bathed in the colours of the rainbow..." Ardak crawled tortuously and slowly towards the water... "Almas!" she called, weeping. "Dear Almas!" If only he could have carried her now in his arms to the depths of the lake. And yet the deceitful lake moved ever further and further away.

Then Ardak's directed all her hopes towards her mother: "Mama, dear mama, save me! Was it really so wrong of me to play next to the lake?! Oh, forgive me, Allah, and show me mercy. Oh, the pain! Oh, I am dying, I'm burning up! The fire! The flame! Where are you, mama?! My back is breaking in two! Mama! Ohhhh! Ardak's wide-open, dark eyes froze and clouded over, but suddenly they opened even wider and filled with blood.

"A-a-ah-h!" echoed her desperate cry, far over the lake.

And with this cry, the great thing that everyone and everything had been anticipating burst forth: the one they had been waiting for made his arrival. At that same moment, Ardak's old mother came running over, dishevelled and bare-headed, and she heard the powerful and demanding cry of the new-born person. At that very moment, the sun soared up over the shoulder of Akshoky and its powerful rays turned the high crags crimson, flowing across the mountain and flooding the waters of Markokol. The lake's curling waves seemed to turn crimson with blood and, vainly attempting to outrun each other, they crashed to their destruction on the shore only to swell and rise once more, like the pointless and never-ending enmity between people. No matter how much the waves crashed onto the shore, they would never reach the young mother, lying prostrate on the ground in a pool of her own blood. Just as the waves of enmity and evil will never overwhelm mankind's kindness and kinship.

The all-powerful spirit of nature seemed to bend its vast, shining face over the foothills, over the pure waters of the lake and over the springtime valleys. Grinning with moustaches of sunshine, it seemed to say, *all this is mine! And this child is mine.*

"My dearest daughter, what has happened?!" Kozha exclaimed, running in terror along the shore, also having heard her pitiful cry.

His wife stood in front of him, screening his view from Ardak, lying there on the ground. Speaking in a commanding, imperious voice, she passed something to the old man:

"Here, hold this! And stand over there, out of my way." This was the first order she had ever given her husband in all the years they had lived together. But Kozha did not hear a thing. Raising the infant's crimson body high, the old man burst out laughing and roared for all the world to hear:

"Hey, you, Shalabai and Dalabai! And all you other enemies of mine! Here, take a look at this! Ha! You say that no one will take her in marriage? Well, what of it? I already have a boy! Hey, you, you foolish old woman! Do you understand what I have here in my hands? This is a boy, my heir! The continuation of my line!"

And the old man carefully cradled his grandson next to his breast.

The waves of the clear, bright-eyed lake quietly whispered like moist words: *Forgive me and be blessed. It was I who fostered you. You are my child.* It was as if the lake had taken upon itself all the blame for the advent of this fatherless child into the world. His way in this world would be a hard one but he had been given a life nevertheless.

THE RUSTLER

Beneath the moon - the lonely yurt shines white beneath the moon and the woman in black, the widow, bows low to the threshold.

Beneath the moon - the steppe spreads out broadly beneath the moon, shimmering dark red in its light. And kind and bountiful is our steppe, like a mother to all our fine men, who nestle up, trusting, tired and resting in endless sleep - a last refuge and a farewell song. Oh, our Kazakh steppe!

* * *

The wind howls like a dog from the Tuyetas Ravine. This wearying and wicked wind could topple a rider together with his horse. The face turns to stone when the wind blows from the Tuyetas Ravine and it lingers with a kiss on scarlet lips.

Two crags pierce the sky like shimmering spears, while the green valley ends with an abyss that plunges down to its foot, where the occasional larch has found shelter. The Tuyetas Ravine: the unruly Sharyktybulak stream curses as it spits white flakes of foam into the sky, and the wind howls like a dog as it slides over the cold, sheer walls, ready to burst out into the open, yet it crashes its pliable chest at full force onto the black rock, standing at the very outlet like some ghastly sentinel. This cliff is reminiscent of a giant, wicked camel, and it is from this that the area and the ravine of Tuyetas get their name.

A modest yurt stands pitched close to the very foot of the cliff, which protects it well from the wind. There is no other human habitation here and nor could there be; the lone yurt is surrounded on all sides by steep crags, imposing cliffs and mighty trees. It also seems that life froze here many centuries ago, a remote, misty, silent place forgotten by the gods; a wild and alienated part of another world, living according to its own laws, which are known only unto itself...

A woman, wrapped in a shawl, slips easily down to the stream with a pitcher for water and disappears again into the yurt. And silence falls once more. A quiet that is as thick as the morning mist and which cautiously listens in to itself. This is a wild, desert-like, sombre place...

The mountain stream's guttural cackling can be heard and the ominous screech of an eagle owl breaks through. How sweet the alpine tulips smelled here in spring, but summer has passed by, autumn has croaked its last, scorching the flowers with its icy breath; the flowers have drooped and the grass has turned brown. The mountains now have a bitter aroma of sagebrush and a bitter smell of decay and dryness.

Traveller, stop a moment and you will see a mighty horse, tethered to the yurt, so large that it seems it can touch the stars with its lips, simply by pushing itself from the earth with its hind hooves.

Here it stands, from sunset to the dense darkness; then it goes off, hobbled, to graze in the meadow behind the yurt. And all is dark and only the vestiges of a fire seep through from holes in the felt matting and light smoke wafts above the roof. The wind from Tuyetas Ravine takes the smoke from the home, rich with the aromas of boiled meat, plays with it and sweeps it further away. When the Sholpan Star rises above the crag, the door to the home squeaks open and the horse's master emerges, a round-shouldered, big-boned giant. The man looks at length up at the bright moon, sighs and walks over to check his steed. He strokes it lazily, but his tenacious eyes beneath contracted brows see every last blade of grass.

The sky pales slowly and all around is silent; the moon rolls frantically, barely managing to keep up with the departing night.

The sky is silent. The rocks are silent. Your sleep is heavy, traveller! Your sleep is heavy and all around is silent – the black forest, the blue mountains and the grey yurt. Your sleep is heavy.

* * *

His heavy crop hung on the wall with a copper ball on the end, twisted from twelve strong straps. The crop was the breadwinner, the rustler's saviour. No good fortune would be possible without the crop and the black cooking pot would hold no morsels of meat. He had given a cow and calf to the craftsman for this crop and it stood, as always, in the place of honour.

But what was this? Moisture had appeared on the copper ball, growing and becoming heavier, droplets falling from its end... And now new droplets were falling steadily, drip-drip-drip they fell, although the handle and length of the crop were completely dry. What was this? From where were these warm, weighty drops coming, smelling of almonds and mare's milk? The drops soaked into the sand and new ones followed, smelling of almonds and mare's milk.

Doskei lay there motionless and it seemed to him that heady, delicious *kumiss* was pouring onto him from some magical flask. He lay there motionless and the drops of the magical, heady *kumiss* moistened his eyes and he felt good inside and wanted to tell his wife about this wondrous milk.

But she was asleep and dreaming the end of a springtime song. He could hear her light breathing and he wanted to turn and embrace her and tell her of this wonder but, as if fettered by some witchery, he found he could move neither his arms nor his legs.

"Kamka!" he called to her in a whisper. Fatefully, though, the sleeping woman remained silent.

"Kamka! Kamka!" he screamed in terror. "Kamka! Kamka, wake up!"

But he was met with silence and quiet, as if from the grave. Quiet and silence that chilled the soul.

58

The *kumiss* still flowed from the crop. Filling his eye socket, it now ran over the man's face, this heady, intoxicating, magical and delicious *kumiss*.

"What will be will be!" Doskei decided and opened his lips.

And here he froze in terror and disgust. Blood! The salty smell of fresh, human blood struck his nostrils. Blood!

"It is blood, but whose blood, Kamka? Tell me, do you know? Kamka, tell me, tell me!"

His whole body shuddered and he opened his eyes. His entire face was wet with tears. He cautiously screwed up his eyes, looking over at his sleeping wife, but Kamka still slept and, calmed by the fact that she had not heard his screaming, Doskei jumped to his feet and went out of the yurt.

Before midnight, the sky had been completely clear but now it was engulfed in heavy, leaden storm clouds and grey rain was showering the earth incessantly with fine, watery dust. The chestnut horse had darkened under the rain and stood there, bowing its head sullenly and shaking it as if from a toothache.

The Sharyktybulak had burst its banks and the mountains were wrapped in the cold gloom, sullenly silent and resigned to the inclement, autumnal weather. The earth wilted obediently, weakened by the profusely hot summer.

Doskei untethered his horse and led it under the crown of a larch tree. On his way back he took the saddle, which, having been left in the rain by the entrance to the yurt, was now wet through.

Kamka was still sleeping, snuffling sweetly, now spread out in her sleep, and Doskei felt a spiteful rage come over him.

"Now that's enough lying around!" he screamed. "Get up, I'm hungry!"

He sat at the low dining table, his nostrils irritated by an inexplicable anger. His wife, frightened and feeling guilty, quickly warmed up some goat's meat from the previous day's dinner and placed it in front of him but he didn't even touch it.

"There's a hair in it. Take the hair from the meat," he said blankly and, sending the dish flying, he lay back down on the bed and covered himself in a heavy, camel-hair *chekmen* coat. However, he instantly threw off the *chekmen*, as if it were suffocating him, and he took deep, greedy gulps of air through his mouth. "Oh, Creator!" he spoke and his sighs gave the impression he was sobbing.

Kamka had never seen her husband like this, which is why, both surprised and timid, she sat down on her haunches by the hearth and decided that it was best not to ask him anything. She looked with love and pity at his face, dark with rage, while he tossed and turned, all tied up in knots.

59

"Kamka!" he finally forced himself to say, sitting up. "Kamka, where is my crop?"

"What do you mean, where?" she didn't understand the question. "It's hanging there, where it always is, right there, above your head."

"Throw it out!"

"But why? What are you saying?" She stared at him but he remained silent; she turned, silently took the whip from the wall, placed it next to the saddle and froze there, her head in her hands.

The crop! His heavy crop with a copper ball on the end, twisted from twelve strong straps. He had given a cow and calf to the craftsman for this crop and he had never regretted it, as the crop was the breadwinner and their saviour; the only true friend of the *dzhigit* rustler. There would be no good fortune without the crop and the black cooking pot would hold no morsels of meat! The crop made him strong and invincible, it went with him on all his most daring and dashing raids and yet here he was, looking at it with a look that was strangely lifeless and spent. He had instructed her to throw the crop out but without it, he could not bring food or even survive.

He had instructed her to throw it out and in so doing he had demeaned both the crop and himself. He understood that with this deed he was drawing a line through all his life up to that point, a life full of risk, struggle and adventure. And he had so loved that life, with the whistling of bullets past his ear, the furious breath of the chase and the sweet joy of seeing a defeated enemy.

And now he had thrown it all away, demeaned and cursed the crop and all because he had seen something in a dream. Blood – and what of it?! Had he not seen blood in his life? Had he not always said to the other fine men, with a laugh, that he saw any bread not gained through risk and mortal danger as unleavened?

He ground his teeth, sank onto his side and froze as if dead, his eyes closed. And so he lay there until almost noon and there was no way of knowing if he was awake or sleeping.

Kamka became overcome with genuine unease, for she had never, ever seen her husband like this and a prophetic woman's anxiety took hold of her.

"Lord, can it be true he will be killed?" she whispered, looking into the flames in the hearth where the brushwood was crackling. For the first time since her marriage she felt abandoned and alone and for the first time since her marriage she felt a yearning for other people and for her *aul*. She recalled her mother's kind hands and tears rolled down her cheeks.

Shaking themselves down and clearing their throats with a spit, six horsemen entered the low door and the woman, pulling herself together, stood up to greet the guests. All six where exemplary, young men from the Karatai clan, from the other side of Tuyetas.

"Where is our Doskei?" they asked, not noticing the giant in the half gloom, spread-eagled by the wall and looking like a sleeping bear.

"He's lying over there," the woman replied quietly.

"Has he fallen ill or something?"

"I really couldn't tell you... Perhaps he is indeed ill."

"Doskei! Hey, Doskei! What's the matter with you? Have you fallen sick? It's us. We've come. Come on, lift your head."

But he didn't move.

"Who is that? Is it you?" he asked with annoyance, blankly ignoring the men.

"It's us. Your younger brothers. Autumn has come and here we are. We planned to take a ride out to Kerei in the autumn, that's what we agreed... Hey, Doskei, come on, get up! Have you died or something?"

Doskei got up in a start and the young men, who had flocked around him, all took a startled step back.

"I am not sleeping," he growled. "And I haven't died yet, either. As for you, go home. The journey will not be fortuitous and misfortune lies in wait for us in the *aul*. I know this."

"But, Doskei, we have so looked forward to this day," said the young men, with their spirits dampened and looking at him imploringly, as if they were not trying to talk him into some plundering, but wanted to travel with him to Mecca to visit the holy sites.

"I know this," he repeated stubbornly. "That's it! Get out! That's enough!"

And he turned back to face the wall. The young men, hovering there and unable to conceal their disappointment, made their way one by one out of the yurt.

Doskei was silent. Should he tell his wife about his dream? But what would a woman understand about a man's business? And what did she understand about anything, the bitch, and what could she do? She couldn't bear him a son, after all. Doskei let out a malicious laugh.

"Hey, Kamka!" he cried out rudely. "Yes, you with the dried belly! So when are you going to regale me with a son, eh?"

The woman groaned as if she had received a slap round the face and raised her eyes, full of tears, to meet his.

"But why? Why are you being like this?" she gasped.

He could not bear her bitter, hopeless look; after all, she had never heard such cruel words from him before. He jumped up and ordered,

"Stop your bellyaching! I am fed up with your whining! Call those wolves, I'm leaving!"

Sobbing, she went out of the yurt and he looked at her with pity and regret.

"What on earth is happening to me? What is the matter with me?" he whispered.

* * *

The horsemen finally emerged at the Maraka Pass and the deep, silver bowl that was Lake Ainakol opened up before them, on the banks of which spread the *aul* of Kerei.

The *aul* was clearly visible from above, much like a bone die in the palm of a schoolchild. A good dozen horses stood tethered, women in white headscarves were milking the sheep, but there were no pointed men's hats anywhere to be seen. Allah forbid that any of them down there would raise their heads and notice them there! But, to their good fortune, no one did look up.

"They cling to their sheep like ticks!" Doskei smirked, briefly swung his crop, doubled up in two and the men noiselessly made their way down with only the red stones, rustling like lizards, sliding after them. Soon the horsemen concealed themselves in the undergrowth by the shore and melted away from view.

This autumnal day was unusually bright and it would have been madness to attack the *aul* in broad daylight, where the men were, of course, armed as ever and could crush these rustlers in a rebuff, not least because there were only seven of them, including Doskei, who was standing guard. However, a combination of impatience, need and *braggadocio* still moved the young men to attempt this bold pillage. Doskei could see as they drew nearer to the *aul* that they had emerged as if from under the ground and, in a single movement, they urged their racers forward silently, hunched down close to the manes.

The *aul* horses were grazing among the cat's tail and bullrushes in the flooded meadows by the shores of the lake. With the approach of unknown horsemen, they instantly sensed something was wrong and scattered in all directions. Only a small herd flailed about in confusion, stopped on one side by the lake and, on the other, by a sheer cliff. The young men shepherded the herd to the Maraka Pass and Doskei couldn't help but admire their catch. There were deep-chested racers, fiery, unbroken horses and slender pacers with swan-like necks. Yes, the Kerei people really did have decent, proud and strong horses!

Doskei looked toward the *aul* and saw that the horses, having recovered their senses, had started dispersing, pushing one another with their croups and that his comrades were unable to keep hold of the herd they had captured. He was a sharp-sighted and experienced guard and the watch, of course, could not have been trusted to anyone else, but he fell into a frenzy at the sight of the helpless goings-on of the young men. "Faster, faster!" he whispered to no-one in particular. "Come on, you blockheads!"

Then he heard the blood-curdling voices:

"The Karai rustlers! The Karai rustlers! Horse thieves!"

Oh, if only the *aul* had not become startled, he could have herded the entire catch away by himself, while these whippersnappers would have only had to make it to the pass. But they had slipped up. He would have herded them all off by himself...

But it was too late. A moment later, six horsemen were galloping out from the *aul* at full pelt.

This did not bother him; he had been in skirmishes far worse than this. He stood cold-bloodedly and proudly in the path of their pursuers.

In their hurry, the Kerei horsemen had forgotten their cudgels and long-handled *soil* clubs, leaving them holding only whips, and this meant that providence was on Doskei's side.

The riders flew fiercely forward. The rustler lurched his horse sharply to one side and the deluge of pursuers rushed by. Laughing with all his might and calling upon all his ancestors, he sent his horse after them, thundered into the group of horsemen and again broke out into the open, taking all six whips from his unfortunate opponents as he went. He had pulled the whips from their hands and held them to his saddle with his leg, like a goat in a game of *Buzkashi*. Circling round and managing to tie his catch to the saddle, he cast an involuntary glance over at his men and his lips broke out into a wicked grin. His comrades had huddled together and were watching the battle anxiously. Of course, they had let every last horse escape.

"Hey, you lop-eared curs! You brainless pups!" he roared.

And, with teeth clenched, he raced his horse towards the frightened huddle of unarmed Kerei men. His hot horse skipped, jumped and charged forward, trying to bite itself in the chest on the gallop. Doskei, though, was no longer pursuing the Kerei men, but his own blundering fellows and his face breathed fury as he went. Seeing him, his men scattered in all directions.

However, a menacing bark stopped Doskei in his tracks:

"Stop, stop, you dog!"

Looking back, he saw a middle-aged, broad-shouldered *dzhigit* on a tall racer with a white star on its forehead. The enemy was charging straight at Doskei and his eyes shone white with anger; in his hand, he clenched a heavy cudgel with sharp metal spikes. With no time to take fright, Doskei rushed to meet his new enemy, realising all too clearly that now this one-on-one battle alone would decide which side would come out on top.

"Yearning for the grave are you?" he snapped, directing his steed face on.

But he missed the mark and, lashing the horse right on the star, split his skin such that even the mount's bone shone white without a single drop of blood being shed. His opponent did not even manage to raise his terrifying, toothed cudgel, as the horse spun around on the spot from agony and the Kerei rider, not expecting such a swift strike, was unable to master him. Doskei managed to adjust the scarf covering his ears and struck another blow, this time landing on the Kerei man's back. The horseman's sheepskin waistcoat split and the horse's croup became coloured in dark blood; the next moment both horse and rider crashed to the ground.

Doskei looked gratefully at his crop, lashing it through the air with a whistle and, proud in victory, charged his racer towards his own men.

* * *

He was sullen and silent as he descended from the pass ahead of his gang; the horsemen were also silent, afraid to interrupt his silence. The excitement of battle and the rage at the recent skirmish had all gone and they rode in silence, realising their guilt and their blunder. The catch had been lost for good and this burned them with shame, as their disgrace was great – the disgrace of cowardice before their leader Doskei. But he said nothing. It would have been better if he had leathered them with his whip, but what then would have been left of them? The entire region knew of his heavy hand and his terrifying crop.

They completed their descent. They were riding through a clearing, thick with bushes... They made it to Sailau. Doskei held his horse back and, dismounting, he tethered the bridle of one horse to the tail of another, that to a third and so on, in so doing, forming a circle.

And yet Doskei still remained silent. He unhurriedly removed his outer gown, stretched his numb right arm and made a number of sharp movements with it, to get the blood flowing. Sitting down on a rock, he tore some grass and reached for his knife. And here he shot up sharply, as his belt held only an empty sheath.

"Oh, damn! I must have lost my knife out on the hunt," he muttered and six daggers were instantly offered to him.

Snorting without looking up, he took one of them, cut the blade of grass and began rooting around in his mouth with it.

"Wait for me here," he said suddenly.

"But where are you going?"

"Where do you think? There, that's where! There has not once been an occasion when I have returned from the Kerei people empty-handed..."

"We'll go with you. We've had our feathers singed and we have learned our lesson, so there'll be no more mistakes from us," the young men spoke out.

"No," interjected Doskei, continuing to poke around in his teeth. "We'll not manage to steal the herd now, as everyone in the *aul* will be on the alert. But I'll try to take the steed from the *dzhigit* on the watch."

64

"Doskei, take us with you," the young men pestered.

"Wha-a-at? You aren't a match even for an old woman, let alone an entire herd! You want to lead me on a merry dance, you wet-tailed asses! Sit tight here and don't go sticking your necks out!" said Doskei contemptuously.

The young men said nothing out of shame. Doskei leapt up onto his horse.

* * *

The autumn sky was unstable and changeable. Just one hour before there had not been a single cloud, not even a mackerel pattern in the sky, fluid as mercury, but now it was densely packed with heavy, leaden storm clouds. What is more, the westerly wind too had picked up. The tops of the trees began to rustle, ominous and depressing, and the waves heaved on the Ainakol, crashing onto the unfriendly shore. The storm clouds, dressed in ragged furs, spread desolation over the land.

Doskei tethered his chestnut horse to a tree and stealthily approached the guard's hobbled horse. He listened closely but his keen ear caught no anxious sounds, just the waves splashing and the trees moaning in the wind.

The horse would not give itself up to the stranger. From whatever side Doskei approached, it would turn its rear to face him. Realising that, by playing it cautious, he was only losing time, Doskei straightened up, grabbed the horse by the tail and forcibly pulled it to the ground. The stallion wanted to kick out at him but was unable to lift its unexpectedly heavy rear. That was just what Doskei needed and, untying the fetters, he was just about to jump up onto the horse, but someone, beating him to it, leapt like a cat onto his back and Doskei found himself on the horse's back together with this unexpected load. Casting his right arm behind his back, Doskei pressed his attacker so tightly to his back that the man let out an involuntary groan, unable to wriggle free or even move a muscle.

Doskei spurred the horse and galloped away. Once a little further away from the *aul*, he pulled his captive out from behind his back, threw him across the saddle in front of him and, looking him up and down, smiled in surprise:

"What the...! He has the weight of a goat kid and the strength of a sparrow and he goes off to attack *dzhigits*!"

The guard, small and thin and looking like an adolescent, held his tongue in fear, his head shrunk down to his shoulders, and Doskei suddenly felt pity for him.

"Alright, the hell with you; I'll let you go," he muttered and pushed his prey a good distance with his powerful hand. The guard, landing safely in the bushes, shook himself down and in an instant set off on his heels. Doskei shouted after him:

65

"And tell your people that you came up against Doskei the Rustler. That's me and Allah protect you should you encounter me again!"

Then he sought out his chestnut steed and set off once more, through the darkness and the bad weather, leading the stolen horse.

* * *

When they reached the Black Mound, snow was falling, interspersed with rain. It was dark all around as if everything had been stained with ink; there was not a bit of sky to be seen, not a glow and not a single light. It was a black, cold night in this deserted, wild place...

A blizzard picked up. The wind beat like a slap of the back of the hand, blowing out what was left of the warmth from his sleeves and creeping under his collar. The horses pressed close to one another, finding it hard to place one hoof in front of another.

The road was becoming more and more impassable. A road? What kind of a road was this?! The track, barely visible, was covered with snow and they walked forward on intuition alone, guided by their senses and guesswork and not knowing the right route to take. Perhaps they had actually long since lost the track altogether. Doskei rode up in front, leading the other horse by the bridle. Following close behind came the young men, striding like wolves in a line. They stumbled and fell as they went, as they had long since lost all sense of time and direction. Where were they to go? Where were they being led? And why, when the track has long since been lost? What was this aimless journey and what was the point of advancing further; where were they to go? Further and further from home?

"Doskei! Where is the road? We'll be done for here, done for!"

"Wha-at?"

"We won't go on! We have no strength left! We are lost, lost I tell you!" whined the young men.

"Well then! Let the Kerei dogs devour you then!" shouted Doskei cruelly and, spurring his horse, rode forward.

The young men were taken aback. They knew that it would be no easy matter getting out of there on their own and, gathering the last of their strength, they trudged on after Doskei, grumbling like whipped dogs.

The storm, though, became stronger and stronger and there was not a glimpse of light in the thick fog of snow. Tired, spiteful and hiding their faces from the wind, the gang members looked at their leader with hostility and angrily urged their exhausted horses on.

Doskei came to a stop.

"Hey, one of you! Come over here!" he barked. "Have a rummage around and see if you can find my knife."

One of the men rolled off his horse and scrabbled in the snow where Doskei had indicated.

"Got it!" he cried and the group murmured merrily. A week before the attack, Doskei had carved up the carcass of a mountain goat and it was here he had dropped his knife. That meant that they were still very much on the right track and that they were in the vicinity of Tuyetas; therefore, home was not far off.

"Well done, Doskei. You won't lose your way with him beside you!" shouted the young men but they made no haste to move on. They knew all too well that a dangerous abyss lay up ahead and not one of them wanted to risk their life here, just a couple of steps from home.

And yet their leader fell into thought and it seemed that his thoughts were contriving a game of *Buzkashi*, tearing and ripping his heart to pieces, each thought pulling its own way. This was grave. The wind was howling, like a dog for its deceased master, and the soul, too, howled and ached. Like this deserted place, his soul was grey and empty, as the foreboding of a terrible misfortune troubled him.

He had lived alone and proud, never currying favour or ingratiating himself before anyone. He went on raids to get his blood racing and to fill his black cooking pot, to have his fill and feed his wife. However, it had become harder and harder to handle his crop. Not because his hand had weakened with the passing years; his strength was not something that occupied his thoughts. More and more often he had got to thinking while changing the leather wristband on the crop handle after each raid, that there was someone else left lying in a pool of blood, with a crushed skull or crippled spine. So his years had passed, impetuous and grey, thinking of his daily bread today and his next raid the day after. Oh, Allah! And yet he had never held a grudge against any of his opponents. He rarely even remembered their faces, in fact, while there were many who remembered and hated his. But who was he to worry about people's malice when he was so strong, bold and independent? No, he had no enemy. He believed that he did not have a worthy enemy. Over the course of his life, he had not encountered a true enemy, savage, intelligent and cunning... He had endured bloody battles, but no, he had not encountered a true enemy...

So with whom had he been fighting all his life?

The young men had let him go on ahead and he was quietly dozing in the saddle.

The track ran over the abyss, a hair's width across and sharper than the blade of a knife. This was the track over the Suykshat Abyss.

The horsemen hurried and led their horses by the bridle. Here they had to be especially careful: one wrong step and you would fall to the very bottom of the abyss, right to the Sharyktybulak stream, and there, on the jagged boulders, you would find your last resting place. It was for good reason that the locals called this track the *Bridge of the*

Righteous, as they believed superstitiously that were anyone to be unfortunate enough to crash into the abyss, in the eyes of a true Muslim, they would forever be deemed a sinner.

Doskei walked in front and his hapless gang limped along behind him, like a pack of jackals. His brow was sweating from the tension as he felt around for the treacherous track with his hands and his crop.

"Take care!" he managed to shout out as he slipped down and the crags of the Altai echoed his last warning many times over.

And, once more, a sinister silence fell over the mountains. The six men made it safely over the *Bridge of the Righteous...*

* * *

Doskei had been terribly crippled but his mind and his memory remained clear.

They wrapped soaked willow twigs around his cracked skull. The wood pressed hard and caused him unbearable pain, despite the several layers of calico they had placed under it. The blue veins on his forehead became dark and swollen and his hands shook.

And the mighty rustler would not have made a fuss even with this wound; he would have got up and walked, despite the hellish pain, but his right leg had been crushed. Even so, he never called the bone-setter. "There's no point," he muttered. "There's nothing any healer can do... It's pointless..."

They crammed ribwort into the skin of a freshly slaughtered young sheep, where the film of basting fat shone white, and they firmly swathed the maimed leg with it, tying it tight with a thick thread of wool. Doskei thought it made it a little better.

Many visitors lined up to see him. The *aqsaqal* and *karaqsaqal* elders, relatives and peers all came to see the brave *dzhigit*. They all tried to persuade him to join his people and not be obstinate before grave misfortune befell his home. But he would not submit to their persuasion; the rustler had grown up in the wild, shying away from people, valuing his solitude, his cramped yurt and his dangerous, dark craft more than anything in the world.

"If I have to die, then Tuyetas alone will be my grave," he barked one day, flying into a rage, and his relatives, sighing, stopped imploring him to move, seeing that there was no overcoming his stubbornness.

The *dzhigit's* once powerful body had quit on him, but his spirit still remained strong. When the grey elders came to see him, he sat with them at the low table, dragging his sick leg along and barely able to stop himself screaming with pain. He shed tears from the pain but he squeezed his leg with his fingers and laughed:

"The devil take this leg! What do I need it for? It has shattered into tiny pieces, the cursed thing. I squeeze it and I can feel my bones shaking."

However much he concealed his suffering, however much he laughed off his misfortune, the people could still see the furrows in his brow, how pale he was and how much cold sweat poured from his body. There were times when he would lose consciousness and fall senseless the moment people had left the yurt.

Kamka wept silently and the crop hung alone on the wall. Only the two of them, just two in the entire world, the wife of the rustler and the rustler's crop, remained witness to this cruel battle between life and death, which was playing out over his bed.

He was once even visited by *dzhigits* from Kerei, the *aul* upon which he had brought so much misfortune. Some of them gloated over him but others pitied the sick man and could not help but admire his courage.

And so his bitter days dragged on. Once, at nightfall, Kamka gave him some hot tea and he stroked her silky hair at length.

"I was thinking about stealing a beauty from Kerei, but this fall prevented me," he joked.

His wife wept and, in his desire to cheer her up, he chatted at length about nothing in particular, telling true stories and yarns alike, but then he unexpectedly fell into a deep sleep.

Kamka looked hopefully at his jaundiced and sunken face and she suddenly thought that all was not lost and that one day soon there would be a miracle and her daring husband would turn a corner. This weak star of hope warmed and glowed in her heart.

She went outside and looked at length at the mountains.

Then she brushed the forelock of the chestnut horse, embraced its slender neck and wept once more:

"My kind, true friend! Can it be that you and I will be left alone?"

* * *

Warm is the liquid that drips and drips from the crop, this renowned, heavy crop with the copper ball on the end, the crop, twisted from twelve strong straps. Breaking away, the drops fall into his eyes. These drops are bright and clear. He stretches open his parched mouth and dry lips to capture them. He catches them greedily and swallows this pure liquid, but the bitterness burns his throat as these drops are tears... His tears...

With difficulty, Doskei awoke from his slumber and he felt rougher still from the realisation of his own helplessness and profound remorse. He looked at his wife. Kamka was sleeping and just a faint smile shone radiantly on her jaded face. He carefully crawled over to her and sniffed greedily as he breathed in the dear scent of her skin. Drawing himself up with considerable effort, he tore the crop from the wall.

The edge of the hide that swathed his leg had folded away and his nose was struck with the pungent stench of rotting meat. He stood there a while with his face screwed up, either from the pain or from a bout of nausea. Recovering his breath, he crawled once more on his hunkers, leaning on the handle of his crop and grinding his teeth.

Leaning on the yurt post, he slowly straightened himself up and, limping terribly, he hobbled to the door. Once there and having gathered all his strength, he pushed back the flaps and the October cold burst into the yurt.

The rustler made it outside and for a good while he was unable to regain his breath.

Moving as before, by crawling, he gathered up the scattered ox hides and placed them in a neat pile. He had accumulated these hides over many a year – the hides of animals he had rustled. With a groan and almost losing consciousness, he collapsed onto this pile.

Then he unbandaged his leg and, pushing his fingers on the loose, dough-like skin, leaving deep marks, he chuckled and shook his head. Looking back, he saw his horse had turned to face him and made as if to jump up, preparing itself for a whinny of victory, rear up and then carry him away from his pursuers, from misfortune, grief and sickness or even almost from death itself.

You divine creature! You understand everything, don't you? he thought tenderly and, there and then, he jumped up as if stung by a wasp. A strange force he himself had not known lifted him up and made sure he didn't fall. Grinding his teeth from the pain, he lashed the pile of dry hides with his crop and split every last one of them as if with a sword!

He shook from side to side. He looked over at the distant, snowy peaks, the deep, misty abysses and his entire life flashed before his eyes.

Did he regret his youth, when the wildest steeds had fallen dead at his feet? Did he regret the sweet glory of the bold horseman, whose name had reverberated across the steppe? Or was he thinking of the fleeting life, short as the handle on his crop, which was now departing? Or of the wormwood bitterness of his existence? Or perhaps loneliness had finally crept up on him and had sunk its fangs straight into his heart.

Who knows... But something sweet did ache within him and, for the first time in his life, he burst into tears. It was difficult for him and he was not particularly adept at it.

But he wept. He stood on his good leg and his sobbing shook his mighty body. Then, like an oak, felled by a storm, he crashed heavily to the ground.

The sky turned crimson. Dawn was nearing. An alien sky and an alien dawn, for the rustler was no more of this earth.

* * *

70

The strongest of the men were unable to unclench his fist, so firmly did he grasp his crop. Here he fell into eternal sleep, his crop in his hand, strenuously heeding a peace that was not of this earth. The elders ordered that his hand be cut off to save the crop, but Kamka objected.

"He has no son to whom he could have bequeathed his weapon," she cried through her sobs. "In life, they could not be parted, so let them be together in the heavens."

And so Shari'ah law was breached and, for the first time, the rustler and his crop were buried side by side. This happened many years ago and much water has flowed past since then.

* * *

Beneath the moon - the lonely yurt shines white beneath the moon and the woman in black, the widow, bows low to the threshold.

Beneath the moon - the steppe spreads out broadly beneath the moon, shimmering dark red in its light. And kind and bountiful is our steppe, like a mother to all our fine men, who nestle up, trusting, tired and resting in endless sleep - a last refuge and a farewell song. Oh, our Kazakh steppe!

NOVELLAS

THE MAN-DEER

The Kazakh land ends with the village of Arshaly, beyond which stretch alien countries and lands unknown. It was here that a young man was born and grew up, who came to be known as the Man-Deer. He had not ventured over to that other, foreign side, but he had heard that Kazakhia was as vast as several large nations put together and yet he could imagine that, were he to gallop from the east or from the other end, say, from Crimea, his horse's nose would point without fail to the centre of the world, his native Arshaly. Everywhere beyond these places seemed to be shrouded in mist for the Man-Deer, both mysterious and improbable. In his childhood, he had heard old Asan say: "Hey-y-y! Do you really think there is more land out there than that we have already trod or mountains that we have not crossed? After all, we galloped all the way from Karashoky to Shubaragash and we made it back again! There is truth in the saying that if you are drawn to strange, foreign food then you are bound to give it a try. Just think – a road has already been laid all the way to Katon-Karagai!"

How could the Man-Deer possibly have known that the old man was speaking about a route stretching a mere seven or eight kilometres? It is certainly true that one's own hill seems higher than all the mountains in places far away. The village of Arshaly has some sixty houses, yet if we were to find ourselves here in the heat of the day, we would be amazed at the lifelessness and silence on its streets. Not a dog barking, not a horse neighing, not a woman's voice to be heard; the only sign of life in the entire village - the thin stream of smoke, curling from the chimney above the short, stout end house, like a thread of saliva from a cow's wet mouth. The chimneys on the roofs of the other fifty-nine houses are all bricked up. The empty houses seem dead and the large human settlement, like a cemetery. And the lone house at the end, with the smoke creeping from its chimney, appears like a sentinel, watching over this mournful graveyard. Indeed, this is perhaps how things are, for the village has not died but simply moved elsewhere, to the central country farmstead. And the only hearth of life, from where the smoke emerges, belongs to the guardian of the settlement who doubles up as the forester, watching over the riches of the surrounding, dense taiga.

It has already been mentioned that Arshaly is the point at which the Kazakh land ends. However, the Man-Deer had heard that Kazakhs lived further on, too, beyond its borders: they had left these parts in times gone by, when, as they say, even the sun had turned its back on the people. The people fled, some on horseback, others on foot, saving themselves, driven by fear and dark rumours. From the richest to the poorest of the poor, they all fled to the mountains and were times when Aktan, who came to be known in the village as the Deer or the Wild Beast, could not help but think with sadness: *How many of them are wandering around out there in that foreign land, suffering beatings and humiliation? But what does it matter to me?!* Aktan believed it meant nothing to him, even though his father was one of these outcasts and refugees. He had spent his entire life without him; not once had he heard the words "my son" fall from his father's lips and now he had no need for them.

There is no road to Arshaly and no car could make the journey, but if you were to follow the winding path, tracing the babbling course of the Akbulak stream, it would lead you as if by the hand, straight to this deserted village. In the winter, when blizzards rage and snowdrifts obstruct and conceal the way, there would be times when no-one could make the journey and the village would be cut off from the outside world until the spring. The villagers were fed up with living like this, putting up with nature's fickle cruelty and, as soon as news reached them that the smaller, outlying villages were to be joined with the central country farmstead, the people resettled outright. Watching them, the Man-Deer was amazed: they were actually prepared to fly to Ust-Kamenogorsk, jumping for joy in their saddles as they went. What frivolous people they were, like tumbleweed, driven on the wind of rumour; how absurd they were...

He did not leave, oh no; he learned that a guardian was needed for all the good things that had been left and so he remained behind with his mother, to watch over Arshaly. He had the intelligence to understand—despite being nicknamed the Wild Beast—that, in the inscrutable, impenetrable depths of his soul, he would never change, no matter how much he may be moved about the face of the earth; he knew that the celestial heights above the Altai, the constant sense of being in flight and the cold, mountain water from the stream, always quenching his thirst, were still the most important and irreplaceable things for him. And the truest perch for a hunting eagle such as him was still the saddle on the back of his grey steed with the star on its brow.

When the villagers heard that the Man-Deer was staying and would not be moving away, not many were surprised: he was the Wild Beast, after all, what more was there to say? It was only Aktan's mute mother who, learning of his decision, quietly shook her head in an expression of mild reproach.

* * *

He always rose early. On this day, the silent fog covered the mountain from first light, swallowing up the forest-covered stone crags that loomed high above. The fog was so thick that you couldn't make out the fingers on your own outstretched hand. The white haze consumed the smoke from the chimney, too and the air was so thick that it was hard to breathe. Heavy droplets fell, either from the sky or from the trees. Aktan emerged from the doorway and his face and chest, bare in his open shirt, were spattered with the moisture; a shiver quickly overtook him and he turned back into the house. On entering, he could hear his mother's groans, a sound so customary to him and yet so baffling: what was it all about? The black cat emerged from beneath her at the end of the bed.

Aktan dropped to his haunches by the iron stove and started the fire. The light of the flames that shot up above the dry, long-cured logs illuminated the walls of the room to reveal signs of human life out of the darkness of that autumn morning... And so it was each day – the customary tasks would be seen to at their given and allotted time.

He wrapped himself in his deerskin and lay back down, watching the flames dance in the open fire. He would not fall back asleep; he was already overwhelmed with his thoughts. The Man-Deer even failed to notice this, as he had long since grown accustomed to these thoughts. And they were always the same: they had been the same yesterday, the day before yesterday and the year before that; they never changed...

He would rise every day before dawn. He would step outside and, like a wolf, sniffing the passing wind, he would consider the weather. Then he would return inside, light the stove and fill the kettle on the plate. After that, he would wrap himself in his deerskin and lie there, watching the fire. The flames would dance in the Deer's eyes, his thoughts drifting far away. At times a spark from the hot spruce logs would fly from the stove and fall on the deerskin or the black cat, looking to warm itself, would accidentally brush against the red-hot stove. Deep in thought, Aktan found it impossible to restore himself to his senses until the irritation in his throat from the burnt fur had subsided. His dreams overwhelmed him—a man invariably becomes a dreamer when he is lonely— painful dreams that became all the more agonizing and mournful as time passed.

Sometimes the flight of his enchanted soul would be interrupted by his slumbering mother's sudden snoring, snuffling and lip-smacking. Or, on the contrary, when she gave no signs of life for too long, he would get up, walk over to her and, bending over, listen in the silence for the beating of his mother's heart. It beat evenly, freely and unflaggingly. Aktan never heard his mother's voice. And now that they were left completely alone, he realised that the most difficult thing for a normal, strong man was when there was no-one to exchange a word with, when there was no opportunity to unburden one's soul of its unspoken thoughts... Once again, he started thinking about his father...

What had happened to him: had he died or was he out wandering somewhere, under a foreign sky?

Perhaps the earth already held him in her embrace, he thought. If he had not died, then why was it he had never returned to his native land? And in coming to his native land, could he not find it in himself to visit them here; even a dog knows his own home. He could have come running in, muttering something like "My wife is all alone, my son is orphaned. Oh, Allah, there is no-one to look after them and they are probably sitting there in hunger..." Yes, that is certainly how it would have been, were he alive. Could there really be a man, a father and master of the house, capable of abandoning his own hearth and home?

There were rumours that his father was still alive and that he had gone to the hills. He had disappeared from the village, not in those dark times, when everyone was leaving and when a father's protection was needed; no, he had disappeared after the Great Patriotic War. At that time, many of the old refugees had already returned home, without their horses, with only a saddle on their shoulders, even those who had taken thousands-strong herds of horses with them. Not one of them had been raised to an elevated position or accepted in any of these foreign lands... So, how could his father, knowing of all this, have left him and his mother? Aktan waited long, hoping to see him one day among those returning. But his waiting was all in vain.

Well, what of it?! These things happen: a man marries in a foreign land and starts a new family...

Aktan's mother was mute and the village itself had not really provided the son with much information about his father. As a boy, Aktan heard that his father was a tall man, taller than anyone else in the village and his temple bore a large, dark birthmark. He also learned that his father strode around in enormous boots with felt legs. And that was it. The village did not particularly commemorate the man. No-one went looking for him. People only went looking for those about whom letters of condolence had been received, seeking their graves in far-away places. Finding them, they would find solace in that they had seen the last resting place of their nearest and dearest. This solace, however, was not something the Man-Deer was able to find; his father had not died in the war...

At times, Aktan fancied he saw his father in the house and, shuddering, the young man glanced around at the dark corners of his one-room wooden house. Or he would imagine that his father was hiding in the shed...

His mother had evidently been greatly offended by the boy's father. Whenever Aktan started speaking of him, she would shake her head, turn away or walk out, muttering something or other to herself as she went.

78

Rising from his bed, he shuffled the logs about in the stove. The fire perked up. It had become lighter beyond the window. His mother was snuffling and it was unclear if she was still sleeping or had woken and was lying there, simply daydreaming about something. Aktan went outside once more.

The fog had begun to recede, drawing closer to the land. The top of Karashoky—the Black Mountain—emerged in the distance. The black outline of the peak stood out clear and sharp in the hazy whiteness. The air was cold, damp and heavy, as before. Were you to walk through the bushes, you would be wet with dew from head to toe in an instant...

The light, colossal Akshoky—the White Mountain—came into view through the white haze, free of the fog from the chest up. Like flakes of sour milk, its fibres crept down into the deep forest below.

The sun had yet to rise and something oppressive and heavy was diffused all around, but a thin strip of the sky shone white above the mountains as if driving away the fog, which had absorbed the stifling fumes of the night. A cold wind blew. The harsh Altai November was upon them.

Aktan pensively followed the tails of the fog, disappearing between the trees and, recalling his pending tasks, he headed for the shed. This small outbuilding pressed up against the wall of the house, like a frightened colt against his mother. The rusty door hinges had been moistened with water and the door opened without a squeak. White Eye had managed to eat all the hay; the horse had a somewhat voracious appetite. Seeing his master, he stamped his hooves and whinnied in welcome. Aktan put on the bridle and led White Eye out of the shed.

He rode to the river, flowing by the foot of the mountain. White Eye had a thick, wide back and he was fairly tall in the withers, but Aktan's incredibly long legs, hanging to the sides, still brushed through the grass. The horseman was broad of shoulder and tall, just like his father, they would say. In his childhood, too, Aktan had a reputation for being the tallest of his peers.

And here was the river, wrinkled with ripples; it had taken three days of rain for the water to get here. Here and there by the rocky banks, the river raged and foamed and the waves tripped and danced; the black rock that had been protruding above the water the day before had now disappeared, to be replaced by the swollen mound of the taut, supple stream. As it hit the bend, the river produced wild vortexes, greedily lapping against the rocks and, surging over them, it roared powerfully, flooding the channel and rendering it considerably wider.

Stopping his horse, the Man-Deer looked at the running water, listening to its fearsome growl. The river, as if sensing it was the only living thing around, roared all the louder: it must have seemed to the river that if it were to fall silent, then all life would come to an end here in this deserted spot. "If my waves were to die down, you would become completely deaf and dumb!" the mountain river thundered, boldly splashing and shouting its challenge to the gorge through which it ran. And this quiet, dusky place submissively tolerated its insolent cacophony and wilfulness. Akbulak was the only child of the surrounding mountains and who other than an only child could be so brazen, mischievous and capricious!

White Eye wanted to drink. He filled his belly long and hard; it was not for nothing he had spent the night chewing hay. So as not to slide into the water, Aktan shifted himself from White Eye's saddle to his broad croup. And while the horse was filling itself with water, he seemed to nod off. He drifted into a sleepy stupor and his entire body was overcome with drowsiness; what wouldn't he have given to go back to the warm house, climb under the deerskin coat, curl up in a ball, close his eyes and just lie there... Yet he would have grown tired of this. There was nothing else for it but to wend his way down into the valley like everything else? His mother was old and frail. There was no-one but him to boil the tea for her. He had been like this for a month already as if tied down by a lasso, unable to step away from the house...

It transpired that White Eye had long since drunk his fill of water and also appeared to have nodded off. Water dripped from his wet lips. The rider dug his heels into his mount's swollen belly. Sighing, the horse turned and lazily climbed back up the steep bank.

* * *

The smoke above Aktan's house on this day was neither black nor grey; instead it was somewhat faded and colourless, weak and forlorn...

The water came to the boil in the kettle. He poured it into an old, dented, copper samovar and threw hot coals and kindling onto the burner. He brought in the remains of yesterday's venison and the dry bread that had been baked in the large *kazan* pot. The cat was the first to approach the freshly laid table that was so lavishly decorated with dark scorch marks. The cat meowed, looking at the meat with bright eyes. Aktan signed to his mother to come over. She rose, stepped outside, returned, performed her ablutions and, with a groan, opened the chest, pulled out some beads and began praying, turning to face Mecca. Sitting on her mat and moving her lips, she whispered something incoherent. That was her prayer. She never prayed five times a day like other righteous people. It was enough for her to

80

perform the morning ritual of prayer before eating and then the same in the evening, before retiring for the night. Only once during the entire prayer did she bow down, touching her forehead on the old mat on the floor. For the rest of the time, she simply whispered and moved the beads over her fingers.

Today her prayers were not protracted. Aktan watched her calmly and vacantly. While they sat there like that, the tea turned cold... Completing her bowing motion, the old woman bent her back, her brow nestled on the prayer mat and there she froze, unable to straighten herself back up.

Aktan went over and helped her; the mute old woman looked at her son through wide eyes and shook her head, pointing with her chin in the direction of the samovar, as if to say: *you sit and drink, and let me pray*. When the old woman had finished her prayers, displaying a sufficient degree of loyalty and obedience to Allah, her son threw more kindling under the samovar, to heat up the now cold water...

After breakfast, he washed the dishes with the remaining hot water and washed some of his and his mother's rags. By the time he had hung out the washing, it was fully light in the yard. The small, hazy sun hung between the mountain peaks. The dusky, wet rocks shimmered against this vague light.

Steam rose from the roofs of the houses and this gave the deserted village a slightly more jovial appearance as if it had returned to life. It was as if the people had returned to their deserted hearths. Aktan always felt out of sorts when he looked at the deathly houses, but today he was prepared to greet each one as if they were people and to run through the street, knocking on the windows and demanding *syuinshi*, a gift for bringing glad tidings... The Man-Deer's soul blossomed with elusive hope and he saw himself as the wielder of some magical power that could instantaneously return the people to their old hearths and the living spirit to their dead homes. He jumped briskly onto his horse, straightened himself up and trotted out of the village with a double-barrelled gun across his saddle.

However, as he drove his horse further away from the village, it was as if he was simultaneously drawing nearer to his past, vivid with its never-fading images.

He knew the most incredible intricacies of each home, whose windows were now boarded up with old, criss-cross planks. These clay huts had once witnessed loud and vibrant feasts, at other times they had been places where lives had been honoured in death and children born and given worthy human names... The hearths had blazed there and the smoke had curled above the chimneys. How could they have chosen to put out this flame with their own hands, he pondered, or pour water on their own hearths! If just one or two had been extinguished, then so be it, but fifty-nine had been put out in one go. In despair, he whipped his

81

horse and galloped off, as if wishing to leave his sad thoughts behind as fast as he could.

In one particularly sorry hut, there had lived a vivacious, quick-tongued old man called Asan. The village boys liked to sit with him beyond the village, somewhere on the silky grass by a dung fire, listening to his tall stories and long tales until the stars shone bright. Everyone in the village laughed at Asan and he laughed at himself as well; ever the joker and the jester, a rugged fragment of the distant past; the severe and forbidding menfolk would say of such frivolous old men: "Who else is there to laugh at if not the old grey beards?" However, there was no-one to reprove or censure the garrulous old man; he was the only grown man left in the entire village.

Old Asan would say: "Children, a foolish man lives long, like the crow. This village has but one idiot and he has gone on to live to a ripe old age and now he has got in with you children. As they say, this world is full to the brim with tears. We lost all the boisterous, bright and healthy menfolk in the war and now the old women are in the driving seat. I am talking about those women who bring in the water and flirt about. Let me tell you, lads, it's better to have one foolish chatterbox of an old man than ten clever, gossiping women. The village needs at least one chatterbox like me, to sometimes spin you a yarn about this and that and at others to tell you of the courage and great deeds of your respected fathers... Today, though, I would like to tell you a very specific story... Listen up, boys, my tale is about to begin..."

Asan was a good-hearted old soul. And, indeed, the boys in the village really needed him. If a man is born, it means he will die, and if anything had happened to Asan at that time, the village of Arshaly would have been left without any *aqsaqal* elder at all. You don't need to spend long working out why. You only have to count the number of young men, good and strong, who died in the civil war and then the Patriotic War. The youngsters who appeared shortly before or at the same time as the last war have had to learn to stand on their own two feet. And so it transpired that, with the death of Asan, the village would have been left without a single beard... But what is the point of dwelling on that? There is enough grief in this world as it is. The passage of time is cruel and elusive; it deposits layers of life and death, rebirth and ruin. Just take a look at Arshaly on an overcast November day when it has been deserted by everyone as if cursed by fate.

At one time it was called the *Widows' Village*. When war broke out, the men from sixty homes left for the front lines. Only one of them survived and returned, and that was Aktan's father... Of the sixty homes, fifty-nine became the homes of widows. When they got together to mourn those they had lost, the entire valley at the foot of the mountain was filled with their keening. And the women's voices reached the ears of he who is called upon to watch over us from the heavens, or so they say. Bearing letters of condolence in their hands, they wept, like a camel weeps when it sees a camelskin coat. "Oh, my pillar so tall, my support so strong! You are no longer with us; you have passed away and, with you, my hope and my protection!"

Frightened by the wailing all around, the foolish young Aktan had marvelled back then at the strange, unfamiliar words contained in these widows' lamentations. He was especially astonished by a woman called Zibash. The boy had earlier heard people talking about her husband, saying he was like a small bird from the taiga and that Zibash would take him for walks nestled in her arm. And here she was, wailing: "Oh, you are dead, my pillar so tall, my support, my hope..."

Indeed, it was not for nothing that Arshaly was called the *Widows' Village.* Wherever you looked, out in the yards and on the roads and in all the dusty open spaces around them, all one could see were women's white headscarves. Of course, all wars have the same terrible outcome... But terrible too is the fact that it burns, depresses and ages the children's souls early on, instilling a feeling of hopelessness when confronted with their eternal, inconsolable loss. Little Aktan felt sorry for all the men of the village who had died and one day he vowed to perform a deed never heard of before; be it day or night, he would gather all his strength and skill and turn the mountains on their heads, if need be, to ensure the feat was irrevocably worthy of those who had died... But no such mighty deed existed and the boy did not possess the strength to make his vow come true. He ran out into the taiga and climbed to the top of the tallest tree, from where he looked mournfully in every direction as if seeking those fifty-nine fine men from the village who had been killed. K-i-l-l-e-d... But he found nothing, seeing only that same forest, turning black as it stretched to the horizon, and the silent village, sprawled out and motionless like a calf, knocked senseless by an axe. He could climb no further; above him was the deserted sky and this small tree was incapable of reaching this unattainable blue vault. Aktan climbed down from the tree and, tormented by an obtrusive, insatiable yearning, he grabbed fistfuls of the black forest earth and squeezed it tight, crying adult tears of despair. In moments like these, he wanted to disappear from life, dissolve in the river water and flow into the distance or slide away like a black snake into the depths of the earth. He would probably have found it easier if his grown-up, all-powerful father had taken him by the hand, stroked his hair and explained a thing or two to him.

"Father, where have you gone?" he thought now, many years later. "Do you still wear your tall boots with their felt legs? Why is it that, returning to your native land after the war, you never once visited your own home? Other people saw you but then you disappeared altogether. Where are you now? They say I look like you."

Old White Eye ambled along the path he had beaten flat with his hooves. Lord knows how many times he had had to take this route, carrying his grown master on his back. The two of them were the only living souls who knew of this path in the forest. White Eye was not sad (and why would he be?) that people had no need for the path they had made. The old gelding was himself unneeded. Oh, who had he not carried on his patient back over his horse's life? And there had been a good many fools among them who had counted the hay he had eaten in the night, kicking him viciously in the stomach and calling him a glutton and nothing more than a big sack of shit. One of these fools, the one who sprayed saliva when he cursed, had even whipped him in the eye with a thorny branch. Then, deciding to treat the horse, he had chewed coal, mixing it with his toxic spit and rubbed the resulting muck into the horse's eyes. In a word, the poor thing had suffered considerably and from that day on, he had been called White Eye. A creature such as this can never hope to die a natural death. There would come a time when someone would come and take a knife to his throat... And the horse felt no sadness that he was ambling along this beaten path alone...

Nearby, with a crack and a clatter, a herd of Siberian deer ran by, scampering off in fear. The large-antlered stags led from the front, their heads down. How many years have they been fed and watered by humans and yet these free, wild creatures would never grow accustomed to them, Aktan pondered. But take the horse and see the kind of life they have had ever since they submitted to man's will? Aktan scornfully jabbed the handle of his whip into White Eye's croup... It was fresh and damp there in the forest; the moist earth, thickly carpeted with yellow leaves, offered a soft cushion beneath the horse's hooves.

Large drops glistened on the green pine needles; passing by, Aktan struck a pine branch with his whip and the droplets fell thickly to the ground. A lingering, plaintive cry reached them from afar, from the direction of Akshoky. The distant forest in the direction of Karashoky responded with the same sound. And there and then the sonorous cry of the Siberian deer echoed close by. The deer were calling to one another, gathering together into a single herd. That meant their frantic season of nuptials was at an end.

Aktan recalled the first time he had watched the mating rituals of the deer. Ten years must have passed since that time. He had heard from the older children that the deer have the most unusual, wild and frenetic wedding games and he wanted to see them for himself. He packed some food and set off into the mountains. The autumn was dry and frosty. It was beautiful in the taiga and terrifying at night, but Aktan was not afraid. At the foot of Karashoky, he spied a large herd of Siberian deer; he crept up from the side and hid near a large larch tree, laying out a warm sheepskin beneath him. He lay there the whole day but failed to see anything. It only seemed to him that, from all sides, behind every tree, he could hear the frantic voices of the roaring stags. This roar went on throughout the night. And the boy kept his eyes open all that time. He looked out tensely into the impenetrable darkness and all that was needed was for a twig to snap for him to start up like a young animal, ready to dart away to safety. By sunrise, he was overcome with drowsiness but a nightjar suddenly churred wildly and some snowcocks flapped their wings loudly somewhere close by... The rut began when the late autumn sun emerged from the peak of Akshoky. The bucks stepped unhurriedly away from the does and stood in pairs, facing each other off. As if on some silent command, they lowered their heads, took a step back and then rushed forward fiercely. A crack rang out across the taiga as their powerful antlers crashed together. The bucks fought frantically and without mercy from morning to noon. One by one, the defeated, bereft of all strength, swaying and falling to the ground, left the field of battle and only the two mightiest and most indefatigable bucks fought it out for another hour and a half or so, until one got the better of the other, chased him off too and, trumpeting his victory to the skies, headed off to the does, standing some distance away. Gathering them together into a herd, he drove them on ahead onto the slopes of Karashoky... Aktan returned to the village (perhaps it was from that day that he was given the name *the Man-Deer*?) and it was only a week later that he was able to return to the taiga near Karashoky. At the site where the rut had taken place, the victor lay gaunt and weak, looking like a shrivelled corpse. Aktan walked up and touched the stag's antlers; he did not even make an attempt to get up and clearly lacked the strength for this either.

Aktan smiled, recalling the aggrieved and forlorn appearance of that first lord of the harem. Aktan had heard that even the most ardent male has only the strength for a dozen does. What was the point of him fighting for them all? When he becomes exhausted and guiltily lowers his eyes before the waiting females, the stag he defeated last in battle will approach him and lance him below the ribs with his antlers. And that is how a new leader and master of the herd emerges, although he too will not last for long... In turn, a third and then a fourth will come. In a word, each will receive his designated share and the does will bear them little baby fawns. These are the facts of life for the Siberian deer, the mysterious truth of their mating rituals, but Aktan never saw the greatest secret of their lives—the birth of a fawn—and never had he heard of any other who had succeeded in witnessing this.

* * *

85

The calls of the deer could still be heard from time to time as Aktan approached the chain of dark, majestic mountains, the spurs of the Aldan Highlands. He was struck by one incredibly narrow and tall, black rock, shooting into the sky like a spear; a flat rock stood perched on its stone tip and it seemed that a single gust of wind would suffice to topple it over. Yet people recalled that this strange rock had been this way for centuries, with the flat stone on its summit, like a plate, spinning on the pole of some circus performer. It was a mystery, what forces kept this rock in place. This peak was known as the King's Vault – *Tanirkoimas*. At its foot, there was a bottomless pit and the mountain path that passed through here, ran right up to the edge of the precipice as if testing the courage of each traveller who passed here.

Whenever the Man-Deer had to pass this place, his heart would shudder, as if pricked by the blades of many small daggers, and he would hold his breath. He hurriedly cracked his whip and hastened on, as if he were being pursued. Later, Aktan would be surprised at this agitation, almost akin to terror. Could it be, he thought, that there is some force concealed there in Tanirkoimas, which makes a horseman quiver, time and again forcing him to call upon his maker for help?

People were unable to speak, or, more precisely, the old Asan could not speak about this rock without tears welling up in his eyes:

"In the distant past, in ancient times, a tribe of Kazakhs lived here, who rode on short-legged steeds. They lived in peace and prosperity; they put their cattle out to graze and hunted to their heart's content. In a word, they lived happily. However, one fine day, when no-one expected it and when the valleys near Tanirkoimas were teeming with horses, cows and sheep, the *Dzungars* attacked and plundered our tribe. They managed to drive the evil enemy away and the people never left. They disputed the lands with Russian merchants and then the war raged between the reds and the whites. Surrounded by fire from all sides, our people nevertheless refused to desert their native land, even though they could have taken to their carts and departed out into the sands. However, glory to the creator, this never came to pass and we are now all here living next to our native landmarks, each of which contains an untold tale or story. And if a talented writer or storyteller is found in your number, then don't go giving yourself airs like some, who write about singing cockerels or braying donkeys. Rather, tell everyone of the glory of our people, of the highest peaks and the bottomless *Arkhara* ravines of our mountain tribe." How clearly Aktan could now see the old man's wrinkled face as he said all this. Turning away from the young boys and looking pensively somewhere into the distance, Asan would take a pinch of snuff. The golden sheen of the setting sun would begin to slide, leaving clefts and dips in the pale-blue shadow, higher and higher toward the mountain peaks; the small boys' eyes avidly drank in the old man's wrinkled face. But he was in no hurry to continue his tale, coughing long and hard and fidgeting in his seat, until he eventually turned to face his listeners. And at that instant—Aktan suddenly remembered most clearly—a stream of cool air carried a certain smell towards him... So much time had passed and only today did Aktan realise that this smell coming from the windward direction of the forest was the scent of old Asan, who sat there, enclosed from head to toe in his old, worn-out body, inspired and kind, vivacious and warm. "It was an uneasy time, my sons. If I am not mistaken, it was the same nineteen twenties when the Reds defeated the Whites in battle and the carts of refugees came flooding through Arshaly and out of the country. Everything comes to an end and so it was with the flow of refugees, but now the battles reached as far as our mountains. Well, it would take a solid three months to relate all these events, but the one thing I will say is that although the Whites retreated abroad, Baltabai and his gang remained and continued their raids, not giving the people the chance to get back on their own two feet, take off their boots and loosen their belts. This gang slipped away from the red police who had been sent over from the regional centre and they hid in the hills. Our forests and ravines, where only the snowcocks fly, would have provided shelter for an entire army of soldiers, to say nothing of fifty or so bandits. Baltabai took Arshaly on two occasions. At that time, my sons, I was still a young lad. There were fewer and fewer men left in our village; in those dark times, they crossed sides from the Whites to the Reds and from the Reds back to the Whites, with many a poor soul falling on one side or the other. I ran free, my sons, like a wild *argali* sheep. I hunted wild animals but I had no desire to hunt people. Eventually, though, Baltabai's young men came for me and I had to hole up in the mountains with a five-chambered rifle that I had taken from a straggling refugee... How did I take it? It was very simple really. I just clipped him once round the back of the head and, while he was scratching around, I took his rifle. So there I hid, during the day in the mountains and, late at night, after Baltabai's men had lain down for the night, I would come back home. There was one time when I got up after it had only just turned light to return to the hills. Near Tanirkoimas I saw two horses tethered. I approached quietly, like a cat stalking a mouse, and I saw this red-bearded type, snoring there under the larch, lying on his back, with his rifle clutched tight to his belly. And sitting next to him was a young, slender Kazakh girl. Oh lord! Like an innocent baby fawn she was, no more than fifteen or sixteen years old. She was also asleep, and her face, lads, was a picture of unbearable sadness; a single tear had set there on her long lashes as if frozen in place. Well, I came up close to them, as carefully as I could. The girl was sleeping very lightly, like an anxious bird she was, and she was woken by the rustling of my steps. She saw me and was about to scream out with joy for seeing a fellow

87

Kazakh, but managed to keep herself in check and put her hands over her mouth. And she looked at me with such pitiful, desperate little eyes, that I understood in an instant: I was this girl's last hope. Well, lads, I didn't sit around thinking for long and rushed to release her, although, just in case, before cutting the rope binding the girl, I carefully took the rifle from the red-bearded bandit. He soon came to, jumped up, moving his hands to grasp the rifle but, realising I was holding it, he ran away toward the caves of Tanirkoimas. I went after him. Of course, I could have shot him down before he climbed into the cave but I didn't stop him; rather, I did the opposite and ran after him, chasing him down into it, good and proper. I then took the girl to the village and, you might believe me or you may think I'm talking tosh, but I tell you this is the honest truth: this girl became my wife. Yes, yes, lads, she is now my old woman, the one sitting beneath that cow and pulling at its teats. You ask what happened to the man I forced into the cave? Well, lads, I really don't know.

"One autumn I went into that King's Vault myself, a place where a man can't enter without his knees knocking and, Allah forbid, my boys, that any of you should have to experience what I had to back then. It was dusk and it was as black as night in the cave. Tanirkoimas, that heavenly, mournful rock, admitted me inside but would it reveal to a nobody like me the secret of its heart? All I could feel, my children, was the yearning of this dark, mysterious soul of the mountain and I was so cold and so afraid; there is probably nothing colder on Earth than that cave. I crawled into the bottomless cavity, feeling the icy breath of the darkness on my face and, suddenly, I had a wonderful feeling of relief. What could it have been? I was overcome in that impenetrable gloom by a sense of bliss; I stopped in my tracks, clothed in a gentle coolness and I wept from an unknown happiness that I had never experienced before. Who knows what it could have been, lads? This gloomy cave Tanirkoimas that people say hides evil spirits suddenly turned out to be full of motherly tenderness for me and I imagined that I, this unworthy creature, had crawled into a fairytale palace of immortal spirits and this is what my soul had been yearning for all my life... At the same time, I felt a bitter doubt that no-one up on the surface, in the chaotic confusion of the days and nights that we call *life*, would ever believe me. And I could tell no-one that I had travelled to the world of death, where everything for us is alien, but where peace, bliss and grace reign over everything. I lack the ability to relay the greetings to those who walk the earth, either on my own behalf or on behalf of the lords and masters of the cave, with whom I conversed in this blissful state between life and death... Hundreds and thousands of years ago, these spirits—and me with them—were living people, but now we have become brothers and eternal dwellers of the Tanirkoimas cave."

88

Then old Asan fell silent, finishing his tale and sitting surrounded by the boys, staring at him with eyes, round with fear. He suddenly got up, stepped over some of our legs and swiftly strode off in the direction of the watering place. At that moment, the boys imagined that old Asan was under some enchantment as if summoned by secret voices, reaching out to him through the thundering stream, never to return to relate any amusing or horrifying story ever again. The boys weren't yet able to understand that adults perceive the secrets of the world as poorly as they do, which is why they console children by inventing and relating fables and fairy tales. And when this old man, who had adopted this majestic appearance, became hidden from view, the boys also got up and rushed back to the village. It seemed to them that spirits were emerging from the black mouth of the cave and silently moving towards the fire. Aktan was the first to make it to the village, urged on by the frantic beating of his heart, and yet the terrible secret of the Tanirkoimas cave had still not been revealed to him. This was because childhood had passed and old Asan had died, having promised the children that he would take them to the cave with candle in hand. With the death of the silver-tongued old chatterbox, the only living source of fairy tales, legends, fables, songs and merry ditties had gone. The jovial lantern of the old man's wisdom had faded and gone out and a wild wind blew into the empty house without its master. There was no-one left to tell stories to the village boys and the village itself was as good as gone, too. All that was left were silent, forlorn houses under the autumn wind and rain.

We all know well that if a person does not experience wonderful and marvellous things in childhood, once they grow up, they will lose all curiosity for new knowledge and the mysteries of the world. It is perhaps our fairy-tale impressions of childhood and the eerie wilds of the fantastic that give flight to our dreams, like a bird that carries human creativity furthest of all. Only in childhood, when evil is still unknown, do people view the world through eyes that are especially innocent and pure. These eyes see the world of springtime as a green carpet, adorned with floral patterns. And this world will forever remain the ideal we seek; we want to revisit this green carpet but this is not possible because our sins bar our way. There is no way back down the road that leads away from childhood.

Childhood, however, had not deserted the Man-Deer's soul. The passage of time seemed to have had no effect on the blue vault of the skies of his childhood, which remained unchanged and unsullied over his head. Exciting childhood recollections frolicked under this sky, like the fallow deer with their tender teats, playing near their fawns. He sometimes tried to rid himself of these recollections, which re-opened old wounds, but they would always return. He soon stopped chasing them away, realising that, if they were to disappear altogether, he would have no peace in his life. These recollections would usually come unbidden and of their own accord and he could only marvel and sigh wistfully that they remained so dear to him...

Passing by Tanirkoimas, he became overwhelmed by that distant childhood fear, despite the fact he was now grown and felt sure he had the strength to tear down this cliff with his bare hands. The Man-Deer was particularly troubled by this ambiguity of feeling, borne of the boundless loyalty of his heart to the childhood that was embedded in his memory. He imagined what it would be like to climb to the very top of the stone finger of Tanirkoimas and lie on the flat stone that crowned its summit; then, with his chin hanging over the side, he would look down; oh, how his head would spin over that sinister drop into the ravine! Even if you sit on the soft moss by the edge of this ravine on the hottest summer's day, when the water is almost boiling over from the heat, you will still feel an icy chill overwhelm you. The cold comes from down below, like the breath of a monster, and it appears like sorcery. Many times Aktan had wanted to descend down ropes into the chasm, to solve this wondrous mystery, but something always seemed to stop him. No, he had no fear! He was quite capable of overcoming his nerves... Yet there seemed to be a taboo hanging over him and Aktan could not rid himself of it. It was like a deep-seated, powerful taboo, that no-one instils in you but which prevents a person from murdering their own kind or from venturing on some foul and depraved debauchery, even once shame and conscience have been erased. His desire to enter the ice-cold ravine still seemed unattainable and, with the passing years, it had acquired a dreamlike weightlessness and flight. When he became desperately lonely, afflicted and helpless after a particularly strong bout of spiritual suffering, he would begin to think deliriously, "Oh, to go down there and come back alive!" he would repeat to himself incessantly, through clenched teeth. He imagined that if this were to happen, the rest of his life would change, as if at the bidding of a sorcerer, and he would become rich, magnanimous, all-powerful and revered like no other on this earth. All that it would take would be to venture into the depths and return...

Aktan unwittingly held back his horse, following the path that traced the edge of the ravine. "Such weak, vain and deceitful thoughts!" he told himself in dismay. Is it not because we think of riches, benevolence and power that every child already knows some story about treasure, hidden at the bottom of some chasm? So did that not mean that the real reason he wanted to lower himself down there was not to pass some supernatural test, but simply to gain the earthly pearls and gold, hidden there by the *bai* landowners and other rich men after the Revolution? "So you're not averse to getting rich, either, then?" the Man-Deer accused himself, angrily whipping his quite blameless horse.

He turned his horse back; he had no wish to climb any higher toward Tanirkoimas. On that cold day, foggy and gloomy like never before, it seemed that his soul had become overcome with a premonition of impending calamity, treachery and betrayal, weighed down by an immense burden and grief. The fog, which had started to clear, did not really disperse in the autumn air, oversaturated as it was with damp, and soon its turbid banks began to swell once more, drawing everything around it into an obscure, white haze. An icy vapour permeated the forest, marking the onset of winter. Its breath was even more intolerable than the cruel February frost. The time of snow and frost was close at hand, a time when the Altai is submerged in a deep white sleep. In the winter time, the Man-Deer always felt alive; he hunted frequently and travelled out far into the taiga on his skis, padded with colt skin. Now that the people had deserted these wooded areas, the number of squirrels, foxes and other wild animals had increased beyond compare. The village had fallen silent, the sheep no longer bleated and there was more space for the wild forest creatures to roam freely, so the increase in their number had been no surprise. What was unclear, however, was where the mysterious, sacred mouse had disappeared. Aktan had not seen it or its tracks for two years and he had no explanation. Perhaps, he assumed, the abundant May snowfalls over the last three years had done away with the mouse and all its kind. Or, perhaps, they had a premonition of the impending famine, the like of which had never been seen before, and they had left these parts early...

White Eye hurried for home, not feeling the hand of his master but Aktan recovered his senses, straightened up in the saddle and turned the horse toward the distant and as yet unseen Blue Lake. The sickly sun, drowning in the fog, seemed to have jumped to a new place and now a barely noticeable, white disk appeared to the right of Akshoky and Karashoky. These stone giants were now swallowed up by the fog and stirred as barely visible shadows in its womb. So strong was the fog's stranglehold enveloping heaven and earth, that even the noise of the mountain river, always blithe and sonorous, was now muffled by something akin to a thick veil of cotton wool. Aktan galloped through this icy vapour along the riverbank to the Blue Lake, as if he was hurrying to a feast with his relatives.

Kokkol, the Blue Lake, had once been alive with workers, ferrying minerals on their carts in all directions. People came here en masse from the Siberian side and the Kazakh side, armed with nothing but a pick or a shovel, to mine the precious tungsten. The metal, once extracted, was loaded onto camels and sent deep into the country. Aktan had seen none of this with his own eyes. This had been a long

91

time ago; the mine and the factory had not existed for long and now everything had been abandoned and there was nothing to remind anyone of those noisy, vibrant and heady tungsten mining days. Kokkol hid its congealed, dead waters beneath the tatters of the fog. The Man-Deer had a sensitive and vulnerable heart and he was always dismayed to see such images of decay, abandonment and neglect. His soul grieved, but a powerful force still brought him here to the dead mine by the Blue Lake. He only had to be away for a month to feel vexed and uneasy.

In his darkest thoughts, he perhaps compared his fate to this part of the Kazakh land on the banks of the Blue Lake, the border waters of which divided Kazakhstan from the foreign land. And, like this abandoned facility, a vagrant and lone wanderer in the desert, he was doomed to oblivion and a sad demise. The longer his life went on, the more the thin threads of his hopes for joy and happiness would fray. Aktan did not believe that, in losing this hope, he would gain anything in its place, even if it were just some eventual, consolatory wisdom. His conscience harboured a growing conviction that there was no such wisdom, only a large, immeasurable and protracted sense of life. Everything else, including this eventual wisdom, was something people invented, either to deceive themselves or shrewdly to deceive others. But what for? A human being cannot live without either feigning tears or laughing insincerely. As for Aktan, what truths did he know about people? No, he too knew nothing. People exist each of their own accord, dreaming up their own pitiful wisdom and laws. A genius despises empty-headed people and passes them by with contempt, while a simpleton, with only a vague idea of genius, views such exceptional people with disdain and disgust. Thieves travel along this hard life's path with their own laws, inviolable regulations and customs. The saying goes that thieves observe their own laws far more faithfully than honest folk. "And what about me?" Aktan pondered. "Haven't I devised my own laws for myself? I live apart from the hustle and bustle of life, I don't read newspapers or books, I don't listen to the radio, I don't go to the cinema and I live all by myself with my mute mother."

He recalled the collective farm shop at the central country farmstead at Oreli, which sold brick-shaped transistor radios. However, whenever he thought about them, he would scoff and remonstrate with himself: "What the devil does an old dog need a block of metal for?" He had lived thirty years without listening to this radio and somehow he'd get through another thirty without it. After all, his mother had lived seventy years without knowing, hearing or seeing anything. "I don't see that those who have seen things or who have been places are any happier than me," thought Aktan. "Take, Kan the scholar, for example." He had returned to his native land having worked for a while in the regional cultural department and had then been kicked out for his drinking. He had left his wife and children and moved to the village, where he had worked as head of the social club. He had scrounged money from Aktan many times: "I need the hair of the dog, brother. My head is splitting." Everything he earned had been spent on maintenance payments and booze. This world-weary, useless man spent his time wandering around the village, a living example of human shame and disgrace. To think, this fine fellow had been a pen-pusher at some institution in the capital! The question is, does it matter where a person goes astray – in a dense forest or among the hen houses? The thing is, a person like this is doomed to wander aimlessly through life and will never be prepared either to face death or to fight it. "I'd like to see you screaming like a hare, grabbed by the ears, when grim death comes calling," Aktan had thought with a wicked grin, "You don't deserve to be around Aigul, you wretched coward, you vagrant in soiled trousers!"

Aigul!

"I'll rip the heart out of that bastard, give him a good kick up the backside and you'll soon be rid of him, Aigul. You are like a white fallow deer I found in the white fog. All it takes is a single waft of your kindness and my good-for-nothing soul, like a bucket with no bottom, melts like the snow in springtime. At times like these, my sadness subsides and the solitude, from which I so want to flee into the depths of the forest in order to die with my face buried in the damp moss, no longer seems so bitter.

"The books you gave this foolish Man-Deer, the Wild Beast as everyone calls him, were like winged doves. And even though Aktan the Wild Beast was unable to wade through these dull tomes, know this, Aigul: I rested my head on them when I slept and stroked them as I dreamed, as the faint aroma of your hands remained on them. You probably remember that early autumn day..."

Aigul had been sitting alone in the library. The glass in the uncovered window had flared up from the streaming evening sun and the fiery, scarlet shimmer that had fallen from them onto Aigul's face had presented the Man-Deer with an unusually perturbed, anxious and rather stern appearance. It was perhaps for this reason that, standing in the middle of the room, he had even found himself unable to say hello to her. She, too, had been silent, bent over her table. There he had stood, unable to take his eyes off the girl's gentle, scarlet face, and he had sensed an unknown, powerful desperation rising up inside him. Unable to bear the feeling any longer, he had turned and headed for the exit. "Aktan!" she had called out abruptly and then once more: "Aktan!" He had been astounded that the girl had called to him for the first time and had said his name... But this had not been a voice for calling, rather for chasing away. Without looking round, he had run off, slamming the door behind him. Two months had gone by since then.

Prior to this, they had met by chance in the home of the collective farm's chief accountant, or *Beancounter*, as they called him in the village. She spoke with Aktan, asking why he never took out any books from her; after all, he was bright, he had been to school and it must be dull, living all alone in the deserted village settlement. He answered, only not immediately and, when he did, his eyes had sparkled: "Aigul, I know that if I read all the books in your library, I would become much cleverer. But I would also become more cunning and more impudent. Who are the clever, after all, Aigul? Surely it's those people who are more cunning than others, more merciless and more unscrupulous? So, I think I'll choose to be dim and uncultivated. I may not be able to think or weep like they do in books. But I will live in my own way, as I can, and I will never turn my back on my freedom..."

She was taken by surprise, as she had not expected that the Man-Deer would speak in such a way. Then she became afraid, afraid for this rather awkward Wild Beast. Flustered, she looked at him with terror and said, almost in a whisper: "Oh, Allah, but a man like this only wants to live for himself!" To which he responded with a long, dogged and somewhat mocking look, crying and wagging his finger:

"So, tell me, who today lives for others? Tell me truthfully! Only truthfully!"

She could not bear it and lowered her eyes.

And on that bright, autumn evening, Aktan, kicking shut the flimsy library door, headed off to the Widow's shop. The Widow was a saucy young mother whose husband had died, falling from his tractor into the river. The Widow harboured warm feelings for Aktan and treated him with unwavering kindness, treating him as one of the family, as he had been a friend of her late husband, whom she had lost in the prime of her female years. Her quick, black eyes shone joyfully and, as always, endeavoured to express something more meaningful and more suggestive than regular friendly joy, whenever the Man-Deer entered the small shop, bending his head to pass under the lintel. But the Man-Deer did not reciprocate the Widow's silent, playful summons. Planting his elbow on the counter, he conversed with her, courteously enquiring after the health of her children. Then he asked for some vodka, accepted a table glass from her and downed the drink in one, following it with a deep sniff from the sleeve of his coat.

"You look here, you witch," he snarled, grabbing the Widow and lifting her off the floor. "If you go flashing your eyelashes, I'll, I'll... Shame on you, you hussy, before the spirit of the man who fatally upended his DT[1] tractor beccause of you and the children. Have you no shame before your little children?"

The Widow was not afraid. She pressed up to him all the tighter and, her round, rosy face glowing and let out a little laugh.

"Oh, if Allah ever sees to give me another man, I want it to be you. I'd rather you tormented me than anyone else," she answered, laughing, throwing back her head and turning to face up to him close with her soft, large, hot face. "My DT would forgive you. Were he alive, he would forgive you. He loved his friend more than me, his wife."

The Man-Deer released the Widow and pushed her away. The cold, burning vodka spread through his veins and went to his head. He vaulted up onto the counter and sat on it, his long legs dangling over the side. With eyes downcast, he sullenly asked for another vodka. The Widow brought it to him, he drank it down and sniffed his sleeve once more.

"Remember, Aktan, how DT and I used to call you the *Wild Beast*. And everyone at the farm came to tease you as well, calling you *Wild Beast*," chirped the Widow, leaning up against his side. "You really are more of a wild animal than a man, aren't you, ha-ha?! And isn't it time, you poor thing, moved to the farm, got yourself married and made your own home, eh?" the Widow suddenly murmured compassionately.

But it seemed that the Man-Deer had not heard her. Drinking vodka on an empty stomach had turned him deaf. He muttered something incoherent and grimaced:

"All of you... you and Aigul, and everyone... the entire farm... what can you possibly understand? I don't know you... Once a month... I come down from the hills to drink vodka and you all reckon I am just a drunkard and you're all afraid of me. You envy me, I know... I catch animals and sell expensive pelts. I have no father, and you know what my mother is like... and yet still you envy me. And this hand, this fighting hand, will grab you all by the scruff of the neck, in this world and the next, do you see?"

Muttering something else along those lines, he suddenly swayed and fell from the counter. Twisting around awkwardly, he then fell asleep, right there, on the floor where he lay. Somewhat perplexed, the Widow started sweeping up. If anyone were to see him here, rumours would blaze like wild fire, causing her to burn with the shame. And yet the Widow decided not to turf him out of the shop onto the sheet, taking pity on the handsome forester, for whom she clearly had feelings. She covered him with her coat and, looking out the door,

---

[1] A Soviet-made tractor. The abbreviation of the tractor that he drove is also the Widow's deceased husband's village nickname.

closed it, locking it from the inside. Then she sat on a sack of grain and kept watch over Aktan's drunken dreams in silence. She sat there for a good while, before laying out some empty sacks and settled down next to him. Aktan spent the night in the impenetrable gloom of the locked shop, feeling nothing in his drunken stupor and failing to sense the hot, quivering, greedy hands that embraced him. He only came round when the indistinct light of the early morning peered in and then he noticed the Widow, sleeping by his side. She had waited the entire night in vain for a miracle to happen. Her round face, usually pink and flushed, was now a leaden grey and puffy with the fatigue of a sleepless night. She snuffled like a child, babbling something incoherently in her sleep, and all that Aktan could do was pity this helpless woman lying next to him. Who knew what the young, unhappy Widow was dreaming about...

* * *

Two Siberian deer shot out of the forest and ran across the road. The strong, slender deer soared up above the misty earth, as if in a nimble, animal dance and disappeared from view in a flash. Aktan knew that two males had escaped from the nursery and these were evidently them. They had grown strong in the wild and had stored fat. The hunter thought it would be a good idea to track and shoot them, to store meat for the winter. At the same instant, however, he felt sorry them.

Clouds of thick fog raced like billowing smoke and the sun was obscured from view. The horse walked tentatively, slipping on the wet, clay road. The air, clammy and heavy with moisture, streamed down his face and clothes and the horse's body. Once the old horse, lurching cautiously from side to side and feeling out the path, had made it up the invisible little hill, the forest ended and the wet bushes began slapping damp leaves against his legs and face. White Eye's hooves now trod on soft, compliant moss.

The fog soon cleared and the outlines of the rocks and the smoking silhouettes of the trees came into view. Between them, the lead-like surface of Kokkol glistened dimly. This was the deep hollow on the banks of the lake, where tungsten had once been mined from the earth beneath the hill. The hill was now barely visible, covered by a milky-white fog. The hump of the mined hill loomed hazily on the bank, with the oval mouth of a cave at its foot, gaping like the solitary eye of a giant. Aktan headed there, like a tiny Rostam[2] toward an enormous giant.

Long, dark huts flashed by in the ragged fog. These dwellings were now empty and run-down, acting as a shelter for wild owls and

---

[2] A celebrated warrior hero in Shahnameh and Iranian mythology

snowcocks that flew noisily in and out of the empty windows and doors. Aktan wanted to lead White Eye into the cave, but the horse dug in his heels and pulled at the reins. His master then decided to tether him to the bare trunk of a larch. With his crop held tight in his hand, Aktan stepped under the arch of the cave. The darkness grew thicker with each step and Aktan recalled the terrors of the Tanirkoimas cave, of which old Asan had related. It seemed that the evil spirits of Tanirkoimas had gathered here in secret in order to track their uninvited guest. Soon the main body of the cave split into several passages and Aktan stopped, unable to make up his mind if he should go on. His heart beat frantically and the icy damp breathed on his face from the underground gloom. There was no reason for him to venture here, just to overcome his fear and risk being buried alive; the supports had long since rotted and could collapse at any moment. Stumbling over remnants of minerals lying here and there, Aktan began to advance carefully, collecting twigs as he went. Dropping to his haunches, he struck a match and lit a fire. A weak, flickering flame danced on the rock, gradually growing stronger until the flame burned brightly, repelling the cave's darkness to a good distance. Gathering more firewood, Aktan sat down by the fire. Through the crackling of the fire, he could hear a noise by the entrance, probably his hungry horse pulling on his tether... Soon, all noises from the outside world ceased to exist, as he sank into oppressive, obtrusive thoughts. They were especially onerous now, like a dense fog, covering the mountains. The Man-Deer's head dropped low to his chest. Strangely enough, his mournfully inclined head was tormented by a once-remembered joy and by recollections of his carefree childhood. The never-ending games, the bright days that had passed by, never to return, like swallows flying with a swish-swish-swish to warmer climes. These recollections were not, however, a source of tenderness, rather a dull, spiritual ache. This was because his dreams would soon lose their joy and the first, timid thoughts of love, like an outburst of passion, would be trampled by the heavy, canvas boots of wartime... He recalled his schooling that had been brought to an abrupt halt, his father, who had disappeared, heaven knew where and his mother, unable to utter even the single word "son"... Time and again he shuddered from these recollections, as if from heavy blows to the body... The time for children's stories had ended for him and it seemed like a thousand years had passed and that they would never return. Now was the time for grey, joyless solitude. He had not spoken to a single soul for two months now. Day and night, he was always alone. At times, Aktan would rebel, saying, "Can a human really turn its back on itself? And why am I eking out this pitiful existence, like an old man who is out of his mind? What do I lack that stops me from living peacefully among other people?"

97

He didn't know what he lacked; there was only the darkness behind his closed eyes. Streaks flashed, white and blue... Where are you, spirit of Old Asan? Why don't you come? I so loved your brightness, youthfulness, humour and wisdom? How can this Man-Deer live in this world without your tales and strange stories?

This was one of those old tales of Asan.

The village of Arshaly was especially beautiful in the evenings. A peaceful, fragrant smoke would rise above the rooftops, golden from the evening sun. The herds would be returning from their distant pasture, flooding onto the village street and the hustle and bustle of evening life would simmer in the yards. Old Asan, gathering the small boys by his hut, would tell them: "In the olden days when one of our great ancestors Mametek the judge was alive, no-one but Kazakhs would ever dare come here across the Kurchum Pass. Mametek was indeed a most wealthy man but Allah also blessed him with wisdom and wit. People spoke of his riches, saying that if all his many horses came to the watering place and took but one gulp of water, the river would run dry. One day, however, a terrible springtime plague, a *dzhut*, struck and all his horses dropped dead; there was not even a single mount to saddle. Mametek was forced to go and ask for horses from his rival, the landowner Tekesh. Tekesh wanted to humiliate proud Mametek and ordered his bondsmen to drive his most select horses past his neighbour, with expensive blankets on their backs; he said Mametek could choose any of them. Mametek, however, made as if he had not understood and he became despondent: 'They were wrong to say that the respected Tekesh was almost my equal in wealth! Not one horse from his ten prize herds will do for me!' And he refused to select a single one. When someone whispered to him that his neighbour had tried to humiliate him, he exclaimed: 'What a simpleton I am! I can only count the big rocks while Tekesh is so clever that he can count the smallest grain of sand...' So even in his darkest hour, he was able to avoid dishonour. After Mametek had travelled to Mecca and Medina, he became known as *Kazhy*, and his fame spread far and wide across the land. He became a supreme judge and now he would make way or doff his hat to no man.

"Even the children would stop crying at the mention of his name. One day, after the times of trouble had arrived, Mametek declared to everyone that he would go and seek a promised land, where winter and summer are one and the same. Mametek took fifty men with him and set off on his long journey. At that time there were no roads marked on maps and there were no paper maps, either. They determined their route by following the sun and travelled in a straight line, following their noses. Well, our Mametek was a very learned man and he knew things that others did not. He led his men out of Arshaly, straight to the distant country of Thailand. Those fine men saw an exotic land, where a wondrous summer lasted the whole year through. It was a wonderful thing to behold - a promised land indeed! Of course, those Kazakhs who rode all the way to the mysterious land of Thailand were bathed in glory. And you couldn't even get there by aeroplane today, could you? So, now you understand... They returned home, fit and well, three years later. And they told their people that something grows there that is like wheat, but which can be harvested all year round. It is plentiful, needs no sowing and just grows of its own accord. So, the following year, Mametek prepared to migrate to this Thailand with his people, the Karatai that is, with our people, but he never made it, for he died soon after (at this point, old Asan was deeply moved and shed tears, drying his eyes with the sleeve of his old shirt). If he had not died, at least one tribe of Kazakhs would now be living in that wondrous land of Thailand, my sons."

That tale still affected Aktan. When he was at his loneliest, he would almost lose his mind thinking about it: "If," the Man-Deer thought, "this indeed took place, did my great-grandfather go to Thailand? That would mean I might have been living there, where winter never comes! And what would I have done? What job would I have had?" And strange thoughts such as these would fill his mind.

However, although Mametek's descendants never made it to Thailand, they did leave Arshaly and had been living some five years in Oreli now. Old Asan, although he had refused to budge, also ended up going there. His son was a teacher and he had said to his father: "Who will I teach in an empty village? I can hardly teach you and there will be no-one else." The old man had to concede defeat. However, he did not last a year in this new place and died. According to his final wishes, his body was taken to Arshaly and buried near the abandoned village.

* * *

Aktan warmed himself by the fire; the wet clothes he was still wearing gave off a smoky steam as they dried. His back still felt a chill, between his shoulders, and he sat with his back to the fire. He didn't know how much time had passed or whether it was winter or autumn outside, if the fog still persisted over the land or if white snow had long since covered this mountainous country. It was silent. He could hear neither the snorting nor the stomping of his horse, tethered by the entrance. He should have gone out to take a look, but all Aktan did was turn back to the fire and poke the burning wood. He was listening attentively to a peculiar conversation that had been going on for some time now, not in his head, but somewhere thereabouts. They were speaking and arguing, one the intelligent, sensible Aktan, the other, the wild, obstinate Man-Deer.

99

Aktan: look at you! You're barely in your thirties and you've already gone to seed. So what have you achieved in your short life, eh? And what have you given the people or the world? What are you sitting around here for?

Man-Deer: I know full well that I am just sitting around... I was all alone and so I will remain. But you can be lonely even among other people. After all, they say that if it is the Creator's will you can go astray even in the day with a light to guide you... I have indeed achieved nothing and I have given nothing to the world. And it is true I have gone to seed, a wild man among the people. Yet I still remember all of Old Asan's tales. But they have forgotten them. And now, I alone carry them in my soul.

Aktan: And why do you cling to all these tales? Do you think there is nothing else of value in life? Do you think that so little of what people dream ever comes true? Nowadays, people dream something at night and the next day they see the same thing on television. Your tales aren't worth a fig; not even the children have any need for them.

Man-Deer: You think I don't know this? I have long since realised that only old Asan and I loved these stories. We are the last ones who hold them dear. Say what you like, but you'll never prove to me that there is anything wrong in that. What is it you don't like about the legend of Mametek, who wanted to resettle his tribe in a country where there is no winter and where everlasting bread grows on untilled earth? Would you even dare to call this a foolish, empty yarn?

Aktan: The old man did have a touch of eccentricity about him... And this Mametek – he could have brought ruin on his people, had he led them away from Altai, where the fierce winter rages for six months in the year. People would have died from disease in the hot climate. That's what abandoning oneself to an empty, perilous dream leads you to! Instead of recalling the ravings of a dead old man, you could go down into the valley and do something useful, while old age has not completely got the better of you...

Man-Deer: Something useful, you say... And what does "something useful" actually mean? I think the best thing would be to learn how not to kill off the faith of another person, who, like you, lives but once and dies for all time. And you don't have to live in Oreli to learn this. Here, you see, I don't have to practice cunning and guile on anyone and I am not an object of envy or malice... Perhaps my life is not a bed of roses, but at least my conscience is clear.

Aktan: You are so naïve to make assumptions like this. Who needs a devotee like you, eh? You're such an innocent angel in your own eyes. You are so concerned with your own purity that you haven't even noticed how you've gradually become this lonely Wild Beast. You're the laughing stock of the village and perhaps even the entire region! There are those who envy you for catching and selling on those

100

valuable furs, but shoot me down in flames if there is even one person who envies you your life. What is it they say about you? Aktan, they say, has grown completely wild. Why isn't his own mother afraid to live with him and how has she not gone out of her mind? He's past thirty and still not married. Perhaps he's not all man, but, you know, only half way? Where does he disappear to sometimes? It's like he is swallowed up by the earth. Let's face it, it's not for nothing that people tell each other the devil knows what about him...

Man-Deer: I am a hunter. I go for long periods into the forest, it's perfectly simple... But let the people say whatever they want and let them call me the Wild Beast. It's better for me to be the Man-Deer than the Man-Machine. Over in Oreli, I know there is no-one who can make up stories. Unless they start telling tales about me to frighten badly behaved children.

Aktan: But why does anyone need fairy tales these days? They grow up and get clever, their childhood and adolescence come to an end, they forget their innate, timid humility, and is that such a bad thing? That means we have finally attained freedom, and that is the result of progress.

Man-Deer: Don't be so fast to rejoice in the future, Aktan! You watch, man will become over-confident and self-assured thus losing his generosity of heart and the best of his human qualities?

Aktan: And what about you? Why have you placed your own heart under lock and key? Why are you hiding your generosity of heart under a bushel? Or are you afraid of someone?

Man-Deer: I have no-one to fear. I have no enemies.

Aktan: Which means you have no friends, either...

And at that moment, when the argument between Aktan the man of reason and Aktan the Man-Deer was distracting Aktan the Hunter's attention as he dozed alone in the cave by the fire, something looking like a long snake slid out of the darkness, cleaving the air with a whistle and wrapped itself tightly around the man's neck in a wet, hairy noose. The noose, drawn tight with an incredible, furious force, was as hard as a steel hawser. It was pointless fighting this invisible opponent and Aktan stopped still, leaned back and tried to loosen the noose with both hands. With incredible strength, he was able to loosen the rope a little and take a convulsive breath. Trying to hold himself together and not thrash about in the terror that had overcome his entire, half suffocated being, the Man-Deer did his best to show his unseen opponent that he did not intend to resist. However, the rope began to squeeze on his throat all the more and he wheezed and staggered; at that second, the noose loosened a little. Recovering his senses, Aktan heard steps behind him and breathing close by and he realised that a person was standing behind him. The Man-Deer wanted to turn to face him in an abrupt movement but the other beat him to it and, with a knee against his back, tightened the noose once more... It was not so much the pain that tormented him, rather the helplessness with which he was laid prostrate at the feet of his merciless, unseen enemy. Everything inside the Man-Deer was rent asunder and roared with helpless fury; he wanted either to die there and then or get his hands on the bastard who was so cruelly tormenting him, to slam him against the stone wall of the cave...just to see his legs flail in the air.

Aktan mustered all of his willpower and forced himself to calm down, for the battle and for his revenge. However, slanting his eyes a little, he looked with a strange feeling of sadness and indifference at the dying fire and a thought crossed his mind that this was when he would die, in a minute from now, and that he would die pointlessly and ignominiously, without even knowing at whose hands he would meet his fate, with the wild animals of Kokkol dragging his bones from the cave... And he would leave nothing behind on earth: no brothers and no children to live on in his place; he would die once and for all eternity...

It was then that a dull, languid indifference overcame his soul. This great life—with all its humdrum daily cares—seemed about as valuable as a copper coin. It was nothing but a worthless, black and oppressive heap of trouble. What was the point of clinging to it? And yet, as if contradicting this fading of the soul which was falling into a dying languor, the Man-Deer's young body and belly suddenly shook with tormenting convulsion of hunger. A fierce growl surged from deep within his stomach that had not seen food there since early morning. Plump deer, leaping in the mist, flashed once more before Aktan the Hunter's half-closed eyes and he now realised he had been wrong not to kill them; how much meat there would have been... Where was his gun? Where was White Eye?

Bending down, he grabbed the noose and, with all his strength, he rushed forward, to one side and then the other. The heavy knee was still pressed tight between his shoulder blades, however, and the fibrous noose pulled even tighter. This silent battle continued for a considerable while; Aktan rushed to the cave's exit, but someone's mighty arm pulled on the rope and forced him back to the stone floor. Eventually, Aktan was able to prise his strong, vice-like fingers, like the claws of an eagle, beneath the noose's loop. Stretching the rope a little, he took a full chest of air and, with all his might, pulling the noose away from his neck, he crouched down, rushed forward, head bowed low; then he turned onto his back in sudden movement and, as he turned, he kicked up powerfully with both legs. The technique proved successful and Aktan's giant, wet boots struck the face of his opponent like two battering rams, sending him flying into the half-gloom of the cave. The choking noose fell slack. He threw it off his head and, roaring hoarsely, he jumped to where he thought his enemy lay sprawling. He got up from the stone floor and Aktan kicked him as hard as he could in the back with the heel of his boot. He might have broken his opponent's back with such a kick but his enemy dodged the blow and escaped a direct hit. Aktan almost fell and when he got himself up again and turned back again in a rage, his enemy had grasped a smouldering firebrand from the fire and was brandishing it in Aktan's face. Aktan slowly stepped back, but the unknown assailant relentlessly closed in, forcing him into a stone corner. Danger once more loomed large over the young man and, in this second, Aktan the man of reason thought that an unknown man couldn't possibly harbour such a deadly hatred for him, for he had no enemies. There was something unclear here... He would need to ask for mercy, soften him up and then things would become clearer...

"No! Death is better than this!" protested the Man-Deer in fury. Fight honestly and be victorious in open battle or die. Heavy beads of sweat ran down Aktan's face, filling his eyes and tickling his lips. What should he do? There was nowhere to retreat; his hand touched the cold wall of the cave. At that second, the mighty, fierce roar of a horse came from beneath the stone arches. White Eye had unexpectedly decided to give voice! The unknown assailant started at this unexpected turn of events and looked round; before he knew it, he was on the ground, floored by a powerful blow. He tried to get up but was stunned by the next blow to the back of his head. Darkness overcame him, lying prostrate on the stone floor of the cave...

Aktan staggered toward the exit. The anxious White Eye wheezed and pawed the earth. Heavy snow was falling all around. Aktan pressed his face into the warm muzzle of his steed and kissed it. "You remembered. You saved me," muttered Aktan, overcome with emotion and stroking the horse's warm croup. He wept for the first time in many years. For the first time, he sensed how dear his life was, with the white snowflakes falling and the hazy forests and mountains barely visible through the dispersing fog in this trembling world of sudden and unexpected snowfall. How indescribably wonderful this life was, like a clear vessel, full of moist, delicious air. The Man-Deer thought that he could even live in a hole, feeding on ants and enjoy the burning happiness of the everyday. Again, he sensed that fierce, bestial groaning hunger in his belly and at that moment, the Siberian deer flashed into his mind and he joyfully thought: "How wonderful that I didn't kill them."

He wanted to smoke, but he had no cigarettes. He struggled to bend his beaten, weary body and sat down on a moss-covered rock. Rummaging in his pockets, he found a hard lump of *kurt* cheese. He shoved it into his cheek and savoured its delicious sourness. The sky then mingled its interminable rain with flakes of snow and it seemed as if it had decided to release every last drop of moisture in its possession.

103

It was only then that Aktan remembered he had a gun. He jumped up, searching around in agitation but then calmed down: his gun was standing where he had left it, not far from the entrance to the cave, by the trunk of a young larch. He picked it up and, returning to the mossy rock, placed it between his knees. White Eye faltered nearby, hanging his head and repeatedly drew in his hungry belly. The meltwater ran off his wet mane and wide croup, from the saddle and the reins, splashing onto the ground in heavy drops. The poor animal was patiently and obediently enduring the foul weather. Suddenly, his ears pricked up. Aktan looked around: the beaten, unknown assailant was crawling out of the cave, dragging himself along by his arms. He appeared pitiful and helpless. "A tough old dog, that one," thought Aktan, who had long been waiting for him his appearance. Drawing nearer, Aktan saw that his enemy was completely emaciated and was more akin to a ghost than a living man. He came over hot with shame: so this was the man he had been fighting a battle of life and death with... Could it be that this half-dead bag of skin and bones had almost got the better of him? The Man-Deer hurriedly bent down, grasped the man under the arms and, lifting him up, sat him on the ground. The man bent up his legs with difficulty, placing his hands round his knees, and looked up at the overcast sky with a vacant, dull gaze. His eyes were dead and barely seemed like eyes at all, more like deep, scarred pits. He breathed silently, wheezing, and Aktan could not understand how this emaciated body, now writhing in pain, could have mustered such ferocious strength to fight him. The Man-Deer was overcome with pity and all thoughts of vengeance dissipated in an instant.

"Who are you? Where are you from?" he asked, touching the stranger on the shoulder.

Suddenly, Aktan felt a deep-seated fear: the bloodless, seemingly dying figure opened his eyes wide and the Man-Deer saw a sparkle in his dark pupils, which flared up in malice and rage. Aktan stepped back, readying his gun, but the man took a dagger from his bosom with unexpected dexterity.

"You are a young hunting dog, but I am an old wolfhound," he said, "and you will not defeat me. If you kill me, it would be no great loss for I have already lived out my years. However, if you were to perish from my knife, it would be much worse for you, for you have yet to taste life. But hear this! If I had wanted your death in the cave, I would have strangled you then and there. But I didn't... You, too, truth be told, could have killed me, but you didn't. That means that we are even and we owe each other nothing..." Uttering these words, the stranger hid his knife in his boot and stood up with a lurch. Straightening to his full height, he stepped towards Aktan. His eyes, which had only just been burning with a wild invincibility, suddenly glazed over and sank back into their sockets. His legs crumpled at the knee and he began to reel.

Aktan quickly caught him. Bearing him up by the shoulders, he led the stranger into the cave and laid him down by the dying fire. Adding twigs, Aktan waited for the flames to rekindle and he bent over the unconscious man.

In the glow of the flame, the face of his vanquished enemy had become an ashen-pink, like a shabby, burnt calico cloth. It seemed that he was already dead and had passed his last, fatal moments in a state of terrible torment in atonement for his once cruel nature and his sins. Drops of cold sweat had frozen on his motionless brow. Aktan gathered snow and put it into his pot, so the stranger would have water to drink when he came round. His mysterious appearance in these desolate borderlands made Aktan uneasy. He decided to learn from him who he was, where he was from and, perhaps, he would learn something about his father.

Warmed by the fire and having greedily drunk the water Aktan offered him, the stranger muttered something, staring motionless at the fire, as if delirious:

"I am a poor man, who has nothing left in life but to die but die I cannot because life is so sweet... And yet I cannot live either because life's hard knocks continue to rattle my bones... I am unhappy; I have lost my people... For many years I have hidden from people, not daring to enter my own village, over which the curling smoke billows... If I were to die now, bury me and leave for the valley. Go back to the people. Beware your accursed loneliness! If you come running round here again, like some wild argali sheep, you will suffer torment at my hands. You will inherit my fate, like a dead man's clothes. You can be certain of that. Living here is like being in a prison, with the mountains rising up like four walls on all sides... You will be lost forever, like your father."

"What happened to him? Where is he?!" cried Aktan, grabbing the stranger and lifting him from the ground. "Tell me now, where is he?"

Up close, Aktan saw the pockmarked face in the rosy reflection of the fire and his eyes, like scars from old wounds, like ancient, sunken wells... And Aktan recalled old Asan's distant, half-forgotten, eerie tales about a werewolf, living in the hills and attacking lone travellers. So this was the time and place they were destined to meet!

"Your father? Your father took it into his head to venture into the icy ravine in search of treasure in the Tanirkoimas cave but he fell and was dashed to pieces in the chasm..."

"And is he still lying there? In the ravine?" exclaimed Aktan, incredulous and unsure whether or not to believe this tale.

"Yes, he is there," muttered the stranger, "along with another dozen or so men, entombed in its icy depths. Each with their pockets and boots filled with gold and there they froze on top of all that gold."

"How do you know all this?" asked Aktan doubtfully, looking closely at the stranger's face.

"I must be on my way," the stranger said, starting and jumping up as if it had been a totally different man lying there like a limp rag just a minute before. "I have to get there while the fog is still hanging, I must hurry, others are waiting for me..."

And there and then he ran out of the cave, rushing headlong and bent double in the billowing fog, his head barely above the ground, and the Man-Deer watched him go with fear and disquiet. What part of his ravings were truth and what part were nonsense? And who on earth was he? A man or something conjured by the devil? Whoever he was, this madman who had almost strangled Aktan with his horse-hair lasso had now disappeared, concealed from head to toe in the fog, which continued to billow for a while and stretch after him, marking the route that the now invisible man had taken...

* * *

After that day, Aktan couldn't wait to move to the big village. Never before had he experienced anything like it. Previously, he had only ever ventured down to Oreli out of necessity—on business or to visit the shop—and he had gone there with a sense of burden and wretchedness, but now he felt an uncontrollable desire to go there and he finally decided to ask his mother's permission to go... He could not forget for a minute that strange, half-mad fugitive. The glassy stare that could barely be discerned in the sunken depths of his eye sockets had appeared to the Man-Deer in his dreams. Aktan dreamed that he was trying to shoot him but could not hit his target, even though in waking life he could have hit the thin edge of a razor blade from a country mile... In his dreams, he felt that the appearance of this stranger harboured a terrible threat to all and, when he awoke, he would realise in the cold light of day that there was no such threat. There was only one thing he knew for sure: the fugitive was right to warn him that he might inherit his fate like a dead man's clothes... This sorry thought intensified his yearning and accelerated his decision to come down from the mountains and live among people again.

It was an overcast day when he descended down to the road again. The occasional drop fell from the sky as if the sun was weeping sparse tears, having irrevocably lost its way in the gloom of the shaggy clouds overhead. Swollen with moisture, the log walls of the houses and the turf roofs and dividing walls of the barns and outhouses had all grown darker. The earth itself had absorbed the moisture with an

106

indifferent melancholy and now liquid mud splashed up from under the horse's hooves. Only the crows, obtuse and indifferent to nature in all its beauty and profanity, cawed loudly and mindlessly as they flew from one perch to another.

The horseman rode with his head down, lost in his familiar old obsessive thoughts as well as new musings, which only made him more anxious. These new thoughts had arisen after his terrifying duel with the wild, half-crazed man. Aktan now wanted to know what he could learn from that strange encounter. Was it just a senseless case of evil doing? The incomprehensibility of it all made the Man-Deer uneasy. This was the first time he had experienced such genuine anguish, as he began to realise that he had been unable to distinguish between good and evil. And because of this, he had been quite helpless, for it was the ability to distinguish between good and evil that separates man from the beasts. Aktan could now understand this just as he understood what separated life from death, or poverty from wealth.

He also thought about the ability of humans—and of humans alone—to imagine a future. And in this future, he had seen his descendants, the healthy shoots from the seed he had sown, the reason for his brief existence on this earth...

As he saddled up White Eye and then, as he trotted away, Aktan recalled the Widow's body, nestled up against him, her hands, her hot, fitful breathing, her shameless laughter and her shameless touch. While imagining the distant future, intertwined with his many descendants, for some reason the Man-Deer hadn't once stopped to think about the tender, timid, wide-eyed Aigul.

The village of Oreli appeared to be completely deserted; the inclement weather kept the villagers indoors, with their noses to the window, viewing the occasional rider passing by on a wet horse along the slushy street, or the filthy dogs running along the road and deserted alleyways with their clay-spattered bellies. Occasionally, a cow would low, restlessly and wildly, as if during a famine. And yet the peaceful life of the village still carried on. A woman passed by with a couple of pails on a yoke, the wide legs of her boots slapping as she went. For some reason, there were no men to be seen: they were probably sitting in the warm, swigging their infernal vodka and wasting the day away. What was there to do, when the muck was impassable, the rain fell incessantly and there was no venturing outside? Large drops of water ran briskly along the wires, chasing one another as they went.

Thick smoke curled above the damp houses, which were snuggled up to one another beside the long streets. The plumes of smoke merged into a single eddy over the village, striving upwards towards the heavens that were shrouded in heavy, grey storm clouds. The numerous smoke stacks told a tale of no work and menfolk sitting

107

in their homes, idle, their DT and Belarus tractors quietly soaking in the yards.

Aktan turned into the farm and tethered his horse. The old door to the office, studded with torn felt, opened with a creak. Beancounter (the chief accountant) was in the room located in front of the manager's office. The reception area was always full of people and the smoke was thick enough to cut with a knife. The walls and ceiling were grimy and dingy and light entered from a solitary window, the lower panes of which had been knocked out and stuffed with crumpled, old, oil-soaked work jackets. Beancounter sat at the desk next to this window A short sharp and acid-tongued man.

Without raising his head, he looked askance at Aktan and muttered from under his moustaches:

"What brings you here? Missing the wenches, eh?"

Aktan didn't respond. Restraining a sudden surge of sorrow, he looked beyond the accountant's head out of the window. The street outside was a sorry sight as well. The damp, unwelcoming village appeared wretched and joyless. Dusk had come early, yet there were no lights flickering. It was stuffy there in the room with its stench of smoke. Aktan even began to feel sleepy; he wouldn't have minded finding a place to lie down and rest his eyelids for a while...

"Has the cat got your tongue, Aktan?" the accountant asked, writing something on a piece of paper. "Or are you afraid that your silver spoon will fall out of your mouth, eh?" He pronounced this sarcastic barb with particular pleasure. He then threw down his pen, leaned back in his chair and, stretching luxuriously with a cracking of joints, he yawned expansively, contorting his face in the process. "So, why the silence? Have you got a smoke? All these idle bastards in this village do," cursed Beancounter, "is take my cigarettes." He took a filterless cigarette from the pack of Prima that Aktan had offered, stuck it in the corner of his mouth and gestured with his hands for a match. "In they come, the bastards, take a match and then leave, taking the whole box with them." He took the matchbox from Aktan, lit up, extinguished the match and pocketed it. "So, what's new in our legendary local *batyr's*[3] mountains?" asked Beancounter, releasing a stream of smoke through his moustaches. "How many marmots have you shot this year, then? Enough for a fur hat, I hope?"

The Man-Deer remained silent and Beancounter, fixing him with a fierce stare, cried out loudly, thrusting his forefinger toward the young man's face:

"Listen, you may be a local folk legend but there's no need to be ungrateful with me! I've been counting up your money for ten years

---

[3] The Kazakh word for a folk hero

now and I've nearly worn my eyes out. So don't tell me, I don't deserve those lousy pelts! And I've also heard that you found some *mumiyo*[4] up in the hills. All that anyone who moves here from Arshaly talks about is this *mumiyo*."

"Well, what they say is true... I did find some," replied Aktan quietly. "Only I'm not sure it's actually *mumiyo*..."

"Well, you bring some to me and I'll tell you if it is or not," Beancounter responded with a wink.

"Oh, so you're an expert on this as well now, I see," responded Aktan with mock respect. "Your talents know no bounds!"

"Well, damn it, what's the mystery?!" bellowed Beancounter with exaggerated and feigned anger. "All you need to do is give me a bit, I'll taste it and tell you what it is quickly enough. But what I really want to know, you unconscionable, vagrant, old rogue, is this. Do you have any ground, dried deer horn powder for me? You see, the thing is, my wife won't let me near her at night, if you know what I mean." And, with that, the stocky Beancounter laughed out loud and almost fell backwards out of his chair.

"If I had what you are talking about," Aktan began wearily (Beancounter's loud, intrusive banter was beginning to grate on him), "I still wouldn't give you any. You'd be the first to go and report me for deer poaching. And I'd be the first to be held responsible if you end up taking too much and blowing off with a bang... People have died from overdoing that stuff, you know."

"You know where you can stick your deer horn, don't you? I hope you choke on your precious dried deer horn! You'd be better off keeping it for yourself and trying it on for size with our poor put-upon village wenches. Anyway, if you're such a big lady's man, why don't you make your old mother happy and bring a wife home, eh?"

"Oh, give me a break!" Aktan interrupted sullenly. "And don't you go poking your nose where it doesn't belong. You know what they say, if you tighten the strings too far, they might just snap..."

All this repartee was a bit of an effort for the Man-Deer and he began to feel an overwhelming fatigue well up inside him. He had made this long journey in foul weather to hear human voices and this was all he had got for his trouble.

Both men fell silent. The darkness in the room became thicker. The ends of their lit cigarettes glowed like red dots. The men's faces became indistinct and grey and it became impossible to distinguish one from the other. The light beyond the window flickered weakly, dwindling at the feet of the encroaching night.

---

[4] Also known as *Shilajit*. A thick, sticky tar-like substance, found predominantly in the Himalayas, the Caucasus, Altai, and Pakistan, believed to possess medicinal properties

With a strange crackling noise, the wick of a lamp flared and guttered out. Beancounter cursed it richly and roundly.

Aktan was actually quite fond of this outwardly disagreeable and unattractive man. He could be cantankerous and foul-mouthed, that was true, but he was neither greedy nor genuinely malicious. In all the other farm offices, the accountants and cashiers were forever being replaced or sent to prison but Beancounter had been at his post for some twenty years now. Perhaps Allah was protecting him, not wanting to see the tears of his small children, or perhaps he was indeed an honest man, who knew... He was Aigul's older brother, and that held a particular significance for Aktan. It would only be thanks to him that Aktan would be able to see the girl today... And, as if guessing the young man's thoughts, the accountant said:

"Come on then, folk hero, that's enough small talk for now, why don't you come over to our house. Where else is there for you to go? You have no relatives to visit. You can stay at ours for a bit and pretend my wife is your auntie; true, she's not good for much, but at least she'll make you some tea... And as for the *mumiyo* and dried deer horn, don't take it to heart, I was only pulling your leg! What the devil do I need that damned stag power for anyway, eh? There's no-one to leave the missus for and with so many brats running wild in our house, there needs to be someone around to give them a thrashing now and then."

Aktan was touched. In an instant, his melancholy mood lifted and his heart was warmed. What a kind-hearted man! And so jovial and jolly with it! he thought, following Beancounter out onto the street.

The November darkness had already descended, embracing the earth and taking root. The street lights weren't working properly, flashing into life for a second or so and then going out again, so bad was the wiring. Streaks of light seeped out here and there from the windows and, falling onto the wet mud, dimly lit the way.

It was not late, but the early darkness had seeped down from the surrounding hills and accumulated in the valley. Night had not arrived at its allotted hour. They were closer to Akshoky from here than they were from Arshaly and now the mountain had turned black, looming large like a hungry cow standing patiently at the door of the house. The foothills were submerged in the darkness of the night, with only the snowy caps of their summits peeking out a ghostly white. The Man-Deer's log cabin stood somewhere beyond those dark expanses, with his mother sleeping in the impenetrable gloom. And not far from that house stood another, the hearth and former home of the short, moustachioed man, who was now showering the engineer from the power station with obscenities and calling him a drunkard and good for nothing... But what did Beancounter care that, far up in the mountains,

110

the boarded-up house where he had once lived was now completely damp and gradually falling into ruin?

"It's a good thing you trotted up," said Beancounter, rocking behind Aktan on the back of White Eye, "I reckon I would have drowned in this muck if I had had to walk home. Just look at it, there's no light and the darkness is as thick as pitch it is... Calls himself an engineer, the old git... With a salary of eighty roubles a month, and for what?!"

An engine grumbled into life somewhere off in the distance and bright light began to surge from the windows throughout the settlement, followed by jubilant cries across the village from children and adults alike. In the distance, off to one side, a single light winked as bright as the eye of a bent and crooked witch.

"You see that light?" Beancounter pointed to the distant glow. "That's the engineer's house, that is, the bastard. There's not a single street light working in the village and there he's gone and created paradise on earth for himself with that street light hanging right in the middle of his yard."

With unprecedented agility, White Eye suddenly lurched to one side and, before he knew it, Beancounter, engrossed in his idle gossip, had flown from the horse into the liquid mud. Aktan subdued the horse with a couple of angry blows and then, having calmed him, turned back. Beancounter was upbraiding someone loudly enough for the entire village to hear:

"You silly bugger, what the hell are you doing getting under the horse's feet like that?"

"Oh yeah, and who got under whose feet in the first place, eh? It was the rotten horse itself that got the jitters."

"What the hell are you doing out here in the middle of the night, you lazy so and so? May God strike me dumb if I'm lying but I bet you're off to the Widow's shop again, aren't you?!"

"Well, even if you're right, what are you going to do about it? Grab me by the trousers and stop me from going, is that your plan?"

"Have you no shame, man?!"

"So what! I'll just have a little vodka and grab a bit of something to warm myself with. What of it?"

"Have you no scruples in front of her children?"

"What's it to me, if their mother has no shame?"

The Man-Deer recognised the voice of Kan, the head of the social club. His first instinct was to grab the scumbag by the scruff of the neck, hold him fast to the side of his horse with his knee and give him what for but, catching the nauseous smell of alcohol coming off Kan's breath, he restrained himself and kept out of the conversation.

"Well, get lost then!" growled Beancounter, climbing back onto Aktan's horse. "I've been dragged through the dirt, good and

111

proper; that'll give the wife something to keep her busy. Now as for you, bugger off and good riddance! I won't take you to court for the damage you've caused me this time. After all, Kan, you're not from round these parts and what would I get out of you anyway?"

Aktan couldn't believe what he had heard. The wife of his dead friend and this stinking drunkard. Like everyone else in the village, the Man-Deer was well aware of the head of the social club's weakness for women. If he had counted the number he had wooed, the list would probably include half the female population of the village.

"Now, lad, I know what's going on in that head of yours," Beancounter muttered sullenly. "But you just forget it! If you start thinking about every dirty rumour you hear about, let alone let them get to you, you'll end up losing your wits. Our two-legged animal back there often traipses around there through the mud even in the cold light of day, when everyone can see him, and God knows what he gets up to in the middle of the night... But don't listen to anything that that Kan says: she's no fool, that widow of your friend DT, and there's no way she'd let that mangy dog get his paws on her. She's like a she-wolf that one... she's not going to let some mangy old mongrel get his paws on her, now is she? The bastard's probably sitting and drooling on her doorstep even now as we speak..."

All hell broke loose when the father of the house arrived at his door and a crowd of little children came running out to meet him. Some of the smaller ones, hanging from Beancounter's neck, didn't even have any trousers. They looked the guest up and down and, nudging one another, exchanged whispers, which soon turned to full-blooded yelps and exclamations: "It's the Deer! The Man-Deer! The Wild Beast has come!" Their father shooed them away. Beancounter's plain-looking, redhead wife, appeared with a barely audible greeting and then disappeared from sight again, picking off the clinging infants from her hem as she went.

Beancounter's home consisted of two rooms. An iron stove, stuffed full of firewood, roared in one room; its sides glowing red-hot and the tongues of hellfire forcing their way round the carelessly half-closed firebox door. A mound of dry wood shavings had been piled up right next to the ash-box and it was a small miracle the entire family hadn't gone up in flames. A small boy sat on a bench by the stove; he was a little older than his bare-bottomed brothers. His plump, round, apple-like cheeks wiggled as he chewed on a piece of hardened pine resin, repeatedly spitting with relish at the glowing side of the stove and listening with evident pleasure to the angry sizzling it emitted. Aktan hung back indecisively, not knowing what to do with himself. Beancounter went into the other room to change. The children dispersed to their various corners and returned to their previous

112

activities and no-one paid any further attention to the enormous Man-Deer.

"Hey, what are you standing there like a post for?" cried Beancounter, emerging from the far room. Take off your coat and hang it up there by the door. You'll have your fill of tea before you go. I'm afraid I can't offer you a place for the night, we haven't got the space..."

Beancounter's wife slowly readied the samovar. This squat woman with her red hair was renowned throughout the village as one for never being in a hurry and, even if the earth were to tear asunder beneath her feet, she wouldn't have hastened her step. She just waddled laboriously about the house like a duck, completing her chores without the slightest haste. Calmly, with the same, unhurried pace and without a superfluous word, she had conceived, carried and borne all these children, every last one of them a boy, raising them and attending to her husband's needs at the same time.

While this commendable woman was preparing the tea, Aktan and his host played a few rounds of draughts. Beancounter's ten sons flocked around them, attentively following the game and grabbing the pieces as they were removed from the board. At times, a furious melee would kick up over the captured pieces, fists flew but no-one broke them up and the parents didn't seem to notice a thing.

The door opened with a squeak and Aigul entered the house. She greeted Aktan with reserve as if he were a stranger. Beancounter's ten sons rushed to the girl:

"Auntie Aigul! Auntie Aigul! Did you get any sweets?"

The children swarmed around her bag like pups around a bowl, their fists flailing and slaps, shouts and cries ringing out but, as before, the adults made no attempt to reprimand the children. It was as if the boys were growing up like motherless lambs independent of a parent's watchful eye.

Aktan turned to look at the girl at the door as she removed her coat and he thought he could sense the fragrant warmth of her body on his face. This strange glow roused an excited yet groundless joy inside him and gave rise to dreamlike imaginings of unknown happiness. The Man-Deer froze, his entire body feeling weak, weightless and hot. As if realising the state the man was in, the girl instantly dropped her eyes and disappeared into the other room, keeping as great a distance between them as possible. The Man-Deer didn't dare suppose that the girl might be entertaining the same feelings of excitement for him as he, for her.

"Hey, are you going to move, or not?!"

Exclaimed Beancounter, rudely returning Aktan's attention back to the game and the Man-Deer's joy dissipated instantly and

113

irretrievably, after all, a timid soul has little command over an illusory moment of wonder.

"I concede. I give in," he replied.

"Well, that suits me just fine," said Beancounter with satisfaction. "That's another one for me to chalk up!"

Afterwards, they sat in silence around the samovar and the host's languid, red-headed wife, like some cult figure from the steppe, poured tea into the bowls. It was evidently the custom in this house to have to push your empty tea bowl right under the hostess's nose to persuade her to pour the tea as, otherwise, the half-slumbering wife would fail to notice that more was wanted. Aktan was unaware of this house rule and received nothing more after his first serving. He quietly left his bowl on the side of the table and there it sat, quite forgotten. It was awkward simply sitting there at the table and Aktan moved back, together with his chair. Aigul didn't emerge from the far room.

When Aktan began to get ready to leave, Beancounter got up from the table and, with a yawn, said:

"Oh, it must be pitch black outside now. Folk hero or no folk hero, you'd better spend the night here. We'll find you a spot, somehow."

"No, it's fine. I'll be going. I like riding at night," Aktan replied.

"Yes, I know that," said Beancounter. "We all know you're a funny lad... You're not afraid of the dark like any normal person. But just tell me one thing. Aren't you fed up with wandering about at night while everyone else is sleeping? Isn't it time you started thinking about starting a family? After all, thank God, you are a still a young man and a bright one at that and you could become the first among all the men here, you could, seriously! Why is everything in life turned on its head, eh? Why do the addle-brained sit where the smart ones should be, and vice versa? Why are you sitting all alone up there in Arshaly? You want to prick everyone's conscience, do you? You're wasting your time, lad. A fool's errand! You won't prick anyone's conscience around here. And you'll end up rotting away there in Arshaly for nothing. So you have to decide but before you do just ask yourself this: do people get better as they get older, or worse?"

"Alright, alright, I'll think about it."

"Well, that's that then! Only don't go thinking about it too long, eh? I don't care whether that great bonce of yours is full of great thoughts or completely empty, we are only on this earth for half a century or so and that's it. So don't you go giving me the runaround, like my Aigul, who does nothing but promise to think about things. You young'uns nowadays do nothing but think. And for heaven's sake, stop living like a lone wolf, give it up and put it behind you!" he concluded angrily.

Aktan smiled. Already stooping at the door, he looked round and noticed the attentive eyes of Aigul in the half-gloom of the neighbouring room, eyes that followed him anxiously.

It was as dark and gloomy outside, as the aftermath of a funeral; the distant lights barely penetrated through the thick, wet darkness. Aktan even had trouble finding White Eye, tethered to the fence. He mounted and was about to head for home when he suddenly remembered Kan, trudging his way along the muddy street. Had he really been heading to see the Widow? The thought gnawed away at him and, in an instant, he had forgotten about Aigul's sad face, shining out of the darkness and the hearty, rosy Widow and her free and easy manners dominated his thoughts. Could it really be that she had desecrated her husband's bed and let that rogue Kan in? Aktan turned his steed's head sharply in the darkness and galloped off along the long street, the dirt splashing and flying up from his horse's hooves as he went.

"Get out, you dog! Get out, I said!" Aktan heard the words as soon as he reached the door of the Widow's house.

He shuddered: the cry was so unexpected and so furious, that it seemed as if the woman had been screaming directly at him. Still not knowing what on earth was going on, he froze at the door. However, his perplexed dithering might have been mistaken for eavesdropping. The Man-Deer already wanted to be done with everything, turn and leave, when he was stopped in his tracks by the screeching cry of the man he so hated:

"You worthless bitch! What difference would it make to you if you were to say yes just the once, eh? With your reputation, it'd be no skin off your nose. So, stop playing hard to get. You're probably going out of your mind wanting it? Or are you waiting for that wild Man-Deer to come running? It's Aigul he needs, not you, you fool! He arrived here today and went straight to her place with her brother; old Beancounter was riding with him on the back of his horse."

Aktan pulled at the door so hard that the handle came clean off in his clenched fist. The Widow and Kan turned round and for a moment they froze in surprise and fear. The Man-Deer was a terrifying sight in his shaggy hat, completely soaked through and spattered with mud. He stood at the door, his head brushing the ceiling, staring silently with rage at Kan. Kan, recovering from his fright, raised his eyes which flashed with an impudent sparkle. The woman looked from one man to the other, not knowing what to think.

The head of the social club spoke first:

"Go on then, hit me! You're stronger; what's the point in me trying to stand up to you? You can get the better of me now, but time will tell who comes out on top. What are you standing there for? Hit me! Don't you want to? Well, that's not like you at all! No, I don't recognise you, Aktan the Beast-man. You were always as straight as a die, but now you've become all sly and underhand. Tell me, what were you nosing around here for? You think this house is a barn or a stable where you can just kick the door open and wander in? And this woman – do you think she's just some filly that anyone can ride when the fancy takes them? You need to ask your host's permission first before you drink his water. What are you doing here in the middle of the night, anyway? What have you come for?"

The Man-Deer didn't know how to respond to this high-pitched torrent of words. And for a moment he thought to himself: *why have I come here?* He knew he wouldn't be able to respond directly and honestly and that lacking his opponent's cunning, he would lose the argument. Averting his gaze and looking down at the floor, he muttered gloomily:

"I...I only came to ask what you were doing here."

"Interesting, and what right do you have to come around here asking questions like that? Maybe it's me who should be asking you the same thing! Let's ask the lady of the house, which of us is entitled to what here."

"I'll tell you this for starters," cried the Widow angrily. "Neither of you need to get ideas above your station. I'll get by just fine without you two! And if I do need a man then I'd be better off choosing someone who at least wants me than some young upstart who has no need for me and is about as much use to me as an impotent cockerel to the hens in my yard. So there you have it!"

Kan chuckled, wiping his hands. He jumped up from his place, went up to the Widow and gave her a loud slap on the back with his hand:

"Well, that's put us in our places, you clever minx!" he cried with a laugh. "You've tied and bound my enemy and thrown him at my feet! Thank you, my dear, I'm much obliged to you!"

The Widow giggled too, looking at the Man-Deer challengingly. The latter's eyes darkened with rage, hatred and shame. Forgetting himself, he threw the metal door handle at the two of them, who were so openly ridiculing him. They barely managed to dodge the missile. Then he took a swift step forward, grabbed Kan with one hand and hit him over the head with the other. He turned him over on the floor and tied his hands together with the belt he had pulled from Kan's own trousers. Opening the door, he grasped the trussed-up Kan and dragged him out onto the street. The Widow could hear Kan's muffled cries and, shaking with fear, she timidly said to herself:

"Oh, what a brute! What did this poor man do to him? He'll end up killing him..."

The Man-Deer returned.

116

He had flecks of white foam on his lips and he fixed the Widow with a heavy, frowning gaze.

"Now, take your clothes off!" he screamed. "Don't make me force you... After all, for a yard hen like you, it's all the same to you who sows you their seed! You defiled your DT's memory long ago but it's better that I do the dirty deed than that stinking degenerate."

Losing her nerve, the Widow went numb. Her arms hung limply by her side like a pair of riding whips. Then the enormous, furious and broken-hearted man strode towards her and turned out the light.

The day was overcast just as the day before it had been. A huge, black rock stood between Arshaly and Oreli. A cemetery spread out at its foot, the resting place of the dearly departed from the two villages. A grown man in clay-caked boots and soaking, filthy clothes lay on one of the fenced graves. The man embraced the mound of earth in his arms and wept bitterly and inconsolably, his broad shoulders shaking. A saddled horse stood next to the fence, its head hanging dejectedly close to the ground.

The man, who had at times been capable of contemplating life's most complex mysteries and who considered his greatest gift to be his knowledge of and reverence for nature, had utterly fallen from grace. His knowledge alone had not been enough to prevent him from committing a grave sin against nature. Life, it turned out, was wholly indifferent to whether a man's nature was light or dark, whether he was good or bad, pure of soul or sullied with imperfections. Aktan realised that nature's greatest creation was neither entirely base nor entirely noble, neither an outright murderer nor a complete saint. Sometimes it is as easy for a man to commit the most appalling atrocity as it is for a butterfly to flutter into a blazing fire.

"My dearest friend, poor DT!" wailed the Man-Deer, weeping bitterly. "Can you find it in yourself to forgive me? I am nothing but a fool, a wild and lowly Beast; I have sullied your bed when all I wanted to do was to protect your honour from these scum. I know... I know, you won't return to this place where people steal from one another in order to improve their lives, where everyone puts on a mask to deceive others, where... Oh! I am so ashamed, DT! Oh, my dear friend! If you were to return to this place now, you would have wanted to live your short life so differently. Oh, DT! You would never have wed that woman... No, no, perhaps you might have wed her, to ensure you had offspring. In this respect, you have been more fortunate than me. But, if you were to return back here, you would have tried to find out who was really responsible for your death. So who... who is responsible? Why did you need the money you worked so hard for? Why, it was to cover your wife's squandering in the shop. So, at night, after work, you

117

would transport hay to people or travel all the way to Arshaly on your tractor with no brakes to bring firewood. And that was why you fell from your tractor into the Akbulak! You wicked river, why couldn't you at least have given up his body to me? I searched for a whole month but all in vain. It was others who found him. And I... What is there to say? It is all like a dream. Just a dream. I didn't want to repeat what you have done, DT, but I ended up in your nest all the same and took the place that is rightly yours. Why, oh why, do I have to follow in your footsteps? Why is it that even the tiniest modicum of happiness always comes at the price of someone else's pain? And what is human happiness, after all? It is nothing but the fruit of another person's grief. Things are good for me but they're bad for another. Why is that? Do you remember how we used to gather dock and sorrel when we were children? Looking at the tall, stone tower of Tanirkoimas, you said: 'When I grow up, I will be a pilot. I will fly a plane beyond Akshoky, all the way to America!' And, in my envy, I replied: 'And I will become a great marksman and shoot you down.' But, ever the diplomat you answered: 'Then let us always be friends! And when we become fine *dzhigits*[5], we will take one girl to be our wife! And we will all live together!' At the time, I didn't know what to say to this; I found the idea rather awkward and lowered my head. What is the meaning of this? Could it be that even back then I had a premonition that I would sully the purity of our friendship? Forgive me, my friend!"

Aktan got up from the grave and wiped his wet face with his sleeve. The wind hurled itself at him and White Eye's long mane and tail fluttered in the grey air. The sky darkened over as if preparing itself for a downpour. The cemetery crows cawed, circling high overhead, it looked like it was going to snow. The earth had become callused and crusted over with frost in the cold. The last of the autumn mud had started to turn to stone, preparing a hard bed for the long, winter snow.

The Man-Deer turned to face the village he had left. From this high vantage point, the log cabins, nestled together against the river bank, were like two rows of beads in a necklace. He shook his fist at them. How innocent these little nests appeared to be. But he could well imagine the wicked rumours that were now circulating there. And Aigul would hear them. And the Widow, too. On their parting, she had said to him: "Aktan, you have to answer for what you have done. If you want to save me from disgrace, you must move in and live with me. But if you never come back to me again, then a curse be upon you and I will not shed a tear for you. If nothing else, at least think of the good name of your friend."

---

[5] A word of Turkic origin which is used in the Caucasus and Central Asia to describe a skillful and brave equestrian, or simply a brave person. In certain other contexts it is used to describe menfolk in general.

The Man-Deer stood there a long time, facing the strong wind that was blowing in from the valley. It seemed that he could sense the sour breath of the human dwellings and the smell of smoke... What is a man? Why is his face such a closed book? Who are you, Beancounter, you long-nosed, stump of a man? And who are you, Aktan, the man they call the *Deer*? Kan had said, "You may have got the better of me for now, but time will tell who comes out on top". Come out on top? What was he hinting at? "If you never come back to me again, a curse be upon you and I will not shed a tear for you," the Widow had said. And Aigul? Who is Aigul? Why were her eyes that followed him so sad?

The snow fell and a storm picked up.

He thought that he would soon go mad. The deathly silence of solitude seemed to play games with his mind. This was the silence of grief, filling every dark corner of the shack and it concealed a host of Azraels, angels of death that were in close proximity but as yet unseen. A dull light from the grey sky streamed through the little window. The sighs of his mute mother and the black cat with its brown scorch marks reached him from the stove. If he had got up and looked out of the window, he would have seen a white, silent, estranged world out there. He recalled Aigul: she always entered his mind when he saw anything pure, radiant and beautiful. Now, though, he only felt pain, realising that all this magical whiteness and radiance meant nothing when confronted with the futility and deception of a beauty that only dazzles the feelings. It would be for the best if he were to wish for nothing and just stretch out on his bed and stare up at the smoke-blackened ceiling.

Suddenly, he imagined he saw something flash by his window. The shadow shot past and melted away. Then the light spot of the window began to darken over and he could see the ashen, dead face of DT, pressed against the glass from the outside, peering into the house.

"My friend, what is that around you?"

"White fields, nothing more."

"Just white fields... And nothing more... My poor man, are you not cold?"

"I don't know."

"You married early, old friend. Too early."

"I probably knew I would die early..."

Aktan's mother approached him silently and placed her light, cool hand on his forehead. He grasped her dry hand and pressed it to his lips. Then he sat up and, burying his face in his mother's breast wept, sobbing and shaking like a small child.

"Oh, mother, what can I do?" he said through his tears. "I am utterly confused and I don't know where to go..."

His mother responded with bitter silence.

It was another day and the sky was bright and blue. The mountains, cliffs, rocks and forest undergrowth were cloaked in white snow. The blue vault of the sky was so close, you could have touched it with your hand. The radiance of the snow and the bright glitter of the heavens caused the eyes to ache. The virgin snow on the fields was marked with the patterned tracks of small wild animals. The air in the taiga was imbued with the scent of pine resin. A squirrel scuttled over the branches, disturbing the evergreen boughs and knocking off loose clumps of snow and star-shaped splashes formed on the tender, white, downy bed under the trees. Breathing in the delicious, resinous air, the Man-Deer thought that life was still wonderful and that he had been reborn in order to understand this. The sheer pagan joy of this day was perhaps even a source of regret for it meant that his feelings and thoughts were precisely at one with everything in nature and therefore just as susceptible to change as the fickle weather.

He was wearing skis covered with doeskin and a double-barrelled gun hung over his shoulder. He needed to hunt the wild animals but was quite incapable of bringing himself to violate the majestic peace of the winter forest with a sacrilegious and thunderous shot. The frost stung his cheeks and the snow lay deep all around; so deep, in fact, that a horse might have disappeared up to its withers in the drifts. The tops of the young firs stuck up out of the snow; these were saplings that Aktan himself had planted. He had once planted 350 of them in the old clearing. Back then, when he was still finding his feet at the logging farm, he had asked the manager to give him work that didn't involve felling the forest... His friend DT, however, had chopped trees as if there was no tomorrow. The more superstitious among the village folk believed that it was this offence against the wild forest spirits that had caused his untimely death. On that fateful, last trip into the taiga, he had felled ten young larches and, coming down the mountain at night, he and his tractor and trailer had slipped off the forest track and disappeared into the river... In just one year, an entire, one hundred-year-old forest had been felled on the slopes of Mount Belukha. This is how mighty trees and fine young men meet their end.

Standing on his skis at the edge of the glade with his fur hat in his hands, the Man-Deer's dark curls seemed to have been dusted with a layer of white hoar frost. But it wasn't hoar frost! Aktan's head was now covered in a thick, new growth of grey hair.

* * *

Not long later, Kan came to see him. He was also on skis, with a gun slung over his shoulder and carrying two bottles of vodka. Still

120

standing in the doorway, he grabbed one from his pocket and held it up high by the neck, like a trophy.

"I've come to make peace with you!" he said, breaking into a broad smile. "Come on, up you get and welcome your guest. No need to look at me like that! Who else is going to come over and see you? No-one, that's who! So we quarrelled over some rotten woman. Well, to hell with her! Let's have a drink and let bygones be bygones, eh?"

Perplexed, Aktan didn't know what to say and he slowly turned his broad and bulky body to his mother, looking at her questioningly. The mute woman responded with a resigned nod of agreement and then, grunting and groaning, she climbed down from her bed and set about laying the table. She had no tumblers or shot glasses, so she placed two tea bowls on the table.

"Well, that's just fine," said the guest approvingly. "This is much better than eking it out, drop by drop." And he proceeded greedily to gulp down the vodka that he had filled to the very brim of the bowls. He screwed up his face, grabbed a chunk of toasted bread, ripped off a piece and crunched it between his teeth with a satisfied look on his face.

The Man-Deer gazed into this broad, puffy, utterly vacant, masticating face and thought to himself: *Oh, yes. People like you live many a year.* Suddenly the guest's jaws stopped their chomping, his narrow eyes opened in amazement and he asked,

"Hey! What's happened to your hair? You haven't dyed it, have you?"

"It's turning grey..."

"Well, knock me over with a feather - so is mine! Half of my hair is grey already. Well, these days you get five-year-olds going grey, so what can you expect for the likes of you and me, eh, Beast?! I'd like to raise a toast to women, to hell with the lot of them, the bitches! How could a fine pair of men like us have possibly come to blows over them... I have forgiven you for everything; all is forgotten. And you must do the same! That's why I've come all this way. To make peace, that's why. Well, to be honest, that's not the only reason. Ha-ha-ha! I thought I might ask you for a little fix of that dried deer horn, they say you've got."

I ought, to beat you like a dog and turf you out of my house! the Man-Deer's dark scowl seemed to reply. However, it would have been awkward getting into a fight in front of his mother.

"Alright, alright, calm down, forget about the dried deer horn. Can you just give me a little piece of *mumiyo*; I've got this terrible stomach ache," Kan whined. "Are you really going to begrudge a sick man a bit of medicine?"

Aktan got up, went over to a chest, upholstered in strips of tin plate, opened the heavy lid and took out a small leather bag. Breaking

121

off a little *mumiyo* from a large piece, the hunter silently handed it over to his unwelcome guest, making it quite clear from his expression that all he wanted was for this man to get out of his house as soon as possible... However, Kan, folding the medicine in a piece of paper and hiding it in his pocket, was entertaining no thoughts of leaving; he made himself more comfortable than ever at the table and began to strike up a long conversation.

"Good for you. You live like a real man and I really respect you for that. It's a shame we don't see eye to eye. So I decided to come and see you myself and let you know that there are no hard feelings. Neither of us are fools, so why bang our heads together like two stubborn billy goats on a narrow bridge? Of course, in life, everyone wants to prove that they are right; every man is convinced that his mountain is the tallest. But I'm not that sort of a fool; I am prepared to yield to you because I respect you and if I ever have another son the only name I would ever consider giving him is Aktan..."

"Where do you plan to get him from?" asked The Man-Deer curtly. "The last time I checked, you didn't even have a wife. Are you going to give birth to your own children?" he concluded with a sneer.

Kan fell silent for a moment and cast a long, meaningful look at the man sitting opposite. But he mastered himself and calmly continued:

"So, you're a bit of a joker, it would appear... I had to leave my wife and two children in Alma-Ata. To be honest, I'm not sure they're mine, but I still have to pay maintenance for them."

This time it was Aktan who looked at his guest for a long minute. The Man-Deer realised that the man sat in front of him was completely unscrupulous and unrepentant. Kan's eyes narrowed and sparkled.

"So, you have nothing but contempt for me, I see. Well, the feeling is mutual," Kan continued with a sneer. "And, what is the good in that? And what's the point? After all, people dislike you and me in equal measure. They don't like us, old son! But you and I, we couldn't give a damn. I've read a heap of books and I've learned all sorts of things; there is no-one around here who has seen as much of the world as me. And you know what? I couldn't give a damn about any of it. I've learned many a truth and yet I have nothing but scorn for the lot of it. Why do you think that is? Are you judging me? Well, what about you? Why have you shut yourself away from everyone? Tell me! And don't be in such a rush to judge a man before you've learned a little bit more about what is stored up in his soul." Having said his piece, Kan shifted a bit closer to Aktan and slapped him on the back. "You know what, Beast-Man, it's people like you who are all the rage in the big cities now, not smart alecs like me."

"You must be joking," replied Aktan. "There's not even a place for me in the village."

"You're lying! You could easily forge a place for yourself in the village or anywhere else, for that matter. But you're clearly unwilling to give up your freedom and your easy life. I'm much the same, I like to be my own boss too."

Kan's words suddenly dried up and he seemed to visibly deflate. He now sat at the table downcast, no longer the wicked, barefaced rogue that the Man-Deer thought he was, but rather a weary, half-grey, weather-beaten old man.

The iron stove had gone out and quickly gone cold, and the room was growing cooler and cooler. Aktan rose and, taking an old fur coat from the wall, covered his mother who was bent double, tucking her in on both sides with the edges of the coat. Walking to the window, the Man-Deer looked out. The snow was falling quietly. All was calm and quiet, nature was preparing obediently for the long, lifeless winter. Looking round, Aktan saw Kan, sitting motionless, almost asleep.

Aktan set about getting a bed ready.

They lay down silently in the dark. At times, Kan snored and coughed heavily, tossing about and sighing. Suddenly, turning sharply to face Aktan, he said in a confidential tone: "You may be a strong man, but always remember this: never believe a word anyone tells you and always be the one to strike first." Then, with a snigger, he added, "Otherwise you'll end up dying an unnatural death."

And, saying this, Aktan's guest turned toward the wall and ceased disrupting the cool, viscous silence that settled over the house like the cream on the top of the milk.

In the morning, Aktan shot up from his bed as if he had been jabbed with a needle. Light peered in through the window but the darkness remained thick in the corners of the hut. Red clouds, like bloody sea spume, hung in the distant sky, clearly visible through the glass of the window. A deafening silence reigned in the house, but something unfamiliar and uneasy worried the Man-Deer. He was surprised to see that the bed where his unwanted guest had been was now lying empty.

Sliding his bare feet into his cold, heavy boots, Aktan went out of the house. There was no-one in the yard, just the glistening, pure, blinding snow. The door to the shed stood ajar. Aktan went in and saw White Eye lying dead and frozen on the floor. His head lay in a puddle of blood that had leaked from his mouth. A blood-smeared axe lay on the ground nearby. Squatting next to the dead horse's fallen head, Aktan lifted the black forelock that was matted with blood and saw where the cruel blow had hit home.

123

He went back to the hut to wake his old mother and noticed something else that he had failed to see in the dark earlier: the lid of the chest was open and items from within it lay strewn across the floor. The leather bag with the *mumiyo* had gone. Everything became clear to Aktan.

Before leaving, Kan had broken both of Aktan's fur-covered skis in half.

"No! I can't stand it! I can't live like this any longer!" the Man-Deer cried in anguish. "Tell me, mother, why do I run from all that is good because I want nothing to do with evil, and yet evil still finds me, no matter where I flee. Well, if that is the case, I will stop stepping aside from now on. From now on I will advance to meet this evil head on! I will go and I will catch this dog! Gather your things, mother. We are moving to the village."

This was the first time the old woman had seen her son in such a rage. He looked uncannily like his father who had once, many years ago, become so enraged by other people that he could find no way of living in their midst and had spent his whole life acting in defiance of them. She knew that he had left the village, leaving her and her son behind purely because of this disposition and this hatred which she was totally incapable of comprehending. But this one, on the contrary, wanted to go to the village.

"I'll decide who gets the better of who!" he bristled in his fury. "We will pit our strength against each other there in a straight fight and not by threatening one another from afar. I will live among them and let them all know who I am and what I am capable of. And my enemies will learn the meaning of grief! Why did that dog kill my horse? Why did he break my skis? He probably thought that I would be afraid of the snow and never chase after him. Oh, what a fool he is if he thought I would remain in these snowy hills until death itself comes to claim me. Mother, get your things together this instant! And don't go taking too much; without skis, we won't be able to make it very far in any case."

In silence, the old woman took her son by the hand and pulled him after her. She led him to the entrance of the tumble-down cellar that had been dug out beneath the house. Taking a lit candle, she descended down below, groaning as she went. Aktan followed her. In the stuffy, damp gloom, caked in cobwebs, the old woman tinkered about, then straightened up and handed her son something, wrapped in a skin and tied with string. They were the old skis his father had left behind – the man who perhaps now lay at the bottom of the Tanirkoimas ravine.

Aktan, known by adults and children alike as the Man-Deer, resolved to leave Arshaly for good. He fitted his father's skis, covered with the hide of a colt, to his feet, took his double-barrelled gun and

124

went up to his mother, who was standing by the gate with a bundle in her hands.

"Well, sit up on my back, mother," said Aktan, looking impatiently out into the distance. "Go on, don't worry. You carried me for five years when I was small, and now it is my turn to carry you."

He sat his wizened, stooping mother on his back and then raced away on his skis like the wind, his teeth clenched in fury. Before him stretched the two-line track of his enemy, who had fled into the valley, while behind him there now lay two tracks, running side by side. It was as if all the opposites that lay at the heart of this endless, borderless world of light and shadow, good and evil, cold and warmth, death and life were now stretched out in the tracks of the two enemies, into the distance, into an unknown, mysterious tomorrow. And it remained a mystery who would get the better of the other, who would come out on top and who would fall to the ground first. Everything was concealed behind the foggy expanses of the quiet, blue valleys. And only the eternal tracks of the enemies ran and twisted alongside and crossing each other, running ever onwards. They were leaving Arshaly forever, traversing the white snow and leaving behind the old village that everyone else had deserted, where the last tale of the secrets of the Tanirkoimas cave had been told.

For now, we have no idea if a single hearth will ever be lit in that deserted village ever again.

Perhaps, the Man-Deer will not be able to rub along with the folk down there in the lower village and perhaps his soul will yearn for his wild freedom; perhaps his blood will rebel and he will rush back to Arshaly, as if to a trusty, old shelter. Perhaps he will want to unravel the mystery of his father's disappearance and venture into that icy ravine, into which no one has ever entered and no one returned. Who knows? For now, though, he was hurtling down towards the valley like a man possessed. Suddenly, a vision appeared before his wide eyes of a DT tractor falling from a high bank and into the mountain river below... A splash, rushing waves and then silence.

The old woman, silent for more than a quarter of a century and long since known as mute, sighed bitterly and, with barely a whisper, she uttered:

"My little foal... Do you think we'll catch that rapscallion?"

Arshaly was left far behind. Ahead lay a long, long journey. Be strong of soul and remain vigilant, Man-Deer.

THE SCREAM

Billions of people trample the face of the earth and the world groans from their screaming. A huge, bellowing world. It is now hard to hear an echo, let alone hear oneself and then realise that our thoughts, our aims and even our actions are just an echo of the thoughts, aims and actions of others. They include those who are no longer among us and who sleep under the ground.

If they could come back from that place where there is no "time", no "possibility" and no "forgivness", perhaps they might be able to teach the living not to direct cruel words at each other, not to torment one another but just to live on this wide earth, as the birds and the beasts live in the open pastures, where there is room for everyone, with the sun shining above us at day and the Pleiades radiant at night, the stardust glimmering and the herdsman's star, Sirius, smiling down from above.

But the world just screeches and, in this bawling and bellowing, it is impossible to make out the lone scream of a single person. When this person stands all alone in the midst of this enormous, silent world, nothing but an echo replies to their scream.

I remember how, in my adolescence, I would go on twilight walks on my own. My path would leave the village for the forest like a bright line of stitching. I walked this path with my heart aflutter because, at times, as soon as the sun hid in its nest of gold, a strange echo would fill the dark valley. An echo bereft of any scream. Then it would occur to me that this was the voice of an unseen messenger and this messenger was concealed somewhere out there, in the thick, blue heights, proclaiming the end of the brief interlude between day and night. And that the darkness was coming and people needed to prepare for it. But then I thought to myself: Only a person tied to the land forever would be able to do this because he has been born of this place. At other times, though, I would imagine that it was the cry of our world's boundless and wonderful sovereign ruler bidding his earthly dominion good night and farewell before the dark mantle covers the tall mountains, the cool valleys and the silvery lakes flashing like the scales of a fish. But, now I know that this reverberating echo was the resonance of a cry that was dearest and clearest to me. The cry of a Kazakh who is keeping watch over his herd of horses.

With this cry, the herdsman informs the world and the inaccessible sky that he is alive, that he is not lost, that he is not rotting to death up in the mountains, has not lost his way in the valleys, and that the rushing river and the narrow ravine have not swallowed him up.

And then, after the evening echo has dissipated, a wonderful

127

moment would ensue, like a herald or a premonition of some pending day of judgement. A flickering flame would burn on the elevated peaks of the Altai, and the western horizon would become like an enormous, blood-red eye, the eye of Mother Earth, weeping for her poor children; the red-brown mountains would quiver as if trembling in some passionate embrace. This would all last but a moment but it was strange that in those distant times I often sensed this moment, standing still on that path, and it remained with me forever. Later, I lost the ability to conjure up this vision in my mind, but I do remember it. I remember how the path, shining white in the twilight, split into two as it ran up against the forest, like a snake's forked tongue, as if the snake was tasting the dark obstacle in its way. One of the forks disappeared into the dark undergrowth, while the other stopped at a strange gathering of hillocks that looked like overturned feeding troughs.

The village of the dead. A mysterious force had led me there. I recall the anxious beating of my heart; it seemed to me that thousands of irrepressible young horses were tearing about within my chest and my knees shook like a new-born camel, and yet I pressed on because I could hear the whispering of a multitude of voices. This whispering melded into the roar of a mountain waterfall and I desperately wanted to make out just one voice, or understand just one word.

I was convinced that the souls of the deceased would soar like a bird all day long over the heads of the living and at twilight, would return here, to report back to others what they had seen and heard.

Perhaps, if I had been able to make out and discern that dull muttering, I would not have made all the mistakes I have made, I would not have uttered empty words and I would have better understood the meaning of the words and actions of others.

However, with a quivering heart and faltering steps like a child who has only just learned to walk, I made my way to the far end of the cemetery, to the hill, dominated by a herdsman's long birch *kuruk* stave with a lasso on the end of it, the only monument in this distant heathen, holy place, in this remote corner of the world.

The hill was not fenced round; it belonged to all the earth and was accessible to all who walk it.

I would often encounter a man near this place. If I hadn't known who he was, I might probably have lost my mind, because frozen to the spot, he looked as if he was half buried in a grave, his face turned towards the setting sun, and he was muttering something akin to a funeral prayer.

"My soul, my rod and staff in all that I do..." I could barely make out. "Where is your trail that distinguishes me from the wild beast; what does it mean?"

He protruded from the ground like a stone idol and did not notice the lad standing stock still nearby.

128

This man's name was Aspan. He was a herdsman and he had become the most revered man in these parts.

He did not shudder as the echo rang out; he did not interrupt his muttering, paying the echo no heed. This was the most mysterious thing and it was this that tempted and drew me here in the evenings, leading me away from the warmth of my family home.

* * *

At the start of each day, a person cannot know in what way and how it will end. They awake in anguish or in joy, considering in their mind's eye all that awaits them; they look out of the window, reach for a cigarette (if they are inveterate smokers) and then address the customary morning chores that do not distract them from their thoughts. Perhaps there are only a few mornings that stand out for each of us from the monotony of the everyday and the unremarkable.

And all the same, when a person begins their day, they don't know...

That particular winter crept up gently and deceptively, but the snowstorms arrived in February. The worst of them, which lasted for four whole days, flattened every living thing and nothing was able to raise its head. The people and the land, drowning in this endless, viscous snow, choked in the embrace of its great silence. Everything and everyone was overcome by torpor.

No-one wanted to eat, get out of bed or leave the house. The village in the mountain ravine took on a vague and pitiful appearance, as if it wasn't so much the snowstorm but some wicked force that had caught it unawares, covering it in a dense blanket of snow and, all that could be seen from under it, which not long before had had meaning and importance, now appeared to be nothing more than the flotsam and jetsam of life.

Timid plumes of smoke now rose from the roofs of the houses like vast wads of cotton wool, indicating that there was still life here, albeit entombed in the snow, and this smoke seemed to dissipate into millions of snowflakes.

The chairman of the collective farm, Aman Tengrinov stood in the midst of this whiteness and told himself that he would have to leave the house straight after breakfast. He would have to do this in a matter-of-fact manner as if there were no blizzard out there, as if he were simply setting out on a sultry summer's day to inspect the pastures. He also wondered who he would take with him. There was not a soul about and, surrounded by the seething white snow and unable to distinguish east from west, he felt like a military commander who had been deserted by his troops in the middle of the battlefield. He could have gone from house to house, rousing the men who were slumbering and warming themselves by the hearth, but he ended up deciding that he would go with the first person to arrive at the office. This was a day of destiny and he had decided to trust in destiny from the off. It was not that Aman was specifically thinking that today would be a day of destiny, but he just felt and knew it and appointed it as such himself. Today would be the day.

"As long as it doesn't all end in a blizzard," Aman muttered, blowing the snow from his lashes and snorting like a horse and he went back into the house.

His father stuck out of his bed like a nail in a block of wood. Usually, he would rise later and Aman was planning on leaving before he had woken up.

Out of a sense of discomfort, as if he had been caught doing something he shouldn't have, he was unusually irritable with his sleepy wife:

"What's the matter with you, has an evil spirit got you pinned to your bed or something?! Get up this instant!" His father frowned and called out to him with authority:

"Hey, Aman, come over here!"

This powerful, pockmarked giant, the father of five children and a fully-grown man, stood in submission at the threshold, fixing his gaze obediently on his father.

"Sit down," said Old Man Aspan, pointing to a spot on the bed.

They called him *Old Man*, though, only out of habit. An enormous man with a copper-coloured face and moustaches without a single strand of grey, to all appearances he was ageless; the personification of male strength and might.

He silently and inquisitively looked at his son with large eyes, pupils as black as coal and incredibly clear whites that shimmered blue like sour milk.

"What's got into you, grilling your wife first thing like an ear of corn? What's with all this bellowing before you've even eaten your morning bread?"

Aman remained silent.

"Go and heat the stove!"

His son got up with an unexpected willingness and, ducking beneath the lintel, shot into the kitchen.

Aspan smiled. He liked the fact that, with a single word, he could order this mountain of a man about, this chairman, a giant and the breadwinner for five children, just as his own father had ordered him about when he was a small child, with just a twig. This, his only, beloved son, his future support in whom he placed his hope for his later, bitter years.

Aspan rummaged under his pillow and found his smokes. He

130

pulled out a cigarette from a half-empty pack of *Prima* that had been folded into two and inserted it into his chewed holder. He looked for his matches and, finding none, flew into a rage.

It was the same every day. The family would take the box and then forget to return it. They would lose their matches, come to him for some and so it would go on. He had now started hiding a box under his mattress but this, too, had proved fruitless. Could they not understand, damn it, that this was yet another source of petty annoyance for him? One of millions. What did they think: that he would get used to it and didn't care?

He understood that there was another reason for his anger and this was Aman's silence, in the readiness with which he rushed to fulfil his order, not wishing to remain alone with his father. He had tested his son all his life and knew him as well as he knew himself. He also knew that today his son had set himself his most difficult challenge yet. But this was not something they could speak about. His son would reply that it was his duty to visit the remote wintering grounds and this would be the truth. However, he would withhold the real truth and Aspan would not insist on hearing it; there are certain things the finest young men simply will not speak about. After all, he had always tested his son in all things and it seemed he had taught him to endure trials such as these, unknown to and unnoticed by all but the two of them.

His rage needed an outlet.

"Hey, Aman, where are you?" he cried out in a thunderous voice.

"I'm in here!" his son replied from the kitchen.

"Well if you pass this way, could you give me my matches?" said Aspan, stressing the *my*, so that no-one would dare touch them again.

Aman appeared slowly and handed over the box.

"The kids took them again..."

Mentioning the grandchildren was a request for leniency but his son avoided looking into his eyes.

"Even if they were to go and burn the house down, I'd still insist on them buying me a new box at the shop. And fast! Now bring me some water, I'm going to wash my face."

Again his son appeared slowly, bringing a jug, a bowl and a towel around his neck, submitting to each and every command. *I won't get a word out of him, even if I hit him over the head with my crutch,* thought Aspan. *Such an obstinate, headstrong colt.*

Although Aman was Old Man Aspan's only son, he was not his only child. After Aspan the Herdsman had lost his legs, his wife had given him two daughters. One of these daughters worked as a librarian, the second was just finishing school.

Like all Kazakhs, he had a soft spot for children and he had spoiled his girls and now his grandchildren, sitting them on his shoulders and, if he could, he would have even protected them from the birds flying over their heads.

He had also raised this big fellow without insult or offence, although without the spoiling: that had not been a time for over-indulgence.

And here stood this giant bear of a man, silently handing him a jug and a towel. The usual morning routine only, suddenly, for no apparent reason, his son was trying to do up the buttons on his shirt.

"What are you doing?!" Aspan exclaimed, pushing Aman away with his hand. "What on earth has got into you? Go and help your foals; it's too early for you to be tending to me!"

Ever since Aman had become the chairman of the Yenbek collective farm and had chosen the finest steed for himself, his father had given him no peace, picking up on his every move. Aman understood this unexpected and dramatic change: his father feared that this paltry office of authority might go to Aman's head, that he might start to walk with a swagger and develop an inflated opinion of himself. If this big-headed he-goose were not regularly reminded of his place and not kept in submission in the home, he would quickly begin to talk condescendingly, belch while eating, cultivate a fat belly and, most dangerous of all, start wielding a stick over the heads of his fellow men.

Old Man Aspan lit up a new cigarette while waiting for his breakfast and, smoking out the small room, which, over the last thirty years had become a refuge that he seldom left, he looked out of the window with an almost dog-like yearning. That night he had had a nightmare. He had taken a considerable while to get to sleep, tossing and turning as if someone had placed brambles in his bed and he only nodded off near morning. It was then that he had had the nightmare.

He was carrying firewood on a sledge when suddenly someone called out to him; he turned and saw two legs in high boots, running after him. His own legs. He was frightened and began whipping his horse, only the legs drew closer, crying out: *Don't be afraid, we want to be with you!* They ran in broad strides as he had once done, the snow crunching beneath them. Aspan's soul left him like a fly and, overcome with terror, he mercilessly thrashed at his chestnut mare.

I am done for! cried Aspan and fell onto the broad, low sledge.

Hey, Aspan! came the cry from behind him. *We can see that you are all high and mighty and are living a happy life. Your children have all grown, so now it's time to remember us; have pity and take us with you!*

The firewood tumbled off the sledge and clattered to the

ground as the mare galloped away at full pelt.

Aspan woke up. It was his son who had thrown down an armful of firewood next to the stove with a clatter. The old man realised that today he would be going to the Alatai wintering ground; today he would cross the Devil's Bridge...

Aspan was both terrified and enraged. The lousy so-and-so had prevented him reaching the end of his dream. He had really needed to see how it would end. He must have had to come to a stop, waited for his legs and taken them with him. That would have been a good omen. Now, though, nothing was clear...

He looked through the frost-covered window and pondered about what he seldom allowed himself to think. About his own life.

After he had lost his legs, he had come to understood many things in this transient world. Before, he had lived like any other round-headed creature, preoccupied with his day-to-day concerns, with a fear of death forever smouldering under the surface. He had lived through this and, now a cripple, a sore thumb sticking out for all to see, he had come to realise that he had been deluding himself throughout his previous life.

Oh, lord, when his arms and legs had been as strong as sledgehammers what good deeds had he ever done for anyone? Whose life had he improved? Everything had been just for himself. It seemed that, by becoming a cripple, he had gained the perfect right to live for himself alone, but this had proved unnecessary, as he realised that he had become a cautionary figure of fear. Secretly pointing at him, the other old men would tell their grandchildren: *See what being headstrong does to a man. Live a modest life and don't go standing up to anyone, or you'll become like Aspan.*

Could it be that he had returned to life and avoided death, just to become a figure of fear for others? He remembered well how proudly he had come to the office on his prosthetic legs. Mumbling through a toothless mouth, the old elder had said:

"You've got better. Just look how well you handle those wooden stumps!"

His peers had gathered around him, touching the artificial limbs, clicking their tongues in approval and slapping him on the back. And yet what he had seen in their eyes was joy: joy that they had escaped such a fate; *glory to Allah that this has not happened to me.* Aspan had returned home, removed his prosthetic legs and he had never put them back on again. He hadn't liked it when others slapped him on the back; he hadn't wanted to become a successful cripple, a cautionary object of fear. He had learned how to ride on horseback, squeezing the haunches with his stumps; he had fathered two daughters, cut the hay, worked around the house and sheared the sheep. The villagers had secretly observed his battle with life. Strange people, devoid of pity. But Aspan was just the same; he knew no pity and nor did he want it. He had no wish to prove anything to anyone. Except the Herdsman that he had once been and who had now departed for the heavens. He had wanted to prove something to him. If he could voice some vague judgement, it would sound like this: while a person lives, they cannot disappear entirely. They simply become a different person. The Herdsman had disappeared and only Aspan knew this. What remained was Aspan, a stump of a man. But time had gone by and now no-one noticed his disabilities. People had argued with him and feuded with him; people were friends with him, sought his advice and cursed him to blazes. But they never shouted or screamed at him. No-one was allowed to scream at Aspan. And everyone knew this.

The frost outside had intensified. Aspan could see this from the pattern on the window, which had become more distinct. He placed his hand on the glass and the frost melted away. The snowstorm died down, but Aspan knew this would not be for long.

"Let's go have some tea, old timer," said Aman behind him.

"Oh, god, you again! You've been hovering around me since first thing; you'd have been better off sending one of the children."

"The snowstorm is having a bad effect on you."

"Not for the first time." Unable to help himself, he continued needlessly: "It's just that I have a heavy heart. I had a nightmare."

"You shouldn't believe your dreams."

"So what should I believe?"

The son bent his head; he had always been a slow thinker.

"What should you believe?" he asked again with greater emphasis.

"You said that I shouldn't believe my dreams and I asked, what should I believe? What's got into you? You are acting rather strangely. Is something bothering you?"

"My work is what's bothering me."

"So what do you plan to do today?"

His son was silent.

"You'll have your work cut out to stir those drowsy youngsters from their homes."

"Yes, you're probably right," Aman concurred absent-mindedly.

"So, what is it you plan to do today? There'll most likely be a blizzard."

"I have to check on the remote wintering grounds. Find out if they need any help."

Aspan's heart jumped and then fell. *Why ask the question when it would be better not to know*, the faint-hearted thought flashed through his head.

"Well, it needs to be done. It needs to be done," he repeated.

"Father..."

But Aman was cut short by a joyous cry: "Grandpa!" and Aspan's favourite and most mischievous grandson ran into the room, leaping up and wrapping his little arms around the old man's stone neck.

"My little foal!" Aspan squeezed the boy to his chest and sniffed his forelock. My frolicsome little Yelik![6]

"Tell me about Yelik," started the boy. "Tell me, you promised."

"A long time ago," said Aspan, "a long, long time ago, one delightful summer's day, I had driven a herd of the farm's horses to the foothills of the Altai and had gone to pick berries..."

"Grandpa hasn't drunk his tea yet," Aman said to his son. "Let him be."

"I don't want any. Drink without me... So, anyway, I had gone to pick berries. They grow at the foot of the mountains, where there are a large number of *caragana* bushes. The grass is so tall there that it reaches right up to a horse's belly. I had this marvellous, jet black stallion. Smart and brave, he was. Suddenly he became startled and almost threw me from the saddle..."

"Nothing could throw you from the saddle," said the boy.

"Not now but back then it was possible. Listen. I thought my horse had been frightened by some bear droppings; they're absolutely terrified of them. I began urging him on but the horse stayed where he was. I looked into the undergrowth and there I saw Yelik the little goat kid. He was curled up, sleeping. I got off my horse and spent a long time looking curiously at this carefree little goat. He was so fresh and young, so pure, like a babe in the crib. When you were still suckling, when you were full of your mother's milk, you would sleep in just the same way, in a deep, honey-sweet sleep. I couldn't help myself and took him up in my arms like I took you in my arms as a baby. The goat suddenly woke up and struggled to break free. But he couldn't wriggle out of my strong hands and eventually calmed down. I put him inside my coat and brought him to the yurt at the pasture. From then on he lived with us. I made a little house for him and fed him well. He became accustomed to drinking milk from a bottle and eating from our hands. He became attached to us herdsmen and never went far from the yurt. With the November cold, we moved to the Alatai wintering ground."

"Will we go there?" asked the boy.

"We certainly will."

"And will we cross the Devil's Bridge?"

---

[6] *Yelik* is a mountain goat but it is used here as a proper noun

135

"How do you know about that?"

"All the boys talk about it. They want to cross it too."

"But why?"

"To become a true *dzhigit*. A man only becomes a true *dzhigit*, if he has crossed the Devil's Bridge, like you. Well, go on."

Aspan was silent.

"Carry on telling me about Yelik."

"Yes, yes, about Yelik... He lived in the shed, like a pet, completely tame. The dogs at the wintering ground became so accustomed to him that they even used to chase each other around, but never caused him any harm. And my heart glowed as I watched their frolicking. That was Yelik for you."

"And then?"

"What do you mean, then?"

"What happened to him? Did he run away?"

"No."

"Was he savaged by a bear?"

"No."

"So what happened to him?"

"I accidentally killed him."

"Killed him? But why?"

"I told you, it was an accident. I didn't want it to happen. I didn't sleep three nights afterwards. And I understood that it was inevitable that this would happen."

"But why?"

"Because I had taken away his freedom. A child of the wild mountains should not live as a house pet. There would have come a time when he would have run away himself because Yelik was not a dog, accustomed to being tossed a bone or fed on slops. But we don't understand this. We live according to rules and so we want wild animals to live according to rules, too, without freedom. Wild animals, however, are better than some people. They have horns that stick out and serve as protection. Some people have horns that are concealed within. Yes, that's right: they have unseen, sharp horns and ruthless hooves and they use them to attack others."

"And who are these bad people? What are their names?"

"They are called THEM."

...On one of the last days of November, ONE OF THEM had arrived at the wintering ground with his dog. It had become an annual custom for the chairman, to go out for the last time to check on all the livestock before the first snowfall at Alatai, then, over the course of the six months of severe winter, he wouldn't show his face again. But it was during the winter that he was needed most of all or, to be more precise, it was help that was needed. Help with medication, with feed and simply with information regarding the health of our nearest and dearest and with news from the village and the wider world. Yet only the hunters would wander on rare occasions out into the inaccessible depths of the Alatai.

He would turn up as unexpectedly as the snow that falls on a person's head, to ensure the inspection was a surprise. Aspan the Herdsman had heard an unusual noise and had darted out of the shed to see the chairman's dog snapping at Yelik, while the big boss egged him on with whistles and whoops. Yelik was crying out in heart-wrenching screams and the dogs at the wintering ground, sensing blood, had jumped one another to settle old scores.

Maddened by Yelik's cries and the deafening howls and squeals of the dogs, Aspan had grabbed a stick to chase off the mad canine intruder. However, in all the turmoil, his stick missed its mark and struck Yelik, who fell, lifeless.

Aspan immediately ran into the camp, grabbed his rifle and took a shot from the porch at the dog, who was tearing the helpless body of the little goat to pieces. He discharged his sixteen-calibre gun into the hound, even though the chairman had grabbed his arm, shouting something at him. He had pushed him away. The chairman was in a furious rage.

"You have shot my dog over some useless, wild animal, he was my support in my lonely and dangerous travels!" he had cried, his eyes as cold as alpine ice. "You have lit the flames of enmity between us and you have lost your end-of-year bonus. What will I say to my twin brother; the dog belonged to him, after all, and it was me who failed to take care of him? From now on you shall no longer be the senior herdsman. Now bury our hound as is fitting."

"I will bury him," Aspan the Herdsman had said. "He is innocent. It was you who was egging him on. But first I will bury Yelik, whom I was caring for like a child."

"No, first bury my elder twin brother's dog. He was a wolf among dogs, while your Yelik is nothing but a stupid, wild animal."

Aspan had picked up a shovel.

"First I will bury Yelik," he had said, looking straight into the icy eyes.

"Well, I never! Not only have you caused me harm, but now you are showing mindless obstinacy. You'd better watch your back!"

"Try as you might, you can't belittle a simple herdsman any further than you have already," Aspan had said.

The chairman had departed without tasting the *beshbarmak*, without looking over the farm and not once looking in the direction of Aspan the simple herdsman.

"Could your aim really have been so wayward?" asked the boy.

137

"That was what happened."

"I don't believe it, grandfather. You can easily hit a cross with a knife from ten paces."

"I can now but I had to train long and hard. I sat throwing, practising for hours on end. And my arms are much stronger now than they used to be."

"But why did that man egg on his dog? Why did he make you angry with his shouting? No-one is allowed to shout at you."

"Well, not now they aren't but back then they used to shout at all of us."

"Papa never shouts, but he is a chairman, too. I think he was upset that you didn't drink tea with him. He's gone without saying goodbye."

...Aman had been sitting alone in the office for what must have been over an hour. No-one had been in a hurry to get their assignments, although Aman was sure that many had seen him heading for the office from their windows. Because of the harsh, Altai winters, the windows in the houses are tiny but, when they have to, the villagers can see everything from these tiny portals.

Aman could feel himself being overcome by drowsiness. Thousands, millions of snowflake butterflies fluttered beyond his window; everything out there was as white as could be but, in here, it was warm and dusky. The village, always as noisy as a travelling fair, with cows lowing, dogs barking and countless children squealing, was now silent, as if it had been swallowed up by the earth.

Aman thought that this deathly silence might drive a man out of his mind; it engendered a bleak sense of unease that suppressed the beating heart.

But perhaps this unease was down to something else? he asked himself. *Perhaps it was the way my father looked at me this morning, me leaving without saying goodbye and the foreboding of the long, hard road ahead that has deprived me of my usual calm and strength?*

Aman looked at the clock. It would soon be nine.

If no-one comes, I will not go from house to house, he decided. *I'll go alone. What the devil is going on?! Either you cannot kick them out of the office with their loafing around, smoking and laughing for hours on end, or they refuse to show their faces as if they have fallen through the snow. They know what's afoot - a journey to Alatai. Yet they prefer not to know about this, even though they understand how important it is to make it through to the wintering grounds. A strange people, these Kazakhs, so unthinking and yet so self-reliant. But when all's said and done you're not so different yourself...*

A silhouette of a man flitted past the window and in came Erkin the stock breeder. He was perhaps the last resident of the village who Aman would have chosen to accompany him. An outsider, who had come here from Moyynkum two years previously, he was not much of a companion. Moreover, there had been another thing, a slightly awkward matter that had arisen between them. But today was a day of destiny and, what is more, travelling to the wintering grounds was Erkin's duty.

Erkin lingered on the threshold, shaking off the snow that had coloured him white, and he looked in with his face screwed up. After the white of the street, he found it hard to get accustomed to the gloomy room.

"Are you well, Erkin?" Aman welcomed him and Erkin smiled back happily and a little embarrassed.

"So you're here, boss! Are you well? Why are you here on your own?"

"Everyone probably got themselves stuck in the deep snow. There's no-one about. I am glad that at least you have made it in one piece, thank God."

"Do you have a spare smoke?" asked the stock breeder, shaking a box of matches.

"Oh, Erkin! Always the same... Your greeting is always accompanied by a request for a smoke. Here, I'll give you ten roubles and you can go and buy yourself a sackful of cigarettes. How much longer do you plan to wander around here with your hand outstretched, shaking a box of matches, eh? You're not married, you have no-one to hide your money from, so what's the problem?"

Aman immediately regretted remarking that the stock breeder was still a bachelor; a joke like that could lead to trouble. After all, it had been Aman who had refused this outsider his sister's hand in marriage.

Erkin, though, did not pick up on it and laughed good-naturedly.

"Oh, I am so forgetful with my tobacco! And you are forgetful when it comes to matches. You never have any around either."

He took a cigarette from the pack that Aman had offered him and lit up with a flourish.

The mention of matches sent a shiver down his spine. He recalled how his father had been angry that morning; he recalled his truncated body, protruding from the bed. *Bismillah! Bismillah!*[7]

Erkin struck another match and extended it to the manager.

"One man is in need of something, another provides it. I think this is the best way to live."

Aman didn't reply.

---

[7] Meaning "God willing" in this context

They both sat in silence, drawing on their cigarettes. Even the smoke was invisible in the gloomy room; it disappeared as if passing through the walls.

"Only on my way here, I saw the old man; your old man," said Erkin, coughing. "He was tying down his trapper hat dead tight and sitting firmly in the saddle. He called me over and sent me for a bottle of red. I asked him what he wanted it for and he replied, 'What's it to you? Do you want to report me to the police? You can tell you're not from around here. Don't you know what they do with wine? They drink it, mister. And rather than ask me idle questions, you'd best be going to Alatai, or you'll end up saddling up a *kuruk* and not your horse.' And he was right."

"And where was he heading?" asked Aman.

"In the direction of Mota."

"I see," said Aman. "He was in a bad mood this morning. He had a nightmare. He's probably gone to say a prayer at the grave where he buried..." Aman hesitated, looking for the right words. "...what was once his."

"Oh my! I heard that Old Man Aspan has been going there nigh on thirty years now, drinks a bottle alone and then comes back. An interesting prayer. Sorry, *aga*, perhaps you don't like talking about this but the story about Old Man Aspan's strange custom was one of the first things I heard when I arrived in these parts."

"Every village has its stories," said Aman coldly. "In our village, they're largely about my father's odd habits."

"You understood me wrong. I wanted to say that after the burial of *what was once his*, he did something that amazed the people and everyone has great respect for him for that."

"They respect him for his courage in saving a large herd of horses."

"Yes, yes, of course! But I think the village needs this grave and needs a person who pays it homage. Respect for the dead always evokes respect among the people."

"Yes, he is a man who has much that is worthy of respect," Aman muttered, looking out of the window. His face was grey. "This morning he said that he hadn't seen a snowstorm like this in the last thirty years. It's falling so heavy that you can barely lift your head above it. I say that not to be funny, but because I'm afraid that the yearlings and foals at Alatai might give up the ghost, every last one of them. How many head are out there?"

"About two hundred..."

"And there is no feed for them nearby and where are we going to find the strength to cut a path through snow that is as thick as a man is tall, to bring them hay from the ricks? Natural calamities always catch us unawares. I had hoped until today that the herdsmen would be

140

able to make it through to us, but even the horsemen from the nearest camp at Tarbagatai have not made tracks for three days now. It looks like they are also prisoners of the snow out there. What are we to do, Erkin?" He stubbed the butt of his cigarette into the ashtray and looked at him expectantly.

"We need to think."

"No matter how much we think, there is only one way to make contact with them: someone has to get on a horse and ride out there."

"And who is that someone going to be?"

"You and I, for example."

"You can't just leave the central office to the will of Allah."

"Meaning you're not going? Well, you have that right."

"I am not talking about rights but about duties. We have our duties, as set out in the regulations."

"And on the basis of which regulations do I have the right to send other people out on a dangerous journey in this frost? We'd have to cross the Devil's Bridge."

"Why that way? There's the concrete bridge."

"That would take us a day longer, it's a large detour. And if we are being serious, we can't delay for a single hour. We'd need to take medication and, most important, we'd need to get there, so they don't think we've just left them for the wolves. We'd need to go as far as Tarbagatai, get a team of *dzhigits* together and, flattening a path through the snow along the way, we'll reach the Alatai camp. That's the immediate goal; circumstances will dictate what's to be done after that. You decide. Look," he said, tapping on the window pane, "there'll be a blizzard soon and that means there'll be all sorts of trouble, the sort of trouble that can end up with a man losing his mind. This is what my father senses. Thirty years ago, when he was swallowed up by an avalanche, the very same sort of impassable snow was falling and it ended with a terrible blizzard that lasted many days."

"Are you trying to scare me, *aga*?" asked Erkin.

Aman got up, put on his trapper hat and quickly did up his buttons on his half-length, black fur coat.

"Shall we take some skis with us?" Erkin reached for his fur coat.

"We'll pick some up from the herdsmen at Tarbagatai."

"Are you going to head back home to say goodbye?"

"It's not as if we are heading to a certain death, to warrant such a solemn send-off, now are we? The less fuss about our departure, the less heartache they'll suffer."

"What's it to me? I'm not married. No-one here will suffer heartache on my account."

The thought flashed through Aman's mind: *Why am I taking someone who is not a friend? After all, he is hinting that he is single because of me...*

But again: *Today is a day of destiny; my father also rode out with a man he could not call a friend. We'll see if anything has changed in this world.*

The snow was now falling differently, striking them sideways in the face. The drift on the crust of the snow was like the roof of a cow's mouth and the huge mountain, always looming immediately overhead, was concealed in the hazy whiteness. Yenbek was snuggled up so close to this mountain that, from December to March, the sun would cross on the other side of the peak and its rays never reached the village. During these months the people enviously eyed the villages on the opposite bank of the Bukhtarma, where the sun shone brightly and the spring always came earlier. However, during the sultry days of July, when those on the opposite side were languishing in the heat, the livestock and people sweltering under the incessant blaze of the sun, the people of Yenbek, enjoying the soft coolness of the ravine, were invigorated and at ease thanks to the light breeze and the absence of the pestilent green flies that always accompany a herd when it is hot.

They would say: *What can you do? The bounty of nature is preordained and those who have spoiled themselves with overindulgence when the winter was bountiful are now suffering the consequences.*

The infernal snow, the like of which had not been seen for over thirty years, made itself felt all the more, descending like an innumerable host. Having started out as a light snowfall, it had been falling incessantly and obstinately for three days, engulfing every living thing and only later was it followed by the wind, carrying millions of hard grains. It either moaned like an inconsolable widow or howled like a hungry wolf. This evil force, goaded by some unseen foe from the south-west, had taken hold of the world, sweeping over the mountain hollows and gorges, in its search for prey.

It had seemed as if every hungry wolf in the Alatai was standing with its mouth gaping, ready to leap.

A blizzard is a rare event in the mountain gorges but if one comes, it really makes itself felt. It builds up and starts hammering away at such a rate that you cast your mind back to the past as you prepare to meet your maker. It is at its most terrifying when all the snow-packed gorges, peaks and crags begin keening and howling at random. The Great Noise commences and it feels as if the shards of the sky are falling to earth with a roar.

Old Man Aspan had been caught in the blizzard the moment he reached Mota. He had been prepared for it when he mounted his horse and so felt no fear. He folded the bottom of his half-length fur coat under his knees, sat side-saddle and set off, his head tensed up to face the wind. The chestnut mare was contemplating turning back but

142

the old man struck her a couple of times with his twelve-tail crop and, with a sharp tug on the reins, he cried:

"Don't you go getting all cute on me, big belly!"

Trudging through the blizzard, he stubbornly forged his way ahead. The cold mocked and tormented him, penetrating his fur coat and burning his chest and back.

Well, it's a challenge just like any other, only my stumps are giving me grief something rotten, like huge, aching teeth.

He could barely see his hand in front of his face, he did not know east from west and he was like a swimmer, floundering in a viscous, roaring, seething, white ocean. A tiny figure lost in an abyss. And, as if mad with rage that it had failed to crush and finish off this obstinate creature, the storm, wailing and roaring like a dragon, crashed down, again and again, trying to rip the man's clothes from his back. But all in vain. The man, huddled like a clenched fist, would neither buckle nor bury his face in his horse's mane. Only the horse, unable to withstand the wind that beat directly at its muzzle, advanced sideways.

"Oh, Allah, save me from fresh hardship," he muttered to himself. He was but a stump of a man, so what more terrifying ordeals were there that could possibly frighten him? And what grief was there that had forced him from his home? He could have stayed in bed, enjoying the peace and quiet, the babbling of his grandchildren and the warmth of the stove.

Perhaps he had a death wish; perhaps he was just tired of life with all its trials and tribulations. If so, then why was he fighting so fiercely against this death-wielding force?

The blizzard, which had been yelping like a she-dog as it began its violent onslaught, was now baying threateningly like a wolfhound. And this baying contained an audible threat and a furious desire to force the man to spit blood.

It was as if the blizzard was destroying and swallowing everything in its path without even bothering to chew it first. It had created its own screaming world, over which it ruled supreme, playing with millions of burning whips, lashing anyone who might happen to come into range. However, Old Man Aspan, having set out to pay his respects to that *which was most dear to him*, which had once been taken away by a blizzard much like this one, was not the slightest bit afraid of dying in nature's embrace and threw his gauntlet down at nature's feet, returning its challenge.

Neither side would yield. The blizzard was relentless, like a colossal, white fire, but the man doggedly continued on his way.

The chestnut mare was an intelligent and experienced creature. Unable to find the strength to withstand the blizzard's onslaught, but feeling the iron force of the man's stumps against her sides, she ploughed forward, her hooves biting into the snow.

143

Reaching Mota and turning her nose to the grave, discernible only by the barely visible *kuruk* sticking out of the snow, she stood stock still, riveted to the spot. Her master did not immediately realise he had reached his objective. He was in a dream-like state, rambling under the weight of his joyless thoughts. Then he came to and muttered: "Well, well, my dear, what's got into you?" The mare refused to budge. Then he opened his eyes and saw the end of the *kuruk*. He patted the mare: "You clever thing, I was wrong to rebuke you," and he dismounted in a single leap.

The snow, as thick as cream on milk, softly swallowed up the stump of his body, leaving just the man's head above the surface. Pushing off with his hands in fur mittens, Old Man Aspan slowly began to advance towards the *kuruk*, leaving a deep furrow behind him. His advance consisted of several, sequential actions: first, he cleared the snow in front of him, then he reached down to the dark-brown earth and, taking a firm hold of this solid firmament, he shot his body forward.

The legs of his quilted trousers were sewn up, reliably secured with heavy stitching and the damp had yet to penetrate the thick layer of padding. But how slow his progress was! In summer he could move as fast as an able-bodied man but now he was crawling with such difficulty that the wind was able to drift the snow over his path. Behind him, the snow lay smooth. This was truly a creature that left no tracks!

He barely made it to the *kuruk*, quite out of breath, with his lungs burning hot. Reaching his goal, he collapsed face down, unable to catch his breath. Sweat poured from his brow, his body was covered in perspiration. Steam billowed from him and all this was despite the fact that the distance from his horse to the head of the grave was no greater than the *kuruk* that was embedded in it.

And even this short path had already been covered by the storm.

Old Man Aspan looked back. The last section of the furrow he had created was filling with snow and then it disappeared altogether. What would a person say, seeing his graven image, protruding from this untouched whiteness? Would they think he was a werewolf, fallen from the skies? A stone idol in human clothing? A madman, who had wandered here from who knows where? And where were his tracks? A normal man leaves tracks, but this one didn't... Perhaps, he was not a person after all, but some ghostly apparition.

But he was a man and he had brought a man into this world. It was his son who was now travelling through the snow, accompanied by another man who was not his friend, breathing down his neck. His son was struggling to reach Alatai and his way lay across the Devil's Bridge. He knew his son and he knew that without a shadow of a doubt he would be crossing the Devil's Bridge. And he also knew that they

144

were halfway and would, perhaps, encounter the *one who had screamed.*

It was because of him that Old Man Aspan was now a man who leaves no human trail. Yes... At first, after leaving the hospital, he had hot-headedly put on his artificial limbs. He had even deigned to show off in them, the fool. But he could never get used to those poor stumps of wood. They had had a life of their own – a life dictated by the wood they had been fashioned out of; they did not understand how to flop down onto the green grass, how to remove boots, dry footcloths and wiggle their toes in the fresh air.

If that was to be the case, then to hell with them! Aspan had decided, seated with his backside on the blessed earth. *I couldn't care less for all that meaningless hopping and skipping! A man needs no props for anything. And if my soul has no use for them, why should my body have any need for them? I can still ride a horse without them, cut the hay and do the chores around the house; what more could you ask of an old man from a village in the middle of nowhere?*

As if curious to learn what the man would do, now he had crawled his way to the grave, the blizzard began to quieten down. Everything around, shrouded in a blanket of white, awoke and the mighty mountain peaks came into view. The chestnut mare breathed heavily, drew in its belly and paced from foot to foot.

"It will snow again soon," said Old Man Aspan loudly and pulled out the bottle of vermouth from inside his coat. His horse, frightened by his voice, pricked up its ears and looked cautiously at its master. Old Man Aspan tore off the yellow foil cap with his teeth and released the cork by slapping the bottom of the bottle with his hand. Then he stroked the *kuruk,* giving it a shake it to check that it was firmly in place. He was pleased: this *kuruk* bore witness to his youth, his mighty strength and his woes. Many years before, Aspan the Herdsman had stripped the bark from the trunk of a young birch and the staff had shone like a young moon; it was with this staff that he had first ventured out to take the horses to pasture. Back then he could not have known that his staff would prove stronger than him, that it would remain in one piece and when he had realised this, he had pushed it into the grave in memory of Aspan the Herdsman who was gone forever.

The storm now transformed itself into a light, sparkling snow shower, falling gently from the heavens. Nature, once deceived, was now happy to be relieved of its howling misery; the River Bukhtarma gave voice and the sun broke into a forced smile through the grey shroud of the sky. Overladen with a mass of dark firs, the Altai seemed to straighten its shoulders with a weary sigh.

Old Man Aspan took a small swig from the bottle and, screwing up his eyes to view this familiar but ever-changing picture of the places he knew so well, thought that everything around him—the forests, the riverside woodland, the streams, the wildlife and mountains—were now engaged in a barely perceptible and joyous celebration that they were still alive and had been spared by this great onslaught. Everything was united in its joy, just as every element had been created for the other. The sky had been created for the land, the land for the water, the water for the animals, insects and even the riverside woodland, and they, in turn, had been created for the barely noticeable, thumb-sized sparrow. What need had they for human beings? What need had they for Aspan the Herdsman, for example? He had died but had the stars in the sky been changed? Had even a single fir tree stirred? He had caused nature no harm but nature had caused his demise with an avalanche. So nature has no need for humans; perhaps nature is actually forever seeking an excuse to be rid of them for good. Aspan the Herdsman, you have become unneeded, you have joined the countless ranks of people who have departed, while the mountains that destroyed you remain standing; the snow that froze you still covers these mountains; and as for the one who had screamed...

Wait. Say that again. As for the one who had screamed... So, it was not the snow or the mountains that destroyed him; a human did... And what end awaits me, Old Man Aspan? When will they bury me in that same grave? And will there be many mourners? And, most importantly, what purpose do I serve, crawling about on my belly like a lizard without a tail in order to frighten the living with my appearance?

Oh, how he tormented himself, seeking answers to these questions! What was the purpose of returning to this place when there were disputes, suffering, injustice and lies aplenty without him? Would it not have been better to have departed in the tracks of the Herdsman? Would it not have been better to let them cover him in earth and place a heavy rock on his chest, pressing down good and proper to make sure he would never rise again, never interfere in any dispute over happiness and fortune and, most importantly, never reveal the crime that had been committed or spit in the face of *the one who had screamed.*

Aspan the Herdsman had decided to take his leave and now he was lying in this grave, and the man who remained had no desire to stoke the feud or continue the endless settling of scores or the search for guilty parties. Is it really possible to stand up against time? And was it not because of this, lying under the winter sky, glimmering with stars, cold and remote, that he had traced the movement of this time and, when it had played out, he had emerged from nothingness to bear witness to the need for his life and his modest purpose.

When Old Man Aspan reached the middle of the bottle, the day had become quite clear and the frost had slowly begun to take hold. For now, only his cheeks stung a little. The chestnut mare had perked up and was seeking out the grass, clearing the snow with her hooves. The sparrows, which had hidden away somewhere for the course of the

146

blizzard, had now settled on the tops of the trees. However, the snow clouds, like lumps of curdled milk, floating in a sky of pale blue whey, were moving slowly towards the mountains. They gathered on the shoulders of Tarbagatai and hung close together on the tips of the pines as if they had become lodged on them.

Old Man Aspan looked back to see if any of the shepherds had emerged. Using the lull in the storm, the shepherds might have made a move for the village now. This would have been most inopportune, for he would have had to share his wine with them and, hunkered down like a marmot, he had no desire for company. What was more, they might have plagued him with questions: what had possessed him to leave the house in such a blizzard and why had he dragged himself to this grave? Or, worse still, they might have said nothing and, moving on, tapped their fingers against their temples and laughed.

Could he really explain to anyone that he had come to sit on this frozen hillock so that Aspan the Herdsman would not feel so alone during this *dzhut,* this terrible snow-bound famine?

And there was another secret: guessing that his son would be heading for Alatai, he understood that, despite the snowstorm and the danger of getting lost and disappearing for good, he had simply had to come here. With scant regard for his own pitiful, limbless life, he craved indulgence for the fate of his son.

His son had set out on a difficult journey. His journey.

...Thirty years ago, he had also headed out to Alatai. Back then the same, heavy snow had fallen; the precursor to famine.

Grief is like a contagious disease and like a contagion, grief can take a hold and be transmitted from one individual to another. Aspan took fright at his thoughts and whispered to himself: *Oh, Lord, turn this onslaught away from us! Turn it away! Perhaps the man in his grave has taken the thread of his misfortune with him... Yes, misfortune has a habit of clinging to a family. The village is filled with unfortunate souls like these...*

A man named Durzhin had been shot dead at the mountain pass in 1930, his son disappeared seventeen years later, his grandson was sent to prison and his daughter died during the war. It is God's will that some people make it through life unscathed, behaving like a bull in a china shop, their forelock waving in the wind, while others who wouldn't harm a fly see misfortune cling to them like lice to a beggar.

Turn aside! Old Man Aspan shook the bottle, churning the wine, and took a large swig. *Oh, if only he might return in one piece and feel no fear while crossing the Devil's Bridge.* He uttered these words loudly, like an incantation.

He knew his son was heading for the Devil's Bridge. He would take the short route; it was not for nothing that he hadn't wanted to wait out the storm. How Old Man Aspan now regretted the words he

147

had once uttered in a moment of weakness. *Don't follow my fate,* he had said.

Who knows, perhaps it had been because of these words that his son had now chosen to take the route over the Devil's Bridge and, perhaps, because of them, he had copied his father in everything he did. Was it really possible to discern who had been supporting who all these years: the father had raised his son and the son had helped his father survive...

The chestnut mare suddenly let out a loud and plaintive neigh.

"Graze away, my dear," said Old Man Aspan. "What is left for you and me to do if we do not eat and sleep?" He scraped the snow away from the head of the grave and whispered quietly: "You must intercede for Aman's life and his safe return. If people wished one another well, there would be no need for the likes of me. If this had always been the case, I would not be sitting here, grasping my stumps... But in these times, life has not treated our kind well, leaving us without strength or time to think of others. And never mind others – we have forgotten about ourselves. Crossing the Devil's Bridge, I had failed to utter *Bismillah* and was left there under an avalanche. And there I remained for many days and there were few who rushed out to search for me and fewer to even say a prayer for me. But it's time I got up instead of prattling on with this nonsense..."

He leaned forward sharply and, recalling he was as helpless as a small child, he cursed himself roundly.

"Damn your head, you crazy Old Man, which devil tricked you into forgetting that you are just a rotten old stump..."

He scolded himself mercilessly and thought that it was indeed a good omen to have forgotten about his lameness while his son was making his way towards hell.

The horizon approached once again, while the sky descended, looking as bad-tempered as a herdsman who has lost his horses.

It was barely afternoon, yet twilight had set in and everything all around was silent, laying low in anticipation of an impending woe.

The playful Bukhtarma, the great beauty of the Altai, began to moan in a muffled fashion, like a newlywed bride who has been scolded in her husband's home. And now she wept uncontrollably and the sound echoed like a mournful howl throughout the woodland.

Nature will witness much weeping. Old Man Aspan gulped down the last of the wine and pushed the bottle into the snow; he would come back to collect it in the spring. How many of them would have accumulated here in thirty years! Enough to erect a beautiful monument to the Herdsman. A pyramid of bottles. Bound in cement. They would glitter in the sun in summer and play a humming requiem in the echo of the Altai wind in winter.

Old Man Aspan regretted that this wonderful idea had come to

148

him so late. It was hardly likely that he would now accumulate enough empty bottles before his life came to an end to construct a large enough pyramid. He secured his hat under his chin, fastened his coat and pulled on his fur mittens. He called to the mare and she obediently trotted over. It seemed that even she dropped a little curtsey. Old Man Aspan, using the convenience of the grave mound, grabbed the saddle with his powerful hands and flew straight up onto his mount.

"Oh, Lord, protect and preserve my son!" He wiped his hand across his face and, urging the mare on, set off for the village.

The mound with the flattened snow and the birch *kuruk*, playing its endless, melancholy song in the wind, remained behind him. A song that reflected a persistent anguish, an unfamiliar dream and the secret of a man's soul. Aspan did not look back, just coaxed the chestnut mare into a trot, to get home all the sooner and see to the livestock; after all, his son was at Alatai and tomorrow would be the New Year. In any case, he had heard that *kuruk's* song many a time before and already knew it by heart.

* * *

By noon, Aman Aspanov the chairman of the Yenbek collective farm had reached the foot of the Tarbagatai mountains and it was here that he encountered the storm. He couldn't even see the ears of his horse. He rode with care, listening attentively to the steps of his steed. He climbed to the summit along a path that wound like the print on a person's thumb. It had been built by prisoners-of-war back in the First War with Austria-Hungary.

This route was called *Irek* and it wound its way to the only pass to the other side of the Altai. It was the route that all shepherds and herdsmen took. They made their way across with prayers, asking God's indulgence and repenting for their sins.

Another path lay a little to the side but it was narrow and only a single horseman could pass along it and not just any horseman either, but a *dzhigit* above all *dzhigits*, with a bold, bristling heart and a steed above all steeds. In the cruel winter days, no living person could pass through here without risking their neck.

In the summer months, cars rush along this route while in winter it is only passable on horseback, in silence, and without haste.

Therefore, the people in these parts are able to converse in silence because a single shout or a loud cough would be enough to dislodge the thick snow that balances on the shaggy firs that overhang the edges of the crags and send it crashing down in one fell swoop to smother the road and sweep away everything in its path, living or dead.

A deluge of snow from the mountain can crush a horse and its rider, dragging them into the deep chasms that gape at the foot of the

149

mountain.

If you are spared this trial, however, a more difficult one lies in wait further on. A track called the Tar leads down from the pass to the Alatai wintering ground. Its very name, which means *narrow and cramped*, speaks for itself. It twists along the Kaba River, spanning it many times with numerous bridges and then wanders between the mountains before departing for the south. This narrow thread cuts through rocky crags that seem either ready to teeter over and fall at any moment or fly skyward like a spear. Its bridges are like strands of hair that repeatedly traverse from hell to heaven and back, many, many times over. You have no strength to catch your breath. In winter, the track is covered by two metres of snow and only experience can help you guess where it is. However, once you have overcome all of this, the untold beauty of Alatai is revealed to you like a great trophy. In winter, the expansive, white valley is framed by dark mountains, overgrown with mighty firs, while in summer it is an emerald set in a ring of mountain peaks.

Throughout the summer, the village of Yevbek in this pasture prepares hay for the livestock that will spend the winter at Alatai. The herdsmen drag the hay to the wintering grounds in the cold and are then cut off from the world for months on end to live quietly, like marmots in their burrows. They stock up on provisions when the land is still black. And so the process is repeated throughout the herdsmen's lives year after year. One day, the ice storms and the *dzhut* arrives and all help from anyone or anywhere is severed. Your only hope is to rely on yourself, and if you have not hauled enough hay for the animals, you will not be able to drag anymore from the distant stores and not even the *tebenyovka* grazing will be able to save you either. You will have no option but to sit and watch hundreds of guiltless creatures simply starve to death.

The two travellers in the blizzard knew this and were on their way to help. But would they reach the distant wintering grounds in one piece?

They had already made it over the Irek pass and had emerged at Tarbagatai. The blizzard, which had been howling persistently, was suddenly behind them as they crossed the pass and peaceful flakes of snow glistened in the air. The Sharyktybulak plain opened up before the travellers, like a sleeping girl with beautiful breasts. The wintering ground was hidden beneath the snow, somewhere in the middle of the plain. The shepherds of the neighbouring villages of Shyngystai and Pilorama lived here and it was a place to get warm, rest and have something to eat. The traveller out in front, however, directed his horse in the direction of Alatai.

When Aman and Erkin reached the wintering ground, at the very mouth of the Tar, it was already growing dark.

The riders dismounted from their horses, which were steaming with sweat, and headed for the wooden house in the camp. Aman lashed at the head of a wolfhound who was barking crazily, snapping at his coattails and opened the door. The herdsmen sat stock still, like sparrows at the sight of an approaching cat. Settled around the metal stove, they were playing cards, their legs spread apart and guffawing loudly. After a moment of consternation, they leapt from their seats and rushed to their guests with exaggerated attention.

Aman did not offer his hand and did not respond to their *assalamualaikum*. He threw down his fur coat, sat on his haunches before the stove and warmed his hands. After their moment of perplexed embarrassment, the herdsmen darted forward to shake the stock breeder's hand. He greeted them and also went over to warm himself at the stove.

The silence lingered and then the youngest of the herdsmen, a whiskerless young boy, said, almost apologetically:

"We should heat the *kumiss*. You must be frozen to the bone.

The young men, who did not know how to prove their mettle, rushed over to the *saba* horse-hide bowl. One stirred the *kumiss* while another readied a tin bowl. Taking care not to come too close or bother the chairman, the boy placed the bowl on the stove.

"Aman-*aga*, is all well in the village?" the herdsmen Alke broke the silence.

"You want to know how things are in the village but we want to know how things are in the Alatai wintering ground," Aman barked, contemplating his frozen hands.

"And we thought you'd tell us what is going on back there."

The man who uttered these words was the only person who had not made a fuss, remaining seated furthest away from the hearth. Poorly illuminated by the flickering of the fire it was impossible to make out his face. Aman guessed from his copper-red moustaches that he had known this herdsman from childhood. His presence always evoked a strange, wearisome feeling. A memory returned to him of a hot summer noon, a colt on weak, thin legs and two boys who were friends. The boys knew the custom that when twin colts are born, one must be slaughtered. Yet, the poor things had glistened so brightly in the sun and the mare had murmured over them so tenderly that they wanted to save them both. They knew that the copper-whiskered herdsman had himself been born a twin and so they had entrusted their secret to him in the hope that he would save it. However, by evening the colt was gone.

Copper Whiskers or his brother (you could never tell one from the other) had been the chairman of the collective farm in that terrible year when the avalanche had taken Aman's father and made him a cripple. Now one of them was a simple herdsman, the other – a simple

151

shepherd. Aman sensed the challenge in the words of the copper-whiskered man and everyone else sensed it too. All the herdsmen all fell silent. Erkin wanted to say something, but Aman stopped him with a motion of his hand.

"So, are you enjoying paradise early out here lads?" he asked calmly, although he had wanted to cry out. "Why are you sitting here idly like a groom with his bride, playing cards, chomping *kazy* sausage, belching and knocking back the *kumiss*." Grabbing the bowl from the stove, he began drinking it in large gulps.

"Comrade chairman, leave me some, will you?" said Erkin with a simple joke, trying to dissipate the tension in the hut that now crackled with a malevolent charge.

"Strike me dead, but can you tell us what you are so angry about?!" the boy implored.

"Can't you guess?"

"I honestly don't know, sir."

"Perhaps some of you older ones can guess?" Aman asked two of the others.

"We know our business," muttered the copper-whiskered man in the gloom.

"Then I will explain," said Aman, threateningly. "Answer my questions simply and honestly. How many days has it been snowing?"

"Today is the third day!" Alke the herdsman piped up happily, a quiet man who had suffered a long, protracted illness. He had been particularly bothered by the sudden tension that had overtaken their merry and peaceful company at the wintering ground.

"How much heavier is the snow compared with previous years?"

"There's about two metres more of it."

"Have you ever seen such a protracted snow storm in all your brief years?"

"No, sir. But my father told me that when I was an infant, there was a terrible blizzard"

"Did he not tell you what real *dzhigits* do at times like these? Why are you sitting here as if it's the height of summer outside? Why has no-one gone down to find out if the livestock has enough feed? Why has no-one thought to find out how things are going with the men holed up higher up the mountains, where things are even harder?"

"That's what management is for, it's their job to think about others and it's ours to worry about ourselves," said the copper-whiskered man.

Aman's silent rage washed over the hut like an invisible wave but the same blind enmity rose to meet it from the dark corner, and everyone present could sense it.

Erkin grew tense. He sensed that there was some secret reason

152

why Aman had been so angry. A clash of an enmity this great could generate a storm more terrible than that which raged outside and Erkin said in a calm voice:

"Which is why we are here because we are thinking about everyone. What interests me, though, is how things are with the feed..."

"Our hay is running out..." said Alke quietly.

"Then you will go and make a path to the ricks. And when we return from Alatai, there will be hay waiting for us."

"But how can we make a path?!" asked Alke pitifully. "You can't even stick your nose outside."

"You will do it, even if this weather blows in drifts of blood instead of snow. Now get us some horses; it is time we were heading off."

"But chairman," said Erkin with a shake of the head, "where are we going to end up, stumbling around in the middle of the night and what difference will it make if we set out at dawn?"

"If you're afraid, you shouldn't have come with me. You knew this was going to be no joy ride."

"The stockman's right," said the red-whiskered man. "Even if things aren't looking good for our four-legged friends at Alatai, at least those on two will be able to survive. Thank God, there are enough provisions. And you might end up finding yourselves stuck between the camps and get lost on the way, and then you might die only to be carried away by the River Kaba. You don't even know where an avalanche might be waiting for you. I think that would be beyond the call of duty."

Why is he baiting him like that? Why is he trying to push him over the edge? thought Erkin, trying to make out the copper-whiskered man's face in the dark.

And here I am his ally. Oh, how things have turned sour.

"Spend the night here, chairman. We'll see in the New Year together," said the boy in his open-hearted, childish way.

"Listen, boy, you have yet to experience misfortune," Aman said slowly, "which is why you aren't thinking about the fine men who are stuck up there in Alatai. Can you imagine what a desperate and exhausting New Year they must be enjoying? Are your hearts really not troubled by the terrible plight of those two hundred head of foals up there? After all, if your feed is used up, there's probably not a strand of hay to be had up at Alatai. What kind of New Year will it be for them if we just loaf around here? I don't care if a new year is approaching, we must still be on our way."

"Well, each to their own; feel free to do as you like," snorted the copper-whiskered man.

"And who is free to choose to do as he likes?" asked Aman.

"We are. Go if you want but you can't make us come running

at your beck and call as if we were your sheep."

"That's where you are wrong, *aqsaqal*. Whoever I order will go wherever I send them."

"But there's no-one here to be giving orders to. You can't touch the boy; he has yet to see life. Alke is one of the bosses too, albeit not of your standing. He is still a senior herdsman and has to stay with the livestock. And what's more, his health isn't up to it either. And the stockman needs to inspect our animals; some of them are in a bad way..."

What is he after? He wants to go up there with him, it suddenly dawned on Erkin. *He really does want to go. And what really makes no sense is that Aman also wants him to.*

"So you'll go," said Aman.

"I need to think about it. I am much older than you and I know what it means to be out on a stormy night. And you of all people should know what a man who sets out in this sort of weather can expect."

"Hey," said Erkin, "whoever goes, I still haven't forgotten what day it is and I've brought a bottle with me. It is New Year, after all, so let's get it down us sharpish, eh?"

With a flourish, he pulled a bottle from his felt boot and banged it down in front of the stove. The herdsmen licked their lips and burst into a peal of merry laughter. Erkin even imagined that the copper-whiskered man winked at him.

"Get the other one out," said Alke, pointing to Erkin's other boot.

"I don't have another. Now bring the glasses."

The boy shot off to a far corner to get the glasses.

Alke brought out some cold meat and *kurt*. Erkin set about cutting the *kazy* sausage, with only Aman and the copper-whiskered man left sitting motionless. Aman never took his eyes off the bottle, which shone as it thawed by the fire.

That seems to have done the job, thought Erkin happily, carefully laying out the appetising morsels on a plate.

"Well, comrade chairman, give us a toast. The appetizers are ready," and he offered the plate to Aman.

Aman started and looked around at everyone as if he had only just come out of a reverie. The herdsmen impatiently held out their glasses, their faces lit up with expectation and the scarlet glow of the flames.

"Yes, give your poor men something to be inspired about, even if it is only for short moment," chuckled the copper-whiskered man.

The young boy piped up:

"Yes, give us a speech. A real one, like the ones we get on the radio."

154

Only Alke didn't seem to share their high spirits. He looked somehow dejected. His heart was aching with a melancholy pity. He felt sorry for them all. Those who would soon be departing into the blizzard and those who would remain behind, lost in this white, whirling snow, perhaps more lost than anyone else in the wide world. In order to dispel this melancholy, he clinked his glass against the bottle that Aman was holding and asked quietly:

"Pour us a drink, *aga.*"

"Are you serious, men?" Aman asked, turning the bottle to the light as if looking at it for the first time. His voice sounded unnatural and cracked as if it weren't his own.

"Oh, come on, you can't be serious! Don't keep us waiting on tenterhooks?" said the copper-whiskered man in the shadows, his words hanging over the bottle like a cloud.

"Don't torture us, chairman; say your *Bismillah* and do the honours," laughed Erkin, raking up the fire in the stove.

Aman could only sense their selfish greed. None of them had even spared a thought for the men caught in the storm up in the mountains. As soon as these sorry brutes had set their eyes on the vodka, they had forgotten about everything else.

Damn this wretched vodka! he thought and smashed the bottle down onto the table, cracking the glass.

Silence reigned.

"Oh, chairman, you should have been more careful," Erkin exclaimed and slapped his knee in his vexation.

Dovlet, the young boy looked at Aman in terror and bewilderment, his lips suddenly began to tremble and he burst into bitter tears. Bitter tears for the hope of what he might have experienced together with the adults, the hope of seeing in this special occasion as an equal with his wise and respected elders. He had known few joyous moments in his short life. He had never had a holiday, he hadn't even been to a wedding. He had so wanted to experience just a little bit of kindness, a sense of spiritual harmony, a bit of conversation.

"Oh, and what a wonderful aroma!" said the copper-whiskered man, wetting his hand in the puddle of vodka and dabbing it to his brow.

Only Alke remained motionless, staring at the fire as if he had foreseen what might happen. He had seen much in his life and he was indifferent to alcohol. Erkin, though, spat angrily at the metal stove and his eyes filled with blood.

Pretending not to notice the others' angry reaction, Aman calmly ordered:

"Go and find some suitable horses. Ours are completely spent."

The herdsmen left in silence.

155

"I see you've tightened your girth and are ready to vent your spleen," said Aman derisively, when he and Erkin were left on their own.

"It would appear that you're as righteous as an angel, chairman," Erkin replied. His pupils aflame, either from the reflection of the fire or from his anger. "A man could end up travelling all the way to heaven with you. Oh well, the festivities didn't work out, so let's get going. But I wonder whether our journey will be a wasted one with enemies at your back?"

"What are you talking about?! What nonsense! What enemies?! These sorry animals who are so selfish and greedy, you can see them positively trembling at the sight of the bottle."

"No, I'm not talking nonsense and they are not animals, just normal people. And people who from this moment on will have no respect for you. The only power you will have left over them is fear. As for myself, well I'm sorry, chairman, but I don't have the words to tell you everything I think."

"Can you really have so completely lost your senses over a swig of vodka?" said Aman, sarcastically slapping Erkin on the back. "Calm down, if it's so important to you there'll be plenty more where that came from."

But his sarcasm concealed his confusion and indignation. The young man's words had cut him. Who was this nobody, this outsider who had taken it into his head to teach him how to behave? Of course, the right thing to do would have been to hit him. But no, he mustn't...

"No, that would not be right, comrade manager," said Erkin, as if reading his mind and Aman even took a step back in surprise. But the stock breeder was talking about something else.

"You don't understand the human soul. Do you know what the dearest and happiest moments in life are? You have deprived these people of a rare celebration. And why? It makes no sense. There is no explanation for your actions and that's what makes it even more upsetting."

Aman remained silent. He cracked his knuckles loudly.

"Your father would never have..."

"Leave my father out of this; don't go bringing him into this."

"I have no intention of blackening his name. Quite the contrary, I have nothing but respect for Aspan the elder, he is the pride of our village. You have let your spite get the better of you, but your father detests all evil, whatever its shape or form and however it may be screened by good intentions. They are not drunkards and you know that and that is why they won't forgive you for demeaning them in that way. It's not as if we are sitting in your office back at the farm, at the end of the day, we are their guests here. We should have shown more respect to our hosts."

156

"I must say, I was not expecting such eloquence from you," said Aman and, getting up slowly, he reached for his coat and began to put it on. "You speak most eloquently, my friend, you really do. But I doubt you have the slightest idea about what happened back there. This is only the second year you have been living in these parts and you don't know our people."

"People are the same wherever you go," said Erkin, without taking his eyes from the fire, "and instead of beating them about the head like pups, turning them into cowards, as their leader you should give them the chance to learn to respect themselves..."

The herdsmen came back in, preventing him from finishing his sentence. They stood in silence by the door, crestfallen at what had happened.

"The horses are ready," Alke reported quietly.

He stole a secretive glance at Erkin and was surprised at what he saw. This taciturn, modest young man had an unexpected brave streak. A strange thing had occurred while they had been outside: it was as if Aman the man mountain had somehow become shorter and more diminished, while this skinny lad, who had been quietly carrying out his duties for the last two years—keeping count of and tending to the livestock it—had appeared to grow in stature. No, no, people had been wrong to have called him an outsider. He was not like other men, he was a brave man. Aman would never have forgiven someone for spitting in anger at a smashed bottle of vodka and here he was, having to forgive him. And now everyone was looking at him with respect or surprise; it was clear they had had strong words while they had been on their own. But who would he take with him? Choosing a companion on a journey like this was tantamount to choosing one's destiny.

Casting a glance at the gloomy faces of the herdsmen and at Erkin's tense, stony face, Aman sensed that he had suffered a defeat.

Suddenly, Erkin got up sharply.

"Right, it's time to go."

"You will remain here. Alke will go with me." There and then, Alke got up and obediently went to his corner of the hut to fetch some warmer mittens.

"Alke, wait. I think you have plenty to be getting on with here," said Erkin, stopping him.

"We need Alke," the boy piped in, pitifully. Aman turned to the copper-whiskered man:

"Then you will have to accompany me, even though you fear it greatly."

"No one changes onto an unknown mount before taking on the crossing, boss," said *Copper Whiskers* with a challenging stare, "and we are going to be facing a very dangerous crossing. I reckon it is someone else around here who is afraid, someone who trusts neither

157

me nor the stockman."

"I trust the stockman and that is why I am leaving him here. Gather together any other herders from these parts and make a path in the direction of Alatai. We'll drive the yearlings and foals to meet them and then we'll all bring them into the lowland pastures. There is no other way. Use the hay and the feed sparingly. It's much too cold now to get the livestock out to the ricks. If the sun comes out, lead the mares out onto the *tebenyovka*. If we can't get the larger animals with solid hooves to feed on the *tebenyovka* winter grazing, the heifers will get it particularly hard."

"Icicles are already forming on the horses' muzzles. They'll find it difficult to stretch their muzzles to feed off the ground," said *Copper Whiskers* in a surly voice. "We can't make any promises that we'll be able to make it through the winter with just the winter grazing to help us."

"Don't worry, you'll make it. Make sure you clean all the horse's muzzles and drive them out to graze the *tebenyovka* under the snow. Even if you have to clear the snow for them with a shovel, you'll get through to the spring without losses."

"Well then," said *Copper Whiskers*, "if I make it back alive, I'll be sure to clear the snow."

Erkin understood that the older man had got what he wanted. He was travelling out with the chairman. He understood something else, too: the more he insisted on continuing the journey with the chairman, the more stubborn Aman would be in his decision to test fate.

He could sense that these two people were bound by a secret enmity and that the copper-whiskered man was cunningly and underhandedly drawing Aman into a trap.

"Oh no, *dzhigits*!" he said merrily. "He who begins a journey together must return together. But seeing that there's some disagreement about this, let us resolve it by the only fair means available. Let's draw lots."

"That would be the right thing to do," Alke concurred and the boy simply jumped for joy: at last there would be at least some kind of fun.

"We are going to draw lots, chairman, would you mind checking that the horses we chose are suitable."

"Oh, you *dzhigits*!" said the manager and went out.

"The thing is that there's a curse that hangs over his family and to go out in a storm like this would be to tempt the devil himself. But ultimately I believe in fate," said the copper-whiskered man, the moment the door had closed behind Aman.

"And I thought the bottle was the only thing you believed in," Alke spat out with unexpected vehemence, and Erkin thought to

158

himself: *He also understands that they should not be allowed to travel together.* "Give me one of those bottles you've finished," Alke ordered quietly, "and then we'll see what fate has to say."

Copper Whiskers spun the bottle on the felt mat and it came to a stop, pointing at the door.

"That's about right," said *Copper Whiskers*. "My bottle didn't let me down. He should go on his own. He gets more money than the rest of us, let him take the risks."

"There's something about your jokes that I'm beginning to like less and less," said Erkin, snatching the bottle from his hand. "You spin it this time, Alke."

Alke placed the bottle on the mat and hesitated for some reason.

"Well, go on... spin it!" said the boy, unable to hold himself back. Alke glanced at Erkin with a frown and Erkin, understanding him instantly, lowered his eyes a little.

The bottle spun and stopped, pointing at the stock breeder.

"Oh, damn it," exclaimed the boy, jumping up like a kid goat, "I never get any luck! Uncle Alke, why couldn't you have fixed it so that it picked me?"

"I couldn't," replied Alke seriously. "There was no way."

When they went out into the yard, a light snow was drifting. The night was as black as a nightmare and it seemed that it could silently swallow up anyone who dared leave the building. The frost was picking up and the men's teeth chattered.

The horses waited impatiently for their riders, whinnying to them in the darkness.

"One of them is useless," said Aman. "He won't be able to drive us a path. Go and get one of the stallions from the herd."

He didn't ask them, which of them was going to be joining him, like some impatient woman; he just stood there, massive and immobile, smoking a cigarette.

"Give our horses some hay and cover them with a blanket," he ordered Alke. "We're still going to have to return back on them."

"Why not put them out to graze under the winter snow?" cracked *Copper Whiskers*. "As you advised us."

But Aman pretended that he hadn't heard him.

When they brought over a huge stallion, Aman burst into a peal of laughter.

"He's massive, more like a mountain than a horse!" He slapped the stallion affectionately and the horse neighed wistfully.

"He senses the hard journey ahead," said Erkin as he helped the chairman onto the giant steppe animal.

"I think it'd be better if I took the skis; I can tell this one's going to give you trouble all the way. He's not accustomed to this sort

159

of journey and might play up."

Aman almost bent down from the saddle, as if he wanted to give the stock breeder's face a good look, but then he straightened himself up.

"Alright. You take the skis."

"And you, sir, should take the gun," advised Alke.

"What for?" growled Aman, disgruntled.

"It's better to be safe than sorry. There's a pack of wolves wandering around near the Devil's Bridge and they might attack."

"But we need the gun ourselves," said *Copper Whiskers* from out of the gloom.

"If Alke says we need it. We'll do what he says. Now, take the gun, *aga*. And as for you my friend, there's something I don't quite understand about you. One minute you're a reckless braveheart and the next, you're afraid to go to bed without a gun." And with that, Erkin corralled the copper-whiskered man to one side with his horse, as if by accident.

"What calibre is it? A thirty-two or a pea-shooter?" asked Aman, towering above on them on his mighty stallion.

"It's a double-barrel, sir."

"Where did you get it?"

"I didn't steal it if that's what you're asking. I bought it from some drovers."

"Well, next time get me one," said Aman. "I'm relying on you, Alke, to get the local *dzhigits* together and get that path driven to Alatai."

"We'll make a start as soon as it gets light. Don't worry about us. Just make sure you come back safe and sound."

And although the silhouettes of the two horsemen were instantly swallowed up in the night, the three herdsmen stood there for quite a while, looking after them into the black abyss. They had mixed feelings.

Alke felt anxious and worried. Despite having devoted the greater part of his life to his constant, grinding, hard work and risking his life many times, he had not become hard of heart. During his rare meetings with them, he would spoil his five children and he envied and bore no ill will to anyone. But now his simple heart was filled with trepidation for Aman and Erkin. However, he also felt admiration for these men who had voluntarily set off on an unimaginably difficult journey without so much as shivering at the stormy night and the savage frost. It didn't occur to him for a moment that over the course of his hard life he had taken just as many risks that had been no less hazardous. After all, his work was his life and that had included many long months of wintering in the mountain pastures, with blizzards, incredibly hard, physical labour and much more besides; things that only a herdsman can know.

The men returned to the house, while Alke still stood there, listening to the night. Then he went back inside. The copper-whiskered man was drinking *kumiss*; the boy was dozing, wrapped up in a sheepskin.

The boy was dreaming about Alma-Ata, where he had been to visit the year before. The jets of the fountains crisscrossed, forming an enchanted tunnel that glistened in the sun. He was walking through this tunnel and the splashing water somehow never touched him. He walked for an eternity and suddenly felt afraid that he would walk all the way to the mountains and never get to see the city. It was then that he walked towards the jets of water and they made way for him. He saw a beautiful, tall building, topped with a golden crown and realised that this was now his home. Suddenly, a ragged herd of horses came to an exhausted stop around the building; the boy understood that the horses were hungry and needed to drink. The people strolling along the pavements, however, failed to realise this at all.

The boy really wanted to go into his home and let someone else worry about this herd. But the people strolling around nearby didn't seem to have the slightest intention of tending to the horses. It was then that the boy realised that only he could feed and water the herd. He didn't want to spoil his new trousers and red shirt, but he remembered how the waters had parted before him. He jumped up onto a stallion and drove the horses to the fountain. The trolleybuses and buses stopped still and the cars came to a halt to let the herd through, but the people on the pavements continued to rush past, busy with their self-important affairs.

The boy drove the herd to the fountain; the horses drank their fill and began nibbling at the juicy grass on the lawns. Then the boy cried out: "Hey, look! Look, everyone!" And the people suddenly looked around and saw the jets of water parting before them, letting them into the watery tunnel, cool and glistening in the sun.

The boy cried something unintelligible in his sleep and smiled. Alke folded up the loose end of the sheepskin and placed it under the boy's head. *Copper Whiskers* belched, got up and went over to his place. He lay down with his back to the fire so Alke would not be able to see his face as he slept.

What he feared most was to be watched while he slept. After all, he was defenceless when asleep. In the light of day, there was no man who could fathom and guess his thoughts. But when he was asleep, he was unprotected, after all, for him, the only sure protection in this life is provided by cruelty. And cruelty must be vigilant at all times. If a man is to rise to the top of this struggling pile of humanity that people call *life* he needs to be cruel. And cruelty is what he needed if he is to remain there. But he hadn't remained there. It hadn't been his fault. Time had been at fault. But there was still life in him yet and the reserves of his cruelty were still not exhausted; he would bide his time.

Alke brought his watch closer to the fire. It was nearly nine. In three hours, there would be a New Year. Mankind would be another year older. For Alke, old age was drawing ever nearer. But, all the same, he did not fear it. He had five sons and that was sufficient to allay any fears of old age. Had his life been a good one? It had been a life at any rate, and it had seen its fair share of good and bad. The one thing there had not been enough of, was time spent with his family. Only a few times had he spent this holiday at the family table with his wife and children, back there in the village in the foothills. Or any other holidays for that matter. Once he had become a herdsman, he had no longer been able to celebrate holidays or see the joyous faces of his family and shower them with kisses. It was as if he had turned into an elk, a lonely beast of the mountains, traipsing all day and all night after the herds of brush-tailed horses?

He raked the fire and threw more wood into the stove. Suddenly he heard the distant howling of a wolf. He grabbed *Copper Whisker's* gun from the wall and darted out onto the verandah. He listened. It was quiet. It was as if the snow had begun to lose its power, beating more weakly now against his face. But the sky was dark and there was no moon. Alke went over to the enclosure where the horses stood. They started and in the dark, he could sense that they had turned to face him. And then he heard the now distinct howl of a wolf. Alke pulled the trigger. The shot echoed out many times over the mountains and across the valleys. Once the echo had died away, the silence returned, a silence in which a man might lose his senses.

Well, that's my New Year seen in, thought Alke.

* * *

Old Man Aspan had been kicking his heels all that evening, unable to find anything to keep himself busy. Even his grandchildren had gone to a New Year party, so he was altogether out of sorts. He had dined in silence with the old woman and his daughter-in-law and the women had started doing the endless chores around the house.

Suddenly the old woman said:

"It seems our boy has gone to Alatai. Seeing as he left in such a hurry, it would appear the livestock are in trouble up there. Wherever did he find such a thankless job?"

However, the old man and his daughter-in-law made it clear that they were not in the mood for such a conversation. Old Man Aspan sat on the bed, smoking. His tranquillity had deserted him, he could find nothing to keep himself busy and realised in dismay that a sleepless night lay ahead. He recalled the book he had long since been

162

unable to finish as if a spell had been cast on it. He pulled it out from under the mattress. That foolish *Alitet* was never going to make it up into the hills[8], the letters jumped and the words refused to form themselves into meaningful sentences. Aspan shoved the book back under the mattress. He laced his fingers behind his head. *The most important thing was to try not to recall anything. Not to recall what had happened thirty years ago. Back then an identical blizzard had been raging.*

"Just as long as he doesn't lose his nerve and makes it across the Devil's Bridge," he muttered.

"Father, did you say something?" his daughter-in-law said, popping her head into his room.

"No, my dear, I was just mumbling to myself," he replied.

Yes, back then an identical blizzard had been raging... What a coincidence... Oh, god, what an unhappy coincidence, and what if the family was again cursed with a disability and misfortune... Oh, stop that! An idle mind is always filling an empty head with nonsense. If only I had a sleeping draught, like the one they gave me back then in the hospital. I could just pop two or three pills into my mouth and lie here, all bundled up... Oh, lord, what an unhappy coincidence... And these words returned again and again like a bee, buzzing day in and day out around the hive. Returning and then flying off again. And then returning once more...

* * *

In that year, the snow had also fallen endlessly. Three of them had been putting the yearlings and foals out to graze at the Alatai wintering pasture. It had been a cruel winter with a fierce frost which had kept a firm hold, grasping them by the throat. Feedstocks had been low and the livestock had been growing leaner by the day, the poor animals were barely able to stand. An order had come from the central country farmstead to select fifty of the most famished animals and bring them to the winter pasture at Tarbagatai. Aspan the Herdsman had set off, taking fifty sorry-looking horses with him. He had made his way along the River Kaba, along the terrible Tar path. Although there had been storm clouds up above, the blizzard and inclement weather had abated. The yearlings had found it difficult to walk, but that was only to be expected looking at the poor exhausted creatures, wandering along the path like a trail of sorry ants. They had made their way with Aspan out in front on his powerful gelding, forging a path in the thick snow as he went and then returning and driving the young animals through the narrow furrow.

---

[8] Bokeev is referring here to a novel by Tikhon Semushkin entitled *Alitet Goes to the Hills*, which was popular in the Soviet period and even turned into a film.

Tired and jaded they had had to halt every hundred metres until they finally made it to the Devil's Bridge.

Back then it had been the only bridge across the river. Built during the First World War, it had become completely dilapidated and could only support the weight of a single horseman. That meant the horses had to be led across one by one. Aspan the Herdsman had dismounted and, throwing a rope around the neck of the first year-old colt, he had led it across the bridge. All skin and bone, they were so wretched that the animals had no interest in making any mischief and they had obediently plodded after the herdsman. As soon as he had led the last foal over to the mainland on the other side, he returned to the other bank and mounted his powerful gelding.

Hey, Aspan! The Great Scream boomed, reverberating with a fathomless noise, which caused the skies to shiver. Aspan the Herdsman had turned around sharply, wondering what that thunderous noise could have been, driving thousands, if not millions of horses? And then he saw it:

Directly from the sky, from where the crags penetrated the heavens, a whistling and screaming avalanche came down, crushing everything in its path. And it was rushing straight for him.

With a cry of "Oh, Allah!" Aspan the Herdsman lashed his gelding. So hard had he struck his horse that, before they knew it, they had found themselves in the middle of the bridge and it was here that the white dragon reached them, crashing down with all its terrible might.

The entire world: the bridge, the sky, the mountains, the haggard foals, huddled close together – everything disappeared in an instant. Who could have imagined that death could strike so suddenly? The avalanche, falling from the mountains, had picked up the herdsman, together with his horse and hurled them into the freezing waters of the river below. The dumbstruck foals remained on the bank, watching in terror as their master initially disappeared then reappeared in the stormy waters of the Kaba.

In the mountains, an unseen devil, laughing loudly and slapping himself on his thighs, had jumped for joy, his laughter reverberating in an evil echo.

An avalanche.

This is the only danger, the one silent enemy who lives in the Altai mountains that people are unable to tame. Aspan the Herdsman had not been the first victim of the accursed avalanche and he would not be the last. It had brought tears and woe to many a family. What is it that makes people cross the Devil's Bridge, knowing the danger that awaits them? Because it is the only route to the pastures of the Alatai, the promised land that is so vital to their prosperity and survival. And everyone prays that this fatal, tear-washed bridge remains intact, even

164

though it carries the threat of impending death.

But now it had been destroyed completely, the wreckage carried away along the River Kaba. All that remained were the bridge's orphaned posts.

Some would regret the passing of the bridge. Perhaps. Maybe those who are prepared to pay any price for paradise. Others would be glad. Perhaps. Maybe those who think: *paradise is not worth a human life, is not worth his fear. And, at the end of it all stands Alatai, a paradise for the animals but it is the humans who pay the price for it.* And there are those who look at it in simpler terms: *The life of a mountain people must accommodate danger. Several generations have crossed this bridge and even those who do not leave their own land are also doomed to cross it, albeit at least on one occasion. If they are afraid to cross it, they are weak and will achieve little and nature's merciless cruelty will crush them. They gradually begin to yield to it but one should never yield an inch to nature's cruelty. It is on this balance that the lives of the people hang in these parts.*

Hurtling along on the furious current and choking on the icy water, Aspan the Herdsman sensed that his end had not yet come. The pieces of ice that pressed against him from all sides had kept him above the surface as if the river was refusing to swallow him up.

His unfortunate gelding had been carried past him, its head stretched back and its teeth bared, sitting with its croup awkwardly on the ice; it was as if a host of devils had been driving him on ahead, squealing playfully as they went. Even in his own lamentable state, Aspan the Herdsman had thought to himself: *Oh, the poor thing, I feel so sorry for him. He is being dragged to hell. Farewell, my kind, gentle steed!*

Back then, Aspan could not have known that, until his dying day, he would see the same pity reflected in the eyes of his nearest and dearest when they looked at the *poor thing* that he would become. The icy water, roaring under the battered ice, tossed and turned the herdsman, eventually dragging him to the bank.

He had been grateful for that. Just to be able to grasp onto the trees, hanging over the water. There had probably not been a man in the world with arms more powerful than his. Now though, their ferocious strength, able to tame any wild horse by grasping it by the ears, stopping it by the tail, had now seemed superfluous.

Oh, but what joy! The relentless river that had dragged him along, plunged him under and threw him up to the surface again, playing cruelly with this helpless doll of a man and suddenly carried him up close to the bank. The distance, no longer than a *kuruk*, reduced until he was no more than an arm's length away.

"Oh, God, give me the good fortune and the strength!"

He had tried to throw himself onto the bank, like a fish that

165

has taken leave of its wits, but he had no support from which to launch himself.

And then a miracle occurred: a powerful impact from an unseen saviour of a wave struck him sideways and he landed on solid ground. However, a blinding pain whipped through his legs; his mind, still circling near him overhead like a bird, fell and crashed and Aspan lost consciousness.

After that, nothing registered in his mind: neither the sound of the water, nor the pain, nor the cold, nor the terror, nor the blinding whiteness of the snow.

He had held the cup of his existence in his hands preparing to drink the last and bitterest drops from it, before departing to the other world. But is there anything in this world more resilient and indestructible than a human being?

When Aspan came to, he realised he was hanging over the waters of the Kaba, caught in the branches of a fallen cedar. He saw a white, white world, frozen in anticipation around him. In anticipation of death or resurrection: this white world was quite indifferent to the outcome.

His legs were lapped by the water, but Aspan felt no cold.

His blessed arms had grasped hold of the branch with an eagle's grasp. And his head had remained on his shoulders, so he was still capable of thinking. So there was no reason for him to be hanging there, like a wolf in a trap. He had to act – to get out onto the bank, wring out his clothes, get a fire going and dry himself out. But what was this? Some dishevelled, devil-like figures had surrounded him and, swaying from side to side, they drawled out a dull, tiresome song. Others had flocked in behind them—a considerable number of them—swaying their enormous heads.

"*Bismillah*," Aspan had whispered, closing his eyes.

When his eyes opened, he saw that the devils had left without a trace, to be replaced by giant cedars, their crowns rustling. The entire world, with its enormous boulders, trees and mountain peaks, stood in a solemn stillness, while his poor body was being left to rinse, swaying in the icy water below.

"Oh, Allah," Aspan had sighed, "I must not remain here hanging between heaven and earth, like some marmot pelt. But what is that pain in my chest!"

Aspan gathered up all his strength and with an almighty heave pulled his mighty body out of the water and straddled the trunk of the cedar.

The flame that had lapped at his chest jumped like a black cat from the stove and a sense of relief passed over him.

He pressed his blue hands to his cheeks and breathed on them to warm them. What a thing of wonder these hands are, it turns out!

166

While they were still in one piece, he would have the strength to pluck the moon from the sky.

Now, though, he would have to wait a little, gather his strength and, at least on all fours, creep to the bank along the fallen trunk. He had tried to get his legs to grasp hold of the cedar trunk, but a pain seared through them below the knees like a thousand needle pricks. Aspan's terrifying scream had carried to the heavens and he had fallen, face first onto the rough bark. So great had the pain been that it was as if his legs had been sweeping a bottomless chasm, filled to the brim with all the torments that the universe could devise.

Aspan had lain, pressed against the cedar, a fever-like heat alternating with an icy chill and all he could think about was not to slacken the grasp of his great hands.

The sun set and a black shadow had fallen over the ravine. The lead-coloured clouds thinned out and spots of blue appeared in the sky. The river's water grown stiff and thick and its lion's roar had quietened. The fierce frost of the Altai set in and filled the mountains and valleys, turning everything transparent and brittle, ready to crack into pieces at the slightest murmur.

Aspan opened his eyes and the pain immediately gnawed at his legs, like some rabid cur.

"Oh, heavens!" the herdsman cried but the cur would not run or leave its prey.

Grating his teeth, Aspan crawled along the trunk, grabbing at the twigs and branches. His legs were no help, but his arms, his poor arms—what would he have done without them—had dragged his bear-like body onto the bank. Now he had to get up, no matter what it took... He roared and collapsed into the deep snow. But he managed to turn over onto his back and calm down. The cur crept up and began to lick his face with its rough, prickly tongue; but it was not a dog, but the frost, beginning to encase him in its iron armour.

He opened his eyes and saw the deep, dark blue sky, the silvery stars and the black crests of the cedars.

"Oh, god, but I am still alive!" For the first time, Aspan stretched his copper lips into a smile.

His heart beat loudly and evenly. The beats counted down the time; a time without end.

The prostrate man kept his gaze on the sky, like a loyal slave, pleading for his life from a wrathful sovereign.

The moonlight bathed and warmed his frozen soul. How wonderful and hot this moon was! It was quite different to any moon he had seen, either the day before, the year before, or twenty years before that. Oh, fate, what torment it was to be so weak, like a child that has still not learned to walk! How desperate it was to lie there, submerged in the snow, his soul burning and his thoughts thrashing about and quaking like a bird in a snare!

This was indeed a silently screaming world. The January night was long, like the bowels of a sheep.

Only yesterday he had been running and jumping about like a mountain goat, but now he lay there, shackled in his suffering, hanging between life and death, unable to lift even a single hair from the ground.

The moon was hidden in the cleft of Mount Muzbel and as it disappeared, Aspan experienced a great anguish, the same anguish that he always felt when entering a forest of deadwood. Yet when the stars began to fade, he began to think of the sun, with joy and hope. All that he could do to extend his tenuous hold on life was to continually rub his face and ears with his hands; he had shovelled snow over himself with his hands and was now sheltering under it. And so he lay there, covered in a shroud of snow.

Will anyone come to look for me?

The sun had kept him waiting long and in torment. Its weak rays barely made it to the bottom of the deep ravine; Aspan's eyelids could sense them, he opened and then shut them immediately. The pure liquid light was intolerable.

Aspan knew, however, that in ten or fifteen minutes the sun would disappear once more beyond the mountains. He lifted his head and forced himself to open his eyes wide, in an attempt to receive as much as possible from this brief encounter with this life-giving force.

And then a miracle occurred: unconsciously, like a sunflower turning to the sun, he managed to lift himself up into a sitting position, like a ground squirrel sitting by its hole.

Oh, the happiness he felt!

So many times later, in his greatest moments of desperation, when this sitting position had become an eternal feature of his life, would he recall this first sense of happiness, his cry of joy, and then his desperation would recede.

Aspan had tried to move his legs but to no avail. They felt no pain as if some evil spirits had divided up his body, one of them taking possession of his legs. He realised that this was to be his lot for the rest of his days.

The water that had filled his knee-high boots had now frozen solid. He had to warm up, light a fire. Yes, but the matches he had always placed under the tops of his boots were now hopelessly frozen into the ice and had been rendered quite useless. He had wanted to eat. He had stuffed a hand into his coat. Thank heavens, there was still some *kurt* dried cheese left in his pocket. He had to be careful and eat only a little. He threw a small piece into his mouth and began sucking it, carefully hiding the rest away in the inside pocket of his fur coat, close to his chest.

168

He laughed.

You fool. Aspan: who are you hiding your kurt *from? Who is going come out in this weather to look for you in the Tar ravine, where no human ever sets foot, even in summer? First, you'll eat the* kurt *and then the wolves will eat you. Or vice versa: they'll eat you and your* kurt *together, so there's little point saving it up...*

And yet only the devil lives without hope. Perhaps, after all, some hardy soul might set out to search for him? That notion had given him something to do: count the brave souls who might save him. There was Dovlet, Bolat, Kanoat, and then there was... He got to ten. A decent number. As for the other villagers, they were fair weather friends, allies today, enemies tomorrow waiting for you to slip up.

His handful of relatives would have rushed to Kamka with tears in their eyes and, of course, they would have reminded him of his stubbornness and told him that he had only himself to blame. That is what his closest relatives would have always said. From the moment he had first mounted a horse, this orphan had never gone to his relatives with an outstretched hand. He had fed and watered himself like a small insect feeds and waters itself. He was not the sort to take advice from others and he had survived without them.

He registered the fact with indifference: he had survived up until now and that was the main thing.

...Yes, he had survived without the advice of others. Advisers had appeared when he had a name not only in the district but in the region as a whole. *Exchange that foal for a yearling, no, exchange that mare for a yearling,* and so on. He had paid no heed to any of them because he lived a simple life and would continue to do so. Let them laugh: *Aspan is so honest he would share a horse's hair, even if it was all he had in the world.* And there was another thing his kinsmen could not understand and that was his independence. They simply considered it foolhardiness. It is much easier to forgive evil than independence because evil at least makes sense. So, he had been mistaken to have considered there might be as many as ten men ready to help him. There would not be ten. There wouldn't be anyone. No-one would beat a path towards his snowy shroud or read a funeral prayer over it. His parents had long gone and his son was still just a little child. Neither his heart nor his head had reached maturity. That meant that fate had chosen a suitably inglorious death for this solitary herdsman at the bottom of this ravine, in the depths of a deep forest. Well, not even a man sitting in the house of Allah could run from it.

He imagined he heard the sound of a twig snap. It had either been made by a man or some wild animal. He listened attentively and with curiosity. He was not afraid; he had been carried away by an avalanche, after all. Someone or something was wandering close-by. *Man or beast? A beast would be preferable. Oh, God, send me some brute beast! Let him devour me; that would better than having to endure this shame and suffering. My crimson blood and my bones will turn dark on the snow and the meltwater will carry them away in the spring. And there will be nothing left of me in this sinful world. I will disappear quietly or I will turn into the wild animal that has eaten me and so begin a second life. My son has a mother; whatever happens to me, he won't be lost or abandoned...*

To Aspan's right, crushing and apparently swimming through the snow, appeared the ambling, club-footed master of the Altai. Aspan looked at him and roared out laughing, overcome with joy. He even cried out gracelessly:

"*Assalamualaikum,* dear bear!" The bear had frozen in astonishment. "Come over here, come. Don't be afraid. I have no weapon." Aspan had beckoned him over with his hand. "Come on! My fateful avalanche and the scream that caused it probably frightened you out of your lair into the feisty winter. Forgive me. But I will reward you. Come, come. You must be hungry, so get your fill of my flesh, my dear bear. I will put up no resistance, so eat me up in large, thick pieces. Let's unite our souls and wander around these hills. I am speaking the honest truth, this is no trick. Eat me and may God grant me your freedom and your dull wit. There is no scream that can terrify a man who has been transformed into a bear. Come here, my bear, chomp away and eat me up."

The bear had stood there motionless, looking attentively at the strange creature that cried so loudly, waving its paws about. He had stared at it and then turned and slowly walked away.

"Come back!" Aspan had cried after him. "Why not try human meat?!"

The bear had walked away, crunching the snow and the cracking of the deadwood became quieter and quieter.

"He did not wish to bloody his claws on such easy prey. Eh, my kind bear, you didn't want to feast on food, caught without a struggle or a fight. So you have a conscience. And that means it is my fate to live. To live as a cripple, with no purpose and no joy in life."

Aspan felt for the sheath on his belt. He drew out the knife with its ox bone handle, ran his finger over the blade and was satisfied. Then he brought the knife to his chest.

Stop, it might not penetrate my coat and reach my heart.

He unfastened the buttons and opened his coat.

My native land, my good people, be healthy and happy, whispered Aspan. *I leave my only son to you, the proud mountain to you, the wind to you, the black earth with your covering of snow to you, the sky to you, the rivers and lakes, the birds and the beasts. I leave him to all of you. Farewell, Aman!* He had raised his hand above him when, suddenly, someone had cried out pitifully from above:

"No, no, no!"

"No, no, no!" the unknown voice had repeated above his head and then muttered something he could not make out or understand. Its mumbling had turned to a wailing sound that cleaved the soul.

Aspan raised his eyes. On a cedar branch, an enormous black bird sat with a beautiful woman's face and he recognised her as the girl from Sarmonke.

"So you have come to me, my beauty," Aspan whispered quietly. "You have come to mourn me."

"No, no, no," the bird-girl had moaned in response.

The knife slipped from his hand as if obeying some silent order. The moon flared, filling the world with its silver light.

"Sing to me," Aspan had asked. "Sing to me, my dear girl."

He closed his eyes and the bird had sung that the sons of man cannot ask God for happiness or for death unless their appointed hour has come. *A man will only die if it is his time. Are things really so bad for you, lying in my embrace, hot as a flame and cold as ice? Why the hurry to escape from this vibrant world? Your home has yet to welcome all its guests. You have not yet drunk your fill from the cup of torment. Your father named you Aspan, after the sky; look how high it is, how inaccessible, yet we are all on our way there and the first to make it there will be the one who will have to pay for all his sins and the one who is weak of soul and can no longer help the living. Sleep, Aspan, you need to build your strength before your final farewell. Sleep – I will keep watch over you.*

A deathly silence spread over the tall mountains and the broad valleys. The river, shackled by ice, the cedars with their covering of snow, the peaks and ravines, the bear, the snow slides and the scream had all fallen asleep. And at the bottom of the deep ravine, a man also slept. An ordinary, unguarded man in a pure cradle of snow.

The sun had risen and set above him. The stars had completed their slow, solemn journey. The Great Bear lay on its side, Sirius had risen and the Pole Star shone serenely.

At times, he opened his eyes and saw the sky, cast in pale skimmed milk blue, or pearly pink, or endless black. His favourite star, Sirius, the herdsman's star, had shone and burned in this sky, mysteriously winking down at him.

He was awoken by the fluffy snow that fell on his face, filling his eyes and nose. A large bird disturbed a cedar branch as it took off. Aspan hurriedly shook off the snow to see what it was, but he had only managed to catch a shadow, sliding across the slope of the mountain that hung over the ravine. This bald slope was lit up by the sun and it sparkled, washed by a million mirror shards. The huge boulders on the river bank, covered in snow, seemed to be like polar bears, coming down to drink, while the dense forest on the shady side of the Altai remained stock still, like some innumerable army in white *chapan* quilted coats, awaiting their commander's call to arms.

How cruel and yet how beautiful this world is, Aspan thought. *It would be a shame to leave it.*

He felt extremely hungry, threw a piece of the *kurt* into his mouth and sucked it, smacking his lips.

What wonderfully delicious kurt. I don't think I have ever eaten anything quite as good. I will definitely tell Kamka when I return that she really makes very good kurt.

For reasons unknown, he was now sure he would see his wife, his son and his native village, and that someone had already set out to find him. He just had to wait. Gather his strength and trick the time that endlessly ticked by. Just as you cannot trick death so you cannot trick time. But you can turn it back; it will happily return to the past, to childhood, say, or to the years of one's youth.

Without warning, the senior herdsman had caught a horse and departed to Markakul, under cover of night. Later, the girl who he had gone to visit at the place called Sarmonke had been taken by another... Before that *later*, there had been a fire lit on the banks of the lake, many a song, the earnest games of young *dzhigits*, silent trysts, a trembling hand in his and a kiss, then more kisses... Entwined together by a lasso of desire, they had glanced at the moon, floating in the silvery sky and, in their mind's eye, they had asked it to make them happy. The moon, though, did not hear their silent prayer. The girl remained on the other side of the river, the young herdsman, on this, with only the hair-like thread of the Devil's Bridge linking their banks. In the middle of winter, Aspan could not go to her: an avalanche had fallen onto the Tar and blocked the way to his love. He failed to arrive at the promised time and he did not come later. By the spring she had disappeared. She had disappeared, like the snow, as if it had never been there. She had been carried far away and he had lost her forever.

Now he could not remember if he had pined for long or married as fast as he could out of desperation. All he knew was that, after his only son Aman was born, his great, unhappy and unfulfilled love had faded away and then it was as if he had forgotten about her altogether. So it turned out he had not forgotten; lying there, whimpering at the gates of death, he had remembered her. Was this bird with the face of the girl from Sarmonke a figment of his delirium or a heaven-sent vision?

If it is a vision, then, Lord, send me my father; let me look at him at least once more, let me say the words to him that I didn't manage to say and didn't know how to say.

I loved him like I love my life but for some reason, I concealed my love from him. But he never stroked my head once, never kissed me, never said the endearing ainalaiyn, *never took me on his knee and*

172

never took an interest in me like other fathers take an interest in their children. But all the same, we could not have ever become any closer and when he passed away, I lost more than a breadwinner, more than a protector, more than a father. Why is that?

Aspan had grown up a strange boy – a strange boy from a strange father. He had not been one to take part in the noisy amusements of his peers that generate so much discord between children and adults alike. From dawn till dusk he would follow his father around like a bag, tied to the saddle as if he sensed their pending separation.

And no-one knew that his father, who had been severe and sullen and not one to spoil his child like others around him, would look at his son—whose eyes never left him and who helped him in everything he did without rest—and almost melt from tenderness. And he would think: *Oh, hoof to my* argamak, *continuation of my life and flame in my hearth, I am grateful to fate a thousand times over that you are here. You are a celebration for my heart, but how quickly you have grown and departed from the boisterous, joyous bazaar of childhood.*

Aspan had never once heard these words. He would never forget his father for, having borne a son, he heard in his soul all the words his father had never uttered and he understood that they had been passed to him by the deceased and he understood that his father had allowed him to grow up as God had intended.

Now, when the frost had enfettered him in a chain mail of ice, he recalled his childhood and his love with gratitude. And his soul was overwhelmed by a strange anguish as a cloud overwhelms a mountain peak. But this was not the anguish of one who has gone, never to return; it was the anguish of foreboding. The foreboding of a pending farewell. He knew that it would not be a farewell to the mountains, the cedars or the peaceful valleys. The foreboding of another farewell touched his soul and he sensed that it was dissolving away in this snow, in this sky, in this boundless suffering, like an echo dissolves as it breaks up against the ravine. He didn't wipe away the tears that ran quietly down his cheeks like a mountain spring. When they wetted his lips, he licked them with pleasure, because they quenched the thirst that was plaguing him, an anguished thirst. His tears had been as sweet as honey or first milk; these heavenly tears that poured from the wounds in his soul that was melting with his thoughts of his only son Aman. How he had wanted to touch his hair, hold him tight and set his fatherly love free. God, how happy the animals are and how strong they are for forgetting their offspring! They don't know they are mortal; they don't know the meaning of love. Aspan had also wanted to live a foolish life without feeling; a life that was needed not for himself, but for others. And he had rejoiced that the soul of the forest, the bear, had passed before him.

173

Lying in his cradle of snow, swathed tightly in ice and rocked by death, the infant-like Aspan had thought about the sort of legacy that *someone who spends his whole life chasing about after horses* might leave. There were two things of great value: the path, trodden out to the Alatai winter pastures and the *kuruk*, hardened to an iron state. And, in any case, what sort of Kazakh would ever be bothered about garnering a legacy for his descendants?!

How strange my people are, living their lives without a care and saving up only wise words and customs. Aspan had not even covered his wretched hut with slates; it only had to start raining and the water would come pouring in through the ceiling. But what could be expected of a poor herdsman who had been straining his sinews and dragging his cart of life since childhood? It would have been good if he had at least left his hungry son a mortar, fashioned and planed from poplar wood, and a dried up washtub to boot.

How wretched! A wretchedness borne of complete fecklessness. No matter how hard you try to explain things to your Kazakh brothers, who live in the middle of a forest and yet go looking for wood in the desert, the only reply you'll ever get from them is a carefree tra-la-la. And you are no different. *The world passes by and mankind is no more than a nomadic caravan.* Yes, and you sang these same songs and you rambled aimlessly from village to village with your compatriots. And you will continue rambling until misfortune strikes some poor devil like me. Then you will pull up your horses, look at me and realise that there is no point in putting your hope in God and waiting for one fine morning when he will bring you happiness in his saddlebag.

A noisy magpie landed on a young fir and reported something hurriedly with a guttural chirp.

Curse that tongue of yours, Aspan had whispered, *is anyone really going to come to help? Hold your horses, herdsman, perhaps fortune will smile on you yet...*

The magpie had been a good omen. It promised the arrival of a traveller, returning from wanderings afar, or some honoured guest.

Or perhaps it is waiting for this herdsman's death in order to fill its belly. Well, you'll have to wait, you prissy thing, for we have yet to say our farewells. Our time is not yet up; it has still to return from its distant "then".

Then the war had broken out. He had already turned eighteen and he had been taken by wagon to the regional centre.

Aspan had not been a coward during the war; it was just that there had not been enough time to look round and take stock to feel mortal fear. A private in the infantry, finding it hard to scratch simple letters to his mother, he had had no thoughts of glory or rank. And so he had lived through the entire war without promotion or decoration,

174

although a good many medals were handed out. And there had been this strange thing: it was as if someone had said that this unfortunate fellow should be left untouched: not a bullet, not a contusion. He had returned to the village without so much as a broken nail. And then it had all kicked off. The widows in their mourning seemed to forget that he was an orphan with all the misfortunes of an orphan and looked at him with hatred as if it were he and not Hitler who was responsible for all their woes. And it was as if their malevolent, silent glances had drawn the black cat of bad luck upon him.

Perhaps one of those old curses has caught up with me, the herdsman had thought, looking up at the sky.

Oh, you poor, foolish women, how could you know that the anticipation of the bullet is far more terrifying than the bullet itself?

Once he had waited three days for his bullet. He had had to make it across a large river. At night. Swimming. For many this had appeared to be more dangerous than an attack itself; the water in the dead of night was a terrifying thing. For many, but not for the herdsman. Having grown up on the banks of the Bukhtarma, with the word *Bismillah*, he fearlessly dived in and swam. He had been one of the first to swim to the opposite bank and had begun digging himself an entrenchment. He had won some time by swimming across first, losing no strength to a fear of or resistance to the water. After the ferocious Bukhtarma, this calm and smooth river was heaven. The other lads were not so lucky; they were showered by a hail of bullets. But then he too ran out of luck. One morning, after a battle, they had captured the opposite bank and the herdsman had joined what was left of his platoon. His friends had been surprised and slapped him on the bank, saying: "You must be some kind of hoodoo worker". But the commander said: "You didn't swim across in the night but went to ground and survived you bastard. You'll be court-martialled for this."

He was made to wait for three days, expecting his execution bullet at any moment. His comrades saved him by telling the commander what had actually happened. The major-*osobist* slapped him on the back, saying, "If you can survive that mess, you'll live a thousand years yet."

The herdsman had received slaps on the back later, too, when the war ended. That year, when he had raised ninety-five foals from a hundred mares, the Soviet farm chairman Khali, too, beat the dust from his back with a laugh, calling him a fine fellow in his peculiar accent. That last summer, the collective farm, the *kolkhoz*, had become a Soviet farm, or *sovkhoz* and the new director Samoilov had patted him on the back, saying, "*Aspanchik* is a fine *dzhigit* who won't let us down!" He had always been happy to receive praise and glowed as if he had received a choice gift.

Aspan pictured himself as he was when he was a herdsman, a

hulking, awkward man happily and foolishly grinning from ear to ear, and he had smiled at his past. The moon had watched this smile until dawn, as had the crags, Sirius and, perhaps, another, whom we are not given to see, but whose name all mortals know as Fate.

The nearer dawn approached, the fainter the smile became until it eventually turned into a tormented grimace.

He had woken from an unbearable pain that seemed to be breaking his bones and which had covered his whole body in sticky sweat.

"Oh, Allah," he had groaned, "I am in torment here, please let me go!"

His patient soul, which had never asked any quarter from fate, could stand it no longer and cried out for mercy. The herdsman began reciting a funeral prayer, which took the form of a request for forgiveness to everyone whom he had ever offended in this life.

"Never mind the offended," someone had whispered, "what about those you have killed."

"There was a war on," the herdsman had replied.

The herdsman remembered. Germany. They had broken their way into a nice-looking, multi-storey building. He had been creeping carefully from room to room, his rifle at the ready. It had been silent, the only noise the crunching shards of glass under his boots. Suddenly there was a knock at the door like an explosion, followed by a dull echo. He had fired a shot, probably faster than he had been able to turn to the noise.

If I make it back from this hell, Aspan whispered hotly. *If I make it back, I will teach everyone who cares to listen to me what silence means. I will teach them to refrain from cruel words, not to think evil thoughts; I will teach them to love their wonderful land, their mountains and their defenceless wild animals; I will teach them to love and pity one another and never to scream at their fellow man. Because a scream causes the soul to shrivel and dry up; because a scream generates an echo. Those who I killed during the war, screamed on the squares of their towns; they screamed so loud that the echo reached my own village. It reverberated from the mountains and came back, this time with a deadly force that killed those who had done the screaming. I was crushed not by an avalanche, it was not water that enfettered me in this armour of ice and it was not the frost that tormented me with slow torture. I was killed by the echo of that scream in the village office. Yes, I now understand that. Back then, the division manager thumped his fist onto the table in the office and said, "You will go to the Alatai wintering pasture".*

"My mother is seriously ill and my wife has just given birth. Please let me stay in the lowland pastures; give me the hardest work you can think of, just let me be nearer to home."

"Silence! That is an order. If you want to disobey it, write out a request and we'll release you from working with the horses..."

What else did the man say? What else..? Oh, he had plenty more to say and all of it screamed at the top of his lungs and accompanied with threats...

Did a herdsman really deserve all these threats and, not to mention, in the presence of another, the representative from the district.

After all, this herdsman was a fine fellow, the newspaper had printed his portrait; he had never previously refused a job and had never grumbled.

"Just remember," the chairman had said, "there's a witness here: you will be responsible for everything that happens at Alatai; you will be responsible for any trouble at the wintering ground."

"You and I are both herdsmen, so there is no need to lie so brazenly. Any trouble at the wintering ground will be through no fault of mine. I travelled there the day before yesterday to look over the pasture and I saw with my own eyes that there was not enough hay stocked for even half the winter. The haymakers deceived and misinformed you. The foals and yearlings will perish and you already know that..."

"Now write down a resignation request to leave the farm and hand over your party membership card."

"It wasn't you who issued me my party membership, so you'll not have it from me. And I won't fall for your threats about leaving the farm. I've got your number."

"What number?"

"Everybody knows that you force any person you're afraid of to write two requests: one, for acceptance into the collective farm, the other, for their discharge that is left undated. You insert the date yourself whenever you need to be rid of that person. You report upstairs that this person has left of their own accord and then you just kick them out of the village. But you can't kick me out. Neither you nor the good God almighty has the power to force me to leave my native land."

"Oh, I'll make you leave, alright!" the chairman had bellowed in a rage.

"Oh, no... it is not for you to decide my fate," Aspan had replied without fear.

"It's against the regulations to scream at a worker like that, *aqsaqal*," the district representative had said with authority. "But if what he says is right," he said, levelling his spectacles with a finger and looking sternly at the chairman, "we will send out a commission to inspect the feed at Alatai..."

"Send them out," the chairman had replied without flinching. "Right now, if you want. Only the road to Alatai has been blocked by a rock fall. You can punish me if I tell you in winter that there is not enough feed and the animals are starting to perish. For now, there is no cause for any to speak ill of me. Whatever I do, I do after careful consideration."

And that is how the dispute in the office had concluded. The chairman invited the representative to his house, the commission forgot to come, Aspan's sick mother and weak wife remained at Aspan's home and, when he saw the herdsman off to Alatai at the office, the chairman had said to him:

"Evidently, you can't see clearly for the fat around your eyes. Name me one of your ancestors who had a run-in with his boss and got his way? You're not thinking clearly about the consequences of your actions, boy. If you just thought a little with that fat head of yours, you'd realise that it's not me that gives the orders but the collective farm, chasing to meet the five-year plan while the district, in turn, passes false information upwards and so on. Just you make sure the next time you're chasing truth by the tail that you don't go falling off a precipice!"

Throughout his long journey to Alatai, the herdsman had relapsed into sad thoughts, reproaching himself, justifying himself and then reproaching himself once more. He thought to himself:

You and your pig-headedness, Aspan. When will you realise that, standing at the bottom, you can't go screaming up at those in charge at the top? They are the only ones who are allowed to scream. There is a reason they teach you the saying: rich is the man who finds a comfortable place to park his backside. But you don't want to be wealthy; you want to do what you do in an honest manner. So just keep your head down. But I don't want to just keep my head down and watch while some scoundrel destroys the work of so many people's hands. After all, everyone around knows that he's a snake who uses his cunning to milk every advantage he can out of the villagers. But everyone keeps quiet. When misfortune comes their way because of him and you ask them who is responsible, they look down at their feet and mutter something along the lines of "Well, you know as well as I do who it is, so why are you even asking?" And he is always screaming his head off at people, to disorient and confuse them with his bellowing. His screams fill the air with an echo, which follows you round like a dog. When he had led the last of the foals across the Devil's Bridge and mounted his horse, a scream rang out. It flew between the mountains with a powerful echo and the snow, hanging half-slumbering, broke from the crags and slopes, the Great Avalanche crashed down and carried him away, together with his gelding.

But where had this scream that filled and reverberated around the entire world come from? And who had produced it? Yes, yes, someone came over from the other side. And he screamed. There it is,

178

that is the answer. You foolish, fat-headed herdsman, now you will never hear either scream or echo. You have finally escaped. You are free.

He had been buried deep in the snow. It was silent. This silence had finally been granted to him so that he could think about who he had been. About Aspan the Herdsman.

Humans have come to understand nature, they know how to respect the earth's interior and they study its surface. So why is it that they are unable to get to know themselves properly? If there is something in this world that remains a mystery, it is we, humans. Isn't that how you lived, herdsman? What good have you done for others? And what have you done that is evil?

The bottomless sky bowed low over Aspan. The moon did not rise and the ravine quickly became shrouded in darkness. The mighty firs and cedars stood immobile as if awaiting a response.

What can I tell you? Aspan had whispered. *I can tell you that the frost will recede and that the end of the ringing winter would appear to be close at hand and spring will come early this year. And that if my puny soul remains intact, I will see in the new spring together with you. Even the very earliest spring comes only in April, the snow on the mountain peaks, in May. If you only knew how I yearn for this lazy Altai spring! I have always yearned for it. If only you knew how I yearn for my home! Wherever has the Kambar star[9] got to? There is the impassive Polar Star, already in its place, and there rises Sirius, but I can't see Kambar. She is hiding somewhere in the east. I knew back in the summer that this winter would be a harsh one when Kambar and the Moon had been in conflict. And now Kambar has done her worst, she has disappeared without a trace. She is clearly feeling ashamed for causing my torment. And yet there is Sirius, shining like a flame.*

Of all the stars in the celestial skies, Aspan the Herdsman had loved her above all others. And even though she had offered him no assistance, he had always looked at her with compassion, just as he did now. She was probably also bidding him farewell.

Well, farewell, then, Herdsman!

Godspeed, herdsman from the Yenbek farm! Now you will never sit on a steed or take the kuruk *into your hands again. How many pacers and how many argamaks, jumping to the moon, have you saddled?! And now you are dying in the snow, forgotten by everyone. Maybe you should have planned your life differently? Should you have become a mineworker in Zyryansk as your father advised you before his death? "If you have the strength, don't repeat the mistakes that I*

---

[9] In this context, a star in Kazakh astronomy used as a point of reference in navigation

have made in my life. The wolf cub follows the wolves not because it is intelligent, but out of a foolish, habitual fear. If you are strong, find your own path. I have grovelled with my eyes to the ground, like some grazing cattle, and I thanked life for that. Have you ever seen a bird fly far away from the hand that feeds it? Walk this earth, while you have your arms and legs; don't tell me the world under the sky is not a vast and spacious expanse. Is it really written on the faces of our kind that it is in our natures to go crawling in front of others?"

Well, Aspan had been too young to understand the meaning of these words, blurted out in the heat of the moment. However, he had not followed his father's advice, not because he had failed to understand these sad words, but because he couldn't leave the place where his umbilical cord had been tied. Like a fettered horse he couldn't leave, not from fear or a weak will; it was simply that he had had no wish to exchange his native hearth for places full to bursting point and leave the work he was accustomed to and that fate had allotted him, to take up other jobs.

Why do you now regret becoming a herdsman? Why do you now recall your father's words that he uttered so long ago and which you had seemingly forgotten?

But this had been only a passing weakness before it disappeared forever.

A mouse born in a mill does not fear the noise of the sails and the grindstone, Aspan had said. You see, as soon as you opened your eyes, you saw herds of horses and your father on his horse, forever chasing these herds. You drank kumiss, ate kazy-karta and zhal-zhaya; you have yet to let a piece of leavened bread pass your lips, eating only flatbread, and you have never travelled further than the regional centre. What you saw in your native nest is what you got. What disgrace can there be in repeating the life of one's father?!

Farewell, Herdsman!

All your life, be it long or short, you have never thrown caution to the wind, wearing your hat at a jaunty angle or giving yourself up to mindless merriment. You have not muddied the springs that gave rise to your fate and, although your head has split from pain many times and your legs ached from fatigue, you never cursed a single person and not once rushed to seize and grasp what was not yours. You thought: "There are plenty of people as it is in the world, striving for things they cannot do." You, a herdsman with a single horse, could not fathom the custom of those without flatbread picking at the pleasures of the table or those who dodder along on foot picking themselves a horse, those who are not ashamed of their pitiless nature and view others' good fortune with enmity. You have lived your life, without moaning or groaning. Throughout your life, you have believed that happiness and prosperity are things a person is allotted from birth, a

180

gift from Allah, prescribed to his family. You said: "It is better to have a finger-sized slice of luck than a mountain-sized slice of strength." You had strength, but you had no luck. Earning yourself bloody blisters, you pulled the cart of your fate and all of your colossal strength was spent on this simple, yet back-breaking work. Therefore, if there is a heaven, you will find a place there.

You never wanted to make peace in any shape or form with those, whose injustice tramples over the weak, who spit on the honour and conscience of others.

But how difficult that was! Your integrity actually subjugated you, your honesty pulling you back like a lasso around your own neck. You fought with the cunning, the deceitful and those secretly waging war. How many times did you think how simpler things were during the war: your enemy stood squarely in front of you and you held a weapon in your hands?

But you got the better of them, herdsman, believe me!

If time is water, then simple folk like you never change, like the stones on the river bed.

And are you and I as white as milk and pure as water? Are we without sin? Who knows for what sins this tormenting death has been sent to you? Yet, whatever your sins have been, great or small, try to die with dignity, without moaning and without screaming. There is no point in screaming; a scream does not make death any more bearable.

Oh, God! That scream. The voice that came crushing from the mountains in an avalanche was so similar to the cracked voice of the chairman... He would smash his fist on the desk in the office and scream and scream... Could it really have been him who went up into the mountains in the winter frost to destroy me?

I will not allow anyone to destroy me. And even if I have to be parted from that which distinguishes me from those that crawl along the ground—from my legs—I will not let it be the end of me. I am a human. I will bid you farewell forever, silent herdsman, who once stood his ground but who paid for it with his life. I say farewell and this will be our secret. But I will never forget you and, if I survive, I will bury you as is becoming a true dzhigit.

Oh, how warm this night is!

There is not a person on earth who can say how much strength I have left. Not a single person who can say what the difference is between the death of a famed scholar or an ambitious politician, striving for dominion over the world, and the death of a simple herdsman. If the death of mortals is as similar as their birth, then it is only their life that sets them apart. It is in life that the answer to all questions is concealed. You will not find it in the sky. My poor father – he dreamed of flying up into the sky, hoping to find eternal bliss and atonement for his sins. He believed this, otherwise, he

181

wouldn't have named me Aspan.

No, atonement and happiness are things only of this Earth. It is here that a person must affirm the truth. My enemy may strike me with stones, chase me into a trap and unleash cold and pain upon me, but while there is but one sip of water left in this world for me, I will not part from it.

For the first time, Aspan had realised that submitting to death like that, in obscurity and torment, when his food and water and his daily bread had not yet been exhausted, would mean submitting to his most hated enemy. To evil. He had wanted to stand and scream out, to tell his native land that he was alive. And perhaps the echo from this scream would have brought news to his village.

But Aspan's strength had entirely left him. He had opened his silent mouth, tried to raise his head, but not a single snowflake had trembled on his lashes.

"Oh, god, how tired I am!" he had sighed with incredible effort and forced himself to open his eyes.

The sky had been so close; just one small effort and he could have touched it.

Aspan looked beseechingly at the sky, shaking his head slightly as if rebuking the creator for giving him extremely long arms instead of wings.

Oh, to fly now; this earth has creatures that are able to fly, yet you were created without wings. And why do you need to fly, Aspan? It would be foolish to seek a land other than this one. You have yet to understand its true worth...

Yes, Aspan had to remain on this land, to endure, love and raise his son. He had released the Herdsman to the heavens, as death had released him from all sins... Aspan had no wish to blame anyone or to accuse the pernicious echo; he had called on the echo to see the Herdsman off on his final journey.

Farewell, Herdsman!

Aspan had gathered all this strength together and sat up. The mountains, wrapped in a white shroud, had surrounded him, the mighty trees lowering their white turbans, like old men, congregated for a service of the last rites.

"Farewe-e-ell!" Aspan had cried out protractedly. "Farewe-e-ell!"

"A-a-a," the mountains had echoed in reply.
"A-a-a," the ravine had echoed in reply.
"Farewell!"

It was by following this cry that the men who had gone out to search for him, had eventually found Aspan.

Bringing him into the wintering camp, they were struck by the monstrous smell coming from him. They removed Aspan's fur coat and

182

leather waistcoat and saw the tainted undergarments.

"The man is stronger than the hardiest of dogs," an old shepherd and the master of the camp had said. "We must undress him completely, rub him with snow and then apply badger fat, then he'll survive."

The herdsmen had been troubled by Aspan's boots, which they could not remove. They had to slice up the frozen leather with a knife. Seeing his legs they recoiled, wincing.

"How many days had been lying there under the snow?" the shepherd had asked.

"We don't know."

"I have never seen such an iron will; he is sure to survive."

"May your words prove to be true."

"Look, he is crying."

"No, he is not crying now; these are his tears that froze in his eyes and have now melted. Oh my, his child is so small, so small," the old man had kept repeating, massaging the huge, lifeless body that stank so unbearably.

Aspan saw a blue sheet before him and it swarmed with a horde of black ants, which crawled into his mouth, filling his nostrils, making it impossible to breathe. An intolerable torment and he could not rid himself of it; an unseen force spread him out, pressing him against something hot, sticky and damp. The sheet had then slid away. He had opened his eyes and seen Kamka and his frightened son, pressed close to her. A man in a white gown had stood, his arms crossed over his chest, looking intently at him. He was moving his lips.

"Where does it hurt?" eventually came the distant echo. "Where does it hurt? Where does it hurt?"

"I have an unbearable ache at the end of my legs," Aspan replied and turned his gaze towards his son. "Come here, my little foal," he called hoarsely, his voice breaking up. "Come to me, my one and only."

The boy's eyes were wide with terror and he clung for dear life to his mother and nothing could have torn him away from her.

He doesn't recognise me. My face is probably black and frostbitten, Aspan had thought, looking questioningly at the doctor, in expectation of words of comfort and solace.

The doctor said to him: "You'll live for a hundred years." Then, for some reason, he nodded Kamka to the door, indicating that she should leave.

Kamka had left with the little boy, the doctor following soon after them. There was a window opposite Aspan, with the radiant whiteness of the large yard beyond. Aspan saw a horse, harnessed to a low, wide sledge. He recognised the animal, even though she was covered with frost, with icicles hanging from her muzzle. It was a familiar horse, from his native village. So that meant he was in the district hospital and Kamka had come on this sledge.

Kamka then returned, pushing the boy ahead of her.

"Go to your father," she had ordered firmly.

How could he embrace his son, how could he hold him close when he had two bandaged clubs instead of arms? The little boy came up to his side and was as quiet as a frightened goat kid.

Aspan had looked at the window over his head and, blurred by tears, he had seen the white yard, the frost-covered horse and the blue smoke billowing from the chimney of the small house on the other side of the yard.

Never before had he noticed that tears tasted as sweet as honey and as fragrant as *kumiss*. Never had he seen the world so beautiful and never had he heard Kamka's voice sound so lovely. And all this had been granted to him by the herdsman, who had departed, never to return. However, only the two of them knew that and the day would come when his son, pressed close to his chest, would learn this too. He would also come to learn that wild animals, the sun, the cold and the earth wish no evil on humans and that one need only be beware of black-hearted people.

"God has looked after you and you are still alive," Kamka's voice reached him. "As for your infirmity, well, you'll get used to it and we'll soon carry on as before."

Aspan did not understand what she meant. His legs still ached unbearably.

"Kamka, hey, Kamka," he had called to her as he always did, "stop snivelling. We can't drink the water from your face and, anyway, I was never a handsome fellow. It would be better if you gave my toes a rub."

His wife had stood frozen to the spot and appeared a little strange.

What's up with her?! Is she afraid or something, or have the doctors told her not to? And why has she sat herself down on the bed so strangely, right on top of my legs?

He had wiggled his legs but Kamka had not stirred.

What is this? Has she no feeling, or has all this grief caused her to lose her reason?

He straightened himself up on his pillows and his son recoiled and froze, with the same strange look on his face.

What on earth is up with them?

"Can you get up, Kamka. My legs are hurting."

Kamka had jumped up. How strange: it was as if she had been sitting on an empty bed; as if there was nothing under the blanket.

"Kamka, Kamka, lift up the blanket."

Kamka had stood, locked as if in a stupor, but her chin

trembled. Then she had suddenly burst into tears as if she were at a funeral; the little boy, too, began to whimper quietly.

The doctor came in.

"But we agreed that you would try to hold yourself together," he said, displeased, "and now you've spoiled it all."

"But what does he have left that isn't spoiled?" Kamka had wailed. "Just look at him!"

The doctor had taken her by the shoulder and led her out of the ward.

Aspan looked at the folds of the blanket where his legs should have been and it suddenly occurred to him that they looked like the stomach of a slaughtered sheep.

"There was nothing else we could have done," the doctor had said tersely, returning to the ward. "You had multiple fractures and frostbite. It was a question of saving your life."

"My life?" Aspan had asked in surprise.

"Yes, yours, who else's?" the doctor had said with concern, looking him straight in the eye. "You do remember what happened to you, don't you?"

"Yes, I do."

"So why were you so surprised when I said it was a question of saving your life?"

"Yes, yes, quite right...my life is intact. But what on earth am I supposed to do with it?"

"You are a man, a *dzhigit*. How many men returned from the war with similar disabilities?"

"You don't need to tell me about the war. I saw it myself."

"So you are one of the lucky ones; you have escaped death twice."

"Better say: I *saw* it twice."

"If you like. But let me assure you: life is a great healer; everything will gradually be forgotten."

"Have you ever seen a person who forgot he had no legs?"

"I did everything I could..."

"Alright," Aspan had said, reaching for his shoulder with his bandaged hand, "the noose of fate is clearly something I cannot avoid. But I do have one request."

"Name it."

"Only please, don't be surprised... How can I put it..."

"Try telling me directly."

"Directly is not so easy. You won't understand what I am trying to say... it is a shame I was unconscious when you cut them off because I would have asked you to leave me the limbs that you took away."

The doctor flinched and once again looked long and hard into

Aspan's eyes, black and dark as a moonless night.

"I have my senses," Aspan had replied to this look, "and I would like to bury what is mine, only don't ask me why, because..."

"I understand," the doctor interrupted. "Yes, yes, like that hero from the old legend... but... but don't you go asking me about anything when I give them to you in your saddlebag."

"I won't," Aspan said wearily. The doctor left.

Aspan looked through the window. The horse and sledge were gone, so Kamka and the boy must have left.

So here you are on your own, Aspan. With only what has happened for company... You were created an argamak and now you are fated to crawl like a tortoise... Tell me, do you like this? Do you like remaining alive having paid such a price? You survived, so be joyful, have a laugh, sing a song. Why are you not singing or laughing? You are so full of energy, after all...

He grabbed hold of the bars on his bed head with his bandaged hands and bent them; blood had seeped through the bandages but, feeling no pain, he continued to bend the bars.

"What are you doing?" someone nearby had whispered. "Stop it, please, stop it."

Growling, Aspan had fought with the pieces of metal as if he was in a fight to the death with a wild animal.

A nurse grasped him by the neck and pulled at him with her weak arms, saying,

"Stop it, stop it."

"Get out of here!" Aspan growled.

"You need to save your energy. The worst is yet to come. Bend your will to serve yourself, just as you are bending those bars. You are a man, after all."

Then she went out.

What had she said? That the worst was yet to come? What could be worse than what has already happened? What had she said?

"Ainalaiyn!" he had cried, falling back limply onto the pillow. "Ainalaiyn!"

The nurse entered the ward and sat down on the edge of the bed.

"Tell me again what you just said."

"You know what I said," the girl said, looking at him with her enormous eyes, "there is not a person in the hospital who does not admire your courage. You performed an act of great bravery. If it were in my power, I would award you the title of Hero."

"Thank you, light of my eye, but the act of bravery was performed by another man and he is no longer here. As for me, all that remains for me is to face up to living the rest of my life as an ugly freak."

186

"I don't understand you," the girl said, her smooth brow frowning sadly. "Explain what you mean."

God, how sweet she is. Where is it that I have seen such a tender, touching creature...ah-h-h, at the pasture. Yes, that little goat Yelik... How wonderful, the marvel of nature lives on, passing from one creature to another, to be reborn.

"Don't be afraid, my dear, I simply wanted to say that all of my strength was spent ensuring my survival and now I have nothing left."

"I understand," the girl sighed, "but if only you knew how much the people need you! You have to teach them courage. It is strange, but your face is somehow familiar. I was on duty in the operating theatre, when..." She faltered.

"When they were cutting off my legs?"

"Yes... I cried so much. I felt as if you were an old relative of mine who I had playfully hugged around the neck as a child, and that you could protect me from evil and injustice. Oh, I thought so much about you! Are *dzhigits* like you born these days? Where have they gone? Girls my age think that they were either born too late or too early." She wiped away her tears on a piece of gauze she had pulled from the pocket of her gown and blew her nose like a child. "Forgive me for sharing my troubles with you. You need to get some rest." Then she bent over him and, imparting an aroma of fresh hay, newly drawn milk and something excitingly spicy that he did not recognise, she kissed him on the forehead. "Get some rest." She said and quietly left the ward.

A true marvel! What wonderful eyes and what a fragrance! Piquant, like a mountain poppy, how reminiscent of happiness and youth it was! So my feelings have not yet died altogether, it turns out.

Aspan closed his eyes. In his dream, a bird with the face of the girl from Sarmonke flew down to him and sat on a cedar twig. He wanted to get closer to her but she had flown off to a neighbouring tree, flapping her wings with effort. Again he tried to get nearer; he had really wanted to touch her, but she continually flew further away. Then he realised that he had entered a dead forest and was overcome with terror. The pain in his legs was intolerable; he suspected that he had no strength to go back. The deadwood surrounded him, pressing in from all sides. The bird disappeared. He rushed straight ahead, snagging his face and arms on the bare branches of the trees. There was something bright up ahead. Probably a mountain lake. He would rest there and wash his tired legs, aching from their wounds.

The lake was an unwelcoming leaden colour; it suddenly drew near, spreading out its banks and threatening at any moment to swallow him up in its cold waters. Aspan emitted a groan and woke up. His bewildered eyes surveyed the ward and in an instant, he remembered

187

everything...

"I have no legs," he had said loudly and calmly.

...After three months, full of sadness and anguish, had passed, Aspan was discharged from the hospital. All the doctors accompanied him to the cart. Or to be more precise, the hospital attendants had carried him in their arms while all the others walked to one side. They spoke cheerfully and slapped him on the back. Silently and unnoticed, the surgeon discreetly slipped something into the saddlebag. Their secret.

It was spring, bright but silent, like a modest bride.

"*A man who has not fallen from his horse will never become a brave and bold dzhigit.* This is a wise saying," the surgeon said quietly in farewell.

Trembling in the cart, Aspan looked at everything around him with insatiable eyes. How wonderful this world was! Why had he not noticed this before when rushing over it on his horse?

Kamka whipped the horse, she sat straight and did not turn to look back at him once. A strange woman. Aspan knew that his wife was choking with tears and anguish was tearing at her heart.

The travellers they met on the way greeted them with exaggerated politeness.

The fools: he had no need for their pity; they had no idea how strong he now was!

However, when the plumes of smoke over his native village came into sight, he felt a lump in his throat. Aspan cleared it and addressed Kamka's back:

"You might be better off sending me to a nursing home."

Kamka remained silent.

"So why don't you take me? It's not far. I will occupy myself with simple work. I'll carve wooden spoons and children's toys. I think we still have some spoons at home that some disabled people made. Decent spoons they are too."

Kamka remained silent.

"What sort of bird would want to perch on a rotten old stump, anyway?"

Kamka said nothing but just lashed at the horse harder and more frequently. The cart shook about on the stones, throwing its passengers from side to side.

"What has the poor horse done to deserve such a beating? You'd be better off beating me instead."

Kamka remained silent. Where had this usually teary-eyed, restrained woman now gained this strength?

"Leave me here!" Aspan had cried. "You hear? I don't want to go home!"

Kamka pulled on the reins, bringing the horse to a stop and

188

turned around sharply, her hair tousled by the wind, her face burning and her eyes swollen.

"Aspan," she said calmly, "don't go biting my head off; I am tormented enough as it is. You are not the first person to become a cripple; misfortune has befallen both of us. And if you have had to suffer up until today, now it is I who must suffer. If you die, I will bury you as is fitting. If you don't die, you will live with me until my dying day. So stop working yourself up and stop badgering me as if I was the one who brought the avalanche down upon your head. God has sent us misfortune and you must take the weight of this misfortune on your shoulders. I have the strength to survive your infirmity and the abuse that fate has hurled at us. But don't you go badgering me."

She then turned her back on him and struck the horse. Rocking back, Aspan had barely been able to keep his balance, grasping the sides of the cart.

Kamka's words and her resolution had shocked him. Was this the same silent shadow that he had given so much grief all his life? He had shown no pity, no affection; he could still not completely forget the other girl, the one from Sarmonke.

And she had put up with it all and had gone about her business placidly, never standing up to him. Now he had seen a different woman, perhaps one who did not love him, one who had not forgotten the grievances, but a real friend; he had seen the fire in her eyes, her forceful nature, her strength, her willingness to withstand the trials of life, while his screams and demands appeared to be nothing but pitiful buffoonery. He recalled the words of the attractive nurse. *Be patient. The greatest challenge is to overcome yourself,* she had said.

Kamka had overcome herself and she had overcome the old pain, the hurt of her jealousy and offended female vanity. Now it was his turn. He needed to become a truly different man. After all, it was in that icy silence that he had experienced his own death...and his second coming. Life was what lay ahead and only he could fulfil his duty and obligations before the Herdsman.

Near the forest, very close to the village, he called to his wife:

"Kamka, hey, Kamka. Hold the horses for a little!"

"What now?"

"Leave me here and go and get me a shovel."

"What for?" she asked, disgruntled. "What did you forget at the cemetery?"

"I want to bury what was once mine," Aspan said quietly.

"A-a-ah...yes, I quite forgot. The doctor spoke about that." She scuttled about, trying to avoid his gaze, jumped from the cart and presented her shoulder to him. "Hold on to me and lower yourself down slowly. Carefully, that's right... You're not in pain are you?"

He hung like a child on his wife's back and she carried him to

189

few small hummocks nearby and sat him down carefully on the tender grass.

"Wait here." She jumped up to the front of the cart, lashed the horse and dashed off to the village.

When his body first touched the ground, he flinched all over: *The surgeon reminded me of that wise old saying with good reason. I have fallen from my horse and my god, how cold the earth is!*

He drew the saddlebag close and crawled, dragging it behind him. By the time he reached his father's grave, the sweat was pouring off him, filling his eyes.

Aspan passed his hand over his face paying reverence to his relatives. His hand was soaking wet. He ripped up a blade of young grass, placed it in his mouth and chewed on the still flavourless, tender shoot.

The trundling of a cart could be heard from the direction of the village and a cloud of dust rolled along the road.

Oh, my poor thing, she is flying like a bird. For the first time, he thought about his wife with a feeling of tenderness and gratitude. Kamka had been driving standing up, the wind fluttering the ends of her long headscarf as she went and it looked as if a pair of white wings were carrying her over the ground.

Aspan could not tear his eyes away from the handsome, winged woman, rushing towards him – his wife.

"What are you looking at me like that for?" she asked, hurriedly rearranging the plaits in her tousled hair. "The entire village is waiting for you."

Aspan remained silent.

"Well, where shall I dig?"

"Dig near to my father, but not too close. Better leave a space big enough for me."

"You are just saying the first thing that comes into your head."

"And you have learned to speak as bold as brass." The woman leaned her chin on the shaft of the shovel and smiled.

"I'm doing it on purpose to stop myself bursting into tears."

She cast back a lock of hair from her brow, hitched her skirt up high and had begun digging.

Aspan was astounded by the smoothness and whiteness of her slender legs; she bent her tall frame easily and her black, wavy hair fell loose, sometimes covering her face and sometimes lying in a thick, glossy wave along her back, revealing to Aspan's astonished eyes her dark cheeks, flaming crimson and her shining, coal-black eyes.

How could he have not noticed over the last twenty years that the woman lying next to him in his arms was so stunning?! What with marrying so suddenly and with constantly looking after the horses, he had become blind to the person living by his side. He had yearned for

190

the girl on the other side of the river; he had not been able to forget his first love and this had wounded his wife's soul. Perhaps that was why, after the birth of their first child, Kamka had wandered about as if she were unmarried. No one had understood the reason why and no one had bothered to ask.

Aspan was convinced that, having lost his legs, he would lose his male vigour and this had perhaps been the thing that had tormented him the most during his sleepless nights in the hospital.

Now, though, he unexpectedly sensed what he had felt so long ago with the girl from Sarmonke. He shivered and gasped as if he was lifting the blanket that had covered his loved one.

"Hey, what's got into you?" Kamka had asked, frightened, stabbing the shovel into the earth. "You've probably caught a fever."

"Yes, that's right... a fever. Come over her, my love, and kiss me on the forehead."

Kamka had fallen to her knees before him and Aspan had embraced her with his mighty arms, pulling her close so tightly that she moaned.

Aspan would always remember the smell of the freshly dug earth and the scream of the lark in the sky above and the happy scream of his wife in response to his passion, and the light, semi-translucent, frosting of the clouds in the pale sky, and placing his head on Kamka's knee, he had lain there without an ounce of strength, and she had stroked his face and hair, and touched his lips with her fingers; her cool tears dropping onto him like sweet and blessed raindrops.

Together they buried the saddlebag under a mound of earth and firmly planted the *kuruk* at its head.

In a snowy February, Kamka gave birth to a girl and, a year later, also in February, to another. They grew peacefully and cheerfully like a spring day in May. The youngest of the daughters, Malika, amazed everyone with her incredible beauty while still a small girl and with her peculiar speech and manners like of no-one else from those parts. For nights on end she would sit at her books with the lamp lit while, on one occasion, Kamka showed Aspan several sheets of paper, covered with columns of handwritten lines. And each of these lines had ended with similar sounding words. Aspan explained that these were *poems* and instructed his wife not to touch them. "This happens with girls, but it will pass," he explained to his frightened wife.

* * *

The two travellers, the chairman of the collective farm and the stock breeder, were moving through the snowy-white valley. They were hurrying to the herdsmen on the Alatai, who were being held captive by the deep and protracted snowfall.

191

Their horses were at their wit's end. Aman's white steed would jump awkwardly as if remembering the days when he had been a dashing colt and, there and then, collapse into the snow. The stock breeder's wise gelding continued to batter its way against the endless obstacle of the snow, but he, too, was on his last legs.

Nevertheless, judging by the furrow that crossed the valley, the horsemen had covered a reasonable distance. After noon, the grey clouds that had concealed the sky dispersed and the sun appeared. The snow sparkled in its rays, a million mirror-like shards glistening.

The two men, however, pulled their hats lower; the white stallion, having napped, suddenly lurched to the side in a startled manner and then calmed down, breathing heavily.

"When class differences are finally erased," joked the stock breeder, "will all farm chairmen sit upon mighty stallions with their guns hanging nonchalantly over their shoulders, while lowly types like me trail along behind them dragging the skis."

"Let's swap, if you have taken such a liking to him," Aman replied darkly. "Your gelding would suit me just fine."

"Are you trying to tell me that a *dzhigit* like you could possibly grace the saddle of a yearling like mine?"

"How can I possibly rely on you if you are going to be forever needling me?!" said Aman, seriously aggrieved.

"On a journey as tough as this, I thought a joke would help us through. But if you don't like what I say, I will hold my tongue."

"And rightly so," muttered Aman.

"To be serious, though, I think we should stop for a rest. And so should they," said Erkin, nodding at the horses. "My gelding is on his last legs. It is getting increasingly difficult to keep up with you."

"Yes, perhaps you are right."

While hurrying along, they had disappeared in an instant in a narrow tunnel of snow. Erkin pulled several balls of *kurt* from his coat pocket.

"And here is lunch, *aga*."

Freely salivating, they chewed on the *kurt* in silence. The horses were frozen as if they had been stunned.

"We're not going to make it to Alatai on the horses. It would appear mine has given up the ghost."

"And what if we leave the horses here and head out on our skis?"

"That is not going to be a solution."

The sun, having risen over the white-topped mountains to a noose's height, stood motionless, slowing a little before sliding down and hiding once more behind the same peaks.

A deathly cold and silence hung all around.

"We're like two mice in a sack of flour," Erkin laughed.

"Only instead of flour, it's snow that we can't fight our way out of."

"The sun is going to set at any moment and we haven't even reached the Devil's Bridge, where my father was caught in an avalanche."

"On what side is it?" asked Erkin.

"If we go straight on, it is not far."

"But we'll need to take the concrete bridge! The Devil's Bridge is really dangerous."

"We may need it," Aman drawled incoherently, "But it is twice as far."

"I have still never actually seen this famous Devil's Bridge of yours, although I've been living in these parts for two years now."

"Why would you need to see it? There's nothing good about it," sighed Aman.

"But there are so many stories about it, and they're all terrifying."

"My father once said, 'At least once in his life, every man has to pit himself against the Devil's Bridge. And it has to be crossed. Only those without fear will make it to the other side in one piece.'"

"Why?"

"When you cross, he said it's as if you have a devil sitting on one shoulder and an angel on the other. And if you have sinned heavily in this deceitful world, the devil on the left shoulder will eventually overcome the angel sitting on the right. And this will lead to misfortune."

"And do you believe this?" Erkin asked.

Sometimes he confused the *tu* and the *vous* forms of address because Aman sometimes seemed one of the lads; they were almost of the same age, after all. But at others, though, he seemed as wise as an old *aqsaqal*.

And at this moment, looking at his harsh, hardened face, Erkin thought that, despite their probably having been born in the same year, Aman seemed to have a knowledge of life and people that was somehow unattainable for Erkin.

Aman lit up a cigarette.

"You asked if I believed it? I don't know. I mean, I don't think my father was talking literally about good and evil. That you should never succumb to evil because if you did, you would allow it to devour all that was good in you. My father was convinced that, as the existence of the world is everlasting, so are good and evil everlasting."

"Everlasting?" asked Erkin pensively and looked searchingly at Aman.

He had been working for two years with this mighty man and he had not once seen him angry or raise his voice. He would not alter his calm temperament. It appeared that this immovability was a quality inherent in his family. Malika was much the same... How could one see into her soul and understand... Or how could one understand Aman's explosive behaviour of the day before at the herdsmen's wintering camp? As if responding to his thoughts, Aman slowly said:

"I was not restrained and I blame myself... My father often says to me: *Son, never raise your voice; shouting and screaming will get you nowhere. I am the victim of a scream and this is a burden I will always have to carry with me.* The fact that I failed to heed my father's advice has been gnawing away at me ever since yesterday."

"One of the herdsmen riled you for some reason. I think he was doing it on purpose and, if you don't mind me saying, it was precisely for this reason that you should have held yourself in check. It is hard, perhaps harder than anything, to fight against the hatred you have for another person."

"There are two brothers and it is unclear which of them is worse."

"I am still an outsider in your village and there is much that I still don't understand. However, if what I heard is correct, someone deliberately screamed out just as Aspan-*aga* was crossing the bridge and this caused the avalanche. Do you know who it was?"

"I can only guess."

Something flinched in Aman's face and Erkin realised the conversation he had started was too serious. But they were alone in the midst of a white silence and before them lay a testing journey. The stock breeder loved this man's sister and could not understand her. In the parts where he hailed from, younger men were allowed to speak openly and bluntly and so this is what he did:

"Well, I think that one should look truth in the eye. Are you really still afraid someone might take revenge on you? Can it be that you fear retaliation? Believe me, you shouldn't leave a pot on the fire with the lid closed. Especially when there's a foul smell coming from it. Even the young lads could sense the smell coming out of it yesterday."

"The youngsters have their own journey to make."

"But that is the point: they aren't setting off on a new path; they are continuing along the same path that their elders have trod before them."

"People haven't changed for thousands of years."

"No, each generation is replaced by a different, new generation."

"In what way are they different?"

"They base their actions on reason and not a scream that they do not understand. Take the example of your father. It was in someone's interests to kill the famished horses that he had been driving and then submit a false report about the incident. The best way to do

194

this was to dress it up as an act of God and the fact that your father suffered as result... well, they could just say that it was all just an accident. Yet there is nothing accidental about a scream that generates an echo causing an avalanche."

"Oh, brother, even a dog couldn't tell where it came from so how can we be certain whose scream it was."

"But your father thinks differently, or else he wouldn't have buried something secret in that grave that he visits?"

"Yes, you are right there. No-one knows what he buried in the grave and that is not what is important. What is important is the reason why my father pays his respects to this grave."

"One should never forget the dead – and your father is right not to do so. Only the dead leave no trail on the ground. Their trail remains only in our memory."

"Then you have understood everything, brother. Well, it is time we were off."

"Wait a moment, let's have a think first."

"There's no time to think; we have to move on."

"Our horses haven't been fed since yesterday. They are exhausted. Here's what I propose: we should travel on our skis and lead them by the reins."

"Alright, that is a good idea."

The two men got up and looked each other directly in the eye. This short stop on their journey had changed many things. What had been said and understood between them had closed the distance that had previously existed and it was as if the long, difficult journey, fraught with impending misfortune that lay ahead of them to the winter pastures in Alatai, had also changed.

When they untied the skis, Erkin burst out laughing:

"How inventive that Alke is! For some reason, he has made holes in the ends of the skis and tied twine to them. But I can't imagine what for."

"He did the right thing, if they get buried in the snow, you only have to pull them by the twine and you are free to carry on your way. Look, this is how it's done," and Aman moved forward, leading his white horse by the reins.

"Amazing!" Said Erkin, awkwardly following after him.

"There are no such things back in the desert where I come from. How great this country is. We live in just one republic and you probably don't know how to ride a camel; while I have never seen snow before and I can barely ski either."

The short winter's day disappeared beyond the mountains. Their breath settled on their faces and the fur edges of their hats as white frost and the cold air burned their lungs, but the travellers continued onward. The horses were the first to give up. Aman even

195

lashed the white horse a couple of times. Never having experienced such shame before, the noble animal rushed forward, flattening the snow and Aman could barely keep up with him. Soon, however, the stallion came to a standstill, his sweating flanks in a terrible state. It was evident that no amount of thrashing would persuade him to move forward.

"He has sweated his last drop," said Aman.

"Me too," said Erkin with a forced grin.

"The path is too steep," Aman explained. "Let's rest a little and I will go on alone; you stay here near the horses as they are unable to continue. Soon either Alke's herdsmen will arrive or I'll return from Alatai."

"You don't need to reassure me. I am not afraid. It's just that I don't understand why you should be the one to go on. After all, I am the lighter of the two of us."

"But I ski better. If we were in the desert, you would be going but this is my land and I am better acquainted with its paths and secrets."

"In times like this, honest people draw lots."

"No, brother, this is not the time to play games with fate; there are people waiting. But if you're afr..." Aman checked himself. "If you don't want to remain here alone, we can set off together and entrust the horses to god."

"Even God would have his work cut out prising horses as wonderful as these away from me." The much-vaunted horses stood quietly and listless with their stomachs drawn in tight.

"I don't know about God, but they would certainly make easy prey for the wolves and the bears. By the way, I'll leave the gun with you."

"And how are you going to fight off the wolves? Are you going to invite them to a boxing match?" asked Erkin.

"The wolves will come here. They find livestock much more interesting than people. They might come in a pack, so you won't be able to go to sleep. If you're going to die, you may as well be awake to greet it, don't you think?" said Aman, laughing hoarsely. "I bet you're regretting latching on to me back at the office, right?"

"I regret not latching on to you sooner."

Aman fell silent. He was confused. In his parts, it was not the thing to voice one's feelings so openly, but he knew that the young *dzhigit* was being sincere and he knew the anguish and terror that he would face when they parted ways. And they would part very soon. The meagre supper in the snow was coming to an end. Only a few balls of *kurt* were left in reserve. *How can I leave him more without him noticing; after all, either I have a warm camp with plenty of food waiting up ahead, or...well, or I won't be needing any* kurt *at all. And*

196

he has a long, lonely night to get through. He is not accustomed to these places and the howling of the wolves will sound to him like the cries of hell.

Aman looked at the stock breeder's face, as pale as moonlight, and he thought that grim responsibilities were separating him now, perhaps forever, from the man who had managed to say what was so important and vital for his troubled soul to hear. His father too had told him what was important and essential through the example of his life, which had been broken in two. This was true, but it had unfortunately been only half the truth, while this outsider, who would remain in this place without fear, knew the other half.

"Aman-*aga*," he heard the quiet voice and gathered his wandering thoughts together.

"Yes, brother."

"I understand that you have to test not only yourself..."

"I have to get to Alatai."

"But you also want to find out if life has changed; if the people have changed..."

"You are talking nonsense. It's the moon talking. The moon plants the most absurd notions in people's heads."

"There are only you and I here in these mountains. And if anything were to happen, you would be within your rights to place the blame at my feet. But know this: if anyone dares to chase after you with evil intentions, I will fight to my last drop of blood. I will not let them pass. Go boldly and don't think bad thoughts."

"You've been to the cinema too often," laughed Aman.

"Don't laugh; hear me out. You did not give me your permission to marry your sister."

"I do now. When we return we will lay on a feast."

"Maybe you think there is bad in me..."

"I might, but I won't."

"Don't think bad thoughts. Your courage now is my courage. And know this: I will wait for you here. I will wait for you here, come what may."

"Well, then let God grant we meet again, brother." Aman stepped forward and embraced Erkin tightly.

"Oh, you're going to make me cry now," said Erkin, turning around.

"Make yourself a shelter from the snow. You have enough cartridges to last a good while unless you lose your head and fire them all off into the snow. All the best."

Erkin watched as the dark figure, silent as a shadow, slipped away over the virgin snow, shining silver in the moonlight.

The moon is on the left, he thought. *That is a good omen.* Then he suddenly had second thoughts and shouted out:

"*Aga*! You're going the wrong way! You are veering off to the side!"

"I am taking the straight route, to shorten the journey!" replied a hoarse voice.

"So you've decided to cross the Devil's Bridge without me?"

"Yes."

"It's too dangerous!"

"It's no more dangerous than it is for you to remain here. Don't call out to me anymore; I won't reply."

For a long time, Erkin followed the dot that became darker and darker in the white snow, until it faded from view. He turned back and immediately a terrible sadness overcame him. He felt as if his soul was empty and he was an orphan.

Two years earlier, he had arrived on assignment at the village of Yenbek. After the hungry steppe of Moyynkum, with its crooked saxauls, sweltering heat and sand that crunched on the teeth, the beauty of the Altai had been overwhelming. Now, though, looking at the giant, black mountains and sensing how the icy embrace of the frost was taking an ever tighter hold, he began to miss the dusty heat of Moyynkum. The horses, covered with blankets of ice, were pressed up against one another, forming what looked like a strange monument to a two-headed monster.

The awareness that there was not a living soul for many kilometres all around, that those who were close were sitting trapped in the snow and the thought of Aman, skiing alone in the moonlight, chilled his heart more than the frost itself. Erkin jumped up and fitfully began to shift the snow around him, in order to dig a deep den for himself. He got so carried away that he cleared the snow right back to the soil. The horses pricked up their ears, sensing the *tebenyovka*. Pleased that he had something to occupy himself with, Erkin madly scattered the snow, clearing an ever larger patch of land. The horses helped him. The smell of the earth excited them and chased away their frosty slumber. They moved the snow with their hooves and munched greedily on the grass.

It was as if the still hands on the clock of life had begun to tick loudly once more. Erkin removed the saddle from the stallion and then the saddlecloth and placed it on top of the saddle. It proved a great armchair to spend his night of vigil. But how would he occupy himself? Howl at the moon? He decided to sing a song but, as luck would have it, despite shining at talent evenings when studying at the institute, he couldn't recall a single line. He would have to sing something lively and contemporary, but apart from the line *You'll make it all right, the future looks bright*, he couldn't remember a thing. But something stirred indistinctly in his heart, a forgotten motif of some kind, like small swallows and childhood memories that had settled on the taut strings of his soul.

Erkin closed his eyes and broke into song. He saw the desert and his mother, with her face, prematurely aged and burnt by the sun. The bracelets on her slender arms tinkled as she rocked him, his white cap slipping over his face; how he wanted to reach out and touch it.

How had she managed to raise five children all on her own? He had never once stopped to think about it. Of course, the state had helped with some benefits and they were able to travel to the summer camps for nothing, but who could measure her loneliness when there was no-one to ask for advice and no-one to complain to? All five of them were boys, too. Just see how you'd manage! Their mother was a proud woman and no-one ever saw her shed tears. Once in town, however, when he had taken her for a check-up, the optician had said: *You, my dear, have probably been crying an awful lot.* So, she must have cried at night, then. Erkin's voice rang out with a drawn-out yearning. Suddenly, from the Tar River, he was answered by a protracted howl. The horses started, raised their heads and neighed, rolling their eyes in a frenzy.

Erkin jumped up, grasped them by the reins and stroked them. The poor things, they had nowhere to run, cooped up in this narrow tunnel of snow.

Again, the deathly silence fell. *Perhaps we'll get through this,* thought Erkin, *and, at the end of the day, I have the gun. But what about Aman-aga, all alone and with no gun? Can it be true that a curse hangs over the men of his family? Poor Malika!*

For the first time, he thought about his girl. But could he even call her his own? They met only seldomly and their conversations were strange. Could it be that he would never capture her soul or comprehend her thoughts? Now he knew that such a singular man as Aman must have an equally singular sister. Was she thinking of them now, he wondered. Did she pity them?

When Erkin had first arrived in Altai, a blessedly peaceful autumn had reigned. In his native Moyynkum, nature was green for only a short while and it was as indistinct as a sweet dream.

A dry wind blew almost all year round and the sky was a grey colour, merged with the scorched earth; the dusty saxauls were indifferent both to the heat and to the first, sparse snowfalls. The people were much the same. They lived as if independent of nature, preserving an age-long pattern, but the essence of their nature and relationships was as reliable and uniform as the unchanging state of the desert. But the diversity here made his head spin. Some trees were yellow, others were brown and red; a blue sky hung overhead and the caps of the mountains and the ribbons of foam on the wild Bukhtarma shone white. And the people were strange, no two people alike. They did not cherish their kinship, relying mostly on the strength of their

199

muscles and on flattery; and they were quite incapable of being underhand: they were prepared to voice the harshest truths, even to their own grandfather, like the wild elk that roamed these parts their pride and plain-speaking meant they had doomed themselves to a life of much solitude.

In these parts, wherever you look there are mountainous, rocky peaks. And there is no expanse, stretching beyond the horizon.

So, concluded Erkin, *they have no hope for anything beyond their lives and their day-to-day concerns. This is where these bold natures and this ambition comes from.*

Missing home, where a wooden trestle bed was like a feather-and-down mattress, Erkin had planned to leave on numerous occasions but, while making plans to depart, he had managed to become attached to these mysterious people, living deep in the ravines of the Altai. People only came here by the occasional aeroplane, which sometimes only arrived every few months. The railway was sixty kilometres away; to the south, the border was close and beyond that lay a foreign land and a foreign people.

Friendship here was a rare thing and, therefore, it was valued above all else. Erkin, though, was alone. Once an old shepherd at the summer pasture had said to him: "You are a bird, arrived from warmer parts. If you want to remain here, you'll have to get used to the forty-degree frosts and much more besides. The people, too, will appear cold to you at first. But when you do grow accustomed to them, you'll find yourself a home here and you'll find warmth. The Altai is a thing of wonder; the people are honest and direct. It is true what they say about them being like the steppe ribbon snake: the moment they are born, they slither off in different directions and live their own, separate lives. If they remain together, they will eat one another. However, when they grow up, they earn their place in life and find one another anew and then join up together again. Our people pester no-one, but if an outsider were to aggrieve them, they will join forces, hound the wrongdoer and kill him. So, beware and try not to injure the soul of an innocent person. If you decide to plant roots here, the soil is truly bountiful. Get married and no-one will demand bride-money from you. The Altai girls find themselves a worthy husband and marry for free. You have seen that for yourself. People come here from Uzbekistan and take the girls away with them. Remember this, son: it is no easy matter growing an alien tree on Altai soil. Only strong trees survive, trees that can withstand the cold and other adversities."

What was strange was that the herder had voiced all this in the presence of his beautiful daughter. Initially, Erkin had decided that the old man had been making a hint about his daughter, but it later became clear that she had already been betrothed to someone from the neighbouring village. Like most men, Erkin had been wary of the

200

herder's frankness but, learning that she was already spoken for, he had regretted the missed opportunity.

The father had been wise, the girl, beautiful and sprightly. She remained in his memory for a long time until he set eyes on Malika.

The spring here was always chaotic and sleepless. The sheep, locked in their pens for the entire winter, would creep out to pasture as soon as the black earth came into view. They were gaunt, their bellies hanging low to the ground and their hindquarters protruding. Soon after, when the earth has not yet managed to dry out, the lambing season begins in earnest. The houses are empty and not even the voices of the girls or the cries of children can be heard. However, the gorges, bald peaks and deep valleys are full of young girls, scurrying everywhere with long-legged lambs under their arms. The pockets of all their dresses are full of cloths of various colours.

This is *sakman*, the lambing season. It is a difficult time that never seems to end, with work that is dirty and carried out at high altitude. The lamb has to be delivered, both it and the mother marked with identical rags, and the lamb taught to suckle. Bleating can be heard all around and the lambing girls are out on their feet, running from one sheep to the next; their dresses are filthy and their faces, haggard.

One day during the lambing season, Erkin had dropped into the library to see if all the girls had left for the *sakman*, as he had been instructed by Aman Tengrinov the chairman. Aman was particularly insistent that the head librarian should be out helping with the lambing as well.

When Erkin entered the library, it was completely empty. All he could hear were some steps in the gloom of a passage between the bookshelves. Erkin had waited a little and then headed to the place where the steps had been coming from. A girl stood there with her back to him.

"Hello!" Erkin had said loudly.

"Hello," the girl answered without turning around.

"I've come to call you out for the lambing."

"For *what*?"

"For Kumar's flock."

"Alright. I was there last year as well."

"See you, then." Erkin turned sharply and left.

Well, a fine upbringing they give them here...she didn't even bother to turn around and acknowledge me, he thought to himself of the recalcitrant librarian. He did, however, remember the knot of heavy hair on her slender neck, the earring with the pink stone in the pink lobe of her small ear and her strong chin.

Later, when he was travelling around the flocks to check how the lambing was going, he heard someone's pitiful voice in a small hollow. The tender voice, so sorrowful that a softer-hearted person might have burst into tears, had beseeched: *Oh come on, my dear, come on...* Erkin had bent back a bush and seen the girl; sitting on her haunches she had been pushing a lamb under her mother with a red string tied to its quivering, slender leg. The girl was so engrossed in what she was doing that she didn't hear Erkin approaching. He froze. The sheep had mutely turned its muzzle away, refusing to help the girl. The girl's imprecations became increasingly pitiful and sad and, finally, the voice had reached such point of entreaty that Erkin's heart missed a beat. Even the stupid sheep finally understood her requests and accepted the lamb. With a sigh of relief, the girl got up and straightened herself. Seeing Erkin and feigning indifference, she said:

"Oh, it's you..."

"Yes, it's me."

"I didn't hear you coming. That daft mother is pushing her own child away; every time I have to persuade her. I just don't know what to do."

Her matte, blackcurrant eyes gazed questioningly at the stock breeder.

"Bring a cat; this sometimes works, the mother becomes jealous of the other animal and accepts her lamb out of jealousy," Erkin had said.

"No," the girl had smiled, "a mother that accepts her offspring like that will never feed it properly."

"Then I see no solution."

"Patience."

"Sorry, but I don't know you, sister."

"Perhaps you would have recognised me straight away if another young man had been here. That sometimes works." The girl laughed. "I am the head librarian."

"Ah...the thought initially crossed my mind, but I never actually saw your face. What is your name, sister?"

The girl had looked at him unusually, directly and boldly.

"I see you are not from around here."

Wow, how beautiful she is! Erkin had thought, but said something more carefree instead:

"What a talent you have for guessing."

"It's really very simple. Our young men here never address a girl as *sister*. We only use that term for our blood relatives. If you want to learn my name, have a look in your notebook."

"But why? I have worked it out anyway. You are Tengrinova. But my book will certainly help me with your name... Aha...here it is: Malika Tengrinova, Aspan's daughter."

But the girl had already grabbed the lamb and, driving the sheep ahead of her, set off towards the sheep pen.

"Hey, sister! Malika, what are you doing?" he had called after her.

She hadn't even turned around.

Oh, it is no easy matter cosying up to the girls round here! Erkin had muttered with annoyance and got up onto his horse.

From then on, as if by chance, his horse would turn up at Kumar's flock on a daily basis. The other lambers noticed this and began giggling and gossiping quietly. Malika held her head high and presented no occasion for them to converse alone and this baffling pride had bewildered Erkin.

Perhaps I am just too modest, he had guessed, *which makes me laughable, maybe?* But no. Malika's eyes had looked at him coldly, as if scrutinising him.

Erkin had taken out his annoyance on his long-maned steed, thrashing him mercilessly as he had left the pen. Somehow he arrived at dusk. The day's flurry of activity had died down and the lambing girls had evidently left for the hut to rest. When he opened the door, he saw a simple table laid out, lit by a kerosene lamp.

The girls and young women greeted him with exaggerated good humour and giggling.

"Come and take the place of honour. We've heard you've been singing our praises here, there and everywhere and for that, we would be delighted to offer you some supper," the young woman, who was evidently the ringleader, invited him. An infant had dozed off in her arms. Pretending not to notice the joke at his expense, Erkin had replied with a serious "Thank you".

The young woman covered up her breast—she had evidently just been feeding her child—and pushed a bowl towards Erkin. The girls giggled and pinched one another. Malika was not among them.

This was a bad idea to sit down with them; the jokes and mockery will only stack up.

"You've butchered yourselves too lean a sheep," Erkin had said, trying the *surpa* mutton broth.

"We wouldn't have minded if you'd given us a fat one," one of the lambers responded spiritedly.

"Have I ever refused you anything?" Erkin asked, affronted.

"Of course not," the young woman with the child appeased him, "only you won't find a sheep in these parts good enough for a decent *surpa*; all the mothers have wasted away. And in any case, we're eating heifer and there is about as much fat on a heifer as you'll find in a fisheye. Oh, how we pity ourselves..."

"Who's on duty today?" Erkin interrupted.

"Malika," the girls clucked. "We've called her to eat three times now, but she won't come. She loves her books too much; she's forever with her head in her books."

203

Erkin ate slowly and at intervals. He wasn't going to let them see him jump up and rush off to search for Malika, so he continued chewing slowly in the stuffy room, amidst all the female chatter.

The old cook scolded the young girls for complaining that the sheep they'd been given hadn't been fat enough and told them about the hunger she had suffered during the war. She had had to gather the leftover ears of corn in the fields after the harvest and she had even had to give these to the authorities; after all, it would have been dangerous to be found hoarding any secret stores for the children's flatbread. The girls listened to her words with little attention and, like well-fed geese, they were silent and drowsy. The lamplight fell on their faces. At times someone would open their heavy eyes and, glancing about vacantly, would drop off once more.

Erkin suddenly felt an unbearable pity for these young, pretty girls, who were so worn out by their work. And they were dressed in heavens knows what: canvas boots and dirty padded jackets over their dresses; their headscarves askew, revealing hair that had not seen a comb or brush for a long time.

Catching his eye, the young mother spoke curtly:

"We are going to bed now. There's no place for you here, so you'd best be going. Godspeed! Tell the office that the newborns are all intact, the sheep stock too. And get them to bring us a film to watch."

"Okay, auntie, I'll pass it on."

"Thank you. And I'm not your auntie."

"Do excuse me. Thank you." Erkin rose from the table.

How are they all going to fit in here? he mused sympathetically. *No, I'll have to speak to the chairman; the conditions here for the lambing girls are wholly unsuitable.*

After the stuffy air of the little room, the fragrant spring night went to his head. Erkin stopped on the threshold and lifted his head to the starry sky.

Oh, when will the day come when there will be no difference in the quality of people's lives? In town, girls like these are smartly dressed, sit in cafés, smoke cigarettes and eat ice cream!

His horse whinnied, beckoning his master. Erkin embraced him around the neck and stood by his side for a while.

The snow on the mountain peaks shone with a phosphorescent blue colour; the dark firs, never changing their austere appearance, were frozen motionless.

Their remoteness and beauty reminded Erkin of Malika. There they live, battling resiliently with their harsh life, withstanding everything and, it seems, they must employ every ounce of their strength just to remain standing. But stand in their shade on a hot day and you will sense the fragrance of their nectar, you will be covered by a cool blue, immersed in the bountiful happiness of tranquillity and

204

beauty.

A cold wind blew in from the mountains. How strangely changeable the weather was here and how peculiar the stars in the black sky: they circle and circle as if dancing on the spot. Erkin stopped where he was and then headed off to the sheep pen. The wolfhound got up from his place lazily, half sniffed him and, seemingly satisfied that he had completed an important assignment, returned to his place and lay down. The shepherds' dogs were also strange creatures: they greet any outsider with a malevolent bark, teeth bared, ready to rip and tear, and then just as quickly calm down and show complete indifference.

When Erkin opened the doors to the pen, the sheep fixed their gaze on him from the gloom like a multitude of shining green lights. Malika sat on a low bench, busy with a new-born lamb. She was squeezing its muzzle and blowing into its ears. She was so absorbed in her work that she didn't even turn around at the sound of the footsteps.

"Good evening," Erkin said, clearing his throat. "It seems I am an opportune guest: the mother has given birth to twins."

"Watch you don't jinx them. What are you doing here in the middle of the night?"

"Rustling sheep."

"Well, technically they're yours already, so you can run off with the entire flock for all I care; no-one will stand in your way."

"I think the law might have something to say about that," Erkin laughed.

The sheep shed smelled strongly of manure and wool. This small, warm, little world of peaceful animals sighed, bleated quietly and crunched on the grass, and it was hard to imagine that there might be another life anywhere else, crammed with flashing lights, noisy cars and the roar of aircraft jet engines; where soldiers were fighting and important people were meeting and debating and signing agreements and declarations.

"Tell me what's going on in the village," Malika had asked with a sigh.

"Are you tired?"

"Very. It was almost as if they were waiting for me to come on duty because the moment my shift started it's been non-stop."

"Yes, lambing is not an easy job, that's for sure. But why didn't you go to study at the institute?"

"I wasn't ready, but I will try to get in this summer."

"I could help you with that. My uncle teaches at the pedagogical faculty."

Malika had burst out laughing.

"Then I'll be the first person in Altai to get a place at an institute through an acquaintance. Thank you, I appreciate your good intentions."

"I didn't mean special treatment. What I said was 'help'. That is something different."

"I have faith in my own abilities."

"What interesting people you are: you believe no-one and seek assistance from no-one."

The girl remained silent and looked pensively at the flame of the kerosene lamp, deep in her own thoughts.

"I have been missing you recently," Erkin said quietly. "I always want to see you and talk with you, only I have no idea what about. Yes, it's not easy with you, Malika."

"And who is it easy with?" she asked, without taking her eyes off the lamp.

"Well, I don't know," Erkin had said, at a loss. "The girls around here are very particular."

"Well, yes, probably. Once, a long time ago, some girls went off to gather blackcurrants. They got lost and were mauled by a bear. Ever since that time, that place has been known as *The Six Girls...* There are times I dream about them. If they were still alive, the farm would have had six more lambers..."

Is she out of her mind? Erkin had thought, *What a strange story and what a strange conclusion: ...would have had six more lambers.*

"Seeing as everyone has to leave this world someday, it makes little difference if they live their life as a simple lamber or as anything else. The most important thing is to sustain one's soul... And perhaps it might have been better to be eaten by a bear young than have a bad person kill off your soul. You know, there are times when I want to die but when I think of these tiny lambs that are like orphans in an orphanage to me... or of you..."

Erkin had grasped her hands.

"Malika, I have only now understood what you are talking about..." Malika had not resisted and he had embraced her, whispering:

"Malika, don't think bad thoughts. You are so pretty. I have never seen such beauty." He had held her tighter and tighter."

"You too want to eat me up like a bear." Malika released herself from his overenthusiastic embrace decisively and nimbly. "And you understood nothing. Go home."

And once more their meetings became brief and occasional. When the summer arrived, Erkin learned that the girl was planning to go to Alma-Ata. He had hung around at the bus stop by the district centre for a whole day, waiting for her. His plan had been a simple one: her father would not have been likely to accompany her to town, given he had lost his legs, and Aman didn't have the time. His guess turned out to be right. She arrived on the last bus, jumped from the step and

206

had looked around, frightened. She looked lost and very provincial even in the district centre and Erkin's heart missed a beat: *How will you get by all alone in the big city?*

When Malika caught sight of him, her face had lit up with joy and Erkin immediately forgot about the seemingly endless, sultry day that he had spent waiting at the dusty bus station. However, it turned out that the bus that had been standing growling nearby was, in fact, the last bus to Alma-Ata.

Erkin took the girl by the hand and placed a gold ring on her slender finger.

Malika hurriedly removed the ring, saying,

"I understand the meaning of such a gift. But I believe you will wait for me in any case and I promise to do the same for you."

Suddenly, she held him in an embrace and kissed him for all the local villagers, staring from the windows of the bus, to see. Erkin was confused but the chairman's sister's bold act didn't seem to create any impressions on the residents of Yenbek. They were much more concerned about Malika taking her seat and gestured to her to hurry up.

That autumn, having been accepted onto the institute's distance learning course, Malika had returned to the village. Their time apart had brought them closer and they decided to live together. However, for some reason, Aman had stood steadfast between them. He would not deign to hold a conversation with the stock breeder and in so doing showed him that he didn't take his intentions seriously. At first, Malika had come to him in tears, saying that her brother and her father had wanted that at least one member of their family should study and graduate from the institute and then she began avoiding meeting him altogether. It was then that Erkin decided to talk to the chairman himself about getting married, but Aman had told him that the girls in these parts were free to do as they please and the menfolk round here did not come running to their brothers to complain about it.

* * *

"No, damn it, if I get back to the village alive, I will get married the very same day!" said Erkin out loud. He stood up and stretched to warm up.

It was dusk in the snowy hollow but now he saw the world of the Altai night, filled with milky smoke, and he listened to its inconceivable tranquillity. The clinking of the bridle bits and the crunching of the frozen grass on the horses' teeth melted away in this tranquillity and their dark silhouettes were indistinct. It seemed to Erkin that he was sleeping.

Perhaps it would be better to warm up now in the little shelter and have a little sleep. Malika will probably come to me in my dreams.

207

Yes, but she will come to me in the next life because I only have to close my eyes and eternal rest will lie ahead. So what can I do on this endless night of delirium? Scream? No, for then an echo will resound, the snow will shift in the mountains and Aman will be crushed. Just me all on my own and the rest of the world. As if I were about make a speech on the television. And what if such an opportunity were to arise, what would I say to the people? I don't think I am really very ready to make such a speech... Although, I'd have to give it a go.

Erkin straightened his fur coat and cleared his throat.

"Pour me some water and put it down over there, please" he ordered the horses. "Thank you. Comrades! Thank you for giving me the opportunity to speak at this important symposium. People of the progressive world, it is with a clear conscience that I address these words to you. I hope my speech doesn't drag on too long and that you won't have grown thin and lost weight by the time I've finished. I have never been to any other country other than Kazakhstan so, it's no easy matter for me to address the entire world. Like you, I am also mortal, with a round head and two legs. But just as this world has no country that is greater or lesser than ours, then there is no person who is greater and lesser than me. A country is a country and a person is a person wherever they may be, and neither I nor anyone else in the human race has come into existence in order to kill one another. We are born equal and we are equally subject to death.

"I would ask those of you, who do not understand this, to stop your madness, after all, there are already more people under the ground who have killed one another than those who died a natural death. I am neither afraid of the wolves that prowl around me nor avalanches; the only thing I do fear are you, the madmen of the world. My people, perhaps for just a short moment, when compared with the entire history of humanity, have experienced and come to know the true joy that the simple life has to offer. So don't you prevent them from doing so, you rulers, weighed down and weary as you are with your sins. The smaller peoples need to be left in peace; we have got ourselves up onto our own two feet and we were born to enjoy life. We are not asking you to condescend to grant us this; it is our right and we demand it. We are not mankurts[10] and we shall never allow ourselves to become hostages or slaves. Our people have the power to move mountains. People like Aman, for example. He has set off on a path that will perhaps take him to eternity. No-one can know for certain if he will return, or who or what he has to overcome. People speak so much about great deeds and achievements, but I do not know a single person, be they a herdsman, a shepherd, a lamber or whoever, who does not want the most important

---

[10] A term referring to a person taken captive and who becomes a soulless slave

thing of all – to die a natural death. If a person is granted ownership of their life, why do they not have the right to be master of their own death?

"I repeat: I am not afraid of wolves, the frost or an avalanche but I am afraid of people from the other side of the divide.

"They do not understand, they are so engrossed in organising the end of the world, just as we are only now beginning to discover its expanses, its books, its people and its ideas... What else? Yes... the most important thing is this. We need nothing from you, you people from the other side of the divide, but what we don't want is to be dragged into your trap. We have the right to our own allotted time. My yesterdays are in good order and my future is clear. We have everything we need. I have no desire to turn into a fox or a fish and I am in no rush to take to the skies like a bird, like a child who is besotted and befuddled by fairy tales. I am a person, with my feet planted firmly on the ground. And I have no desire either for myself or my people to become an endangered species.

* * *

Aman travelled at a decent pace, from time to time using the twine to pull the ends of his skis out of the deep snow. An innate sense prompted and helped him to find the way to the Devil's Bridge across the snowy plain.

He thought to himself that what the peaceful people, living in the richly forested Altai with its abundant streams and rivers, suffered from most was the lack of roads. And each road to the wintering ground was the first. If you were going in the opposite direction, from the wintering ground, you would first have to forge a path through the thick grass or virgin snow to the village, after which it would become easier, as a surfaced road leads to the district centre and there would be a stopping place again. Sometimes, people on their way to Alma-Ata would have to hang around in the district centre for weeks at a time, waiting for a plane. The treats and presents in the saddlebags would start to melt, as would the soul's festive mood.

Mind you, there's nothing quite as reliable as your own two legs, Aman chuckled to himself.

When he made it over the hill, he felt the going get easier and realised that the slope down to the River Tar had begun. He began to encounter firs, ramrod straight and striving for the sky, as well as brushwood and *caragana* bushes.

He would need to conserve his energy as he went down the slope. Aman relaxed, looking around him to either side. And then he saw the birches. *Those* birches. He would never forget them because, in childhood, he had been astounded by this huge, five-fingered hand, sticking out of the earth. At their base, the birches were pressed up close together but, as they stretched up to the skies, their finger-like

209

trunks spread apart.

It was here that he had cut hay with his crippled father.

He had grown up rather withdrawn but he had become more dexterous than the other little boys. Being his father's only helping hand, he had been engaged in work from early childhood, not knowing what it was to play and have fun. Having taken to the saddle together with his legless father, he had ridden out for firewood and mowed and ricked the hay with his weak, and as yet childlike hands.

His father worked the scythe, crawling along down the slope on his stumps, completely hidden by the tall grass. A man watching from afar would have taken fright at the sight of the green grass being lopped as if by an invisible hand. Reaching the edge of the plot, Aman's father would pull on the lasso with his hands. He had tied one end of the lasso to the top of a birch tree and the other, to the belt of his padded jacket. In so doing, using the lasso, he would make his way back to the top of the slope and start scything again. Aman had seen the veins bulging on his father's temples, his bloodshot eyes and the sweat streaming from his brow and he had tried to keep up, swinging his small scythe energetically. As for the trips for firewood, when the boy had seen how easily his father had thrust his axe into a tree trunk, as hard as iron, his soul had simply died from admiration. Yes, Aspan had taught his son everything he knew. But first and foremost, he had taught him to be brave and, therefore, the snowy route to the Devil's Bridge was no more difficult for him than cutting the hay had been on this slope in his childhood.

There could hardly be a beauty to compare with that of the Altai in summer. Father and son had sat down to have some lunch when the sun was at its highest. They had drunk their thick tea, quenching their thirst with pleasure. Then Aman's father had crashed down onto his mat in the shade of a fir tree. Either from the heat or to ease the pain, he had removed his trousers and allowed his body to rest. Aman did not have the strength to look at the blue stumps; he had walked off to one side and had wept uncontrollably. It was then that he had understood that the quickest way to rid his father of his torment would be his, Aman's, development into manhood. And so he had hastened to increase his strength, his soul and his heart.

He returned, with handfuls of berries.

"Thank you, son," his father had said. "But I think you are becoming like a little camel who has been lashed too hard; you are becoming timid. See that my misfortune doesn't wound your heart and doesn't break your spirit. Now is the time for those who look life straight in the eye. If you don't learn to be like the pine tree that grows up through rock, crushing it in the process, you'll live your life forever being over-cautious, building up fat on your backside. It would be better to die than to live like a dog, wagging your tail at all and sundry.

Being hard and resolute does not make for a happy existence or a pretty life but it does give you the ability to preserve your dignity, even with nothing else but a knapsack on your back. You are my support; you are the legs I have lost. I had sinewy legs that knew no fatigue or pain in the joints! They were like trees. If, now while you are young you learn to be like an ear of wheat bowing down to everyone around you and fluttering your lashes, you will soon find yourself being trampled by those who are stronger than you. Lift up that head of yours! Look me in the eye! Let me see the fire in that belly!"

Aman had bent down and met the gaze of his father who had been lying on his back and looking up at the upturned sky with the steely might of a prostrate falcon.

"Listen, my fine boy," his father had said, embracing him with gratitude, "I don't know – I will die sooner or later. It is my dream to see you tie the knot and be married off early, so I can still get to kiss my grandchildren. But don't give me granddaughters; they are for others."

And now Aspan the Herdsman's only son was gliding along on his skis, heading for the Devil's Bridge, down the slope that he had trampled as a boy. A boy whose eyes had been opened by the herdsman, a boy who had been doted on and a boy who was to continue the family line. He was headed towards the most dangerous bridge, a crossing that was fraught with risk and which only the best of the best might pass.

Once Aman reached the bottom of the hill, the moon became wary and hid behind the dark clouds for protection. It grew dark. Something murmured; it turned out to be several, small deer, that ghosted by like phantoms. Either the night-time made the journey appear more drawn out, or he was actually not moving fast enough, but it seemed as if some malevolent force was moving the Devil's Bridge ever further away from him.

Aman knew that the best way to shorten the journey was to abandon himself to his thoughts. Travelling around the wintering grounds and the pastures in contemplation of all manner of things is an ancient Kazakh custom. And what else is there for a shepherd to do but to contemplate the world? They stand all alone on their hillocks like sentinel monuments rising and descending together with the sun. Yes, they have but two cares in this world: their sheep and their thoughts.

He could still remember it clearly.

It had been early October. The harvest had been reaped and the autumn fever had relaxed its grip. The frenzied Bukhtarma had also grown calmer and the river, entering its regular channel, had been flowing passively. It had been as if nature had frozen in a brief and conciliatory farewell to its previously tempestuous life. Aman the chairman had also gathered his breath and loosened his belt a little. One

211

day he had risen early, finally feeling refreshed after a number of sleepless nights. He had ventured outside and saw how the sun had adorned the mountain peaks in crimson scarves. Not counting the old men and women, plagued by insomnia, the village had yet to waken from its sweet morning sleep. The joyful trill of a bird reached him from the curly-topped forest. A deer called out from somewhere near the river. The morning dew sparkled briefly before disappearing and it had seemed a shame to step out onto the golden grass it adorned; a white shawl of mist covered the high breast of the mountain pass.

All that Aman had seen spoke of happiness and calm, so what strange sadness was it that was pinching his heart? In order to dispel it, Aman made his way to the Bukhtarma. The river had receded from the banks that it would eat away each spring as it made its frenzied way. Aman softly seated himself on the trunk of a fallen tree. On the opposite bank, several, small deer had blithely come down to the water's edge. And yet there had been something that gave away a human presence; one of the deer had cast its head high, shaking its shiny, wet nostrils and, with a single leap, it had disappeared into the forest. The other deer silently and shadow-like followed suit, concealing themselves in an instant. Aman approached the water, undressed and washed from the waist up. His heavy body sensed its vigour returning. Only now did Aman sense how tired he was. It was time for a holiday. He would hand in a request to the director the next day, get the holiday that he was due and clear off to... yes... to the Black Sea, as they say, that is where everyone goes. He would see different kinds of people, new lands and, for the first time, he would learn about the joys you can buy for the money he had worked so hard to earn. It would be interesting to learn if these joys were worth all the sweat and worn boot leather. Of course, it would also be curious to see other peoples and how the people of other nationalities would look at him. After all, he didn't look that bad, he was strong and not stupid. But here he was nodding to himself like a marmot. So what if he was? Even this tow-haired creature wanders far from its hole in the summer in search of food; it roams about and searches out new experiences and impressions for itself. Was Aman any less deserving than a marmot? No, of course not. Now he would rest as is fitting for a man. In an easy manner, setting his shoulders and back free. *Right, so, rather than sit around like an old man after his ablutions, I think I'll go home, write a request and take it to the director.*

He had stood up and, suddenly, a wild scream rang out. The scream struck Aman like a sharp knife in the back and he fell. A red-hot hammer smashed inside his head, the sky had disappeared and night had come, a thousand red sparks encircling that night.

He could not recall how long he had lain there, prostrate on the river bank. His soul, evidently terrified by the scream, had left him but had then returned, pale and quivering. When Aman opened his eyes everything was oscillating like a heat haze and he thought: *perhaps there is a forest fire nearby?* But then he remembered the scream and the pain. The pain had now gone, only the nausea remained. It would be alright: he would get up, wash his face in the icy water of the Bukhtarma and head for the office on foot. He would write out his request to the director there, sleep it off a little at home and then get on a plane and scoot off to the Black Sea.

Aman tried to get up but thousands of needles stabbed into his head and he fell unconscious once more. Night had fallen once more. Suddenly, though, a bare-footed, bare-headed boy appeared from somewhere out of the dark.

His face was familiar: a shy smile and a peculiar scar on his forehead – a scar that had looked like a new moon. Who had he seen with a scar like that? Why, Aman himself had a scar exactly like that on his own forehead! So that meant that death had come to collect him in the image of his childhood?

You have come too soon, my child, far too soon, Aman had whispered.

Oh, valour of mine, are you alive?! the boy had asked.

I am. But where on earth are you going?

The boy had then walked away.

Where on earth are you going?!

The boy had not looked back...

"Don't go frightening me. Get up, I will support you," his father's voice said. The one voice that could have probably even raised Aman from his grave.

Aman sat up, leaning on the shoulder of his father Aspan, who had been sitting at his side, like the trunk of a mighty pine.

"You have avoided death, so you will live a hundred years," his father told him.

At the district hospital, he was told he had suffered a stroke and would have to rest. He did not go to the Black Sea, instead spending hours on end in the courtyard, wilting in the sun and chatting with his father. He told his father about the boy who had come to him from out of the night.

"Was that death?" Aman had asked.

"It was life," his father answered curtly. Aman had been so preoccupied that he only now realised that he was standing at the Devil's Bridge. His recollections had forced him to forget about the time and his fatigue.

Solitude has a friend, a true, inseparable friend and that is thought. This friend will share both joy and sadness with each and every man until the grave. Who knows, perhaps our thoughts will remain with us out there in that eternal gloom. And it is because of this that people are probably of a higher order than nature and even death.

Aman stood before the Devil's Bridge and sensed that he must act swiftly. He would have to cross this cursed bridge in one go and in haste. Something, however, made his legs heavy and his heart fail. That *something* was fear.

The fear that something like what had happened to him back then on the banks of the Bukhtarma might suddenly repeat itself. That a scream would ring out and he would be left here forever and the herdsmen in Alatai would think that they were doomed to perish alone and unheeded by the entire world.

Aman, who was now past forty and whose nature was as solid and pre-determined, as if it had been moulded from cement, felt a strange transformation. His sinewy body went limp, his fists grew smaller and he came over all hot as if he had entered a steam room or had been wrapped in the skin of a recently-slaughtered ram.

In his mind's eye, Aman entreated the boy not to come to him now, to wait a while. And, while he thought of the boy, he knew that his father Aspan was also thinking of him. Praying for him. He had probably gone again to the grave. His son must know no fear! But fear there was. Those who might scream could creep up on him from behind. Erkin had said: *you have left your enemies behind you.* But perhaps Erkin himself was the enemy. Why should he, Aman, believe his fair, worthless speeches? He would be a fool to ignore his grievance that Aman had not given him his sister's hand or his desire to take his place as chairman. And he would be a fool to ignore the vengeance that the copper-whiskered man harboured, the vengeance of an aggrieved herdsman.

Again he asked the boy to postpone his arrival just a little while longer.

But Erkin had said: *a man can only be frightened by himself.*

And his father had said that the boy had come to lead him back to *life.*

Aman imagined his father sitting on the grave like some stone idol and, suddenly, he realised that there were two of him. One had departed forever on that night on the banks of the River Tar, while the other was his father Aspan, the man who had taught his son to cut grass, saddle a horse and speak with people and with himself honestly. And it was then that Aman understood, standing now before the Devil's Bridge, its name signifying the borderline between life and death, that it was not only he who stood there frozen, but also his father, his son, his ancestors and his future grandchildren. And if the boy had appeared at this moment, he would say to him: *"I told you not to come; go and play knucklebones."*

But if the boy had asked: *"Don't you know that the universe is absolutely indifferent to the lives of that herd of horses and the two or* three people looking after them, who are you trying to save at such fatal risk to yourself?" he would answer: "Yes, my deed is as small and insignificant as the eye of a needle, but I must do it and, to be honest, I couldn't care less how the universe decides to view it."

"And what if a scream does ring out?"

"You cannot know, but I know that no-one will come here to scream out my doom. My father paid this debt long ago along with a great many other people. No-one will come."

"What about Erkin? After all, I know what you used to think of him."

"I was not thinking straight; I failed to take into account that times have changed and that people have changed too."

"And what about Copper Whiskers and his brother? Have they changed too?"

"No. But they are now afraid. Other people, however, good people, have no fear."

"I don't believe it."

"I'll prove it to you."

"You, perhaps, have been overcome by self-centred ambition. You want to be as brave and renowned as your father Aspan, don't you? Your 'ego' also wants to scream, to scream out to the world about itself."

"I simply want to help the herdsmen. At the end of the day that is my duty. So now, be gone, boy, and do not bar my path any longer."

"Bismillah!" said Aman and he stepped onto the Devil's Bridge.

An age-long silence reigned; the enormous expanse of the sky, dotted with stars, seemed to convey an image of the pocked face of his father as he had stood over Aman in his childhood, and Aman suddenly felt ashamed of his hesitation and fear.

"Hey!" he screamed out loudly. "Hey! The only thing a man needs to fear is himself!"

No-one answered.

"Hey! Mountains! Ravines! People! A man should believe in himself and in others!"

No-one answered.

"Hey! I have crossed the Devil's Bridge. I, Aman, son of Aspan the Herdsman! I fear nothing. The most terrifying thing that I feared was to suffer the same fate as my father. My father! My own father! I am not afraid of suffering the same fate; it is sacred. Ah... Ah!"

A-a-ah... came the sudden echo in response and Aman saw the mountain, shake its shoulders and rid itself of the snow covering its back. Whistling and roaring, a river of white came crashing toward the Devil's Bridge and swallowed it up.

215

Lost in a white sea of virgin Altai snow, Erkin heard the distant, dull sound in the mountains and he realised that Aman had made it across the Devil's Bridge.

The next morning, two groups of people walked to meet each other over the boundless, virgin snow, glistening in the sun. From the height of the ridge, they looked like tiny, black specks on the huge face of the earth.

OLIARA

It was during an Indian summer.

The bleak, icy and merciless Altai winds were yet to start blowing and the solemn gleam of the sun slid over the mountain peaks, migrating further and further to the west with each passing day. This radiance of cool light generated a sense of serenity in the Shepherd's soul; on these days it seemed as if he was cradled in a peaceful, autumnal slumber. He wanted to sit there, leaning against the walls of the yurt, gaze over the distant peaks and warm himself in the bright sun's cool rays. And that is what the Shepherd did; he sat there, looking out at length at the only road in the vicinity, a snake that wound its way between the hills, as if waiting for a gallant messenger on his horse to appear. There were times when he wanted to find himself on this road and ride out to the forest that had yet to shed its bright, yellow-green dressing of autumn leaves. The Shepherd raised his eyes and looked up at the sky, marvelling at its clear blueness. He noticed a troubling portent in the unattainable depths of the sky, something rather like a branding iron; it was a flock of cranes, heading south. The flight of birds so high up was always solemn and peaceful, with no sign of commotion, and this meant that no early winter would hurry the migratory birds away. This year, the autumn had been bountiful, the harvest a good one and the hay had been gathered into ricks; it would have been a sin to complain to Mother Nature! The *aqsaqal* elders would say that it had been quiet during the new moon and that indicated that the coming month of *kazan-ay* would be dry and warm.

The Shepherd also recalled how, at this time of year, the elders used to be particularly sad, as their days ebbed away and their lives drew to a close; that, nowadays, the old men had changed their tune altogether and were now almost silent, as if that autumnal grief and humility had been lost for ever. The elders had indeed become more withdrawn and their tales shorter and rarer, with only the young people raising hell and languishing in indolence, having nowhere to go in their free time. The grey-beards would wander among the crowds of youths, steering clear of them, like the doddering old rams in the flock, and, because of their advanced years not daring to raise their voices against the beardless ones. With each passing year, their numbers had dwindled. Those left hid themselves away from the goings-on of the world; they seemed to have no regrets about the past and they were indifferent when it came to the future. They lived for today; all they needed was peace and quiet...

It was an Indian summer in September. At this time, the Shepherd would normally head off to the wintering ground, to make preparations for the forthcoming move there with his family. On this

217

occasion, seated on his horse Mukhortiy, he had set off on his journey, preoccupied with thoughts of the winter, now close at hand, with which he associated vague hopes. Over and over, he whipped his horse into a gallop but, once he arrived at the wintering ground he just stood for a while in front of the plain, little hut and then walked around it. The boards that covered the windows and doors were fixed haphazardly. The Shepherd picked some stones from the ground and launched them at a magpie, perched on the chimney, from which smoke had long since ceased to billow. Suddenly, he felt his heart sinking. He sighed deeply and stood still with downcast eyes. He had seen so many of these wretched, sun-dried houses in his time, with the same old boarded-up windows, all deserted by their inhabitants. There had been a good many of them built in the first years after the war, but this one was somehow still standing.

The Shepherd let out a sigh and, with that, he left the wintering ground. The long journey home was accompanied by thoughts of his children. Three had now started school; he had to buy them pencils, exercise books and some clothes, so he dropped into the village. With five children at home, there was never a dull moment and his Wife was about to present him with a sixth. *What good is there in having a child when we are about to move?* the Shepherd muttered. *So much to worry about.* And thus, muttering away to himself, he rode up to his autumn camp.

His loyal dog Alamoynak greeted him with a loud bark and his five children came running out of the yurt. The youngest two were twins. The children's joyous screams instantly woke the Shepherd from his rather sad and vague feelings and a warm, joyful mood spread through his heart. He jumped energetically from his horse into the throng of his children, who were already caught up in his stirrups. In a moment of genuine happiness, he reached into his jacket and pulled out some sweets, exercise books and toys, and he passed them around. Over their heads, he could see his Wife at the entrance to the yurt, baring her white teeth in a grin. Having each received something, the children scattered instantly in all directions. The Wife went off for water, clattering buckets as she went, and this meant she would soon be plying her husband with tea, now he had returned from his trip.

And so there they sat, the Shepherd and his Wife, drinking tea, smacking their lips and savouring the sour *kurt*. They had been sitting there supping tea for quite some time, their children out in the yard. The samovar was still hot and their swarthy faces ran with sweat. They sat there, just the two of them, silently drinking tea, each immersed in their own thoughts.

Of course, the Shepherd thought, he would have to touch up the winter house a little, and he would have to do it now, while it was still warm. If he waited for the cold to set in, he would have to contend with frost in every corner. However, even though he knew this, the Shepherd would do nothing and, just as he had that day, all he would do was travel to the wintering ground for no reason and walk around it with his hands behind his back. The thing was that it was not in the nature of this Kazakh to worry today about what will happen tomorrow. He was tired, too; there had indeed been plenty for him to do with the flock. The Shepherd's visit to both the wintering camp and the village on that day was down to the uncharacteristically animated, even fidgety mood that had been dogging him in recent days. Usually unhurried and reticent, he would now kick up a fuss over nothing and it was most unbecoming, like an ink blot that mars a clean, white sheet of paper.

The Wife worried herself for nothing over what this change in her husband could mean. In the end, she gave up, deciding that *the fool had come to his senses.* But the Wife didn't know and couldn't understand that even if he was silent, as was customary, then that didn't mean a lack of intellect, rather a restraint and a lack of desire to waste his inner strength for nothing. So now he sat opposite his Wife, drinking bowl after bowl of hot tea, not because he was dying of thirst, but because he was preoccupied, stubbornly trying to gather the thoughts and feelings that had burdened him throughout the course of that long day. His face, tanned by sun and wind, was dark, his swarthy skin drawn tight over his cheekbones. This thin face bore neither beard nor moustaches, just five or six hairs protruding from his chin, which the Shepherd would even take to pulling when deep in thought, gradually one after the other, wrapping them around a finger.

The Wife sensed that her husband had not been particularly happy with his trip. He had clearly not done everything he had needed to but she was unable to learn a thing from the silent Shepherd and this irritated her. She angrily splashed the unfinished tea into the hearth, throwing up the hot ashes with a hiss.

"Well, you could at least have brought us back a bag of flour," she said, disgruntled, looking askance at her husband. "A waste of time it was you going to the village... It might at least have occurred to you to borrow some money from someone, seeing as you forgot to take any with you. And what are we going to feed our horde with, you wretch? So why don't you sit there, tugging the hairs on your chin and think about that."

In a fit of temper, she grasped the samovar that was still hot, noisily splashed the remaining water into a bucket, shook out the smouldering coals from the burner and hung the samovar on the yurt post. The Shepherd observed her silently with calm, sunken eyes. He wouldn't have minded another cup or two, but he said nothing, knowing that now was not the time to bother his angry and far from angelic woman; in ten years of living together he had come to learn this on many an occasion. Still without uttering a word, the Shepherd got up and, taking his crop from where he had dropped it by the entrance, he went out of the yurt. Seeing their father get up on his horse, his children ran up and surrounded him, pulling at his legs, saying: *Where are you going? Are you going to the village again? Bring us back some treats, papa!*

"Of course he'll bring you something," the Wife answered for him from the yurt. "It is for you that he is going back to the village. Just wait and see."

Her eyes were still flashing with anger but, inside, her familiar, old pity for her obedient husband was returning. The Shepherd bent over and picked up one of the twins, held him close, sniffed his forehead and carefully placed him back down, muttering to himself, *No, children, I am off to tend the sheep, not to visit the village.* He dug his heels into Mukhortiy's sides, the horse leapt forward and, in an instant, they were trotting down the dusty road. The dog Alamoynak ran after them.

"Oh, Lord!" exclaimed the Wife with a sniffle, calling on God as her witness. "All my life, all I have ever heard him talk about is his sheep. What have I seen with him apart from sheep? Some people get all the luck: they sit at home, wearing silk and enjoying plenty of everything. Another has a husband who is not some farmhand, but a slender poplar of a man. Oh, how unlucky can you be?!" Dropping to her haunches, the Wife pressed her hands to her wet eyes.

Fortunately, the Shepherd had not heard her words. The sky above him was clear, like a mirror, wiped dry. There was not a cloud to be seen. This was an autumn that was generously warm and graciously dry. A wedge-shaped formation of geese hung over the very edge of the sky. There were too many birds to count and they were all flying free to warmer climes. Were a man like a bird, he would have long since hurried away with the geese and cranes, over oceans and mountains. But the Creator gave people slender arms, not wings, a round, heavy head and long legs...

The flock was grazing nearby. The sheep were clearly in a state of bliss, replete and cool. That autumn had been bountiful with grass and the animals were nicely fat, their fleeces billowing on their backs in the wind. The flock was where it was meant to be and all the animals seemed to be present and correct. Not bothering with the flock, the Shepherd rode on toward Tasshoky Mountain, sitting sideways on his big-bellied steed. Mukhortiy took him to the crest of the mountain, where he was met by a fresh, gusting wind. And it was at that moment that everything indistinct and onerous that had been weighing on his heart these last days and also his Wife's latest fit of temper, dispersed as if they had beeen blown away by bracing gusts of the cool wind. Tethering his horse to a larch, the Shepherd approached a flat crag all folded in a pile like the blankets of a bride's dowry and began to climb. The top of the mountain appeared to extend even higher, the further it rose into the sky, and the Shepherd took a good while to reach the top. In his childhood, there had been a time when he could have leapt up this crag in leaps and bounds, like a young mountain goat. He was not getting any younger, of course, and he was now slower and more cautious... Clambering up to the top, the Shepherd looked down into the void that was the valley below and his head began to spin. He sat straight down on a rock.

The yellow steppe stretched far away towards the horizon; the field, weighed down by the golden harvest, started at the foot of the mountain on which he sat and stretched to the still fresh-green forest. This woodland was about three kilometres long; it was crossed in the middle by the noisy Bukhtarma, whose waters now glistened brightly like silvery *sholpy* hair decorations between the white birches. The yellow-green steppe continued beyond the wood, running up to the edge of the heavens in the deep-blue mountains; to the left of the Bukhtarma, the steppe plain was interrupted by small hillocks and shallow hollows. The hillocks were overgrown with cheegrass and purple osier and, on the leeward side, a number of them were dotted with winter pastures. The Shepherd's wintering ground was on the other side of the ridge, from which he was now surveying the surroundings at the point where the crest met the tall crag where it was always quiet. Turning, the Shepherd peered to that side, trying to make out his winter log cabin through the haze that had now thickened. All he could see, though, was the tall cliff, growing dark in the clot of noonday light... He glanced to the side and there they were: the villages were separated by considerable distances as if they had become weary of one another.

Seated on a speckled rock, covered with lichen, the Shepherd silently contemplated the familiar landscapes. He wanted a smoke and then a drink, but he had no tobacco in his pockets and the water was down below, in the valley. He decided to spit in indifference, but he couldn't even muster any saliva and then started merrily whistling. He wanted to put an end to all the worries and anxious thoughts that were troubling him about his daily bread, about tomorrow, his children's books, the threadbare walls of his winter camp and his cantankerous Wife, who was due to go into labour at any time; he wanted relief from that deep-rooted bitterness of his inescapable concerns about everyday life, which ate away at his soul like rust on metal. It was as if he was free of all this here. The Shepherd became immersed in a blissful, peaceful daydream as if the noonday languor of this fine day had dissolved into his blood.

The Shepherd would find himself in such a state when he sometimes imbibed his favourite *kumiss*. Or when the rain would fall for days on end, when dark days turned to nights almost unnoticed, and he would lie under his warm sheepskin, not sleeping, just irrepressibly day-dreaming, and the long, dark and pale Altai rains would bestow their blessings upon him. They would come soon, very soon...

The Shepherd started and came to his senses as the moist, watery aroma of these imagined late September rains seemed to surge in his nostrils. He climbed down from the rock and crept on his belly to the cliff's edge, to view his flock from above.

There they were, carefree and unconcerned, he thought. But if he were to look around more closely, every mortal creature was no less carefree than a sheep. Down below, against the drab background of the September steppe, the indistinct outlines of someone or something seemed to rise and then melt away before him: hazy figures from a complex world, all united by a single fate... There, down below, was an indistinct vision of what the Shepherd had long known and which always repeated itself: yesterday, today and ten years ago... And yet, in his childhood, things had been different: the world had exhaled novelty and each of its parts had appeared to the boy's eyes distinct and in bold relief. Now, though, this was not what he saw and it was as if everything had drowned in some fog into a bluish, afternoon haze. There was the steppe, the river, the forest, the distant village; there were the mountains, the sheep and, not so far away, his round yurt, standing close to the ground. The Shepherd saw all this as one long, familiar, old picture and nothing in it felt fresh or new. He seemed to know already what would happen next... After the autumn would come the winter, cracking its frosty whip, coating the bare forest with hoar frost, shackling the river in a thick layer of ice, dumping snow and piles of low, grey clouds onto the high peaks and throwing an enormous, white fur coat over the wide steppe. And there among the snowy expanses, as ever, the Shepherd would be busy with his affairs...

And it was then that he recalled what had happened the winter before.

* * *

Little snow had fallen then and the cold was bitter. It had become especially cold by the middle of January when a bleak wind blew for many days on end. The sun barely made it over the mountains—you could throw a stick at it, it was so low—and, there and then, it would slide down the slopes, throwing a sickly reflection onto the clouds; there was absolutely no way of knowing when the sun would rise and when it would set.

The land, cracked from the frost, breathed with a sepulchral cold. Only the sheep, as carefree as ever, happily grazed at the *tebenyovka*, easily reaching the frozen, old grass underneath the sickly

222

snow. Or they took to pulling at thick bushes of cheegrass while the wind pitilessly ripped bunches of twigs from the teeth of any sheep who succumbed to a yawn.

The Shepherd's wintering ground, snuggled beneath the side of a high crag, far from the village, appeared lonely, like a man, lost in the steppe, doing his utmost to catch up with the people he is lagging behind as quickly as possible. Or perhaps he does not want to be among people at all and has left them, affronted, and now he has chosen solitude as his lot and seeks a place to set his hearth and home, away from others.

It seemed to the Shepherd that he had always foreseen a lonely, separate existence for himself, from the very beginning. Perhaps he had indeed been vested with the wisdom to divine his destiny from an early age and he had become who he had become – a Shepherd. If he were now to abandon his work and not put the sheep out to pasture, there would be no point living out the rest of his life and he would perish.

However, this in no way meant that he had not dreamed of starting his life differently. It was now rather hazy, but the Shepherd did remember that at school he stood out from the others with his powers of observation. He noticed even the smallest details, which others passed by without seeing and he remembered everything he saw and heard. With time, he developed a passion for drawing. He drew wherever he went and on any available medium, even on the earth. In his senior years at school, he was well-known as an artist. He had been the editor of the wall newspaper. Once, during a literature class, the pupils had been set the subject *Who I want to be*. The Shepherd remembered sitting at length over his exercise book, not knowing what to write, until he started a new page and wrote out the words: *I will be an artist*. Half an hour went by and he hadn't been able to think what else to write. Needing to hand in his essay, he quickly drew the tall mountains with a small sun shining above the peaks, with a lonely yurt at their feet, a lone horse grazing nearby and a lone man, standing and looking at the mountains... It was this hurried drawing that he handed in to his teacher instead of the essay. But the teacher didn't mark him down. Handing back the work, she looked at him attentively and seriously and said, "I understood your picture. You wanted to say that you dream of becoming an artist. Your thought is clearly expressed and I have given you a good mark. That said, your picture is very sad. The solitude depicted in it will only result in loneliness. But as the saying goes, *just as no walker can ever kick up a great cloud of dust so no person can attain glory on their own...* You, my boy, need a good teacher and then you could become an artist." He couldn't understand what teacher she could have meant. Did he not have sufficient talent as it was?

223

Now, though, the Shepherd, who had once dreamed of becoming an artist, looked over his flock from the top of the hill, astride his big-bellied, patchy-brown horse. Mukhortiy, with a disposition that matched his master's, could likewise stand immobile for hours on end, his head bowed drowsily. He would not stretch to reach the grass; the fire had long since died in his half-closed eyes, his ears hung limply and his tail was chewed by the rams. Yet the steed was plump and strong, unusually mild-tempered and obedient. He tried all he could to get the hang of his master's ways; he had secret morbid fear of the whip and, if caught by a sudden, unexpectedly sharp lash, he would break into a gallop in a panic. However, every time he did so, things would end in the most unseemly manner: his tail swishing, he would evacuate everything that had accumulated in his swollen belly; the stench was horrendous and his master would become most irritated, both from the noisy evacuation and his old horse's subsequent, awkward canter, and he would pull angrily at the reins, making the steed walk at his familiar, unhurried pace. At times, though, the master would lash him with his whip for no apparent reason while checking the horse at the same time and thus stopping him from breaking into a gallop. It was at moments like these that Mukhortiy suffered most. The poor horse would pace about on the spot, nervously swinging his frazzled, docked tail, but would remain obedient and submissive to the will of his human master. How could this unsophisticated shepherd's horse know that his all-powerful master had much in common with his horse and that he too was being worked into the ground; that he too had a master with a sense of life's relentless duties and the conscience of all working animals?

Today, the master's mood was much to Mukhortiy's liking: he had no wish to gallop, tear off impetuously or, in fact, go anywhere, even at an easy pace. Today was a blessing: just to stand in one place the whole day with his nose down, submerged in his sweet dreams... However, he was sure that some madness would follow; people are people and all these two-legged creatures could ever do was ruin the lives of others.

A cold wind blew from the ravine and Mukhortiy, as always, turned his back to it. This was very much to his master's liking. With his chin in the collar of his fur coat, he sat atop the horse like a statue, a stone sentinel of the mountain plain, watching from the hill over his terrain. This, though, was no sentinel idol of the broad plains and no monument; this was a living human with a heart, who was capable of both joy and sadness. Everyone would recognise him as the Shepherd, hardy, sturdy and brave; this was the man who tended the sheep. But few knew what kind of person he really was.

Here, by the tall mountains and the hummocks, overgrown with cheegrass, the gates to life had opened up before him. So many times had he mused over these familiar spaces from his horse; he knew every rocky outcrop and every branch and he thought to himself: *it is warmest of all in one's native land, they say...* And yet he could not imagine what that was. After all, he had not once strayed beyond the place of his birth, so how could he know if it was warmer at home or in a foreign land? It was just that sometimes it could be dull in one's native land too; everything would become tiresome and he would feel the urge to fly off to unknown lands, to see unknown people. The Shepherd would become instantly terrified by such thoughts and carry a feeling of guilt in his heart for a long time thereafter. He had yet to get his fill of the views over the Kazakh steppe and the Kazakh mountains; the Shepherd had never cursed them like his Wife, however wretched he may have felt.

A person is born and they are placed in the cradle; the first thing they see as they enter this world, kicking and screaming, is their own mother and their cradle. That is why mother and cradle are celebrated the world over. A native land is a person's true cradle. It is not for nothing that Kazakhs have a tradition that when a child reaches their first year, they are rolled in their native Kazakh dust and told: *love your land, my child...*

While watching over the sheep, the Shepherd would spend his long waking hours reading books. He had a great many of them, especially on artists. He had once read Turgenev's *A Nest of Gentlefolk* and he had then made a point of visiting the cinema at the district centre, to see a film based on the book. After this, he often took to thinking that there is a grand feeling that is known as love for one's native land and the Shepherd wondered if he was capable of this feeling, so powerfully expressed both by Turgenev and by the director of the film. The Shepherd had already learned that there are lonely souls living amongst all peoples who are capable of departing to foreign lands. And was it not from them that the saying went: if you want to learn the value of your native land, live a while on the other side.

The Shepherd didn't know what yearning for his motherland actually meant. There were times, though, when he had an anxious feeling that he could not quite make head nor tail of. It seemed that something great and unseen was calling to him and his heart would tighten in pain and the tears would come... What was it that so tormented him and called to him? His head would spin, his soul would feel heavy and his chest would emit involuntary, melancholy sighs. It was at these moments that he wanted to abandon these mountains and the steppe, his grey sheep, beating the snow with their hooves, his Wife and children, and depart to somewhere far, far away... But where? And why? He didn't know... And there the Shepherd would sit atop his docile horse and it would appear that he was dozing. But he listened attentively to the breathing and echoes of that distant, inaccessible world of which he dreamed. Then a burning regret would rise in his heart: why, oh why had he not become an artist? And as he had no-one to talk to about this, he sometimes addressed his horse, looking at its sleepy, drooping ears: *Hey, old man, you don't know how lucky you are for being a dumb animal. You have nothing to regret; you just pull down there at the grass. Although you, too, are a poor creature, as I hear you sighing heavily from time to time. I wouldn't mind knowing what about. And how you must be fed up carrying me about and putting up with my beatings. It's a wonder you don't throw me off and trample me good and proper. Have you even once in your life ever had the courage to see yourself as a fine, aigyr stallion? Have you ever given the eye to even one mare in the herd?* The old horse stood there daydreaming, offering no response. And his entire appearance seemed to be saying, *Your rambling will do you no good. The sheep will scatter in all directions and then you'll see...* The Shepherd sensed something kindred in him. You are like a true Kazakh, he thought, who doesn't have a care in the world. In the summer, the flies buzz about your face and bite you, but all you do is snort and swing your head. The cows at least run about here and there, but you just stand there, waiting to be rid of them... How patient and submissive you are. But there is a limit to everyone's patience!

It was winter, a winter with little snow. In the mornings he would herd the flock out to their *tebenyovka* grazing. The winter before, his Wife had been merrier and even joked at times as she accompanied him: *You should trim that beard of yours; just look how it sticks out. A handsome fellow you'd be without it.* He touched his chin, pinching and turning the hairs on his finger, as was his habit.

He pitied his Wife. It could not be easy, he thought, bearing five children in ten years. She had no wish for anymore. And rightly so: if you're watching over children, you're not watching over the flock.

The Shepherd recalled how they had come to be married. They had finished ten classes at school together and they had remained there to work. He hadn't thought about staying on, but an initiative had been announced for the entire graduating class to stay on and work at the collective farm. They even had their photographs taken for the local newspaper. It had been a big event. A separate team of graduating pupils had formed and they had been sent out to cut the hay. Thirty young lads and girls had divided up the field and had started working freely and easily far from the village. They had everything they could possibly want, they were making the hay and then having their young, ardent fun with one another. The future Shepherd had not been bold in nature and his future Wife had chosen him herself. They had got to know each another in the dark time of *Oliara*. Toward the end of the haymaking, she took him to one side by the sleeve and, looking him straight in the eye, declared, *You will be the father of my child.* He didn't know whether to come or go and wasn't sure if he should be happy or sad. But he hadn't been hesitant in his response: *If I'm to be the father, then so be it. So we will live together.* And soon they had already established their own home and their first child, a son, had been born that autumn.

Nine winters had passed since that time. All the graduates of that year were still in the village, having married one another and, like the Shepherd and his Wife, they had brought multiple offspring into the world. Only one of them, the one who had organised the initiative, had not succumbed to the temptation, had not built a family straight away, but had gone to Alma-Ata and had studied to become a stock breeder. Returning to the village, he had remained a bachelor for some time.

It was a winter's day that previous year and, like any other winter's day, it was as short as a raven's beak. It was not yet time to sit down to the evening's meat, but it was already dark and, by twilight, a light snow usually began to fall. It was important to bring the flock into the enclosure before this happened, otherwise, the weaker animals would flounder and get stuck in the snow. The Shepherd gathered the sheep into a circle from their wanderings far and wide across the steppe in search of dead grass, and herded them into the wintering camp. Smoke streamed from the chimney of the lonely hut. He had herded the flock into the enclosure when his Wife emerged from the house. The Shepherd was surprised to see that the morning smile with which she had seen him off that day still seemed to remain on her face. He couldn't remember why she had been smiling that morning and what the reason could have been. However, when the two of them drove the flock into the enclosure, the Shepherd saw a man on a horse near the hillock. It was clear that he was in a hurry, digging his heels into his horse's sides. Looking at the approaching rider, the Shepherd thought to himself, *what could possibly have happened in two evenings? He was here only the day before yesterday. And he is in such a hurry as if he is rushing to bring me joyful news.* The Shepherd was about to walk off, but the Stock Breeder galloped up and reined up his horse, almost knocking into him.

"You look well, old pal!" he greeted the Shepherd.

"I can't complain, thank you," he replied, continuing, without raising his head, to fiddle away with the bolts on the gate.

The Stock Breeder, with arms akimbo, turned to look at the Shepherd's Wife. She returned his glance with a fast, contented look and went into the house.

"You're late bringing in the sheep," said the Stock Breeder, dismounting his horse nimbly. He untied a bag from the saddle pin and placed it nearby.

The Shepherd, who had taken the saddle off Mukhortiy and was preparing to place it on the hay, said nothing in reply but just thought: *I had a feeling that you might pay me a visit, boss, so I tried to herd them in a little later.* But all he said out loud was:

"Will you spend the night? Let me give your steed something to eat."

"There is no need, my friend! The village is just around the corner so returning is really no trouble at all. And the people would scoff...he...he-e," he laughed and, grabbing his bag, he strode confidently off toward the house.

"Well I never, you never felt a sense of shame before the village in the past," the Shepherd muttered under his breath. "You spent the night all those other times before and never gave the village a second thought. And now you are hurrying into my house ahead of me in order to give my woman a good squeeze without interference."

The Shepherd wasn't one for rash decisions. However, once he had a thought he would always tend to say it out loud. Now, though, he didn't want to express any such truths to himself that would only end up making him feel rotten. He pottered about in the yard to calm himself down.

A lamp was lit in the house. But even then the Shepherd didn't go in, standing next to Mukhortiy, brushing his mane. The big-bellied steed, who had only just started to tuck greedily into the fragrant hay, had not expected such a show of affection from his master and, clearly deeply touched, munched on the dry hay with a particular relish. From a safe distance, the Shepherd looked into the tiny window of his hut and saw the Stock Breeder showing his Wife a bottle of vodka, which he had pulled from his bag. Handing the vodka to the woman, he stretched forward and, saying something with a smile, stroked her black hair. The Wife dodged the Stock Breeder with a playful smile. The Shepherd stood in the darkness and burned with shame, either before Mukhortiy or before himself. Then he spat angrily to the ground and turned away.

Between the stems of the cheegrass on the hillock that rose immediately behind the yard, he saw the Shepherd's star, shining brightly. It was always the first to illuminate the sky and it had a festive appearance. With a heart turned cold, the Shepherd gazed at his star for a good while; the star of his comrades, the herders of flocks of sheep.

He gazed at length at the bright, clean, new star and thought to himself: *I should go in there, grab the Stock Breeder by the scruff of the neck and give him a good thrashing... And throw him out of the house onto the street. But he would take me to court, the bastard. And I would have no leg to stand on. I couldn't go crying out for all to hear that my wife had been seduced. And I pity the children; where would*

228

the five of them go? And what am I doing, upsetting myself like this? Maybe there is nothing going on between them at all and I am just...

But then he recalled what had happened only recently: the Shepherd had fallen ill and had been twisting and turning under a blanket, having almost given up the ghost, when the Stock Breeder had suddenly turned up. "How can this be?! There is no way I am going to let death take my old classmate," he declared and called for the village doctor. The doctor had come, felt here and there, listened to this and that and then he had decisively announced that the man had to be taken to the district hospital. Leaving tetracycline tablets and taking three roubles for his trouble, he had upped and left. Two days later the ambulance came for him. The Shepherd had had no wish to go as he was already feeling much better, but no one had paid any heed to him and he had been taken away... He had returned fit and well three days later and his Wife had met him, screaming,

"How long are you going to be coming and going for no good reason like this? It'd be much better if you either lay at home or stayed in the hospital. The animals are standing out in the yard, barely alive. If it hadn't been for your old school chum, they would probably have all dropped dead by now. That's what it means to have a real friend, someone you've studied for ten years together with!" And so she continued screaming in much the same vein, while the Shepherd had just sat there, thin, weak and downcast.

His small son had interjected,

"Papa, yesterday the Stock Breeder stayed here the whole night!"

The Shepherd had then shuddered and looked at his Wife. She turned red and looked away.

"So he stayed the night, what of it? Who else was going to take these three to school in the morning? And he ended up staying not one, but two nights here. We should be grateful to him. And there you are swanning around doing whatever you like. Yes, he stayed the night! And don't you go looking at me like that, giving me a hard time! If I have to, I can do the work for all of us, you can be sure of that. If a woman wants to, she can do things on the go and get what she wants at the same time as taking the ash out, just you remember that."

"Oh, simmer down... They say the best form of defence is attack. What are you making all this noise about? You should be ashamed in front of the children; they're grown up now."

"Right, you think I am afraid of you?! Ha-ha-ha! I fear your ram more than I fear you." And with a shake of her hips, the Wife bolted out of the door.

The Shepherd had sat for a long time at home, embracing his little twins. Then he had gone off to see to the flock.

Oh, lord, there was a time when the all-powerful *bais'* dry old wives were bait for the strong and healthy shepherds and field hands, but now the herders' wives were attracting the attention of the more powerful men in the world, the Shepherd thought, walking behind his sheep. He felt so wretched that he couldn't seem to get a grip on himself. How could he have been such a fool?! No, it was clear the Stock Breeder was a learned man and, even if only by a little, he had got the better of the Shepherd...

That was then, but this time...

"What are you standing there staring at the sky?" screamed the Wife, poking her head out the door. "Or are you going to howl like your Alamoynak?"

The Shepherd headed towards the house... The Stock Breeder was sprawled out by the table in the hot room, leaning on a pile of blankets. The younger children had already gone to bed. The Shepherd's school chum was sweating profusely. There were beads of sweat on the bridge of the Wife's nose, too.

"I've brought you some newspapers," the Stock Breeder said. "So many subscriptions!" And he chucked a weighty bundle of newspapers and magazines onto the table in front of the Shepherd.

The Shepherd skimmed over the headlines and stopped on an article named *Battle with a Blizzard*. He started reading.

"Just take a look at that," his Wife said with dismay. "He won't be happy until he's read the entire newspaper from cover to cover. Drink your tea; there's nothing you've lost there in that newspaper. Well?"

"It's probably about that shepherd again; the one who *battled with the blizzard*, right? Why don't you, my friend go out in a blizzard with your flock, and I'll write about you in the paper; you'll have your name up in lights all around the entire district," the Stock Breeder joked.

"A decent shepherd never remains out in the field with his sheep. He always works out in advance when there'll be a blizzard. And if he does stay out there, then he's only got himself to blame... And I don't think I'd bother spending the night out in the steppe in bad weather for the sake of glory... Glory would be the last thing on my mind, what with my hands and feet freezing and probably ending up in the hospital again."

Hearing these words, the Stock Breeder lowered his eyes and the Wife blushed noticeably. There was an awkward silence for a time. Finally, unable to stand long silences, the Stock Breeder spoke first:

"Hey, and what else are they writing about there?"

"You've probably read them already. They're all old issues, there is nothing new here."

230

"You can hardly read them all! And what's the point in reading them anyway? It's all about the same stuff," said the Stock Breeder with a yawn.

"Really?" the Shepherd replied in Russian.

"Hey, my friend, we're not university academics or party secretaries, so what do we know about politics? Let's crack open half a litre instead. Like they used to say in the old days, how long do we have to pray to the moon?! They were smart back then! Hey, Shepherd's Wife, bring over those glasses!"

The Shepherd didn't answer but continued to read. When he did raise his head, his gaze met that of his Wife, who looked at him with tired, empty eyes. Under the light of the lamp, the diamond-shaped badge on the Stock Breeder's jacket lapel sparkled.

"Drink up," he said. "Why aren't you drinking?"

"I'd never be able to get up in the morning to get the sheep out."

"Oh, to hell with them. If they drop dead, we can always draw up a report that the wolves got them. There's nothing to worry about when you have a friend by your side."

"But you're not the one in charge. There'll be others around asking questions."

"Oh, there's no-one who'll doubt my word!"

"Oh well, birds of a feather, stick together... You'd be better off at least writing off the ones that have genuinely perished from disease, otherwise we'll have to go blaming the wolves for everything."

There was a silence again.

"That son of yours draws pretty well, doesn't he?" said the Stock Breeder. "I noticed that the last time I came... Perhaps they'll make an artist out of him at least."

"Time will tell... But he may well have to take the shepherd's staff rather than a brush, like his father did."

"Send him to the city, like my parents did me," advised the Stock Breeder with another yawn.

It's late, he thought, *perhaps I could spend the night here?* As if reading his thoughts, the Shepherd got up and said:

"It's late. If you don't want to stay the night here, you'd better get going."

The Stock Breeder had nothing else to do but get to his feet as well. The two men, two former classmates, went out of the house into the dark yard. Clouds had covered the moon. The light snow, which had become heavier by the evening, had now quietened down, but the cold had crept in from the mountains. The white peaks were departing into the distance, their edges were getting softer and rounder and they disappeared one after the other. It was the thick of night.

The Shepherd brought his guest his saddled horse, tightening the saddle straps. The Shepherd shivered from the sharp cold after the warmth of the house. The Stock Breeder, however, somewhat under the influence, didn't notice the temperature and, settled in the saddle, struck up a conversation with an amiable expression:

"I can see you have taken offence at me..."

"What on earth gave you that idea?" replied the Shepherd, shrinking back.

"You know full well and yet you still pretend. You're putting on a brave face. You think I can't see? You really shouldn't take offence that I keep coming round to visit you and never invite you round to mine. You need to understand that city dwellers are not the same as villagers. The wife, you know, never gives me any freedom! These days you can't even give your wife a dirty look. And if you do the slightest thing, then she'll be off down to the office to complain about it and that'll be the end of your party ticket. So there you have it, my old friend. Like they say, there's no enemy worse than your own wife."

"Yes, Allah has rewarded us with two she-bears for wives, make no mistake about it."

"Ha-ha-ha!" choked the Stock Breeder from laughter. "Well said! My she-bear could eat a man whole, that's for sure! Well done! You always come up with a choice turn of phrase." And with that, he poked his whip into the Shepherd's chest with a self-satisfied look on his face, while the Shepherd stood there with his teeth chattering. "But all the same, you wouldn't let me stay the night; you must be afraid!" cried the Stock Breeder and lashed his horse... "You're afraid! I know you are!" he shouted, careering off on his horse into the darkness.

The next morning, rising early, the Shepherd took his children to school. He sat them on the wide sledge, wrapped them in a blanket and directed Mukhortiy off on the familiar route to the village, planning to reach it by nine. This was when the lessons started. After lunch, when school finished, he had to collect them and bring them back. He had to make this journey every day if he wanted his children to get an education and subsequently make it in the world. There had been a time when the Shepherd's father had plied his way between the wintering camp and the village in much the same way, taking the children to school, and the Shepherd, too, now had this ambitious dream for his offspring's future. The Shepherd looked back at his little children, sitting under the blanket. The older one was looking somewhere into the distance with his round, black eyes, at the birch forest that stretched along the banks of the Bukhtarma. His rosy, boyish face shone with such a joy, curiosity and delight that his father also turned involuntarily to look at the forest. The white-trunked trees, whose branches were covered with a muslin coating of snow, formed a

232

white grove that reminded him of a huge cup of *ayran* that has not yet been completely fermented. Ravens sat on the poplars near the road, screeching endlessly. With a chuckle, the Shepherd thought to himself: *Those stupid birds do nothing but caw. But what else is there for them to do? I dare say they don't have sheep to tend, children to educate or a wife to bicker with every day. They look as if they don't have a care in the world. And what about me?* He must have muttered the last phrase out loud as his son turned to him and asked, "What was that, father?"

"Nothing, son," soothed the Shepherd. "I think I must have been talking to the ravens. You're not getting cold there, are you?"

He bent over and straightened the blanket over the children. Mukhortiy was barely able to drag the sledge through the deep snow. The fresh powdering by the edge of the road was dotted with mouse tracks. Someone had written their name on a snowdrift with a stick...

"Son," the Shepherd called out quietly.

"Yes?"

"Try better with your studies. Do your best."

"That's what I am doing, father... I saw your certificate in the chest," the boy began to say with a confiding look. "You did pretty well at school, with just three *four* grades, the rest all *fives*. Your behaviour was good, too..."

The Shepherd smiled as he looked at his son's rosy face. *Yes, my behaviour was exemplary. You could even say a full six out of five.*

"Father, it was you who drew grandfather's portrait, wasn't it?"

"Yes, it was me. Your grandfather herded sheep for forty years. People spoke highly of him and sent him to an exhibition in Moscow; he left a whole chest of awards and diplomas as well. And yet he was illiterate; he didn't know a single letter, not like you and me. But what he knew, son, was that it is a great honour to be a good shepherd."

The Shepherd looked attentively at his son. But the boy was distracted and looked closely at the clouds, building up over the steppe. With a sigh, his father thought to himself, *well, perhaps another fate awaits you.*

"And did my grandfather's father herd sheep too?" The boy asked, unexpectedly catching the Shepherd off guard.

"Your grandfather's father? Your great-grandfather, you mean... Yes, he herded sheep too. Only he herded the *bai's* sheep."

"And we herd the state's sheep? Is that right?"

"Yes, that's right."

"There was one *bai*, but the state means many people, is that right?"

"Well, yes, that's right."

233

"So we work not for one person, but for many people."

"That's right. But don't forget that the state actually means us. So we are working for ourselves."

"But why are we held responsible for the sheep that die?"

"Because we have to work so that they don't drop down dead. You have heard what they say: look after the common things as if they were your own. And if we work badly, we'll all die of hunger... Take a look over there, at the slope of that hillock," he said a minute later, pointing into the distance with his whip. "Look really close. Can you see, from here it looks like the side of a cow, only covered in lumps? Can you see?"

"No, papa," his son retorted, casting his eyes over the distant hills. "Cows have only two sides and just look how many sides there are on that hillock. And you don't get cows that colour. I think it is like a sheep lying down. Or an old grave, like grandfather's."

"My word, you're right!" replied the Shepherd with a smile. "I see your eyes are keener than mine." *Perhaps you will gallop away with great strides!* he thought. *Just think.* "Have you seen my books on the artists?" he uttered out loud. "You make sure you read them, son. Make sure you do!"

As soon as they reached the ravine, where there was less snow, Mukhortiy raced off at a pace. The Shepherd didn't hold him back, letting him take them as he saw fit. The master had been lucky with his children and with all the hopes that melted away in his warm heart.

He said goodbye to his children at the school as they ran off to their classes: one to the first class, another to the second, the elder to the third. The Shepherd's firstborn was especially dear to him and he invariably followed his progress and often talked with his teacher, a young, nice-looking girl who had only just graduated from the institute the year before. She was cordial and respectful toward the Shepherd and he liked meeting with her. What surprised the Shepherd most was her open, direct and steady gaze. He was always embarrassed by this look and, when conversing with her, he would turn involuntarily to one side and lower his eyes. Ending each conversation, he would invariably say, in his quiet, dull voice: "*Ainalaiyn*, I am relying completely on you. I trust you with my son..."

He repeated these words on this day, too. He knew that in childhood it was a person's teacher who could, to a great extent, determine their destiny.

"You must be an interesting person, sir," she said to him as she accompanied him to the exit after their conversation. "I assume the boy learned to draw from you? He already draws better than me. And he is very capable all round. He probably takes after his father..."

The Shepherd stopped by the entrance and looked back, somewhat perplexed; was the girl making fun of him? But no, she looked at him kindly and affectionately with her radiant eyes. Then he laughed awkwardly and replied,

"Hey, what use is a comb to a bald man? Is art really something for me?" And with these words, he climbed up and took his seat on the sledge.

"Would you be able to pop in after lunch, sir?" the girl asked him warmly.

And in an instant, this young, full voice awoke something elevated and untouched in the Shepherd's soul. He replied barely audibly, in a sputtering voice that was not his own:

"I will," and moved off.

Looking back, he saw the teacher standing on the steps, watching him as he rode away.

* * *

Sitting now at the top of the crag, the Shepherd recalled this tender, warm look; many months had passed since that day, but that sense of clear joy that had risen in his heart was still fresh in his mind. The Shepherd sighed heavily and the smiling face of the girl that seemed to be floating before him dissolved into the mist, the thick Altai mist that descends so fast in the month of *kazan-ay*. He tried in vain to conjure up that face once more, but it had gone and the radiance that had come from the depths of her eyes had transformed into a distant, autumnal, mountain haze, gliding over the inaccessible heights of the ridges. And a feeling of such emptiness, sadness and gloom overwhelmed the Shepherd that it seemed that one moment more and he would enter eternal nothingness; he would depart to another world, the existence of which he had always known about but which he'd never had the time to properly consider. There had only been one spring when he had he recalled this simple release and had even tried to take advantage of it.

Spring! This was the most tortuous and difficult time for the Shepherd – the time of the spring lambing. Day and night the lambs would come and the Shepherd would have to keep watch over each of the mothers to ensure he did not miss the critical moment. The lamber who was supposed to have come at the start of the lambing had never turned up and the Shepherd had had to spend the first ten, terrible days on his feet almost round the clock. For days on end, he had carried new-born lambs from the pasture in baskets. Some of the ewes had been unable to produce milk immediately and he had been forced to feed the hungry infant lambs, while on other occasions it was the lambs that refused their mother's teats and had to be taught how to eat and survive. His head had spun. A wicked fire had burned in his eyes, his back had ached as if it had broken, while back at home his haggard Wife layed into him with her endless shrieks. It was a dog's life. Once, while he was keeping watch over the new-born lambs, he had sat in the enclosure almost until sunrise; by the end of the night, through all the chaos and the fatigue, a thought had occurred to him: *What is it all for? Is this really why I was born into this world?* For the first time in his life, he felt truly sorry for himself and wept uncontrollably. But the difficult springtime soon passed and summer came.

Summer! Oh, summer! A blessed time. Every living thing celebrates it on a tide of buoyant energy, fluttering, rushing about and playing. People throw out their old rags, burn last year's rubbish, make this and that in the yard, bustle about and all this with such a carefree, satisfied look as if its warmth had come for all time and there would never again be a bleak autumn or winter. The earth takes a deep breath to fill its chest now it is released from the cold cover of winter. The young Altai summer dresses up in its brightest garb. It is a wonderful time. However, the Shepherd had no time to marvel at all this; his day to day worries and cares meant he did not manage even to raise his head to cast his eyes over the flowering expanses in the distance. Life! Probably not everyone would notice that, when exchanging their daily chores for a handful of coppers, it passes just as fast as the fast-flowing summer. You tend the flock out in the pasture and the day lingers; you look after the sheep at night and the night is long. And so it continues with every day that passes: a great deal of work that simply continues to accumulate and the years of one's life pass one by unnoticed, and all at an incredible speed. Its current carries the human like a splinter and there is never any time even to stop and think about life. However, the Shepherd sometimes thought that this was good, that this was what was needed: the summer was warm and gracious; he could rest out in the pasture allowing his body and spirit to restore themselves. Sometimes he would even sneak away from his Wife and meet up with his fellow herdsmen to drink *kumiss*. The Shepherd really liked his *kumiss*. There were times when it was hot and dusty and the throat was dry, but they would bring you a full cup of the heady, foaming drink and cool beads of sweat would form in large beads on the brow. Having quenched his thirst with relish, he would return to the flock and find a place to sit and daydream, unnoticed. He would wake up with a start and the sheep would have all dispersed and wandered off, like his life's dreams, lost, untended and forgotten in the procession of days...

The Shepherd averted his eyes from the haze, floating over the fuzzy line of the distant horizon, and looked down at his wintering ground. His thoughts returned to the present, this warm Indian summer's day and his cares and worries that were the same as they had always been. The Shepherd felt a sense of lingering weariness and, unwittingly, he wanted to forget about all his life's misfortunes when he caught sight of a lone horseman, riding towards his camp. From the man's gait on the horse, he could guess who it was: Shygaibai, Shepherd No. 2, who lived on the northern slope of the mountain where Shepherd No. 1 now sat. The horseman rode up to the yurt, pulled up and spoke at length about something with the wife of the neighbour who had emerged. He then set off and headed in the Shepherd's direction. In all the long time it took the horseman to cross the valley, not once did he spur his horse, preferring to ride at a gentle walk, like a heavily pregnant woman, fearing the unexpected.

The man known by the nickname *Give-em-nothing-bai*, the wealthiest man in the district, approached the hill where the Shepherd sat. Rumour had it that he had an unheard-of amount of money on his savings account. This miser counted no-one as his friend, always kept his counsel, did not like visiting and never invited others to his own house. Only from time to time would he drop in on his neighbour. The Shepherd knew that *Give-em-nothing-bai* had a yurt full of all manner of things, stacked up to the round ceiling, while his little children slept under a single, old blanket. There were plenty of new blankets, but the master of the house forbade anyone from touching the beautifully folded stacks and rightly feared that by being used, the new blankets would become old blankets. In Shepherd No. 2's house, they did not eat substantially, bare children ran around the yurt and the master of the house accumulated and kept his money close, telling no-one why he did. At first, when Shygaibai had kicked up a fuss at some wedding-do or at a funeral feast, demanding five roubles' change from his offering, the people had looked at him in amazement, losing the gift of speech. Then, after many years, they grew accustomed to him and, so as not to bring shame on themselves, they had nothing to do with him, never invited him round and seemingly forgot the very existence of the man. It was as if he had died for the people of this region but that was of no consequence to him whatsoever...

"Hey! What you doing up there, like a rooster at a henhouse?" he cried out to the Shepherd. "Come down here. I've been at the post office and I picked your newspapers up for you..."

He dismounted his horse and, pulling the rolled-up newspapers from his boot, he placed them on a rock. The Shepherd ran down the hill, jumping from ledge to ledge.

"Just one somersault and you'll not be climbing up there again," grumbled Shepherd No. 2. "As it is, you're like a mountain goat, clambering up ever higher."

The Shepherd sat down on the stone next to Shygaibai and asked his neighbour for some tobacco. Shygaibai reluctantly pulled a pack of rolling tobacco from his breast pocket and proffered it, with the words: "Only I haven't any papers, so tear off a bit of your newspaper."

237

The Shepherd was cowed by the miser's proprietorial gaze and, taking the smallest possible pinch of tobacco, he rolled himself a thin cigarette.

"Leave me half, would you, my good man?" asked Shygaibai, looking at the Shepherd with hungry eyes.

The Shepherd said nothing but thought to himself: *Drop dead, I won't leave you a puff.* And he set about perusing the newspapers in an unhurried fashion. Shepherd No. 2 sat there in vain expectation, then looked around and, with surprise, said,

"Hey! You can see the pass from here. Your wintering camp is over there, beyond the ridge, right?"

"So what? It's not exactly the first time you've seen it, is it?"

"The number of times I have been here and I've never noticed it. What a life... You have a decent hut at your camp. And the place is just right. You fancy swapping?"

"Er, my good man! The only good thing about my place is that the camp is in a quiet spot under the cliff, and you even envy me for that."

"Oh, come now, what envy are you on about?! If I am envious of you, brother, it's not for the cliff where you've hidden your house, but personally for you. You are sophisticated and you have an education; that's what I envy you for. Personally, I could never get past three classes at school. Although, if I stop to think about it, why should we bother ourselves with all these bits of paper? To herd sheep, you don't need any kind of theory," he went on, inserting the "learned" word for good measure.

"Yet it seems all you do in life is bother yourself with bits of paper," said the Shepherd, rubbing his fingers together, hinting at money.

"Why are you always going on about that," said Shygaibai, taking offence. "After all, I herd sheep like you, I chew the same rough straw and I wipe my face with it just like you. No, people never say anything positive; they only focus on the negative. And what if I become a cripple tomorrow, with no arms? Who would offer me a piece of bread, eh? You? Or anyone else? No-one will, I tell you. So, my good man, I am thinking about the future, unlike you."

"That's enough, my man! Out in the desert, it's no sin to joke at an old man's expense, as they say." The Shepherd brought the conversation to a halt, seeing that Shygaibai was seriously wound up, but with a sly confidence, went on: "But still, between you and me, without witnesses about, how many thousands do you have?"

"Hey, you sod, you've got a knife to my throat now! Well, I have about ten and a half, what of it? You know yourself: money is like water, damn it! Take these newspapers for example: how many roubles do you fork out on them? And why, I have to ask? They came round to

238

mine as well, to get me to take out a subscription; they almost drove me to distraction, so I took our local *Znamya*: there's no more information in it than will fit on the palm of your hand, but you have to cough up two roubles for it... You think anyone reads it at home? No-one. So why do I need it? Just to wipe my hands after handling meat? But you, though, all you do is just read and read. Such an interesting person! Another person would just read one book and then spend the rest of his life teaching others; there'd be no stopping him. You, though, you never say a word and keep your clever wisdom in your head. Just remember this, my friend: the more you know, the sadder you'll be; neither you nor anyone else will be granted any joy from this."

Shygaibai shook his head in an afflicted manner and sighed. The Shepherd burst out laughing, looking at him, and then looked out to the edge of the sky, where the weary sun hung. In the place where it was supposed to set there was a long, lone cloud hanging over the mountains like a stretched vein, dyed with a red sheen. It looked as if it had soaked up the sun's blood, lending it a particular reverence and a passionate vitality. However, the evening depths of this mountainous country had altered strikingly, now released from the unsteady, pearly haze that had lingered the entire day over the slopes, it was as if it had become wholly condensed and now, glistening with lush greens, purple and golden faces, the dark mountains had risen up in all the short-lived magnificence of the sunset. Nature revealed its innermost charm as if it were a naked, serene beauty, preparing to retire for the night. It was that blessed hour for the shepherd before nightfall, when the peaceful day of feeding the herds was behind him and the sheep, hurrying to take all they could from the remains of the day, were munching the grass with particular zeal. The mountain slope, bent gently in the middle, was turned to face the crimson sun and it appeared to radiate a joyous, powerful light, particularly rich against the background of the hot sky and the yellow expanses of the distant steppe. With bright eyes that seemed to have absorbed all the fiery light of the setting sun, the blazing cloud and the gleaming, red Tasshoky Mountain, the Shepherd looked around and thought: *What a sun. How many human souls on this earth are warmed and shine, like this cloud and these mountains, under the light of human goodness and compassion? While those like Shygaibai not once in their lives stop to think about what they are actually giving to others. Money... they count their money and stick it in their savings accounts...*

"And where are your sheep?" said the Shepherd, breaking away from his thoughts and turning to Shygaibai. "Who is tending them?"

"What do you mean, who? What else is my woman for?" he replied with surprise. Already up on his horse, he said, "You give that wife of yours too much free rein, you do. That woman is a devil and a

239

half. A while back I asked where you were and she gave me a right mouthful... I reckon that if there was a policeman or telephone here, you'd spend fifteen days a month in the cells. At least that way you'd get a regular haircut and a wash, ho, ho... And why do you go around with her like a wet-nurse? Tie her to a tree, the vixen, and give those smooth sides of hers the once-over with your belt. There is no-one else lives in the entire district apart from us so don't worry: I see nothing and hear nothing. Allah will help: you'll rid her of those demons. If you don't want to ruin your belt, here, take my hide whip; there's nothing more reliable. And nothing will come of it. Our women are not the city types, they won't file for alimony and they won't throw you out of the house. A shepherd's woman can't make it without a man around, oh, no!" And meaningfully raising his finger above his head, Shygaibai went on his way. He turned as he went and cried out: "Neighbour of mine, how about you and I get blind drunk one of these days? Just to spite our wives, eh? I am a man true to his word: what I think is what I do!" And Shepherd No. 2, waving his crop in the direction of his neighbour, ended by saying, "Drinking with a fine man like you is something the angels will not see as a sin... How about it, eh?!"

The Shepherd watched him go. The brass cap at the end of Shygaibai's crop shone in the sun as if it were gold. Cheered by something, the Shepherd called out in reply,

"Go on then, whenever you say! Why keep a jug for a thousand years; it has to smash at some time or other!"

He started to turn the flock around.

That night the Shepherd took a long time getting to sleep. When twilight comes, not only does the light fade but the day's worries and cares with it, and man becomes gradually overcome with the spirit of the night. The night gives rise to sin and sin is also concealed within its darkness. Were there no gloom of night, there would likewise be no dark, no criminal desires, thought the Shepherd. It was the desolate night that bewitches man with the thought of some wild, intoxicating freedom. For a moment, it was as if the Shepherd's body was released from its earthly bonds, but soon offence at his Wife and male jealousy seeped into his soul. He wanted to make sure his suspicions were groundless and, with a tenderness that lacked confidence, he touched his Wife's shoulder. But she pushed him away sharply in the dark, muttering angrily: "Get away, you stink of ram's sweat." It was only then that the Shepherd thought better of it, that he was bothering his pregnant woman for nothing, a woman with her own, sacred, secret cares and worries. Embarrassed, he grunted and then carefully rose from the bed and, throwing a blanket over his shoulders, he felt his way out of the yurt. It was pitch black outside; the storm cloud that had built up in the evening blackened the western edge of the sky, the one place where the last drop of light of the passing day could have seeped

240

through. The sheep were munching away peacefully. A weak sound of a gunshot reached him from the northern side of Tasshoky. That had to be Shygaibai shooting. Just in case... That one would never let a wolf get anywhere near any sheep of his. Not a chance. *Perhaps he does live the right way after all; easier than me, for sure,* thought the Shepherd. *He wants for nothing: not a car, not holiday resorts. As long as he has money. And what about me? What's the point of all my thoughts and worrying?* He sat down on the saddle, lying by the entrance and stared at the impenetrable cloud in the west, around the fuzzy edges of which a whitish light spilt out. Mukhortiy snorted somewhere beyond the yurt. A young goat bleated faintly; from afar as if in a response, a roe deer cried out. There was evidently rain falling over the night ridges of the Altai; distant thunder could just about be heard, with flashes of lightning over the sharp peaks. It seemed to the Shepherd that these restless auroras were trembling with their weak, flaming wings somewhere inside him. An unsteady, transparent light, which for a moment lightened the heartfelt pain caused by the weight of the endless gloom, like a spoon of medicine that relieved a headache for a little while... While the gloom was thick and full of a multitude of indistinct, imposing shadows.

And still, even if deceptive hopes flared up like dim auroras in the Shepherd's soul, it was not these hopes that nourished and maintained his soul. Faith, a calm and boundless faith, was what bound him so tightly to life. Faith in knowing that goodness was the right path gave him the strength to live alone and stressfully next to his Wife, who only pushed him away, and near the dumb, unthinking sheep. Realising this, the Shepherd thought with fear: *Oh, lord, what would happen to me if this faith, even if only lukewarm, were to die in me? What would I do; where would I go? Where would I go from my sheep? Would I find a life for myself other than this one, in the tranquility of these great mountains? And what if I were to get up and venture off to distant, foreign lands, to live among foreign people? I would mount Mukhortiy, cross the Altai...and say to all the world: "Hello there, strange, alien people! This is me! Don't shy away!" That's how I would cry out. I have a booming, shepherd's voice; everyone would hear it. The only things that might swallow up my voice are the expanses and the years, the thousands of years of human enmity. And what for? Why do we humans have to be at each other's throats? Have we trained ourselves to do each other wrong? Why is it that we have been squabbling and fighting with one another since time immemorial? Why divide the Earth into hostile, feuding pieces and then play around with them, like boys with knucklestones? Oh, I sometimes think that this Earth of ours is just spinning too fast for us; surely one day this ever-growing speed will see it break up into countless little pieces. Something has me anxious; I would like to take the world in my hands,*

241

place it carefully in my breast pocket, close to my heart, warm it, caress and calm it... I am the Shepherd, the most peace-loving person in the world. I protect the Earth from evil just as I protect my flock of sheep from the wolves. I harbour the strength of a great folk hero. I am a Shepherd and a Human, after all, and yet still I am afraid. I am afraid that not all people think the way I do and that many will laugh at me when they discover what I have dreamt about. "You," they will say, "look after your dumb sheep and don't you go worrying yourself over the fate of humanity. Know your place, your flock and your steppe, and don't bother yourself about the rest of the world." But I cannot help being bothered about it and the well-being of the world means everything for my sheep, for my swarthy kids, for my native steppe and for my hearth and home. The Shepherd stretched sweetly, bent his back, rubbed his spine and got up. His back was killing him. With a stoop in his shoulders, he went over to the sheep and, for a second, there was a flash in the sky, lighting up the mountain slope. The Shepherd thought it was the moon, shining through a gap in the clouds, and he cast his customary, shepherd's gaze over the familiar expanses of sky. But at that moment he remembered that it was the time of *Oliara*, a time when the old moon disappears and the new moon has yet to rise. In an instant, the Shepherd felt a yearning for this night-time companion, who accompanied his shepherd's waking hours. Then the light flared up once more, like a silent shooting star up above. An enormous cloud covered all the sky. Oh, lord, there's going to be one almighty meteor shower, the Shepherd thought. He stretched his arms out before him as if wanting to catch the stellar beams in his hands. A black wind came rushing in from the north with a scream, heralding bad weather. The forest was filled with a booming and a black wall advanced on the Shepherd's tiny camp. Somewhere a vulture woke up and let out a guttural cry. A horse whinnied. At this point, the Shepherd imagined that the moon had emerged over the dark peaks, but it was only a ghost of that beacon, a shadow of his human yearning for the true light. There was no moon and nor could there be; this was *Oliara*! Pull yourself together and be a man, Shepherd! The old moon has died and Tasshoky is in the deep gloom of sleep. This is the time of *Oliara*. There will be light, Shepherd, but for now, you must wait out the storm in this impenetrable, moonless night.

Lightning flashed. At the same time, the wind whirled and howled. With broad strides, the Shepherd headed for the yurt. He knew that in this time before a storm, full of unintelligible terror, the flock could become a shelter for all manner of birds and animals, all out of their minds. He had to take his gun and get to the sheep in double-quick time! If he didn't, they too would lose their minds and scatter to all corners of the night-time steppe. However, entering the yurt, the Shepherd saw his Wife on the bed, glowing in the light of the lamp.

242

"Where on earth have you been, you dullard?!" she croaked. "It has started...it's turning in my stomach...oh!"

"There's a storm coming in... There'll be heavy rain," the Shepherd replied, confused. "I need to get to the sheep, or the birds will fly in and scare them all to death."

"Ah-h! Ee-h! Drop dead with your sheep, why don't you!" his Wife screamed and turned to the wall.

The Shepherd paced about the bed, took his gun and quietly left the yurt. A menacing silence reigned outside. Soon, though, the north wind howled with double the force, trailing close to the ground. With his gun over his arm, the Shepherd began pacing around the yard. The eastern edge of the sky was untouched by the storm clouds and the stars shone there peacefully, nothing hinting at the growing rage of the storm. Flashes of lightning and rolls of thunder still filled the night from end to end. The wind picked up.

Shaitan! If only you would blow from the east, muttered the Shepherd, addressing the wind. *You'd get rid of all the clouds in an instant.*

But all that came from the east was a sleepy beam of stellar light.

The wind, whirling skyward, finally came crashing down with hurricane force. The Shepherd left the flock and ran to the yurt. He hurried as fast as he could but the most terrible thing had already occurred. The yurt was not where it had been. It had been flattened and carried off by the hurricane. Children's screaming and crying reached their father's ears. In the light of lightning flashes, he could make out his little children, huddled close together. Their mother writhed next to them, bringing another offspring into the world. The Shepherd swept round them. He felt around until he found an enormous carpet, a *tekemet,* which could barely be loaded onto the horse during moves from one place to another. Nimbly unfolding the heavy carpet, the Shepherd covered his children with it.

"Sleep, and don't be afraid! The rain won't soak you now!" he cried and rushed back to his flock like a bird in flight.

The sheep had clambered on top of one another, forming a restless heap. *Allah, help me! Help me...* the Shepherd muttered indistinctly and ran around the flock, calling loudly to his dog. The animal leapt out of the darkness and looked frightened, twisting and turning about his master's feet, not leaving his side. Having calmed himself a little over the state of the sheep, the Shepherd rushed back and was soon by his Wife's side. A new, angry flash of lightning showed him her contorted, white face. The woman's black hair was blown out over the pillow. The Shepherd lifted her in his arms and staggered to the forest. It was a little quieter there, but the wind bent the tops of the trees, breaking off branches, and the trunks of the trees,

243

swaying close together, rubbed against one another with a terrifying screech. All these violent sounds of the disturbed forest mixed with the howl and the splashing of the torrential rain and were soon absorbed by it. The Shepherd hastily laid his Wife on some dead wood and rushed to the camp for a blanket and pillow.

The Altai is home to particularly wide-branching larches, whose foliage is so thick that not a drop of water will seep through their canopy. The trees' soft needles, falling year on year, create a thick, dry cover on the earth. You can thrust your hand into this loose covering and it will be warm and cosy there. The Shepherd laid out a goatskin, settled his Wife down on it under the tree and gently covered her with the blanket. Then, with a voice full of guilt, he said, "Well, now it is God's will..." and returned back to the sheep enclosure. Only the frequent lightning flashes lit his way in the dark. He managed to reach the sheep at just the right time. The flock, frightened by the hurricane, had begun to stir in an ominous way and other animals, out of their wits, might have run amok after it. Screaming loudly and shooting into the air to attract the attention of the wet sheep, restless and with wild eyes, the Shepherd began turning the flock toward the forest. His trusty dog Alamoynak, who had initially lost his head in the face of the impending thunderstorm, now appeared to have come to his senses and zealously set about helping his master with a plaintive bark. The Shepherd urged himself on with the last of his strength, trying to make it everywhere, choking in the darkness that splashed with torrential flows. When all the sheep had finally found shelter under the forest's protective cover, the Shepherd turned and ran to the camp to tend to his children. All five of them were lying silently under the *tekemet*. Their father dropped to his haunches by their side and, trying to speak in a calm voice, he reassured them: "Lay here quietly, my dears. The rain won't get through to you here, so don't you worry," but his voice cracked against his will. The Shepherd spoke to his eldest: "You be a good lad and watch over the others, alright? I'll be right back..." He placed his hands around his son's warm head and, closing his eyes tight, taking courage so as not to burst into tears, he kissed the boy. Then he shot up and headed off to his Wife in the forest.

That night the storm, the calamity and the hardship had come down so suddenly that the Shepherd could not apprehend all that had happened and simply rushed from his children to his Wife, from his Wife to the sheep, here and there, backwards and forwards, feeling a fatigue that was like a physical pain in his tense, racing body that moved and acted according to some supernatural force that was not subject to human will. The Shepherd had never known such a terrible autumn storm with thunder and lightning. He had only heard that there had been torrential rain like this back in the autumn of nineteen forty, the year before the war.

244

He sat at the head of his Wife's forest bed under the larch and stroked the woman's hair, wet with sweat. In his state of torpid fatigue he thought to himself, *Oliara has passed with foul weather and that means the new moon will also be restless... The climate is changing; things are getting worse and worse. What can all this mean?* Lightning flashed over the forest, illuminating the restless trees. The Shepherd could clearly make out every last little wrinkle on his Wife's pale face, as she breathed quickly and heavily, and he thought it had never looked so beautiful as it did now in this moment of the utmost suffering, under the lightning flashes. And perhaps never had he had such feelings of acute pity and love for his Wife as he had now. True, he had often had to hear her rebukes which were sometimes undeserved but there had never been a time when he responded rudely. He had never interjected with a curt word or given her the evil eye of the wolf; not once had the Shepherd allowed himself to insult the white *zhaulyk* headdress, the symbol of the virtue of woman and wife. Perhaps his love had chosen an eternal earthly life for him, never knowing the highest heights of self-abandonment and delight, but, that said, he had remained loyal, honest and respectful to the mother of his children. Although he sometimes felt totally alone when next to his Wife, he never once wished for another, even in his thoughts. He was ashamed of his inexplicit, timid dreaming of the bright-eyed, young schoolteacher and he had lowered his eyes guiltily before his Wife when she caught him when he was dreaming like that. He had not managed to stroll with her in the moonlight, take her to a beautiful park in the town or even visit the cinema or theatre; they knew none of that vibrant, fresh love of a young couple. He could not even remember the excitement of the first, awkward kiss. They simply managed to greedily and hurriedly get to know themselves on the narrow bed and life then broke them together, with children coming one after the other.

When he felt downcast, the Shepherd would bitterly regret that he had never known the joys of young love and excitement; when he was sad and lonely, he saw a pained dream with a floating image of a pure woman, a true mother and friend of unearthly beauty and charm, which he wanted to embody in the Wife who lay by his side. And, holding up this dream with great patience, a mild manner and gentle heart, the Shepherd was ready to walk through the fires of hell to stay true to this ideal Wife, the Woman who herself was enduring these same fires of hell and would keep her Husband's honour...

The Shepherd bent over his Wife and kissed her cracked lips. *I believe in you and that is the most important thing, he addressed her in his mind's eye. Human fate is bound by three essences: Faith, Hope and Patience. My Faith is you, my Hope is our eldest son. And Patience is always with me. And if I lose just this, it will be the end of me. I do not hunt for honours; my place is here among the hills, where*

245

my sheep graze. And if you have found it hard by my side, then it is perhaps not I who is guilty but your fate. We met during Oliara, *you and I, when there was no moon. The golden moon did not shine on our love and our life together has been spent in darkness. But I am not complaining; I am happy with all I have. I have a home, a hearth and a family. My children are my continuation and my name on this earth will not be forgotten. And, however hard it may be to spend day upon day by the sheep like a post, I am calmed knowing that in the evening I can sit by the hearth with my children. And what about you, my dear? What is it that is missing? Why are you always angry and why do you weep so often? Why are there times, and I know there are, when you hate me and put up with me in disgust by your side? Who is it you need? Who do you want to hold dear and whisper tender and mad words of love to? Who? Whose flame burns brightly in your soul, that, like mine, feels yearning in these desolate times of* Oliara? *And do you know, Wife of mine, that I understand and pity you?*

You will bear me another son and we shall call him Adil, the Faithful. And our boy will become worthy of his name. And all our grandchildren and great-grandchildren will be faithful to the truth. What else can there be, my Wife? In this Altai steppe, among the mountains and forests, only you can be my support. What could I see in all my life other than these sheep pastures? Who else was there to talk with if not with that miser Shygaibai? After all, you have often not even wanted to look at me or talk to me. Don't kill me, my true Wife, don't kill yourself and our children, as my life is held together by you, you and my spotless honour...

The lightning flashed again and again. A solid clap of thunder fell from the sky to the earth as if someone on the rampage had taken a stick and smashed a window in the dark, immense building of the universe. The Shepherd's Wife cried out plaintively, delicately and heart-rendingly. The Shepherd jumped up and froze there helplessly, looking at her with tears in his eyes. There was nothing he could now do for her. She might have been taken to the hospital on an aeroplane but the Shepherd had only ever dreamed about aeroplanes. During the day they would fly inaccessibly high in the sky, murmuring quietly as they went.

The Wife fell quiet and, finally and in silence, she gave birth. The Shepherd himself received his child, a baby boy.

The mother carefully wrapped the infant, who was seeing the world for the first time during that miserable time of *Oliara*, in her shirt and placed him by her side. At that moment, lightning flashed once more, for an instant drawing the tiny face of the newly appeared human who, opening his little mouth, cried and screamed demandingly.

The Woman dropped her arm, turned her face away and began muttering deliriously, not looking at the joyful Shepherd who was fussing about by her side:

"In this hour, when God himself instructs me to tell the truth, how can I tell you it?"

"What?!" said the Shepherd with surprise. "What?! What?!" he cried a second later, seeing his Wife's face and instantly understanding the fatal truth in all its entirety. "In this hour of great hardship... Yes, in this hour... Tell me the whole truth!" roared the Shepherd in a voice that was not his own. "Only the truth or the god that now listens to us will punish both you and the child. Whose son is he? So he's not mine, is that it? A-ah! I guessed a great deal and I was right. And he should not be called Adil, but Abi-let, the Stray... How filthy you are! Why did you marry me? What seduced you, you deceitful wretch, or did you just want power over your docile husband? Answer me! You are facing death...tell me the truth! Who gave you that child? Who?!"

His Wife turned her head away in silence and only groaned weakly. The Shepherd jumped up and looked around in the darkness. He stepped to the side and disappeared into the night, but returned there and then and crouched down on his haunches. He carefully took the crying child in his arms, bent over his distorted, crying face and said,

"You may have a different father, but you are still the brother of my children and your blood is Kazakh blood... *Bismillah!* Be happy." The Shepherd placed the child with its mother, then knelt down and kissed his Wife's cold, sweaty forehead.

He got up and quietly retreated into the darkness of the forest. After a while, a dull, mad laughter reached the Wife, overpowering the thunder of the storm.

And so, in the time of *Oliara*, the dark period between moons, the Shepherd buried his Faith.

The Wife called after her husband for a long while, but he did not respond. Accustomed to the Shepherd's usually meek obedience, she could not bring herself to believe that he had decided upon some desperate folly. She battled on until morning, unable to rise from weakness and, patiently but frightened, she waited, believing he would still return, after all where else would he go? It was only at dawn when the storm had died down and her son came up to her, did she break down in tears, wailing loudly.

Soon she understood that she had lost forever the most reliable support she could have hoped for in her life. Her husband would not return. Never again would she hear the peaceful cry of the Shepherd herding the sheep and never again would they sit and drink meadowsweet tea together... From that moment on the other women who had husbands would look at her with a secret sense of superiority

247

and she would taste the torment of solitude in all its fullness. The Shepherd had departed never to return.

On a fine, golden Altai Friday, when the autumn sky shone a clear blue with not a single cloud and the grass, which had lived to die a peaceful, gentle death, was enjoying eternal rest, the villagers gathered at the Shepherd's camp and discussed long and hard where he might be found. As the day was tranquil and the warmth of the Indian summer was gentle, the people were also placid and placable; they spoke of the generous harvest that year, of the good stocks of hay and, incidentally, where the Shepherd could have disappeared off to. Some thought that the Shepherd had grown tired of everything and had left for the town to fulfil his long-held dream of completing his education. Others said that he had not gone to study, but rather seek the grave of his brother who had died somewhere near Berlin.

To one side, away from everyone else, the young teacher and the Shepherd's eldest son, his living Hope, sat on the dry grass hugging each other... The boy was crying and the teacher was consoling him tenderly.

What else can be said about the strange and sad tale of the Shepherd? Shygaibai, who had never spent a kopeck on the community, donated 21 roubles and 7 kopecks to the search for the Shepherd. There were those who said that after this unheard-of deed, he somehow lost his way and even took to drink. "Everything now is worth but half a kopeck, you see," Shygaibai now liked to say.

The Shepherd's Wife moved with her children to the village. Another shepherd took over the flock.

The Wife gave the son she bore during *Oliara* the name Alda-nysh. Yesterday she bought half a litre of vodka in the shop and the village gossips are still chattering about who it might be for.

The Shepherd's eldest son recently won first prize at school for his drawing. The young teacher married another teacher from the school.

And the Stock Breeder? They say that towards evening, he had taken to his horse...

THE STORY OF MOTHER AIPARA

1

The camp had moved eastwards. After a week-long, bloody battle, the steppe had quietened, although it had seemed to have lost not only its people but also all thought and all memory. It lay mute, half-dead, tormented, like a weary hero after a great conflict.

The last attack by the bloodthirsty *Dzhungars* had been devastating and frightening. The Kazakhs, separated and dispersed over the steppe, had been unable to reunite, as their enemies had scattered them to the four winds, like a pitiful flock of sparrows.

In every battle there is a victor and a loser. On this occasion, the *Dzhungars* had inflicted a crushing defeat on the *Tobykty* clan, whose warriors had initially met their attack armed only with spears and arrows. The tattered remnants of this once illustrious and numberless but now unfortunate people had been forced to move far away from the places they held dear, in order to lick their wounds after the battle, gather their strength and catch their breath. One day they all rose, from the youngest to the oldest and walked out *en masse* into the expanses of the steppe.

It was a terrible thing to behold these people, all in black, riding horses or shuffling along on foot, silent and dejected. It appeared and so it probably was that they were tired of their tears and weeping and now suffered their grief in silence. It is much the same with a cow who has lost her calf; she lows and calls in vain and then falls silent, seemingly at ease with her loss. However, if you look into her large, sad eyes, you can see the tears, welling up inside, ready to gush out at any moment, and so it is with humans.

Every heart feels pain when confronted with a human in great grief. And here was an entire people, plodding along silently heaven only knew where, only to get as far away as possible from their enemies.

The camp was led by a woman in a tall, black, pointed headdress. Her name was Mother Aipara. She too was silent, deep in bitter thought. She looked up at the sky, at the distant hills in the steppe and yet she saw neither sky nor hills. Looking at the sky, all she could see was a river of deep-red blood; instead of the rolling steppe, she saw a crimson sea.

Grief and sadness bled from Aipara's soul and words dripped from her lips as if of their own accord:

"Weep, unfortunate people! Weep, you people, born for woe and misfortune. Who knows, perhaps your tears will form an impenetrable barrier for future generations against the onslaught of our enemy and then peaceful times will return. Weep, but don't wait for those times to come of their own accord; after all, has not envy and disunity brought us to the sorry state that you find ourselves in?

"Weep, too, orphans! The customs and proud traditions of our free *auls*, all that we once knew and the mare's milk we once bathed in; this is something we can now only dream of. And if we die before our enemy's horse hair ropes are lashed around our necks, then be joyful for this release sent down from on high by a benevolent God.

"Weep, you widows! Let your eyes cloud over, for you look pitiful. You have lost your men. So now sit there, crouching and clutching your poor knees, all skin and bone, withered and alone. There were times in the past when the men returned after repelling attacks, with their stirrup straps rotten from sweat, albeit alive and well, and you got under their feet, bringing them drinks. And now it is you who saddle the horses and it is your thighs that chafe on the stiff saddles. And how many of you have the *Dzhungars* taken away into the unknown?

"You unfortunate people will perish in a forty-year battle and you will leave nothing behind but widows and orphans. Olzhai, my fearless husband and Kandos, my second son, the day has come when my grief and torment are too much. Show yourselves, where are you?

"Weep, oh weep, you withered head of mine! Your son has perished but you remain alive. What use is there in you still living? Allah has not permitted you to die and you drag out your sorry existence, taking the last drop of water in the flask from the children. There is that ill-starred daughter-in-law of yours, all in black, trying to wet her child's parched throat with her tears. I beseech you, preserve the life of this infant. But while he grows to become a protector of the *aul's* honour, who will pay reverence to my grey hairs and where will I find the kith and kin to bury me with all the customs that befit such an occasion? They are no more; they have all fallen in battle.

"The deep water flows silent and speaks of the river's might. And the weeping and wailing of the *aul* is an ill omen; it is its weakness. And in those best of times, when the larks built their nests on the backs of the sheep, you, dear *aul*, wandered aimlessly from place to place. And I was saddened by how you had fallen into such aimlessness. Is there any strength in a tumbleweed? The wind blows and carries it away. A settled *aul* is always stronger. Has there ever been a prosperous, happy *aul* that roamed from place to place? Before you can gather all the nomadic *auls* together, the *Dzhungars* will slash you all to pieces.

"Weep, weep, you poor nomads, but I will not shed a tear. Have tears ever brought anyone joy? You say that wealth and happiness deserted you in a day. But in order to lose happiness you have to have enjoyed it first. You have never been happy, in that life or in this. You could have been happy, but your envy for one another

250

brought about your ruin. No, happiness has deserted you forever, so don't wait for it; it will never return...

"Weep too, oh boundless steppe! There was a time when I looked with joy into the distance: how wide you spread, what goodness blew from you and how much life you held! Now all I see in you is silent, immense resignation, submission and death.

"Oh, boundless steppe! I always knew that you would never gain the peace you desire; all you do is dream about it. But what is the point of your empty dreaming? You will fall, blooded by a *Dzhungar* raid, as a wounded warrior collapses from his horse.

Like a wretch, I always sensed in my soul, seeing your weary and mysterious face, my poor steppe, that you want to leave life's woes behind! Why do you cry so bitterly, like an aggrieved child? You weep all night and I weep with you. Yet I have long since cried my eyes out, becoming blinded by my tears. This was all two years ago. Oh, my broad steppe, there were times when you wept until dawn and then prepared for the cares of the day ahead. Like you, I did not sleep, watching the people in their corpse-like sleep and I guessed how much longer they had to live and how many of them you would swallow up, both cold and hot.

"Weep, weep, oh poor mother! You can be pardoned for everything, as you are not guilty for the people who growl at one another like dogs, who live in enmity in this immense, restless world. At times even dogs are better than people, as people begin to gather and hoard almost as soon as they leave their mother's womb. They hoard until their dying day and then all they have turns to dust. Dogs just growl at each other, but they don't rip each other's throats; they bite, but they don't fight. Oh, Allah, but people even pit themselves against dogs. That is the truth!

"Oh, mother camel! It was not the wolves that ate your calf, but the *Dzhungar* leaders. Three days have passed since you stopped your weeping; all you do now is sniffle. I paid no heed to your weeping as all the *Tobykty* are now sobbing. Your sniffling, however, burns my heart and I see your condemnation of the human race in your bloodshot eyes. Perhaps you want to say that I am now the leader of the camp, even though I am just a woman. That is true, but I am powerless. Poor brute, don't think for a moment that my grief is your grief, too!

"Weep, mother camel, weep! This is not yet the beginning and not yet the end. You will perish before us. The *aul*, which has no future, will always be a place of gossip and it will always dream of its bed. Have you seen livestock growing fatter in a doomed *aul*? No, you will perish before we do.

"Weep, weep, oh winged horse! If a *dzhigit* grows weak and thin, he is like a ghost. If a horse wastes away, it is no longer a horse, rather a shrivelled hide, stretched out on poles. Poor horse, seven days without a thing to eat; what are you now? Before, you were a true racer and prancer, carrying only *batyr* heroes on your back. Now you can barely place one hoof in front of the other, turning and stumbling as you go.

"Will Olzhai return alive? My dear horse with your flaming eyes, has anyone but Olzhai ever sat astride your blessed withers? And whose calves but his have pressed into your mighty flanks? The people are right to say that if the brain shrivels in a small head, it is the legs that have to bear the weight. Are there any lands left that we wouldn't have headed for, or mountains that we wouldn't have crossed? My right foot twitches and I don't know why. There is most likely no living camp beyond this hill.

"I have said my all, proud horse of Olzhai, but there is one more thing to add: even if every living person has to saddle the dogs to continue our journey, I will not pass your reins to another living soul, you true, winged steed...

"My Olzhai once said that if the earth goes up in flames, it will be extinguished with water. If the water goes up in flames, there is nothing to extinguish it with. And if the people go up in flames, what is there to fight it with? The Kazakh people have gone up in flames, lit by the *Dzhungars*. But I know that there is a force that can douse this terrible fire and that is the unity of the people. However, it appears that we had already burned before the *Dzhungar* onslaught and were doomed to become ash, even though not a soul even saw the fire. Olzhai would sigh heavily after words such as these. He was always against our endless wanderings, just like some sorry tumbleweed. 'Why do we roam this filthy steppe?' he would say. 'Did we really make such a promise to our ancestors or are we repaying their debts? Yet we owe nothing to anyone. We need to find fertile land and settle. This vagrancy will leave us with no motherland and no place to call home. We must not copy those steppe birds. It was the *Dzhungars* that attacked this time, but tomorrow other barbarians may strike. Why do we always choose some hill to set up camp and why do we seek deep water and then muddy it? Would it not be better to select a permanent site, even if it is only the size of a ground cloth, and build a town there? Pay no heed to anyone who says his dog will never bite or his horse never trample a soul. Anything can happen in life. The *Dzhungars* are not the beginning and they are not the end of our woes.'

"My husband Olzhai would say, 'We are masters of babbling talk, but we are incapable of doing anything. We should do something useful and not pursue idle talk. Anyone can drink *kumiss* and chase the girls; you don't need a brain for that. But now it is time to fill our heads with thoughts and worries. The world might change and it will be ruled by hands that can put pen to paper. The blind will not do the bidding of the sighted, will they? Or the weak, that of the strong, or the hungry,

252

lake that had only just been a resting place for wild birds and animals, accepted the authority of humans, their peculiar habits, voices and noises. The startled ducks and geese splashed down on the other side of the lake. There was not a single person in the camp thinking about hunting. All the people could think about was how to get through the night without tears or lamenting and each of them busied themselves with preparing the food.

Mother Aipara pondered her recent thoughts. She did not eat, just drank a cup of cold, *saumal* underfermented mare's milk, and sat there in silence, bothering no-one with questions or instructions. Her daughters-in-law, scurrying about their duties, tiptoed in and out, afraid of interrupting her silence.

The once black eyes of the woman now burned bright, white as a shroud. Now they contained more majestic motherhood, more sadness and the calm of a person who has seen plenty in her time. Her slow, free movements were most becoming and when she sat in the fore corner, stout and portly, there were not many who could approach her without fear and timidity. She had always answered her husband calmly and intelligently; never an inappropriate or unweighed word ever passed her lips. No member of the *Tobykty* clan could look her straight in the eye and no-one ever came in to see her without permission. This was not because she had aggrieved anyone; it was simply that her magnitude and intelligence were overwhelming. Although her daughters-in-law would avoid crossing paths with their authoritative Mother Aipara, they truly loved her without fear. And there was plenty to love her for. How could one not love her when she turned her beautiful face to them with eyes full of humanity and understanding?

Today, everyone in the *aul*, both young and old, looked with unease at Mother Aipara, who was now silent and deep in thought. It seemed that she was waiting for some unexpected grief to befall them. The people did not know why she continued to sit there, her brow growing darker by the hour, like a cloud before a storm. They thought it must be because of the delayed return of Olzhai and Kaidos.

However, Mother Aipara was alarmed by the visions of her youth that had flashed before her mind, which had been evoked by the natural beauty of this unfamiliar place. The bloody appearance of the deserted steppe, the red, setting sun and the battle between light and impending gloom that troubled her heart and seemed to warn that tomorrow they would have to prepare for even more terrible ordeals. A coolness penetrated in from the deserted, dying steppe and appeared to carry some terrible news. It seemed that all the *aul's* hopes and dreams would disperse with the last ray of the sun.

The autumnal, withered steppe was harsh and cold. Mother Aipara sighed heavily and thought to herself, *where are you now, Olzhai, oh, husband of mine?* But who could answer her question?

And so Aipara sat there quietly and picked at her beads, still immersed in her grey thoughts. Suddenly she started: "Someone find out what that pattering noise is," she ordered and Zhandos ran outside, returning almost immediately.

"Kotibak and Topai have come back," he said.

"How many times have I told them that it does not bode well when they bring their horses right up to the yurt!" said Mother Aipara angrily. Then she looked at the wife of Aidos and her look softened and she asked for someone to bring her some beans.

When Mother Aipara divined the future in the beans, everyone would leave the home. She would whisper long prayers before fortune telling and then she would run her hand over her face and get down to separating the beans into three even piles. "In the name of Allah, the Beneficent, the Merciful," she muttered, "Oh prophets, help me learn the truth, give me support, oh Lord. If my Kaidos is fated to return alive and well, let the beans fall kindly." The further Aipara progressed, however, the paler she became; her cheeks became sunken and her face, quite grey. The beans had fallen unkindly. "No, I am not destined to see my son," she thought, sighing and straightening her back. "The straps of his saddle are down. His sides are bare and his head is uncovered. He is lost to me, my heart senses it. Oh, Allah, what a troubled world this is! Oh, what grief: beans such as these have not fallen for a long while. Yesterday, when I read them for my husband Olzhai, they showed his feet in the stirrups, his head uncovered and he was resting on pillows in his own home; there was no grief. That meant that Olzhai will catch up with the camp. But I was sure Kaidos would return with him.

"Oh, my poor Kaidos, my treasure, my second son. This means you have remained in the hands of your enemies. You are no longer by my side. Farewell, my son, farewell!"

Mother Aipara ran her open palms across her face. Then she called for her children and her daughters-in-law and she said to them all, "Hold strong for it appears we have lost our Kaidos."

No-one said a word, but many had tears in their eyes. Sitting on her haunches, Mother Aipara spoke: "That is enough crying. Get on with your chores." And she pointed to the door.

The people obediently left the yurt and Mother Aipara could hear their weeping outside. She threw down the beads once more and said to herself, "My husband shall return with the dawn."

Ten days earlier, when the *Dzhungars* had attacked them like venomous spiders, the *aul* had hurriedly fled but Kaidos's wife and their twins Bokenshi and Borsak had fallen into enemy hands. Olzhai

256

and Kaidos had decided to set out with a small detachment to return the prisoners. The *aul* was to move further east, without stopping anywhere on the way. Olzhai had galloped off with the detachment, which was why Aipara was now heading the camp.

With the first rays of the dawn, Aipara went outside, wearing a black cap on her head. Just like the day before, the sky was clear but it grew paler with each passing minute; the stars blinked and disappeared, one after the other. Even Venus had lost its radiance.

A funereal, pre-dawn silence hung over them. The overgrown lake, the dew-covered hills and the sheep were all still sleeping. Only the herds of horses were awake feeding and cleaving through the wet grass with a snort, they went out to graze. Watching all this, Mother Aipara sighed heavily and said:

"My husband Olzhai would say that the Kazakhs' livestock grows, but not the people. And he was right."

She lifted her long skirt to protect it from the dew and set off around the lake in the direction of the hills that were now turning black.

She walked and thought, "There was a time when we lived peacefully and sensibly with our people, without fear or concern. There was no threat of danger from Crimea. Even back then, when the larks nested on the backs of the sheep, the people were already choking from envy, while the children were born not with clenched fists, as they should have been, but with open hands. Could this have boded well? And what games did they play by the entrances to their yurts? They raised small mounds of earth and embraced one another as if lamenting something. Of course, this did not bode well.

"As for my dear, little son Zhandos, he only has to drop off and he'll draw in his belly and sniffle till morning. What good can be expected from that?! If a horse draws in its belly, there will be rain; if a child does the same, expect nothing but grief. And that was how it came to pass. I knew two years ago, that our *aul* would experience woe, hunger and torment and I warned my husband Olzhai of this. And you, my hope and my support, you pulled me up, saying, 'Bad words are not becoming.'

"No, Aipara is never wrong, let Allah strike me down. Of course, I am no saint, but my heart senses when trouble lies ahead. My left eye was twitching yesterday and here I have lost my Kaidos.

"The most terrible thing in the world is when you feel an impending misfortune and you know you can do nothing to stop it. Or you know what another person is thinking. The grief of this *aul* and my own grief are incomparable because I alone carry this heavy burden. If only I could load up a black camel with all my woes and troubles and send it packing as far away as possible. A black camel, however, is capable of lifting only a regular load, not the grief I have to bear.

"Grief and misfortune are the greatest burdens on this earth. What could be worse than recalling the past and fearing tomorrow? But those who live without woe and fear, growing fat on water, are simply fools.

"Oh, you restless thoughts of mine, you give me no rest, day or night, like the pestering mosquito. Of course, like any mother, I look after the health and welfare of my children and my husband Olzhai. Yet it is for you, my sorrowful people, that I worry most of all! Oh, you nomadic people, you are like tumbleweed; I have grown thin from my never-ending prayers for your good fortune. Your disunity pains me more than my grief at the *Dzhungar* attack. People can only fight for their existence and their happiness if they are united. A person may suffer from an incurable disease and lie for years in their bed, from where they curse the world and their sorry fate. However, they see the light at the moment of their death and realise how wonderful the world is but it is no longer something they can attain. This thought brings a person both grief and joy at the same time. They are joyful that they are still breathing and a vague hope visits them for a moment. But an unhappy person soon loses this fleeting hope of survival; the bright, wonderful world around, which has just flashed before them, suddenly fades and turns everything illusory and deceptive, while the years they have lived appear empty and meaningless. But is that true? After all, it all depends on what you live for. Any child, no sooner have they come of age, might strive to conquer a mountain peak and they might spend a lifetime clambering up its rocky slopes, and yet not everyone is able to reach the highest of heights. Not everyone can conquer their mountain. It yields only to those whose first concern is the needs of their people, not their own ambition. And what does a growing child of my *aul* strive for?

"My husband Olzhai once said, 'The hare is destroyed by the reed, the *dzhigit*, by his honour. Oh, Aipara, honour and virtue will both perish.' Then he looked long and hard at his thick, heavy crop, hanging on the yurt frame and then switched his gaze to his large dagger in its sheath. My husband had such a doomed look about him that I thought that he would draw his dagger and slit his own throat then and there. But I knew that my husband Olzhai would never permit himself such a disgraceful death. If he had to die, he would do so like a proud eagle, at the peak of the cliffs and crags.

"Is there a person who has never had a dream? My Olzhai always prayed to Allah for the good fortune of his people..."

It was already dawn by the time Mother Aipara had made it around the lake and had reached the hills. The steppe now appeared more welcoming and it was no longer quite so bleak and sombre. A mist rose from the lake. Drops of dew glistened on the grass. Aipara's *ichigi* boots were wet through and her hair, too, was wet with dew. She

258

walked westwards, following the steps she had taken the day before, in the opposite direction to the camp's route. Her tall, upright figure, her gait and indeed her entire demeanour were reminiscent of a person who had resolved on a certain deed or who was venturing to their death.

The grief that had tormented her heart throughout the night, the heavy foreboding and the consciousness that had tortured her mercilessly had forced her to head out to meet her husband. She suspected that an irreparable misfortune had occurred and she had decided to meet this sad news directly and without panic. Would this misfortune and the torments of a mother with sons and daughters, ever end? No, many misfortunes and sorrows still lay ahead and a firm heart was needed to withstand all that life would throw at her like the earth that she now walked on.

Mother Aipara walked further and further away from the lake and the mist, rising from the water's smooth surface, followed her as she went.

The steppe spread out before her like a giantess or folk hero resting unconscious, weary from a long journey and it seemed that this figure would never rise from their warrior's slumber. The broad, Kazakh steppe was voiceless, stretching motionlessly as far as the eye could see, and Mother Aipara saw it as the adopted child of this large, restless world. It had been seemingly wandering the entire day after the sheep and had slumped into a deep sleep from fatigue. *This slumber is like the sleeping of a poor, wretched orphan*, thought Mother Aipara. *This is just the way a poor orphan would sleep, all curled up from the cold and prepared for any misfortune. One would only need to whistle and the orphan would be up and running...*

She also recalled her husband saying that a *dzhigit* with no sense of unity could be distinguished by the slovenly way he puts on his boots, the heels always worn down on one side.

A long distance away, Mother Aipara spotted a lone horseman and she instantly recognised her husband. The horse, a dappled grey, was so tired it was barely able to place one hoof in front of another but his master would not spur him. It was evident that he too was barely able to remain in the saddle.

The tall rider was indeed Aipara's husband. He had found his camp by following the tracks that had patterned the broad backbone of the otherwise untouched steppe. He had ridden three days and three nights, following these clearly visible tracks, not allowing himself or his horse a moment's rest, almost driving the poor animal to its death.

Usually, Olzhai cut a proud figure when mounted on his horse, but now his broad chest seemed thin, his narrow eyes were bloodshot and he was more like a ghost than a living man.

Aipara's heart missed a beat and she wondered if this really was the man who knew the acrid taste of grief that ate away at the heart

259

like alum, if this really was the man who had so often emerged from bloody battles with his honour intact, who had once faced up to his enemies' spears for the sake of his people's honour, for his native land and who always strove to pay his non-existent debts to his fellow countrymen and to his future descendants. This was the first time she had seen him so deflated and downcast.

When Olzhai got down from his horse and walked towards her, she saw how tired he really was; he could barely stand on his feet. However, he tried to step steadily, evidently not wanting to betray his weakness to his wife, this beautiful, proud woman. But however hard Olzhai tried to stand tall, Mother Aipara still understood that he might collapse unconscious at her feet at any moment.

"Did you make it back alright, my dear husband?" Aipara asked in a regular voice.

"Praise be to Allah," he replied.

Their words had always been sparing and sparse. After a brief greeting, they looked one another in the eye and understood the torments they had had to endure and how much suffering they had experienced in these days apart. Aipara took the horse by the reins and they headed for the *aul*, which had only just begun to wake from its slumber.

A breeze rose from the lake and shepherded the mist onto the banks. Olzhai and Aipara seemed to disappear in this mist, becoming lost forever. Aipara said, "You have done a good thing, Olzhai, for at least retrieving the twins' cradle from the enemy. Otherwise, this would have been a bad omen."

"Aipara, I knew you had sensed Kaidos's death," Olzhai responded. "But what can be done, who can you blame if not fate, which has fallen like a black cloud over our people? I am tormented by the thought that Kaidos's wife and two children remain in enemy hands."

"The wife is not important," objected Aipara. "After all, you yourself said that, however loyal a wife may be, she would weep for her husband no more than a week. And the two children are but two drops of blood. If they remain in enemy hands, this means their blood is tainted."

"I think the same, Aipara."

Olzhai sighed gravely. Aipara shuddered, looked straight at her husband with a degree of sternness and said harshly, "Sighing and weeping are for the women; men endure their grief in silence. You have said that yourself many times. You really have changed. There is no need to suffer so; everything will be forgotten. Is our life not like this mist? Or the road a man treads? It opens up before us but what is left behind disappears forever."

260

"Oh, Aipara, what you say is true, but it does not make things any easier. Life is like a thick fog where there is nothing to be seen; you can barely see a space the size of a hearth before you. We do not know what lies ahead and what has passed is of no use to us. However, if this thick fog disperses, an unhappy future for the people will be revealed and the past will be nothing but dry bones on the road. Then what are we to do? And how will we stand up to our enemies or the people of the other clans? Will they not laugh at us?"

Aipara said nothing in reply, but she thought to herself, *will an argamak horse leave hair where it has lain?* She had no wish to give her support to her husband's reasoning.

She had never acted against his judgement, even though she didn't always agree with him. She remained silent, so as not to diminish her husband's role and stature as the protector of the *aul*, believing that the woman's duty was first and foremost to speak loudly of the man's virtues and conceal any shortcomings, not wag her tongue, but be submissive and have a forgiving heart. Mother Aipara always tried to see her husband's opinion as the incontestable truth and taught her daughters-in-law that they should respect their husbands likewise. Her thoughts regarding the bloody battles with the *Dzhungars* had also proved to be correct. There were now mostly widows in the camp that was moving to the east...

Olzhai's appearance in the *aul* proved too unexpected and none of the men had come to meet him. Olzhai himself had no wish to show himself to the people in such a wretched state. He took the saddle from his horse, the twins' cradle and set the animal free to feed. The starving horse fell to the ground and rolled around, then got up and shook itself. It swept out into the steppe, its head held high.

2

Given that they had decided not to remain long on the banks of the lake, but to move further to the east, Olzhai's ten-panel yurt was not erected. They stayed in the six-panel yurt of his second wife Dariga. The yurt proved cramped for all who came to greet Olzhai and to offer their condolences at the death of Kaidos. Therefore, the people did not stay long and left, saying, "May Kaidos rest in peace and may all others in the home live many long years."

All the best people from the *Tobykty* clan, all the *dzhigits* who were able to take to their horses, remained with Olzhai until lunchtime. The yellow *kumiss* was also coming to an end.

By lunch, fresh meat mixed with cured was taken from the pot three times. The meat was consumed along with the stock and *kurt*. After lunch, the elders of the *aul* performed a burial ritual for Kaidos, placing a man-sized log into a grave.

261

The visitors finally dispersed and Aipara remained alone with Olzhai. Mother Aipara had not wept once during the course of the day. She sat Dariga at the head with the daughters-in-law and it was they who cried.

Since morning, some two hundred people had been in the yurt, but no-one had said, as was customary, "Let the consequences be favourable." Aipara was surprised by this. And, although she didn't assign any great meaning to the words, she had expected them and was anxious to hear them.

Olzhai conducted himself, as usual, sitting with a frown like a storm cloud before the rain and greeting all the visitors dryly and with restraint.

What tormented Mother Aipara most of all was not the death of her son but that her two grandsons were being held, prisoner. For Aipara, battles and the smell of blood were nothing new and she knew that people do not die twice. But the fact that her grandsons were being held captive by these bloodthirsty enemies truly troubled her.

"Is there no way to rescue Bokenshi and Borsak?" she asked, afraid of raising her eyes to meet her husband's gaze.

"No!" Olzhai cut her off.

Mother Aipara fell into thought: *Olzhai, my husband, I understand that rage and helplessness seethe and boil in your heart like a stew in a black pot. You have lost an entire detachment in your desire to save these two wordless creatures, and you have lost your son Kaidos. I no longer wish to test your bravery and intelligence by asking you to find a way out of this situation; you are a man, after all. It is just that we are in a blind pass here.*

What is left after the summer? The bullrushes alone are turning black. And what do we have left after the battle? We have our honour and our virtue. Alright, don't you torment yourself; don't think about your grandsons anymore. The most important thing is for you to lead your confused people and take them safely to Ulytau or Shyngystau, which is what you have always dreamed about. It is clear that you will never become a khan in the domains of the Khan Shyghys. But even without his support, the aul will never find joy, roaming wherever it must. They say that those without grief grow fat on water alone. Maybe, we will make it in a year or, maybe, in a hundred years. Perhaps we will not make it at all and all lie prostrate in the black earth. After all, humans often die, guided by some dream or other. Did not my poor mother-in-law, when she was quite old, leave the house and die chasing after some bird or other? Oh, Allah, she ran like a little child through the thick grass after this bird, until she became quite lost in the steppe, fell to the ground, bereft of all strength, and died. And yet, for this mother-in-law, already lapsing into childhood, this was the bird of happiness. How was the poor woman to know that this aul *was not destined to see the bird of happiness even in its dreams, let alone in waking life? However, may she rest in peace; after all, never once did she look at me unkindly. Before her death, she said, 'Dear daughter-in-law, never offend my Olzhai; he is a man, after all. Never give nourishment to idle gossip and never bring disgrace upon him.' And she set two conditions and stated two truths. If a husband sets riddles and the wife is unable to solve them, that is no great problem. If, however, the husband is unable to solve a wife's riddles, this is not good, either for the wife or the husband.*

Olzhai, my husband, you and I have always set ourselves riddles. But has there been but one occasion when we have been unable to solve them? No, there has not. In difficult times, though, I will not speak in ambiguous words; this is not a time for riddles or mind games. I do not want to belittle the importance of the leader of a numerous people. Your iron crop was clearly not made to teach a malicious and headstrong wife a lesson but rather strike fear in your enemies. Just so long as the daughters-in-law understand all this...

What I am saying is that two of my grandsons are left in the hands of our enemies, but it would be better to say that two wounds have opened on my heart, which will never heal. However much I lament and however much I keen, will this ever return my grandsons? It would be better if they died straight away, so they would not then be baited with dogs. Clearly, my husband Olzhai was unable to consign them to their deaths, as a living soul still stirred within them. I commit them; I offer them up as a sacrifice.

What point is there in me asking help from Olzhai? I will somehow find a solution myself, quietly and without making a big noise about it in the aul. *You won't frighten a strong enemy with strength. My Kaidos wanted to frighten them to regain the children, yet he himself fell at the hands of the enemy. What you need to combat a strong enemy is not strength, but cunning. If you put your mind to it, then you can capture a hare by the tail. Sometimes a child can solve a problem that an adult cannot. If I am not mistaken and my instinct is right, the only one who can free my grandsons is my third son, Zhandos. But what if I lose Zhandos too, in the process? If I say "what will be will be" and take the chance, will it not come back to haunt me? No, this son of mine is capable of a great deal. I see intelligence and astuteness in his eyes. However, I will call him and put him to the test.*

When there was no-one left in the yurt, Aipara ordered that Zhandos be summoned, her last son, who had only just learned to sit upon a horse. His eyes were like two currants; he was broad of shoulder and stout for his age. He was a sharp, energetic lad, who could not sit still for a minute. His face was more like Aipara's than Olzhai's. Zhandos was one of those people who entered Olzhai's home without fear or unease.

263

On this occasion, he appeared so unexpectedly, that Aipara dropped her beads. She wanted to pick them up but Zhandos beat her to it, swiftly retrieving them and restoring them to his mother's hands. Pleased with her son's dexterity, Aipara smiled and sniffed his forehead. Zhandos did not soften at this unexpected tenderness, although his heart did miss a beat. Rather, he knelt down in the way his father did and looked attentively at his mother. There was a question in his inquisitive eyes: "What did you want to say to me?" From the boy's restraint, Aipara realised that her son had matured early and she tried to understand the reason for this. Why was it that the lad had to think instead of playing games and having fun? The difficult, restless days of the *Tobykty* and the recent attack of the *Dzhungars* were perhaps the reason.

"Son, who do you see most often in your dreams?" Aipara asked.

"You," replied Zhandos quickly.

"Well, and who else?"

"The she-camel who recently lost her calf."

"And then?"

"I really don't know. I am forever crying in my dreams. Incidentally, last night I dreamed about Bokenshi and Borsak. A dog was suckling them." Aipara frowned and interrupted him:

"That's enough! You know that every thigh has but one bone?"

"Yes, but the thigh also has a knee-cap at its end."

"In that case, the thigh is Kaidos and the knee-cap is you. You are both lambs, who stretched my narrow thigh and softened my breast of stone. Kaidos died an honourable death. But who remains to live forever in this world? The fatal hour came for the ox and so it will come for the calf. We are like streams in the midst of a giant ocean...

"You know that Kaidos leaves two sons, who you just said were 'being suckled by dogs'. Well, their mother did not bear them lying not on a rock and it was not the wolf's teats she wished for them."

"Sacred mother, say what you want to say."

"Oh, my son of this age of destruction, if you want to hear, then listen now. Bring back your brothers, so they do not have to 'be suckled by a dog'."

"Alright."

"My son, you are rushing in. Think about it."

"I am rushing in and that means I have decided. I had a premonition that I would have to go and inside I have prepared myself for this."

"Alright. Let your journey bring you good fortune. Take your father's goatskin saddlebag, tie it to your thigh and be off. The camp

264

will not wait for you. And make sure no-one knows where
gone. Not even your father. Great deeds are done in silen
your enemy. But you have friends, who will help you in your m.
of need and who will keep you on your feet when you find yourself
stumbling."

"And who are these friends?" asked Zhandos.

"Patience and calm."

3

A pensive, moonlit night reigned over the steppe. A light
breeze rose and the lake rippled as if suffering in sympathy with the
unfortunate camp on its banks. The silence was occasionally broken by
the dull voice of a bittern. The steppe, placid and indifferent to the
people's suffering, bathed in the ambiguous light of the moon. When
the wind came in from the silence of the night, it seemed that the steppe
opened its arms in an embrace, stretched sweetly and froze for a
moment, listening in to its own breathing. Each time the doors to the
yurts opened and closed, the flame from the hearth gleamed in the
darkness like a smouldering candle of hope in the lives of the Kazakhs.

When the wind cleaved the air's silent breast and began
tearing at the sparse grass matting of the yurts, they gave out quiet,
moaning sounds. This moaning sound was akin to the farewell lament
of the Kazakhs who, unable to withstand the hardships of this accursed
life, sigh and weep. Indeed, these yellowed grasses do emit the
melancholy sound of the dying bidding farewell to life. However, a
wise man should never forget that, although the tops of the grass might
turn yellow and sigh in the wind, they have living roots. If you
remember this, you can distinguish in this vale of sighs the kindling of
the faintest hopes and dreams and the emergence of righteous outrage
and the call to battle for honour. Over time, these slight pangs can flare
up and set the steppe alight with a rumble - the final response of a
people who have lost the strength of their arm and all hope of
happiness, a people who are slowly bleeding to death.

From time to time this somnolent, melancholy silence would
shudder from the dogs' barking, not warning of impending danger but
simply from a desire to attract their masters' attention.

Aipara, still silently leading Zhandos by the hand, smiled and
said, "People say that a young, unfaithful filly can always set two colts
at loggerheads. The *auls* are also being set against one another by a
filly known as rivalry."

Zhandos didn't catch what his mother was saying, as he was
deep in thoughts of his own. He knew she was sending him on a
dangerous journey and it was still not clear if he would manage to
return home. He had yet to become an adult and here he was about to

265

be put to a stern test. Although he had learned how to break in wild horses and had come out on top on numerous occasions in fights with his peers, he had never yet had to travel far from the *aul*. Would he fall like grass under the scythe, without reaching maturity and without ever learning to stand on his own two feet? He was travelling to an unknown place to encounter life and death for the first time. He sensed that he had truly become an adult in these last two days.

The previous night had been soft and pleasant as if wrapped in fog or a blanket of moonlight, woven somewhere in the depths of the Universe. Someone unseen had thrown off this blanket and everything around was submerged in silence. On nights like these, you have a more acute taste for life and your dreams, and these dreams become utterly irresistible. Like Azazil, they tempt you in with their hand.

If you set out alone on a moonlit night, the silent, quietly tearful steppe will crush your will, you will become weak, yielding and indifferent to everything and you may even lose your mind in this deathly silence. And if you look at length at the pale, night sky, it might start to jump and dance like a devil before your eyes, ripple like a lake from an unexpected gust of wind or you might be plunged into its deep blue silence and sink for an eternity.

Zhandos remembered the multicoloured rainbow that appeared in the sky after rainfall. He had run after it with the other boys to catch it. The rainbow had hung there, as if within touching distance, like the wooden frame of the yurt.

How was Zhandos to know that he was not alone in his dream of catching the rainbow and that every single one of his ancestors had had exactly the same dream? How was he to know that his ancestors, just like him, had run across the steppe, hoping to catch their rainbow of happiness? The rainbow, however, had jumped from hill to hill, moving further and further away, and failing to attain their goal, they went to rack and ruin, perished and forever entered the hot and cold embraces of Mother Nature.

The son and mother, both wrapped in white, strode out across the hills, each of them feeling the sweetness and bitterness of their last hope and faith.

Mother Aipara did not kiss her son, just sniffed his hair and said to him, "Well then, my son, let your journey be an easy one and let the saints watch over you. If you are unable to return the children alive, be sure to kill them."

Zhandos nodded in silent response. He walked about a hundred paces, leading his horse by the reins and did not turn to look back. Then he did turn and cried out, "Farewell, mother!"

But his mother did not respond to his parting words. Aipara did not wish to utter the word *farewell*. She believed her son would return alive. If she did not have this belief, would she really have let

266

him go? And so she stood there, motionless and silent until Zhandos had disappeared beyond the hills. She was like a sentinel, watching over the restless sleep of the steppe.

For the first time ever, Mother Aipara sensed relief and satisfaction in her heart, as if a heavy load had been lifted from her. This had been the first thing she had done in her life without the consent of her husband Olzhai. Of course, she was afraid, but this was superseded by a faint yet greater sense of joyous consciousness. The faint echoes of joy murmured in her heart and the torment that had plagued her subsided a little. Yet this joy was immeasurably small; her suffering was still greater and more terrible than that of all her people; she drowned in it as if in a boundless ocean. Nevertheless, having done a good deed, Mother Aipara almost felt well. She stood in the middle of the restless steppe and blessed her son, who had set out on a perilous journey at her behest. She did not bless her son in his presence, for she feared that he might relax and become soft of heart. After all, his journey was going to be a long and dangerous one.

Mother Aipara turned to face Mecca and began whispering a prayer: "Oh, Allah! Forgive me and show benevolence. Preserve my youngest son; he has departed completely alone, to perform a true deed – to release our innocent children. Oh, all-powerful and all-merciful Lord, there is nothing in this world that you could not do. Only you alone can now help my young colt on his difficult, crippling journey. It is no fault of yours that we are unable to make our dreams a reality. If we think well about it, we ourselves are to blame for splashing away and spilling our happiness. If you do not wish to take our last remnants of joy and leave us with nothing but grief, then grant my people, who now lie like resting sheep, like horses grazing, and my last son, who has ventured off on a mortally perilous journey, goodness of heart, a sense of justice and pity, and Lord preserve their honour. I know that everyone in this world is mortal and that I will die, but please protect my son Zhandos.

"When grief and torment befall our descendants and they know not how to overcome their suffering, force them at that moment to bow their prematurely greyed heads before your omnipotence and remember who you are. Remind them of your existence, and make them decisive, vengeful and hard of heart. Do not allow them to ever permit anyone to laugh at their expense.

"If my people find themselves at an impasse, not knowing which god to pray to, if my people stop in the middle of the road, not knowing where to turn, show them the way.

"According to Shari'ah law, every person must strive to preserve their life. In this instance, I pray for my son, who is still innocent and has not yet come of age, and I am ready to sacrifice myself for his sake.

"Oh, my almighty Lord, you know that I have always asked you, in all five daily prayers, turning my poor head to face Mecca, to help all my sons live in peace and harmony. And I always recalled one story, where the younger brother does a good thing for his elder brothers, but his goodness brings him much suffering and he almost perishes. He is saved by a dog. Then he is restored to riches again thanks to this dog and no thanks to his brothers. He throws his brothers into a dark pit and throws them scraps to eat, but makes a collar for the dog, adorning it with precious stones, and offers it food on a golden plate. There were times when I feared this. I saw my native people as a camel and this ever-sleepy and humble steppe as its hide, removed and spread out far and wide.

"Oh, father of mine, all-powerful master, if my son dies in his great quest, there is nothing that can be done. But save my people from a bloody battle and do not subject them to the disgrace of slavery. Have pity on the tears of the Kazakhs. Amen!"

4

When Zhandos reached the River Terisakan, dawn was already upon him. The steppe at night, seemingly infinite and flat, had gradually transformed into mountainous terrain, dotted with small hills. The colour had changed, too. The white, feather-grass colour had turned a reddish-brown.

The morning sky was clear, open and benevolent, but thousands of crows flew about like locusts, deafening all around with their hoarse cawing. It seemed that it was they who had awoken the steppe.

There was a little dew on the ground and it had barely managed to moisten the dry grass. The weather had been bright and clear for many days now. The earth had dried out, yearning for the protracted rains of the autumn. All that was needed was a light breeze to blow and the steppe would begin to rustle, emitting strange sounds, as if an invisible being was plucking at the string of some exotic musical instrument. A spider's web floated in the sky, another omen for bad weather in the coming days.

Zhandos, who had travelled on his black horse for the entire night, began to succumb to fatigue; his cheeks were lean and he often yawned and nodded on and off. He desperately wanted to sleep. It was as if, in a single night, he had grown old and hardened, carrying a heavy, crippling burden on his shoulders. After his conversation with his mother the day before, he had rushed into agreeing to this perilous journey; now, though, after the night's journey had left him exhausted beyond compare, he now regretted his decision.

Indeed, if two detachments of men had been unable to release the twins from captivity, there was nothing for him to contemplate. Deciding on this mission was the same as jumping into a bottomless abyss with his eyes closed. Even if he were able to snatch the children back, could he ever catch up with his native camp, which was heading ever further eastwards? Even if he could find the camp by following its trail, could he bring it back the two twins, who were still feeding on the breast, alive and well? What would he feed them on the journey? No, he had embarked on a mission of madness; not even an adult could manage it, let alone a child like him. How could he achieve the impossible? The answer lay in a thick fog.

But what if some good fortune were to come his way; then this heroism would not be such madness after all.

Zhandos brought his horse to a stop and somehow managed to dismount. He realised that the road had got the better of him; he didn't even have the strength to walk in a straight line. His entire body ached and he swayed like a sick man. Perhaps he really was sick, though?

Zhandos lay down on an enormous, flat rock and gazed at the sky. It was blue and bottomless, like the ocean. He wanted to drink. Several times he tried to get up, to go to his horse and drink his fill from the goatskin, but he was so exhausted that he wasn't able. The journey through the night had drained everything from him. Zhandos closed his eyes, but somehow that only made them ache. Then he took to focusing on a single point in the sky as if trying to pierce it with his gaze and view the silky, blue fabric of his fate beyond it. But there was nothing in the sky but the cawing crows. It was as if these birds, the only masters in these parts, were holding his fate and life in their black claws. There weren't even any vultures to be seen.

Zhandos thought of his mother and recalled her words: "Make sure you don't get lost on the way back, son; leave piles of stones on the way. We, too, will leave you a sign on our way." Zhandos jumped up and hurriedly began to gather stones, then he took the saddle from his black horse and hobbled it. He broke out in a sweat and grew even more tired after all these efforts. He wanted to lie down once again, so he settled down on the flat rock and dropped off to sleep.

5

When Zhandos opened his eyes, he saw a grinning human skull before him, eyeing him with empty sockets. For a moment he forgot where he was from the fear, but when he came to, he resolved not to open his eyes. However, the body does not always submit to one's will and not everyone is able to control their emotions. Zhandos felt an irresistible desire to open his eyes again. And he opened them against his will, his teeth clenched. Again, he saw the grinning skull. It was then that it occurred to Zhandos that he had come face to face with the first of the angels of death that come to question the dead. He lay there for a while, not able to comprehend what was happening and then he decided that this was nothing but a dream.

A yellow light appeared before his eyes as if all the world around him had become shrivelled and jaundiced. For some reason, his parents, their faces yellow, sat back to front on donkeys and were angry with him and riding away.

He felt a ringing noise in his ears and someone asked him, "In which ear is it ringing?"

"In the left," replied Zhandos and he asked, "And who is thinking ill of me?"

"Your mother."

"No, no, she would sooner kill me, but would never speak ill of me. I don't believe you."

Suddenly he heard someone laughing, then the whinnying of his black horse and Zhandos thought to himself, *O Allah, but this is just the neighing of my horse. The poor animal is probably dying of hunger. No, enough of this lying around. I must be going. A long journey still lies ahead and my mother remains behind, having blessed me on my way. The twins await me and I must release them. But again, there is that laughter! And I cannot open my eyes!*

And it would have been better if he had not opened them at all for, before him, stood four *Dzhungars*, one of them holding a human skull on a stick. No sooner had he gained his senses than the *Dzhungars* showed him the skull up close and guffawed at his fear. Zhandos realised that he had fallen into the hands of his enemies.

The *Dzhungars* laughed at him for some time, at his helplessness. Then one of them grasped him and pushed him across to his comrade, right over the fire. This comrade shoved him likewise over to a third and the third threw him into the claws of the fourth. Zhandos howled when the flames of the fire surrounded him. But it was not Allah to whom he called for help, but Mother Aipara. At last, his senses deserted him and he fell unconscious...

Most likely, this was not for long. He opened his eyes and saw an ominous, overcast sky, obscured by thousands of cawing crows. The sky appeared to have descended on him together with these birds, but then lightning flashed and thunder clapped. Then there was another flash before his eyes, the world turned white and plunged into a wolfish green light. At first, Zhandos could not understand if this was indeed lightning or something else entirely. Then he realised that he was lying in the flames, burning alive in the enemy's fire. The *Dzhungars* had wrapped him in a mat and thrown him into the fire.

270

In the meantime, the steppe was running riot. Thunder clapped once again, lightning flashed and the crows instantly disappeared from the sky.

A stiff gust of wind struck and the first heavy drops of rain fell. The *Dzhungars*, who had thrown logs onto the fire, rushed to their steeds in their anxiety, dragging their curved sabres behind them. They mounted their horses and galloped away, forgetting about their captive. Perhaps they had thought he was already done for.

The rain came lashing down. Its dispute with the fire, in which Zhandos lay, did not last long. Torrents of water soon overwhelmed the flames. It was as if the entire world was laughing and cheering: *Hey, young man, this is not last time you'll burn and you will see many a bonfire in your life yet, but he who is destined to drown or fall at their enemy's hands will never burn to death in a fire.*

Visions of the past rushed through Zhandos's mind; he could talk with himself and he did not even need to move his lips to do so: *Remember, mama, you said yourself, that Genghis Khan's mother fed him on the marrow taken from a shin-bone and he conquered the world. You didn't feed me that way; I never sucked the marrow from bones. You fed me with milk as white as snow. You decided that I was no longer a little boy and I was not afraid to venture out to the very lair of our enemies, to rescue the children from their plight, even when an entire detachment of heroes had been unable to do this. You entrusted an important task to me. But this trust does not release me from saying my farewell to you. And it is now I say farewell to you. Mama, you are a saint and I think you must have foreseen this misfortune that befell me a long time ago...*

Our last winter was so severe, with the snow up to our knees as early as in October, and yet you soothed your frightened and howling people. It turns out back in the autumn you knew that the famine would come. In early autumn, you warned the people of this and told everyone to build warm enclosures for their livestock. There were those, of course, who did not believe you and who dismissed your prophecy with a wave of the hand. And yet one-half of the Tobykty *people erected warm enclosures and kept their sheep in them. I remember that winter well when we kept the sheep in their pens and fed them with sticks. Father's dagger and sharp spear would have been quite impotent then.*

Do you remember, mama, how the people cursed the protracted ice storm and bent their knee before you for saving their livestock?

Striding proudly, you went outside and looked towards Mecca, then turned to face the cold wind and you said: "The gall of the frost has burst and that means it will now get warmer. The sky is very blue and the horizon has shifted back." You called for the black stallion

271

with the bald patch, inspected him closely from all sides and ordered that he be released into the herd of mares. For a while he walked between them, sniffing, and then he chased them all out into the steppe. You looked out at the herd, galloping out into the steppe and, with a flash in your eyes, you said, "Well, my people, today you will head out into the steppe. Ensure not a single person and not a single animal is left in the gorges and lowlands. There will be a flood at about noon tomorrow and the water will sweep away everything in its path."

Everything you said back then came to pass. The people climbed up to higher places and were saved. The next day a burning sun rose and scorched down so hard that the silent steppe, sleeping under its blanket of snow, suddenly awoke and began to bubble and boil like a man sweating effusively, the beads pouring and running in torrents over his entire body. As early as the evening, the steppe had turned black. When we looked back over the camp of the day before from our vantage point on the hill, we saw nothing but muddy, bubbling water, carrying all and sundry with it: broken troughs, short yurt struts, old roof frames and the emaciated livestock that had been left behind, unable to flee with the others. By the morning, the waters of the River Olzhai were raging, sweeping everything in their path. If it were not for you, what would have happened to the people? There were those who took fright at your second sight, while others shed genuine tears from their hearts.

Oh, Allah, those carefree days when we drank kumiss to our heart's content and travelled our three-year camping grounds, showing off our prowess, are now long gone. The most wonderful thing, however, was that we drank the water of our native land and stoked the hearths of our native homes. Do you not carry a handful of earth from the Olzhai Ravine in your right pocket?

Now we don't know where we are going or how fertile our future land will be. Will we be able to settle there or will we return, like a wild animal returns to a known path after losing its way, even though a trap lays in wait there? Perhaps we will advance to Ulutau, which my father always spoke about. My native camp, you are heading in the direction of the rising sun and, perhaps, you will make it to your promised land, only without me. I no longer exist for you.

But I fell asleep, like a miserable wretch, and I dreamed all of this! The Dzhungars and the fire, too. All I remember is that I lay down on a flat rock and recalled how the lads and I gathered berries on the other side of Olzhai. Oh, lord, why is it that I have not burned and perished? My heart still beats, so that means I am still alive. There is something dripping from above. Is that water or blood? Why am I not burning? After all, they threw me into the fire.

272

But no, he had not dreamed anything. The *Dzhungars* had indeed thrown him into the fire, but then the heavy rain had fallen and doused the flames. Zhandos was still alive...

6

When the boy had fallen into the blazing fire and realised this, he hadn't thought he would ever see this bright world again or that he was destined to experience many a cold winter and many a warm summer thereafter. He had thought that his death was inevitable, that he had been cut down, still young and wet behind the ears, and all he could do was to wonder for what and why fate had determined to grant him such an outcome. He didn't have that many sins, after all. He had had no strength to resist and he had submitted to his indifferent fate.

The *Dzhungars* had wrapped him in several layers of matting, evidently to prolong their cruel enjoyment and get more than their fill from his torment. The boy had endured the torture while two layers of the matting had smouldered; he had not let out a single sound. And it was here that the sky, as if unable to withstand such cruelty, had been horrified by this human wickedness and had released torrents of water from its depths. The fire had gone out and the storm had instilled fear in the enemies, who had galloped away in search of refuge. Perhaps they had thought the boy was already doomed.

Zhandos didn't think that he had been saved by a stroke of good fortune. He was convinced that he had been saved by the all-powerful will of his mother, whom he always considered a saint. She could sense the danger that threatened her son and she had asked Allah to save him. Who knows if that had been the case or not, but Mother Aipara knew of her son's calamitous predicament from her divination beans.

The rain fell all day and the *Dzhungars* would not venture from their yurts. All day Zhandos lay there motionless, with burned hands and eyebrows. When the sun went down and it became dark, he somehow managed to get himself out of the matting and emerged from his shroud. He sat there a good while, trying to regain his senses. He felt an insufferable pain in his toes but, remembering his mother's orders, he jumped up, forgetting about the pain. He was not particularly surprised to be still alive as he had had to survive for the sake of his people, for his mother who had fed him with her milk and to do battle with his enemies and overcome them.

Once out of the matting, Zhandos felt himself freeze. A cold, northerly wind was blowing, heralding the first days of autumn. And the autumn nights in these parts were a terrible thing to behold. The wind promised foul weather and howled like an orphaned cur. On nights like these, the rain would sometimes turn to snow, which would

273

melt during the day, turning everything into slush. The coming night would clearly be the same, rushing through the steppe like a wild, bucking stallion. Zhandos was happy with the inclement weather, which had forced his enemies to seek refuge in their yurts. That meant he would find it easier to complete his mission and bring back the twins Borsak and Bokenshi. All he had to do was be decisive. After all, if the *Dzhungars* had caught him and thrown him in the fire once again, he was hardly likely to enjoy such good fortune a second time. He could not make up his mind and a multitude of questions span around in his head. Which tent were the twins being held in? Were there guards? And if there were, well, a guard is human too and could doze on duty until dawn.

Once the *Dzhungars* were in their leaden slumber, Zhandos crept up to a white tent, where two sentries with spears stood on watch. They were not looking particularly far out into the darkness and they paid it no particular heed. In any event, they appeared to Zhandos to be rather careless.

The *Dzhungars* usually had many dogs, but on this occasion, they were somehow nowhere to be seen. They, too, had probably sought shelter from the bad weather. In every tent, the hearths were still burning with glowing coals. Somewhere in the distance, a horse whinnied and a camel bellowed.

Although it was no longer raining, the sky was full of storm clouds and not a bit of the sky could be seen. One of the guards had nodded off, his head drooping down to his chest, while the other leaned, hunched up, against the wall of the tent.

The strong wind that blew in gusts from the south-west lashed the earth with snow and rain alike. Beyond the plaintive wail of the wind other sounds emanated from the tents: the unexpected crying of a child, someone snoring and another muttering as they dozed. The *Dzhungar* camp was sound asleep. Zhandos, however, was not overly trusting of this inclement night and the carelessness of his enemies. It was all going too well, somehow. With redoubled trepidation, he crept up to the tent like a snake, listening once again, crouching on his haunches. It seemed that his heart was beating too loudly. But however hard he looked into the dark of night and however hard he listened until his ears hurt, there was nothing to see or hear. He became terribly afraid and thought it would probably be better to come face to face with his enemy and fight him head-on, swallowing blood, than like this, surrounded by danger on all sides and not knowing whence misfortune would strike. Zhandos had not experienced such fear, even when he had been thrown into the fire. He wanted to jump up and run as fast as his legs would carry him, or be swallowed up by the earth and become unseen and unheard, but then he recalled his mother and the fear subsided a little and his thoughts cleared. He clenched his teeth and began moving forward. Suddenly his hand touched something soft and Zhandos realised it must have been the sleeping sentry. Thankfully, he was sleeping very soundly. Zhandos sat down on his haunches to regain his senses and calm his heart. The door was closed with a latch from inside. The wind picked up and the weeping of a camel reached him. Zhandos readied the saddlebag, pulled his knife from his belt and slit open the matting by one of the uprights. Now all he had to do was insert his hand into the slit, feel for the latch and open the door. He paused a little: what if the door were to squeak? Zhandos had evidently grown accustomed to the danger as his hands no longer shook. He had decided once and for all that he would free his nephews.

Zhandos moistened the hinges with his spit and slowly pushed open the door. It still squeaked treacherously. His heart missed a beat; someone in the tent snuffled loudly and... fortuitously. Zhandos opened the door a little more and entered the warm room in silence. He was immediately overwhelmed with shivers and his teeth began to chatter. He stuck his thumb into his mouth and bit down until it bled. He gradually became accustomed to the stuffy darkness and began to get his bearings. There was evidently a large bed by the wall on the right, from where the snoring was coming, but where were the children? They could not be heard. As luck or misfortune would have it, an infant suddenly whimpered. Zhandos shot to the side and lay on the floor, covering his head. A woman got up from the bed; he realised this from the lightness of her step. The man on the bed stopped snoring and muttered in *dzhungar*: "If your pups don't fall silent, I will roast them over the fire." Then Zhandos could hear a child smacking loudly at the breast. The woman took a long time to return to her place, even though the smacking sound had long since ceased. From its uncomfortable position, Zhandos's body had gone numb but he was too afraid to move an inch. Finally, however, Kaidos's wife returned to her bed. Zhandos waited for a little and then stirred. Suddenly something soft fell onto him; he shuddered but emitted no sound. Zhandos thought this time he wouldn't get away so easily and that he had fallen into the hands of his enemy for good. For some reason, though, the attacker pressed him to the floor without any strength to speak of. Zhandos risked releasing himself from the clutches of his heavy enemy. To his surprise, his attacker obediently slid from his shoulders. It was just a fur coat, after all. At first, Zhandos almost burst out laughing with relief but then became angry with himself for his cowardice and ventured forward to the cradle.

The bed creaked suddenly again and the woman muttered something in her sleep. Zhandos caught his breath. The man suddenly stopped snoring and rolled over to his other side with a groan. Once again, the boy froze in fear. It was then that he realised that this was Kaidos's yurt that had been captured by the enemy, and Zhandos knew every last inch of it. This realisation gave him renewed confidence. He quickly unfastened the cradle, picked up the sleeping infants under his arm and headed for the door. Kaidos's wife and the man both slept. Zhandos opened the door and slipped outside. The guards were sleeping. It seemed to Zhandos that one of them had moved a little. He dived into the thick darkness, stopped for a minute, shoved the two infants into his coat, covered them with the coat flaps and advanced to the place from where he had heard the camel wailing.

It was as if the *Dzhungar* host had disappeared. The foul weather had driven them all into their warm yurts. And what kind of man would go wandering in the steppe in such harsh weather, anyway? The howling wind brought him the sound of the wailing camel and Zhandos ran hard towards this sound, with the two nephews inside his coat. He felt he could hear the wailing of all mothers with lost children in the mournful groans of this animal. Zhandos sensed that he would make it out alive if he could find the camel in this impenetrable darkness. He ran, occasionally looking back to see if his enemies were chasing him. He ran and prayed, only not to Allah, but to his mother Aipara, putting his faith in her support and protection.

It is true what they say that if a coward is pursued long enough, in his desperation he may transform into a hero. At that moment you could have told Zhandos there was a dragon up ahead and he would have rushed forward without a second thought. Over the course of these several days, he had experienced more trials and tribulation that any adult could have withstood. It was as if he had suddenly grown old and the wisdom of every Kazakh generation had entered his heart. Or was it that danger had awoken his animal senses? The infants suddenly awoke and began to cry. This bothered him. What is more, a strong wind penetrated his chest and prevented him from moving forward. His face was wet, either from tears or from the rain. He broke out in a sweat and instantly froze over. Fortunately, the wailing of the she-camel had not ceased and it led Zhandos in the dark.

The full extent of the cruelty and goodness that nature has endowed upon humans is a thing beyond measure. Zhandos sensed this goodness through some mysterious, powerful force and he thought that it had been transferred to him from Mother Aipara. Perhaps nature was mellowing to her son; he was her son after all and the foul weather would be gone. Only yesterday he had played and frolicked and was as carefree as any child should be; today though, many misfortunes had been heaped upon his shoulders.

Bokenshi and Borsak screamed and screamed and their voices melded with the tormented groans of the she-camel and were carried away on the wind...

That night Mother Aipara did not close her eyes.

7

Zhandos thought it would have been easier to carry two saddlebags of rocks on his back than the two twins. They may have been quite tiny but they were living creatures, forever kicking and screaming. Whereas before he had blessed the bad weather, he now cursed it. He begged Allah for the rain to stop. Allah, though, remained deaf to his request. Quite to the contrary, the wind became even stronger.

Zhandos was incredibly tired and could barely make his way with his restless burden. The she-camel bawled somewhere nearby, but it was no easy matter seeking her out in the impenetrable darkness. After much stumbling, the animal finally came into view. It was evidently the same she-camel that had lost its calf. Zhandos stroked its neck, she sniffed him and moaned quietly. He felt her udder, which was full to bursting point. The she-camel never so much as shuddered. *You poor thing*, thought Zhandos. He placed the children on the leeward side and milked the camel, in order to relieve her torment a little. "*Shek*," he said and the she-camel lowered herself to her knees. She turned her head and began sniffing at the infants. Zhandos decided to rest a little, leaning against the animal's warm side, but remembering the *Dzhungars'* proximity, knew he must fly.

He untied the saddlebag from his belt and placed the twins into its two compartments. Then he cut a little fur from the she-camel's chest and covered the infants with it. All the while he muttered to himself: *May all our misfortunes fall onto the heads of the accursed Dzhungars.* Sensing her fate entwined with that of the orphaned children, the camel easily rose to her feet and with a barely whispered "*chu, chu*" she, the boy and the infants dashed out into the steppe.

Aware that the prevailing winds in these parts blew in from Mecca in the autumn, he steered a course with the wind on his left, knowing that thus he might catch his wandering camp directly. Having thought out his route, Zhandos determined not to get lost and boldly strode ahead. The camel's smooth pace soon soothed the children and their weeping ceased. The wind had died down but the road ahead lay long, joyless and uncertain. By dawn, the wind was no more than a murmur but the leaden sky yielded fine rain for some time thereafter.

So much did it brighten that Zhandos could distinguish each hill and even the sasyr plants dotted on them here and there. The plant was not unknown to Zhandos and he'd gathered its flowers many a time. The plant did not live long; by July it would already droop and wither, but feed the yellow sasyr to a weak animal and it would soon be back on its feet.

Zhandos thought, happy the man who proves his worth to his people, no matter his age, for long will they sing of his courage and deeds. Another might live their whole life and not once prove their use to their people. What would be the point of a life thus lived?

The morning came and the she-camel continued to carry the three sons of the *Tobykty* line on her back. When it became completely light, Zhandos recognised the she-camel from his own *aul* and realised the *Dzhungars* had eaten her calf. So instead of following the *aul* to the east, she had remained at the place her calf had perished, wandering around the familiar surroundings and calling to it.

In the meantime, the clouds had thinned almost to nothing but had not dispersed altogether, and a weak, dull sun occasionally peeked through its muslin netting. However, it no longer offered even the slightest warmth and despite the lessening wind, the cold air warned of the approaching winter. The steppe seemed resigned and prepared for this fate. At times a sparrow would fly out of the scraggy grass with a chortling sound or a ground squirrel scuttle past. Lizards and monitors, which scurried about in the grass during the summer, were now hiding away in their burrows, obedient to their age-old instinct. The feather grass, which had waved like the sea in the wind, now lay flat like the hair of a dead man.

The twins in the saddlebag awoke and bawled in chorus; they were clearly hungry. Zhandos brought the camel to a stop and brought her to her knees. He then dismounted, carefully placing the infants to one side. Raising the camel again he touched her udder, again it was tight. Placing his mouth to the teats, he began to suck the fatty, warm milk. With his mouth full, he bent down to Bokenshi's mouth. The hungry infant suckled his uncle's lips, drinking the camel's milk greedily. Borsak was fed in much the same way and once more they set off, the infants soundly sleeping in the saddlebag.

The journey was long, the steppe was wide, but life is short and narrow. Zhandos rode on half-asleep and his thoughts formed into words, "Bless you, oh, Allah! Could it really be that I have managed to pull my nephews from my enemy's hands? Perhaps this is all a dream? I simply cannot believe that I have performed this deed, a deed that the *dzhigits* were unable to achieve, every one of them but my father perishing. Yet I am still so young. No, it must be a dream. I need to wake up. Why is it not getting light? And where am I? Could it be that I am once again in the burning fire that was stoked by the *Dzhungars*? Perhaps I have died after all and now I must be on the other side.

"The weather has brightened but, for some reason, the sun doesn't warm me a bit. I personally couldn't care less; it is poor Bokenshi and Borsak that I pity. We have been riding a full day and a night. I am out on my feet and I laugh when I recall the serene days of my childhood as if they never existed. Perhaps, when we finally find fertile, peaceful land, which knows no hostile enemy raids, and we start living happily and in harmony, I'll recall this day and all I endured and then I shall weep. And perhaps in my later years I will tell the young ones, like the elders of today: *Oh, children, the things we saw in our time, the things we had to endure.* And if I am suddenly to die, what will become of this mottled sky, with that vulture, soaring up there on high, and this grey steppe, stretched out like the hide of a huge camel? Will they too be lost like me? And what of this pale sun? Of course, everything will disappear together with me. Otherwise, the steppe would disappear if only I closed my eyes. I think that the moment I die, the world will also cease to exist. Yet my brother Kaidos perished and nothing in the world went with him. So that means, if I die, the world will continue to exist as if nothing had happened. The sun, as always, will rise in the usual place and then will set. So that means my death will change nothing in this world. So what is the point of my life? If, however, I had not lived, who then would have rescued Bokenshi and Borsak? So that means I am needed in this world to perform good deeds. My mother said that people only truly come to understand a person after their death. Only then does the true worth of their deeds become clear. Therefore, our people dreamed up the saying: *Even dead cows bear milk...*"

In the meantime, the weather had taken a turn for the worse. The yellow she-camel could barely walk. By evening, the storm clouds had completely covered the sky and the steppe had become a cold and alien place. Zhandos brought the camel to a stop and laid her on the ground. The twins woke up and began crying. Zhandos realised that they were hungry and he fed them more of the camel's milk. The twins cried only when they were hungry; for the rest of the time they slept.

The she-camel lay crosswise to the wind and began to chew the cud. She had appeared to have grown accustomed to her fate and realised that hers was to help these children and take them as far away as possible from the enemy. Hugging his nephews close, Zhandos settled down on the leeward side of the she-camel, snuggling up gratefully for having found such a protector. She had now replaced his own and the twins' mother, feeding and warming all three. Zhandos thought that if fate had not sent this she-camel to help him, he would surely have perished,

Things looked good and they were heading east. Suddenly, though, Zhandos was once again overcome with fear. He came over in a cold sweat and sensed he was falling ill. The darker it became, the greater his sense of fear grew. The illness became stronger. He tried to calm his feelings with happy recollections, but they proved no use. It was then that he realised that only reason could overcome his fear. But what could he do, if his reason was still that of a child? Yet life is dear to a heroic spirit...

Wise folk say that fear and joy have an identical power. The more a person feels fear, the more he wants to live, the dearer life becomes for him, the more acute his sense of anticipated joy. His mother once said to him, "Your father was a fearless man in his youth. He is no longer the man he was, though. He is probably getting old. In the year we were married he brought in a snow leopard on a leash." Zhandos was amazed and asked, "But how did he manage to do that?"

"Very simple," his mother replied. "He wrapped his right arm in a lasso of hair, took a dagger in his left and went out into the rushes where the snow leopard's lair was. When the beast rushed at him, its teeth bared, your father grabbed it by the tongue and brought it back home." Today, for some reason, that story no longer seemed so credible to Zhandos.

The night was like the grave, no place for any living creature. The wind whistled and rustled in the darkness as if it were relating some sad story of the steppe, about its disappointment and never-ending regret. In essence, there never was any steppe land; it had dissipated and disappeared in the cold grey of the night. Any person would find such a night terrifying, let alone a child. It seemed that only the she-camel was oblivious to the moaning of the wind, but perhaps this was only because she couldn't speak. She protected the children from the wind with her back and warmed them with the heat of her body, asking for nothing in return.

This was only the third time in his life that Zhandos had spent the night alone out in the steppe. It was unclear why but the more nights he spent alone, the stronger his anxiety grew and the more he worried. He could have grown accustomed to it by now. They say that a person can grow accustomed to everything.

With each passing hour, he sensed his life becoming dearer and dearer to him and he questioned whether his life was worth sacrificing for that of his nephews. An oak cannot be bent; it can only be broken. If you are overcome with fear that means you have lost your will. He recalled another of his mother's tales: "Once, thieves burst into a house, whose master was known to be a coward. His wife, though, was a brave woman and she rushed out to fight the thieves. They probably would have come off the worse, but the woman's husband grabbed her tightly by the waist and said to her, 'Katsha, go ahead and fight them, but keep me close, so you can cover me with your back.' Of course, the thieves were able to make a clean getaway as a result."

Zhandos smiled involuntarily when recalling this tale, but his worries did not recede. He was shaking all over; the illness was taking an ever firmer hold. *And what if wolves decide to attack?* he thought suddenly. He became afraid and began looking closely into the darkness. And indeed green dots came into view in the distance. Zhandos took his knife from his belt, but the lights gradually faded away and disappeared. He knew that at night, wolves' eyes burn

280

brightly. People say that if a wolf leaps over a camel, it will never rise again. Who knows the truth in such sayings?

Zhandos decided that this was an uncomfortable place to spend the night, so he got the she-camel to her feet and rode on. The journey was long, the steppe was wide and life was short...

It was only on the third morning that Zhandos reached the familiar lake, overgrown with rushes. He did not find the camp here. There was litter, horse manure and traces of yurts all around.

Zhandos felt incredibly hungry. Fortunately, he found a mangy piece of old *kurt* where one of the yurts had stood. He ate it up and this gave him strength but little sustenance. He imagined the smell of *kumiss* and hot, boiled meat. He sought out the place where his yurt had stood and burst into tears.

A lone teal swam on the lake. Crows flew and paced about the ground as if they alone were the true masters of this land. The whole area was deserted and evoked a sense of yearning.

Zhandos, who had had only camel's milk to sustain him for three days, suffered the torments of hunger but the torments of loneliness were worse. He imagined his warm yurt and hot broth. He threw himself to the ground and wept large tears. There was not a living soul around, apart from his faithful she-camel, who listened with surprise to his weeping.

Only now did Zhandos truly realise how dear his native land had been to him and how much he needed his native people. He realised that, without people, the steppe was a place of treachery and indifference. It was a cruel, harsh place. He also learned that it is not time that ages a person, but events. Zhandos realised that people become cruel from having to drag out their bitter existence on this earth like oxen with rings through their noses, who are dragged on a leash to a place no-one knows. He understood that if a person has not perished, they simply exist, thrashing about like a fish on the ice and that the clouds are nothing like springtime, while the impudent, crafty crows who feed on carrion, only wait for one thing - carrion. The lake, though, deserted by the migratory birds, had assumed a grey and mournful state. Without people, the steppe loses its personality.

He thought that if Bokenshi and Borsak were to remain alive and if he were to bring them safe and sound to their native camp and if they were to grow into normal people, this would serve to elevate him. And if they were to grow into protectors of their people, he would be very proud of them. That meant his labours had not been in vain. If, however, they were to become cruel strangers to their native tribe, Allah, protect them, for he would slaughter them with his own hand.

Zhandos lay on the ground and thought to himself: *My* aul *has moved away from its familiar, settled places to somewhere quite unknown. I just hope their new settlement proves to be a happy one.*

are met in their new settlement by enemies or if their
iew them unkindly? Oh, my native steppe, you lie
wed like an infant's blanket. Tell me, whose heels
..a for whom will you become food? What will you do if
..nes fail to come like the Dzhungars *with a brutal attack, but*
..tend to be your friends, with a dagger held behind their backs? You
will not distinguish your enemy; you will meet him with open arms and
a warm smile like a child that runs to its mother. You will lay yourself
bare and your tender approach will be answered with a knife in the
back. May Allah protect you from this! After all, your hospitality knows
no bounds.

Oh, how wide you are, my Kazakh steppe! There you lay with
your bloody mouth, like a mother weeping her grief into her shawl; will
there come a time when the Kazakhs will forget their time-honoured
camping grounds and their pitiful parting from their settled homes?
Will they live without fear and tribulation? For some reason, I
compare you with those twitching crows over there. Has anyone ever
seen a flock of crows take on a live wolf?

I stand guilty before you, my poor, native land. I have
forgotten your generosity and your unselfishness, for it is you who
gives shelter to all, both living and dead. If I think for long about your
future fate, for some reason, I think I want to die. Alright, I will die,
Allah. Yes, I will die.

But Zhandos did not die, although there was a brief moment
when he thought he would...

On the fourth day of his journey, the snow began to fall.
Zhandos positioned the she-camel against the wind and snuggled up to
her warm side to get a little sleep. Bokenshi and Borsak, now
accustomed to the camel's milk, slept soundly in the saddlebag.

The hills that had been black the day before were now
wrapped in a white shroud and were peaceful. The dirty, unwelcoming
steppe had long since been yearning for the snow. It was now no longer
recognisable, so dramatically had it been transformed. The snow
glimmered under the sun's rays, like a scattering of precious stones.
The distant hills shone white, with not a single spot of darkness. In an
instant, the tiresome autumn rain, the howling wind, the dirt and the
impassable roads had all disappeared. The steppe now took on the
appearance of Mother Aipara's prayer mat.

Zhandos slept, snuggled up against the she-camel's side. He
could not have seen two dots appearing on the horizon. At first, they
were no larger than two beetles, creeping over the white tablecloth of
the steppe, but then they began to grow larger. When the riders came
closer, they encountered a truly sorrowful sight. Amidst the white
steppe lay a she-camel, powdered with snow, with two crows and a
magpie sitting on her humps. As the horsemen drew nearer, the birds

cawed, the magpie screeched and they reluctantly flew away. Some pitiful people had taken away their prey from them. The she-camel lay there with her neck outstretched as if she had been struck over the head and it seemed that was saying, "Orphans, I have done all I could for you; now you have to fend for yourselves." And it was strange that, at that last moment, she lay with her head facing Mecca as if reminding the people that they had to look to the Caaba till their last breath. Maybe this is not the case, but this was how it was. Tears flowed from the camel's eyes and the tears had not yet managed to freeze over.

The riders were surprised to see that the she-camel had not crumpled to one side and had not stretched out her legs, but had instead died on her knees.

These riders had been sent out by Mother Aipara to search for Zhandos. When they lifted up the two infants into their arms, their cries rang out once more; clearly, they were hungry again. Zhandos lay there, unconscious. They somehow brought him round and got him to his feet. The first thing Zhandos did was reach for his dagger but, recognising the people as his own, he threw himself into their embrace. Then he stepped to one side and wept for a good while.

Great was his pity for the she-camel, who for four days had saved them from certain death and who had finally brought them back to their own people. He did not want predators to tear her to pieces. He instructed the riders to bring her back or at the very least turn her over and bury her. When the men tugged at her humps, she collapsed onto her side.

The she-camel's death had a profound effect on Zhandos. He did not know the cause of her death, as she had not wanted for food and was not ill. Perhaps she had simply died from her yearning for her calf? "We will bury you," promised Zhandos. "We will return and bury you as is fitting so that you won't become prey for crows. You poor camel; you should have felt nothing but hatred for a cruel and heartless mankind that had deprived you of your calf. But once more you submitted to his authority, you fulfilled your duty, wishing no death upon the infants. You saved them from their enemies, displaying goodness and an open heart. May you rest in peace! You were the last of the camp to leave to the east in lamentation. You seemed to know that there was no hope for a decent existence in this restless and heartless world. You did not believe in a better life for the camp. You saw the pure, white snow for the last time and, expending the last of your strength, drew your last breath. Before your death, you probably wept long and hard and continued to call for your perished calf, but in my stupor I heard nothing. You probably wanted to get up and head off to search for your calf, yet you felt the warmth of living creatures, who had placed their trust in you. You never flinched and not once did you think about withdrawing your warmth from the defenceless and that is how you died."

The dead she-camel was like a piece of the yellow steppe, clenched in a powerless rage.

No-one came from the camp to bury the she-camel, though, as they had had to move on to the east. The greedy, red-eyed wolves tore her to pieces and the crows and magpies picked at her bones. Such is the fate of a fallen animal and such is the law of the steppe.

8

After the return of her son, Mother Aipara's thoughts were both joyful and triumphant: "I had no faith in your generation. But I was wrong. Your courage and bravery know no bounds. And Zhandos has proved this. My son, you are a true *dzhigit*!

"You delivered Bokenshi and Borsak from the enemy's hands and you dragged them from there, as an ox pulls its heavy load, from the very jaws of the abyss. Our grief and our tears reached up to Allah and granted his favour.

"I had wondered what might become of my contemptible people who waxed more rotten and pitiful with each passing year.

"I feared the time would come when they would cease greeting one another altogether, each caring only for themselves. But, thanks to Allah, this is not so. My descendants will remain steadfast in their fight for honour, pure in thought and strong in their faith.

"There were times when I did not believe in a future, but this is not so. Perhaps in a hundred years, perhaps a thousand, my descendants will come to see this; but their eyes will be opened.

"So dry your eyes, my people, you have sons, who will not give up the resting places of our ancestors to the *Dzhungars*. They will smash the enemy to pieces. Do not desert your land, or it will be orphaned.

"Have you ever seen a hungry lion eat grass? Have you ever seen a people with brave *dzhigits* on their argamaks without a shroud or without a burial site, like some fallen animal?

"And you too, you free steppe, wipe away your tears. While you have Zhandos as a son, your enemy will never take an inch from you. And you, you swift steed, don't hang your head for here comes Zhandos my son.

"Don't weep, people. It is not the whistle of enemy spears you hear, but the biting steppe wind. I alone will weep and then it will be for joy and not from grief. I will cry because my son Zhandos has returned. Let my dry eyes become wet again for my tears will bring relief and my heart of stone will soften once more. Oh, I am weeping now..."

284

And Mother Aipara, her tears flowing like the she-camel who had lost her calf, turned to Mecca, opened her palms and said,

"Oh, Allah, don't forget the needs of my honest and innocent people; let your good favour fall upon them. Let our ancestors know no greed, treachery, villainy or guile. Amen!"

The camp moved eastwards. The road was long, the steppe was wide and life was short...

GLOSSARY

Aga
Means 'older brother' or 'uncle'. Kazakhs address all older men as *aga*. However, if a man in his 70s, then he becomes *ata* for everybody.

Ainalaiyn
A term used to show affection for a child. It can be translated as "my dear" or "my little one".

Apa
Means "mother" or "mum". It is quite common among Kazakhs to call their own grandmothers or elderly women in general *apa,* or *apashka* in the diminutive form.

Aqsaqal (Karaqsaqal)
A village elder. A position that commands great respect in the *aul* and in the wider community.

Ata
Literally means "kind grandfathers", but is used as a term of endearment for elderly men.

Aul
Generally means "village". In Kazakhstan, the *aul* represents the very heart of traditional Kazakh values and culture.

Ayran
A cold yoghurt beverage, mixed with salt.

Azamat
A man's name that means "brave warrior".

Bai
A title for chieftain, traditionally applied to the leaders of small tribal groups. Also a general term used for wealthy landowners.

Batyr
A folk hero, warrior and defender of the land.

Bismillah ir-Rahman ir-Rahim
In the Name of God, the Most Gracious and the Most Merciful. *Bismillah,* or *Basmala,* is the name of this phrase which, on its own, translates as "In the Name of God".

Bii
A judge. A *bii* would consult rulers on matters pertaining to the common people, passing judgments on crimes (given the absence of written law in nomad societies) and negotiating with enemies (like a modern-day diplomat).

Buzkashi
Literally "goat pulling" in Persian, Buzkashhi is the Central Asian sport in which horse-mounted players attempt to place a goat or calf carcass in a goal.

Caragana
A bush, also known as Siberian pea.

Chapan
A long, quilted coat worn over clothes, usually during the winter. Usually worn by men, these coats are adorned with intricate threading and come in a variety of colours and patterns.

Chorba
A thick, stew-type soup, usually made with mutton or lamb and vegetables.

Dzhigit
A word of Turkic origin which is used in the Caucasus and Central Asia to describe a skilful and brave equestrian, or a brave person in general. In certain other contexts it is used to describe menfolk in general.

Dzhungar
Also spelled Junggar, Jüüngar, Dzhungar or Dsongar. A people of Central Asia, so called because they formed the left wing (*dson,* "left"; *gar,* "hand") of the Mongol army, which made frequent incursions into Kazakh land in wars, predominantly during the 18th Century.

Dzhut
A famine caused by the large scale loss of livestock either to extreme weather or disease. In winter, often caused by extended ice storms on the steppe.

Ichigi
Soft, leather boots, often decorated with leather inlay and stitching.

Karta
Horse intestines, cleaned, turned inside out and stuffed with horse fat, onion, garlic and black pepper.

Kazan
A large, metal cooking pot, an integral item in any Kazakh kitchen.

Kazy
Sausage made from whole pieces of horse fat and fillet cut from the rib, spiced with garlic and black pepper.

Kibitka
A large cart, drawn by horses and generally covered.

Kumgan
A pitcher with an elongated neck and long, thin spout.

Kumiss
Mildly alcoholic, fermented horse milk. The national beverage of Kazakhstan.

Kurt
A traditional Kazakh dish made from dried cheese and whey, served as rolled balls, in strips or chunks.

Kuruk
The traditional implement used by herdsmen to capture livestock, it is comprised of a long staff with a rope lasso noose on the end.

Saiga
The saiga antelope is a critically endangered antelope that originally inhabited a vast area of the Eurasian steppe.

Soil
An extremely long-handled club for use in hand-to hand combat on horseback and for protecting flocks from predators.

Sorpa (Shurpa in Russian, Chorba in Turkish)
A type of stew made from mutton and popular throughout Eastern Europe and Central Asia

Suyunshi
A Kazakh tradition whereby the bringer of good news is given a present.

Tebenyovka
A form of winter grazing where the livestock scrape away at the thick layer of snow to reach the grass beneath.

Tor
The place of honour in a house or yurt opposite the door where the master of the house sits.

Yurt
A portable, round tent, covered with skins or felt.

Zhal-zhaya
A dish of thinly cut pieces of cooked neck fat (*zhal*) and fillet, rich with fat (*zhaya*). Considered the best parts of the horse.

Made in the USA
Columbia, SC
06 February 2018